263 AND 137 SQUADRONS

263 AND 137 SQUADRONS

THE WHIRLWIND YEARS

ROBERT BOWATER

FONTHILL

FONTHILL MEDIA
www.fonthillmedia.com

A CIP catalogue record for this book is available from the British Library

Typeset in 11pt on 12pt Minion Pro
Typesetting by Fonthill Media
Printed in the UK

ISBN 978-1-78155-245-2

Contents

Foreword

Christabel Leighton-Porter *aka* 'Jane' of the *Daily Mirror*

I really do feel very privileged to be asked to write the foreword of this wonderful book. It has taken Rob several years of research and hard work to produce. It has been so long overdue that it is a 'wizard' achievement on Rob's part especially as he was born some twenty years after the war finished.

The Whirlwind, what a lovely name, such a beautiful aircraft, so graceful and yet so unsung. This had to be rectified in honour of the super young men who flew these aircraft, who through their dedication and enthusiasm helped so much to get this country off 'on the right foot'. Not only had they to contend with enemy action but also were injured and killed by faults with the aircraft. I was fortunate enough to know some of the aircrew very well, especially Reggie Baker, he was so charming, and like his fellow pilots, always cheerful and happy. I knew Tommy Pugh, too, and the Reverend George Wood, who is still cheerful and has a lovely smile. I in fact seem to have spent quite a lot of the war on airfields and in RAF messes. You see they almost owned me; I was their 'pin-up', their anti-gremlin. What a very remarkable breed these boys were, they always seemed to be having a wonderful time and enjoying life to the full, never complaining, or even stopping to consider the fate that could await them. They were not just ordinary, never will they be forgotten and I am sure all that own this book will find it as exciting as I do, and join me in giving thanks to Rob for a record long delayed.

Jane

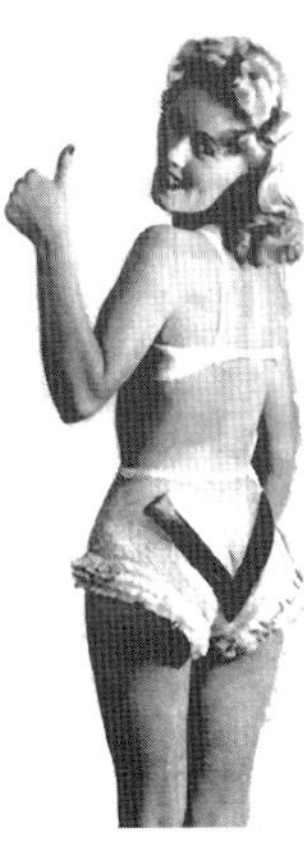

Jane of the *Daily Mirror*. (*Author*)

Acknowledgements

I have received assistance from many people during my research. Foremost, from members of the two Whirlwind Squadrons: Edwin Ashworth, Len Bartlett, Lewis Boucher, Art Brunet DFC, Geoff Buckwell, James Coyne DFC, Iain Dunlop, Henry Eeles, Len Gray, 'Tommy' Handley, Joe Hanmore, Reg Hine, Joe Holmes DFC, 'Hap' Kennedy, Herbert 'Kitch' Kitchener DFM, Len Knott, Arthur Lee-White, Carl Long, Lance Lowes, John McClure DFC, John Purkis DFC, Phil Robson, Cliff Rudland DFC, John Shellard, Doug Sturgeon, Denis Todd, Alex Torrance, Bill Watkins, John Wray DFC and George Wood. I was also lucky enough to meet Christabelle Leighton-Porter – 'Jane' of the Daily Mirror – who graciously agreed to provide a Foreword. Sadly, too many of these exceptional people are no longer with us.

I also received help from relatives: Nigel Albertini, Rick Ashton, Judith Asphar, Carol Banks, Michael Coghlan, Helen Cressweller, Richard Dimblebee, Wendy Douglas, Tom Eeles, Joan Foster, Chris Goldring, John LaGette, Doug McClure, Lilian Macdonald, Jim and John Munro, Andrew Ogilvie, Ian Purkis, Jane Renton, John Rudland and Terry Smith for information on their respective fathers. Jane Donaldson, Beryl Handley and Beth Watkins for information on their husbands. Moira Fletcher, Constance Gray, Gordon Hoskins and Bob Pugh AFC for information on their brothers. Also Nigel and Stuart Bell, Elizabeth Barnes, Jim Birch, Bruce Bovill, Giles Browne, Hugh Burns, Stuart Chalmers, Sir Philip Dowson, Chris Dimblebee, David Ferdinando, Crystal Hambly, Claudia Martin, Kevin Meldrum, Bob Musgrave, Della Payne, Graham Prior, Rosemary Shooter, Dorothy Skellon, Margi Sutherland, John Warnes, Alec Watt, Michael Yuille for information on their relatives.

My thanks also to Chris Thomas for his advice; Victor Bingham, Jerry Brewer, Ben Brown of the Sywell Aviation Museum, Niall Corduroy, Peter Durham, Paul Fitzgerald, Hugh Halliday, Martin Holloway, Ian LeSueur, Bob Mattewson, Walter McGowan, Peter Moore, Tony Poole, Alan White, Revd Adrian Gatrill of St Clement Danes the RAF Church, Edward Probert, Grace Seymour, Petra Silfverskiold, The Old Paludians Association, Peter Kirk of the Rolls-Royce Heritage Trust, Richard Snell of DERA, the Lancashire Constabulary and The Staffs of the Imperial War Museum, National Archives, the RAF Museum, the RAF Escaping Society, the Commonwealth War Graves Commission, Westland Aircraft and finally to songwriter Chris de Burgh for allowing me to quote from his song 'Borderline'.

Finally, special thanks to my wife Elle for her help and encouragement.

Rob Bowater
Renfrewshire,
Scotland, 2013

Introduction

'Westland Whirlwind'. For many the name conjures up the yellow air-sea rescue helicopters seen buzzing around the coasts of Britain in the 1970s, not the sleek twin engine monoplane which thirty years earlier had been the RAF's first single-seat cannon armed fighter, and which was faster than her more famous cousin – the Spitfire.

Designed around the short-lived Rolls-Royce Peregrine engine, only 114 aircraft were produced, a number that was sufficient to equip just two squadrons – Nos. 263 and 137. Between 6 July 1940 and 31 December 1943, the Operational Record Books of these two squadrons list 132 pilots who flew the Whirlwind on at least one operational sortie, twenty-nine who flew them but not operationally, thirty-nine more who although posted to the squadrons, did not actually fly the aircraft, and twenty-six who served with both squadrons. Most are known only to their peers, but several achieved high office and a few are part of the folklore of the RAF.

Henry Eeles CB CBE, the first Whirlwind CO, retired as an Air Commodore, counting amongst his appointments Assistant to the Deputy Supreme Commander (Air) with NATO. Six Whirlwind men attained the rank of Group Captain: Leonard Bartlett DSO commanded 253 Squadron – Viz airfield and then Viz Island off the Yugoslavian coast – and was one of the Group Captains who escorted Winston Churchill's coffin; Arthur Donaldson AFC DFC, cousin of Douglas Bader and one of three brothers who served in the RAF. (Jack, also CO of 263 Squadron was lost on HMS *Glorious* in June 1940 and Teddy held the Air Speed Record just after the war.) Arthur was to have led a Whirlwind Wing but this never materialised; Joseph Holmes AFC DFC was Air Attaché in Bangkok and Senior Operations Officer at SHAPE; Stuart Mills DFC was Assistant Air Attaché to the US where he helped develop British training facilities in America; John Munro took command of the AGME at Duxford and was also involved with the AFDU in secret work; John Wray DFC led 122 Tempest Wing and shot down two Me.262s.

The two squadrons also produced several exceptional Wing Leaders; Cliff Rudland DFC* finished the war leading a Mustang Wing; John Wray DFC as previously mentioned led a Tempest Wing; Pat Lee DFC led a Wing in the Far East, and personally accounted for three Japanese aircraft. Michael Bryan DFC* was killed leading his Typhoon Wing over Normandy in 1944, as was Reg Baker DSO DFC* who began the war flying Sunderland Flying Boats and sank two U-Boats before converting to fighters.

Unique amongst the Whirlwind men was Frank Dimblebee, who flew with 263 Squadron during the second half of 1941, then went on to serve with distinction with 273 air sea rescue Squadron where he saved at least thirty-five aircrew from the 'drink', for which he received the DFC. Post-war he was Assistant Air Attaché in Prague.

Although there were no Whirlwind 'Aces', (Cliff Rudland DFC being the highest scorer with two aerial victories), at least three Whirlwind pilots later achieved that status. Canadians 'Hap' Kennedy DFC and John Mitchner DFC* accounted for twelve and eleven enemy aircraft respectively, whilst American John Curry OBE DFC scored seven victories over Malta, and during the 1960s worked at NASA on the Apollo programme.

John Sample DFC led the section that downed a Dornier Do 18, on 17 October 1939, the first enemy aircraft destroyed since the First World War; Canadian James Coyne DFC appeared as an 'extra' in the 1942 James Cagney film *Captains of the Clouds*. He was also a friend of John Gillespie Magee, who wrote 'High Flight'. Fellow Canadian John McClure became Aide-de-Camp to the Governor of Canada in November 1944 and had a distinguished post war career in the RCAF. Alex Torrance planned Sheila Scott's 1971 record breaking polar flight in a Piper Aztec; Iain Dunlop joined AerLingus where he flew their first Boeing 747 Jumbo Jet; Humphrey Coghlan DFC was head of the Coghlan Iron & Steel Company. Battle of Britain veteran Donald Ogilvie flew with both Whirlwind Squadrons, then as a Liaison Officer to a USAAF P-38 Group flew several missions with them.

The Whirlwind pilot with the most varied flying career was probably Arthur Lee-White DFC. Born in Peru, he flew with 263 Squadron, flew several missions with a USAAF P-38 Group, to whom he was attached as a Liaison Officer, and served with 1453 Flight, flying captured German aircraft. On D-Day he flew a smoke-laying Boston over the Normandy Beaches, and on his second tour he was the personal pilot of Sir Archibald Sinclair, Secretary for Air, before transferring to Transport Command ferrying troops to India in C-47s.

Three Whirlwind men became members of the Guinea Pig Club, Leonard Knott as a result of an accident in a Whirlwind; Donald Tebbit and Peter Wyatt-Smith later in the war.

By far the biggest personality amongst the Whirlwind pilots was Geoff Warnes DSO DFC. Stories of him circulated throughout the RAF, and he was probably the first pilot to fly operationally with contact lenses. A strict disciplinarian, his pilots would have followed him anywhere, as was proved in February 1944 when he was forced to ditch his Typhoon off Guernsey. Australian Robert Tuff baled out to assist him but both men were lost.

This book is not intended to glorify war but is a tribute to the young men who answered their countries' call in those dark days, and to remember those who paid the ultimate sacrifice in that long, bitter struggle for freedom. They came from all corners of the Empire, from England, Scotland, Ireland, Wales, Canada, Australia, New Zealand, South Africa, Rhodesia and the West Indies as well as the United States, Peru, Eire, France and Sweden. 'As only free men can, they knew the value of that for which they fought, and that the price was worth paying.'[1]

Forty-six men lost their lives whilst flying the Whirlwind. A full Roll of Honour appears as Chapter 4. 'We must never forget not only those who were spared, but particularly treasure the memory of the legions that died so young in helping to save their country.'[2]

These are only boys, but I will never know
How men can see the wisdom of a war

PART 1

THE OPERATIONAL HISTORY

1
The Westland Whirlwind

The Westland Aircraft Company of Yeovil came into being in 1935, and was one of five companies that submitted designs for Air Ministry Specification F.37/35, which called for a day/night interceptor fighter armed with four 20-mm cannon, a 40 mph speed advantage over contemporary bombers, operational ceiling of 30,000 feet, and a retractable undercarriage and easy ground access to the cannons.

Westland's submission, the P.9, was designed by William Petter[1] and employed many construction techniques that were ahead of their time and which resulted in a sleek low-wing, twin-engine monoplane with a wingspan of 45 feet, a length of 32 feet 9 inches and a height of 11 feet 7 inches, and a weight of 8,310lbs. The slender wing had an area of 250 sq. feet, and the centre section carried two 67 gallon fuel tanks, oil and coolant radiators; nacelles housed the undercarriage units and the two supercharged 885hp V-12 Rolls-Royce Peregrine engines which turned ten-feet diameter de Havilland variable pitch propellers. There were two sets of slats – the inner ones sat above the radiator air intake between the fuselage and engine and were linked to Fowler flaps along the length of the centre section trailing edge, the movement of which automatically controlled the radiator shutters and root slats. There were also Handley-Page units that extended the full length of the outer wings and were automatic.

The offensive armament comprised of four 20-mm Hispano Mk.I cannon, the lower pair situated slightly forward of the upper pair in order to accommodate the sixty-round ammunition drums giving a total firing time of six seconds at a rate of 600lbs per minute. They were cocked on the ground prior to take-off and fired hydraulically on aircraft up to *P6969*, and pneumatically on all subsequent aircraft. Several other armament installations were tested on *L6844*: four belt fed cannon in a row, four cannon and three Browning machine guns, a 37-mm cannon, and the Martin Baker Company produced a twelve gun nose pod. None of these versions went into production.

The Air Ministry initially ordered two prototypes, *L6844* and *L6845*, on 11 February 1937 at a cost of £45,500 and the new aircraft was given the name 'Whirlwind.' *L6844* was rolled out of the Yeovil factory in October 1938 sporting a dark grey colour scheme, and following taxiing trials was shipped by road to Boscombe Down for her maiden flight, which took place on the afternoon of 11 October 1938. She was tested at A&AEE Martlesham Heath and proved to be so fast at low level she soon acquired the nickname 'Crikey' after a Shell advertisement of the day. Faster than the Spitfire I below 10,000 feet, and equal to it between 10,000 feet and 20,000 feet, she could also out dive it and above 360 mph her manoeuvrability was superior to both the Spitfire I and Hurricane but her

L6844, the first prototype, in the RAE Farnborough wind tunnel 1938. (*DERA archives*)

practical ceiling was only 20,000 feet. Despite this, she is considered by many to be one of the nicest twins ever built.

She had a few idiosyncrasies that could catch out the unwary however. The propellers rotated in the same direction, which caused directional control problems during take-off, although this could be controlled by the use of throttle. The throttle control system was operated by an 'Exactor' hydraulic system and it was essential to prime the system during the pre-flight checks by moving the throttle lever through its full range to purge any air; despite this there was a considerable lag between the throttle movement and the engine responding which made taxiing especially difficult. During landing the pilot had to make an approach with plenty of power to keep the rudder and elevator effective right up until touchdown.

An initial order for 200 aircraft called for deliveries to commence in September 1939, and was quickly followed by a second for a further 800. The first nine aircraft were to be prototypes, and the next sixteen, although better equipped, would not be to operational standard. However, due to requirements they were all were issued to 263 Squadron. The first production aircraft, *P6966*, flew on 22 May 1939, some four and a half years after the issue of the specification.

There are many reasons the Whirlwind has been condemned to obscurity, and whilst most of these are performance related, there was also a political influence. The prototype was over-engineered but when service testing highlighted that modifications were

L6845 with Walter McGowan in the cockpit. 'The plane had just completed a test flight. It was cold so the flight team retired to the pilot's office to debate the results and the ground crew decided to go back into the shop but I was told to "stay and look after the plane." It was 1938 and an 18-year old was put in charge of a top secret plane. Imagine that today. So I climbed in to the cockpit to keep warm. Word came "No more flights" so the plane was to go back into the shop. I was told to sit there and use the brakes. They were activated by a hydraulic hand pump on the right side of the seat. It was not effective. I pumped like fury, yelling I could not hold it. It was a down slope to the shop. Men came rushing out and managed to slow it before it crashed into the Super's office, then they did not open the hangar door enough and took off the wingtip!' – Walter McGowan. (*Author*)

required, Petter was reluctant to make them. This played into the hands of a faction at the Air Ministry where there was no great enthusiasm for a cannon-armed fighter and who were waiting for an excuse to cancel the programme. Westland were not the only target of this attitude: Supermarine had similar problems and at one point the Air Ministry contemplated cancelling the Spitfire. In the end however it was not the production delays or political intrigue that did for the Whirlwind – it was the engines, but not in the way most often quoted. The aircraft was designed and built around the Rolls-Royce Peregrine, the final derivative of the 1930s range of Kestrel engines. Unfortunately by late 1939, a shortage of machinery and manpower forced Rolls-Royce to rationalise production and several engines were dropped. Thus when the first production Peregrine was delivered in February 1940 the decision had already been made to cease production after 290 units. To all intents, the Whirlwind was doomed from that point on, and was limited to a production run of just 114 aircraft. The final 'Whirly', *P7122*, rolled off the production line in December 1941.

There are a great many misconceptions regarding the Whirlwind, the most persistent being that the landing speed was too high, which restricted her use to airfields with long runways. Compared to the bi-planes of the era it was, but it was similar to contemporary monoplane aircraft. An A&AEE report from 1938 stated that the landing was 'not fast or excessively long' at 635 yards, and as all airfields built after 1935 had a landing run of 1,100 yards with a 200 yard overshoot, there was no problem. In fact, during one test flight in *L6844*, Harald Penrose, Westland's chief test pilot was forced to make an emergency landing at RAF Warmwell in Dorset, a small grass airfield only considered suitable for Hart and Gladiator biplanes. Just a few years later, Whirlwinds of 263 Squadron were based there and were operating not only by day but also at night. Another misconception shattered, 'the Whirlwind could not be flown at night due to exhaust flame and muzzle flash from the cannons': a 137 Squadron pilot later described her as being 'infinitely better than a Spitfire on the score of view and ease of flying at night.'

Had the aircraft been ordered off the drawing board, delivered on time, and had the engine not been cancelled, the RAF would have had several squadrons of Whirlwinds during the Battle of Britain. The carnage they would have caused amongst the Luftwaffe bomber formations can only be imagined but, as it was, by the time the aircraft became operational at the end of 1940, the majority of combats took place at 20,000 feet plus, well above her operational ceiling. The Whirlwind had missed its *raison d'être*, but the two squadrons who operated them against the enemy made excellent use of them in a different role – that of ground attack.

2

No. 263 Squadron: 'Ex Ungue Leonum' The Lion is Known by His Claws

No. 263 Squadron was formed in Italy, at Otranto and Santa Maria de Leuca, on 27 September 1918 from an amalgamation of 359, 435, 436 and 441 Flights. Equipped with Sopwith Baby, Hamble Baby, Short 184 and 320 seaplanes and Felixstowe F.3 flying boats, it flew anti-submarine patrols over the Straits of Otranto in search of U-Boats attempting a passage into the Mediterranean from the Adriatic. Eight months later, on 16 May 1919 it was disbanded at Taranto, Italy.

It was re-formed on 2 October 1939, at RAF Filton near Bristol, with Gloster Gladiator fighters, under the command of S/L John William Donaldson. In March 1940 the squadron was ordered to Norway to aid the Finns in the Russo-Finnish War but in April they were sent to support the North Western (Norway) Expedition instead. Transported by HMS *Glorious* to frozen Lake Lesjaskog, less than twenty-four hours after first landing in Norway ten aircraft had been lost to bombing raids and the remainder were flown to Setnesmoen, near Åndalsnes. Four days later, with no aircraft remaining, the pilots were evacuated. During its brief stay in Norway the squadron flew forty-nine sorties, made thirty-seven interceptions, destroyed six enemy aircraft and probably destroyed eight more.

When presenting his report to the Air Ministry, S/L Donaldson was told that the squadron had been sent to Norway as a 'token sacrifice' and that once re-equipped it would return as part of the second Norwegian Expedition. Based at Bardufoss between 21 May and 7 June, they claimed twenty-six victories for the loss of two pilots, but were again ordered to retreat. On the 8 June, ten Gladiators were flown onto the deck of HMS *Glorious* along with 46 Squadron's Hurricanes. Escorted by two Destroyers, *Ardent* and *Acasta* they were intercepted by the German Battle Cruisers *Scharnhorst* and *Gneisenau*. All three Royal Navy ships were sunk with the loss of over 1,500 men, including the ten pilots of 263 Squadron. The ORB noted:

> and so perished a brave and gallant Squadron. S/L John William Donaldson DSO; F/O Harold Edward Vickery DFC; P/O Louis Reginald Jacobsen DFC; F/O Herman Francis Grant Ede DFC; P/O Phillip Hannah Purdy DFC; P/O Sidney Robert McNamara DFC; P/O Michael Amor Bentley; P/O Alvin Thomas Williams; P/O Jack Falkson and Sgt Ernest Frederick William Russell MM. The story of their adventures is already famous and in the future it will have a place wherever the brave deeds of war of members of the British Commonwealth are chronicled.

Maintenance in Norway in a log dispersal bay. (*Lance Lowes archive*)

July–November 1940: A New Beginning

The task of raising the 'Phoenix' from the ashes of Norway began on 10 June, when the remnants of the squadron arrived at RAF Drem, and were issued with several Hurricane Is. By the end of July it was back to its full complement,[2] and had moved to RAF Grangemouth near Edinburgh pending the arrival of S/L Henry Eeles, the new commanding officer, on 6 July in the first of the Squadron's Whirlwinds, *P6966*.[3] His first task was to form 'C' Flight under F/L Wynford Smith tasked with developing the Whirlwind for squadron use. Smith organised a demonstration of the aircraft for the Commander-in-Chief Home Fleet at nearby Rosyth Naval Dockyard. The aircraft was 'secret' and therefore unknown to the notoriously trigger-happy Royal Navy; it was, as he said, 'purely in the interest of self preservation'.[4] Another new arrival during this period was F/O Thomas Patrick Pugh, who was destined to become CO in late 1941 and was the first person to suggest hanging bombs on a Whirlwind and using her in the ground attack or anti-shipping role.

S/L Eeles' task was made that much more difficult as three pilots were lost to flying accidents during July: Sgt Patrick Ian Watson-Parker crashed near Biggin Hill whilst attached to 610 Squadron, P/O Alan Richard Downer crashed attempting to force-land his Hurricane, and P/O Eric Wilfred Bell was killed in Blenheim *L1105*. Having trained on Hawker Hart bi-planes he had been attached to 5 OTU, Aston Down, to convert to 'twins'. He crashed near Frampton Mansell, Gloucestershire, due to engine failure and shortly after the accident the villagers placed a granite block at the crash site with an engraved brass plaque in his memory.[5] F/L Smith almost became a fourth casualty when he wrote off Hurricane *P2991* crash-landing in the grounds of Carstairs Junction Public School.

263 Squadron Hurricanes at dispersal, RAF Drem. (*Munro Family archives*)

Above left: S/L Henry Eeles was the first Whirlwind CO. (*Tom Eeles archives*)

Above right: F/O Eric Bell was killed on 24 July. (*Nigel Bell archives*)

Only two Whirlwinds were delivered in July, prompting the ORB to note that 'A considerable amount of what the Makers are pleased to call "teething troubles" had been encountered.' Whilst these were to be expected with a new aircraft, it meant that all of training sorties were undertaken on Hurricanes. 'C' Flight was disbanded by early August and all pilots were given experience on the Whirlwind, but the Hurricanes continued to provide the squadron's offensive capability so that when the Luftwaffe attacked Newcastle, on 14 and 15 July, two sections were put on readiness although much to the pilots' disappointment they were not called upon. Many coastal and night patrols were flown by the Hurricanes and although these did not result in combat, the pilots who took part are officially accepted as having participated in the Battle of Britain,[6] and official records state that had operation Seelöwen materialised, the cannon armed Whirlwinds would have moved south as 'tank busters'. Quite what they would have achieved is pure conjecture however as there were less than a handful available.

The personnel strength of the squadron was still very fluid, four new pilots reported for flying duties during August, P/Os David Alexander Cummins Crooks DFC, David Stein, and Donald Martin Vine, and Sgt Clifford Percival Rudland. Both flight commanders, who had fought with distinction in Norway, were posted to command squadrons involved in the fighting over the Home Counties. Randolph Stuart Mills left for 87 Squadron and Caesar Barraud Hull for 43 Squadron. Unfortunately, Hull was killed leading his squadron into action a few days later.

Sgt Herbert Kitchener received the first medal awarded to the 'new' squadron, a DFM for his work in Norway, but August was noteworthy for two things, the arrival of S/L John Munro and the first Whirlwind loss.

S/L Munro was charged with the task of 'persuading the cannon to fire without continual stoppages'. The Hispanos had a habit of stopping after just a few rounds, and when they did fire, the blast wave buckled the nose cone. This fairing was initially made from aluminium sheet over duralumin formers, but thicker sheet and the addition of duralumin blast tubes quickly solved this problem. The stoppages took a little longer. S/L Munro was the ideal man for the job as he had written the original armament installation specification for the aircraft, and it was on his instructions that *P6970* and subsequent aircraft fired their cannons pneumatically not hydraulically as originally designed.

P/O Irving Francis McDermott was the unfortunate pilot involved in the first Whirlwind loss on 7 August. Henry Eeles recalled:

> As he took off on a training sortie, the port main wheel burst, the port undercarriage leg buckled and the wingtip touched the ground, but he managed to maintain control and dragged the aircraft into the air then began to circle the aerodrome. I was summoned to the Control Tower, and checked the damage to the aircraft through binoculars. The remnants of the tyre had become tangled in the undercarriage, and it quickly became apparent that it would neither retract nor withstand a landing, so I gave him the facts and told him to make up his own mind, try to land or bale out, although I strongly recommended the latter. He continued to orbit the aerodrome for a while before deciding to bale out. I advised him to climb to a safe altitude, aim the aircraft away from Edinburgh then jump. He eventually left the aircraft between Grangemouth and Stirling and landed safely although he was detained by the local Home Guard Unit and was not released until

> I spoke to the Officer in charge and personally vouched for him. I was tempted to leave him in their custody for a while but thought better of it.[7]

P6966 HE-X came down on Lanton Farm near Stenhousemuir and according to the ORB, 'buried herself thirty feet deep and could not be recovered'.[8]

A Board of Inquiry blamed the poor state of the aerodrome surface for the accident, and this led directly to the squadron moving to RAF Drem. Before this move took place however S/L Eeles was called on again to vouch for one of his pilots when P/O Stein was forced to abandon Hurricane *L1803* over Grangemouth. The oil pressure fell to zero, the engine caught fire and the aircraft crashed on mudflats near the Kincardine Bridge. Stein landed safely in Grangemouth Docks and was taken into custody by the Home Guard, until his identity was confirmed.

The squadron moved to RAF Drem on the 2 September, and Henry Eeles recalled:

> The aerodrome was under the command of W/C Dick Atcherley, one of the winning Schneider Trophy team of 1929 and who had been in Norway during the squadron's brief stay there. He brought back the Norwegian idea of Fighter Pen construction. Instead of sandbags, they were constructed of interlocking logs, and several such pens were constructed at Drem. We (263) only ever used them for photographic purposes; they were too far from the crew-room to be of practical use. Also, the aircraft were originally dispersed on the far side of the aerodrome to the Readiness hut. This severely increased our 'scramble' time, so I ordered that the section at Readiness be parked outside the hut, and we soon reduced this to less than two minutes.[9]

Comprising F/L Pugh, F/O Britton, P/O Wyatt-Smith, P/O Ferdinand, P/O Thornton-Brown, P/O Vine, P/O Stein, Sgt Kitchener DFM, Sgt Milligan, Sgt Mason, Sgt Morton and Sgt Rudland, 'B' Flight, were operational on Hurricanes, but despite thirty-two patrols no contact was made with the enemy. 'A' Flight – S/L Munro, F/L Smith, F/O Olivier, P/O Crooks DFC, P/O Hughes and Sgt Morton – were developing the Whirlwind, and were therefore non-operational. The engines had not surmounted their 'teething troubles' but

Flight Commanders F/L Stuart Mills and F/L Caesar Hull. (*Author*)

the cannons were firing satisfactorily, indeed on one occasion a Whirlwind on an Air Firing Exercise flown by S/L Munro was positively identified by the Observer Corps as a Junkers Ju.88 machine-gunning shipping. A section of Spitfires was despatched to intercept, but as the ORB noted, 'Happily, the encounter did not resolve itself into a trial of arms.' The new aircraft had begun to attract attention however, and during the month the squadron was visited by the Duke of Kent, and Sir Archibald Sinclair, Secretary of State for Air. Both were treated to flying demonstrations by S/L Munro and P/O Crooks. But, even at this early stage of its career, the Whirlwind was not living up to expectations and the ORB continued to report poor serviceability.

On the 23 it noted that S/L Eeles took *P6967* to Rolls-Royce at Hucknall for tests due to erratic operation of the boost control. She was apparently selected as the worst example on the squadron, failing to maintain the rated boost during a climb. An investigation proved that the gauges and pipes in the system all leaked and once this was rectified the boost control was within limits. During her stay at Hucknall she was modified and fitted with external air intakes and oil coolers and Morris low-drag radiators. The original buried intakes were very inefficient, but the drag of the external intake was more than offset by the new radiators, and flight test results showed an increase of 12 mph in speed and 1,200 feet in height at full throttle. Although she was passed to RAE Farnborough on 25 August 1941 for further tests, the improvements were not incorporated into service aircraft.

The Hurricanes of 'B' Flight led a nomadic existence during November; they operated from MacMerry, then Prestwick to cover a 'special target' in the Clyde. This was most probably HMS *Formidable*, but the Luftwaffe made no attempt to attack it. On 27 August they returned to Drem in preparation for a move south where the squadron was to operate exclusively with Whirlwinds.

Norwegian style log dispersal at Drem. (*Tom Eeles archives*)

P6967 was delivered to Rolls-Royce at Hucknall on 23 September by S/L Eeles. (*Rolls-Royce*)

P6981 and F/O Joe Hughes fly close formation on Sgt Cliff Rudland. (*Cliff Rudland archives*)

Ready in a minute cartoon by Sgt Frank Morton. (*Lilian Macdonald archives*)

RAF Drem 30 October 1940: P/O Roy Ferdinand, F/O Tom Pugh, F/L Harold Olivier, Sgt Cliff Rudland, P/O Herbert Kitchener DFM, Sgt Frank Morton, F/O Irving McDermott, F/O David Crooks DFC,F/O Alan Britton, P/O Francis Hendry (IO), S/L Henry Eeles, F/L Wynford Smith, F/O Joe Hughes, P/O George Milligan, P/O Don Vine, P/O David Stein, and S/L John Munro. (*Tom Eeles archives*)

The move was instigated by serviceability levels, on the 4th the ORB stated that, 'Of fifteen aircraft built, the squadron had eight, but four were grounded with engine problems and two were unserviceable, leaving two for training.' Air Marshal Sir Sholto Douglas wrote to Westland's, 'It is now five months since 263 Squadron was re-formed, allegedly on Whirlwinds. I am taking its Hurricanes away and making it operational on Whirlwinds at RAF Exeter. It is up to you to make the squadron's initial strength up to sixteen at once.' The ORB noted, 'It was with great regret that leave was taken of the Hurricanes.' Ten Whirlwinds moved on the 28th under HQFC order 0905, stopping at RAF Sealand en-route to re-fuel. S/L Munro flew most of the flight on one engine, the other having seized, and as there were more pilots than aircraft they drew lots to see who would fly – Cliff Rudland recalled a long, tiring trip ferrying Joe Hughes' car to the new station.[10] Finally, five months after the first delivery, and twenty-six months since her maiden flight, the Whirlwind was declared operational.

December 1940: Operational at Last

The honour of flying the first sorties fell to S/L Eeles *P6974*, F/L Smith *P6975* and F/O Hughes *P6976* when they carried out a patrol over Plymouth. On several occasions over the following weeks the unusual shape of the Whirlwind caused the sirens to sound when they were reported as hostile and numerous times they were fired at by the guns protecting Dartmouth. However, flying was restricted by the poor state of the aerodrome and the ORB noted that, 'the squadron was hourly expecting orders to move with all aircraft grounded except for operational purposes.' Despite this, thirty sorties were flown, although the only interception was by F/L Smith who sighted a Ju.88 near Start Point; it escaped into cloud before he could engage.

The first Whirlwind fatality occurred on the 12th when F/O Britton led a section of three aircraft on an Air-Sea Firing Exercise over Sand Bay near Weston-super-Mare. They carried out their first attack, but the Master of a nearby ship stated that one seemed to fly through the spray thrown up by the cannon shells hitting the water as it made a second attack and dived into the sea off Burnham. Apart from a few pieces of wreckage, neither Allan Walter Naylor Britton, nor *P6980*, were found.

On 16 December, the squadron also lost S/L Henry Eeles when he was promoted to Wing Commander and posted to command RAF Drem. During his six months in command he was able to achieve little, having to contend with poor delivery and serviceability and political machinations between the Air Ministry and Westland. Despite this, to get the unconventional and advanced Whirlwind operational was no mean feat, and says much for his strength of character. He built the foundations for what was to follow, although the ORB noted, 'The remainder of the month was little short of disastrous, and retarded the squadron's progress by several weeks. There have been so many changes in the personnel, due either to deaths or postings that the squadron has, for the second time, been reduced to a shadow of its former self.' F/L Olivier, P/O Peter Wyatt-Smith, both veterans of the Norwegian Campaign, and F/O John Francis Blick (Adjutant) were posted. Of Harold Antony Olivier the ORB stated, 'He was an efficient and competent pilot, as well as being a steadying influence on the younger pilots.' S/L Munro was appointed CO and was

Above left: F/L Harold Olivier was posted on 22 December. (*Author*)

Above right: P/O Peter Wyatt-Smith was posted on 15 December. (*Judith Aspher archives*)

assisted in the task of rebuilding the squadron by the new Adjutant, F/O Leslie Robert Hiscock. Sgt Jocelyn Ivan Yates also arrived for flying duties.

On the 29 F/L Smith led P/Os Vine and Kitchener from Exeter to escort two Catalinas inbound from Bermuda. 'Kitch' Kitchener recalled:

> During the briefing Don [Vine] asked me if I wanted to fly as No. 2 or 3. I replied No. 2 which was on the starboard side of the leader. We took off just after midday, climbed into a clear blue sky and passed over Exeter town at 3,000 feet in perfect formation. Only Smith was issued with a map, it not being considered necessary for us carry one. As we were flying such a tight formation, I was watching Smith's aircraft all the time, but shortly after passing over Exeter, I glanced forward and saw that we were heading towards a thick bank of cloud. Smithy put us into a shallow dive, intending to fly beneath the overcast, and as we entered that cloud I had the impression that we were still descending and the terrain over which they were flying was rising. We continued in R/T silence and briefly broke into clear blue sky before plunging back into the gloom where the cloud became thicker and I lost sight of him. Suddenly forced to concentrate on my instruments, I was aware of two dull red flashes to port and automatically veered to starboard and climbed, as I did so out of the corner of my eye I saw the tops of trees above me! I eventually broke out of the cloud at 4,000 feet and called for a course back to Exeter. After a lot of worry with the controller, I was vectored back to base.

Despite an extensive search, no trace of Wynford Ormond Leoni Smith (*P6975 HE-L*) or Donald Martin Vine (*P6978*) was found until March 1941 when the winter snows thawed and the wreckage of both aircraft was found on Fox Tor Mire, Devon. They were laid to rest side by side in Exeter High Cemetery.[11]

Above left: uk-uk-uk-P/O Don Vine, F/L Wynford Smith, F/L Joe Hughes. (*Author*)

Above right: P/O David Stein scored the first Whirlwind victory on his first Operational sortie. (*Cliff Rudland archives*)

January 1941: Another New Beginning

The Squadron remained at Exeter despite it being entirely unsuitable for Whirlwinds, although all operational flying was undertaken from St Eval and a considerable number of patrols were flown. The most eventful occurred on 12 January when P/O Stein *P6972*, on his first operational sortie, and Sgt Mason took off to intercept Raid 106. They were over the Lizard when the controller told them it had turned away, but he vectored them towards Raid 107 which was approaching Land's End. Unfortunately, they became separated as they climbed through cloud and Mason returned to base. Stein continued and intercepted a Ju.88 forty miles south-west of the Scillies. He manoeuvred up sun before diving on the bomber, which was flying above a layer of cloud at 4,500 feet, and opening fire from the beam with a four second burst, seeing hits on the top of the fuselage and an explosion, but was unable see the full extent of the damage as his view was briefly obscured by smoke from his cannon. The bomber, from K.Gr.806, went into a spiral dive that became vertical as it entered cloud and although he followed he was unable to find it again. As it had not taken evasive action prior to him opening fire, he believed he had caught it unaware but as *P6972* was not carrying a camera gun he could only claim it as damaged. Fighter Command did upgrade it to a 'kill' at the end of February but by then another had been celebrated as the Whirlwind's first. The ORB did note however that, 'The combat is the first occasion on which the Whirlwind drew blood and P/O Stein had no difficulty in catching the bomber which was flying at about 300 mph.' There were two further interceptions during the month but neither resulted in combat. On 13 January, F/O Hughes and Sgt Rudland saw an enemy aircraft thirty miles off the Lizard but were unable to catch it, whilst P/O Thornton-Brown and P/O Kitchener DFM caught a Heinkel

He.111 twenty miles south of Land's End and chased it out past the Scillies before breaking off short of fuel.

Chameleon Patrols

Intelligence reports suggested that on moonlit nights when the Luftwaffe attacked South Wales or South West England, E-Boats would leave Cherbourg, rendezvous fifty miles south of the English coast then lay up about ten miles off Dartmouth acting as Air-Sea Rescue launches for any crews forced down into the sea. It was proposed to attack these E-boats with three Whirlwinds, but due to the specific nature of the intelligence, the operation had to be disguised as a routine patrol. They were to climb to 15,000 feet over Dartmouth, head out over the Channel on 117 degrees and gradually loose height to 3,000 feet at a point fifty miles out to sea, then return to Exeter. They were forbidden to orbit as though searching, and if the visibility was below five miles or the clouds were below 3,000 feet the operation was not to be flown. In addition, at least one of the aircraft was to carry a loaded cine camera gun and R/T silence was to be maintained at all times. S/L Munro, F/L Pugh and F/L Crooks were ordered to stand by daily between 1530 and 1700, and the first 'Chameleon' Patrol took place on 9 January. Despite the meticulous planning however, nothing was seen. Two further patrols on 13 and 15 January also failed to find their quarry.

F/L David Crooks, S/L John Munro, F/L Tom Pugh in front of *P6977* on 9 January 1941 prior to the first 'Chameleon Patrol'. (*Munro Family archives*)

Sgt Frank Morton was killed on 9 January. (*Lilian Macdonald archives*)

Whilst the first 'Chameleon' Patrol was underway, Sgt Frank Morton flew Adjutant F/O Lesley Robert Hiscock to RAF Warmwell in the squadron Blenheim, *L1223*, to take up a new posting. On his return, he was seen to pass over Exeter aerodrome with one engine misfiring, and he crashed near Ebford just south of the aerodrome. He baled out just before the aircraft crashed, but his parachute did not have time to fully deploy and he was killed. The ORB noted that, 'He was well liked by everyone' and the first job for new Adjutant P/O Geoffrey Hugh Hadley was to report his loss.

Another aircraft was lost on 19 January when F/L Pugh took *P6984* on a camera gun test following a daily inspection. During the thirty-minute flight, he indulged in some aerobatics before returning to Exeter, but as he made his approach, another aircraft cut in front of him forcing him to abort his landing and fly a wide circuit at 1,500 feet. About two miles from the aerodrome, he lowered the undercarriage and, almost immediately, both engines failed. Too far away from the runway to glide in, and unable to re-start the engines he baled out at 1,000 feet near Sowton just west of RAF Exeter. He landed safely, but *P6984*, which had flown just ten hours, ended her days in a high-speed crash demolishing several trees and coming to rest in a stream. The Board of Enquiry determined that the cause of the double engine failure was a small gravity switch in the Graviner fire extinguisher system. It was designed to activate only if the aircraft turned over in a crash but as the undercarriage came down it completed an electrical circuit, which caused the extinguishers to discharge methyl bromide into the carburettors and over the cylinder blocks. A ground test on another aircraft recreated the same conditions and resulted in a large cloud of bluish-white smoke and a spluttering engine, which eventually picked up and ran normally. Eyewitnesses reported a similar cloud from *P6984* prior to the crash, and the conclusion was that given sufficient height and time, he would undoubtedly have recovered the situation.

P6984 HE-H ended her days in a high speed crash at Sowton on 19 January. (*Cliff Rudland archives*)

Servicing *al fresco*, winter scene, RAF Exeter, January 1941. (*Munro Family archives*)

On 21 January, the squadron received notice of No. 10 Group operation Order No. 5. Long Range Focke-Wulf Fw.200 Condors of KG.40 were taking a heavy toll of Allied shipping in the Western Approaches, and intelligence sources reported that they flew out into the Atlantic from Bordeaux via Bantry Bay in Ireland, and that on several occasions they had been spotted from the Scilly Isles. This would put them within range of the Whirlwinds, so the squadron was ordered to provide three sections at St Eval each day – one at readiness, one at available, and one at thirty minutes. During the flights R/T silence was to be kept as much as possible, and if an interception did occur, the pilots were under orders not to give a 'Tally-Ho' or to report any action. There were several patrols and scrambles south and west of the Scillies during the following six weeks resulting in visuals of several Ju.88s, but no Fw.200s.

Eleven pilots arrived during the month: P/Os John Furnival Hayes DFC, Bernard Howe, Albert Tooth, Hubert Kenneth Smith, Ivor Ashley St Clair Watson, and John d'Arcy Waechter, and Sgts Glynn Barrow Foden, Douglas St John Jowitt, Cecil Percy King, Robert Burton Skellon, and Walter David Waddington, but Hayes, Smith, Watson, and Waechter left within a week.

February 1941

Thursday 8 February 'gave the squadron its first confirmed Whirlwind victory, but the circumstances surrounding it were mysterious.' F/O Hughes and Sgt Rudland were scheduled for a practice flight from Exeter, but this was delayed when Rudland's first aircraft broke a tail wheel whilst taxiing. Once airborne, they were vectored onto Raid 139 and held in an orbit twelve miles south of Start Point where Rudland spotted a float plane. He informed Hughes then commenced an attack, but as he came down on its tail he saw British roundels on the fuselage so did not fire, and briefly flew in formation with it before it entered cloud.[12] It reappeared about 1,000 yards to port of F/O Hughes who immediately attacked, closing to 200 yards with a five second burst. He did not observe the results of his attack however.

Red Section, F/L Crooks and P/O Graham, were ordered to orbit over Dodman Point in conjunction with another Raid. As F/L Crooks later reported:

> P/O Graham and myself were going to do one hours local formation starting at 0900 hours but shortly after I was airborne I was ordered to point 9 [Dodman Point]. P/O Graham was delayed on the take-off and joined me there. We flew around in formation till ordered to land and were about halfway home when we were ordered to 'buster' to point 9 again. When we arrived the weather had deteriorated and cloud was 10/10 at about 1,000 feet. Unfortunately, I can't say exactly the height or thickness of the cloud, as my ASI, Altimeter and Rate of Climb were unserviceable. I ordered P/O Graham to patrol below cloud and he answered OK, I then climbed through into the clear and patrolled for several minutes having a good look around, then came down through the cloud again. As I emerged I passed P/O Graham, who was going West, I was going East at the time. I did a gentle left hand turn, intending to call him up and ask him to formate on me but he had completely disappeared and when searching around for him I suddenly saw an enemy aircraft come through the cloud in a north-easterly direction on my left. I turned toward it and

> it continued on course, getting lower until it hit the sea and turned over before I got within range. I searched for several minutes but could see no sign of P/O Graham. I reported the crash to 'Donegal' [the ground controller] and was ordered home, so I returned assuming that he had already done so.

F/L Crooks initially identified the enemy aircraft as a Heinkel He.115, but it was in fact Arado Ar.196 *6W+ON*, flown by Oberleutnant Berger, Staffelkapitan of 5/KuFlGr 196, and Leutnant zur See Hirtz, both of whom perished, and was on a coastal reconnaissance. It was almost certainly the same aircraft engaged by Blue Section. Unfortunately, Battle of Britain veteran Kenneth Alfred George Graham and *P6969* did not return from the patrol the Coast Guard reported that two aircraft had crashed three miles off shore, one of them in flames. A thorough Air-Sea Rescue search found only wreckage and an oil slick, leading to the conclusion that he had mortally wounded the enemy floatplane, but was then shot down in flames by return fire. Westland sent the squadron a case of champagne to celebrate the Whirlwinds first kill.

February had begun with the detached flight operating from St Eval, but the ORB noted it was an arrangement that was not conducive to the efficient running of the squadron. Furthermore, the new pilots were detached to Charmy Down to gain experience on the Whirlwind as Exeter was only considered suitable for operational flying. As a result, what remained of the squadron at Exeter became little more than a Maintenance Unit, so it was decided to unite the squadron, and on 24 February a move was made to St Eval.

At the same time, S/L John Gray Munro was posted to the Air Gun Mounting Establishment. His appointment to command a front-line Fighter Squadron was unusual due to his specialist technical background, but once he had rectified the difficulties with the cannon and brought the aircraft back to full operational status, he was insulated from further needless risk. The ORB also noted, 'It cannot be said that during his period of command he was given much assistance by higher authority in his task of bringing the squadron to a high state of operational efficiency. At no time during his tenure of office was the whole Squadron allowed to be on one station.' He had built on the foundations laid by S/L Eeles, and left the squadron with a fully functioning aircraft with which to take the fight to the enemy. His place was taken by S/L Arthur Hay Donaldson, the brother of the squadron's first CO who was lost on HMS *Glorious*.

Five other pilots also reported for duty, Sgts Graham Lewis Lawson, Carl Arthur Long, Donald Frank Jellicoe Tebbit and two Free French pilots, Lieutenants Mauritius Rémy and Jacques Garnier DFC. These were '*nom de guerre*', their real names were Roger Mott and Jean Gabrielli, but they stayed for just three days before being posted away. F/O Denis Herbert Fowler the squadron Medical Officer left for RAF Filton, his replacement being F/O Walter Pollock Weir.

There were several accidents during February the most spectacular of which involved Sgt Skellon. He damaged the tail unit of *P6991* in a heavy landing, then, on the 15th he took *P6976* on a cross country exercise but ran out of fuel. Although he made a creditable force-landing in a field at Cannington near Bridgwater, Somerset, both incidents were blamed on his inexperience on type.

P6969 HE-V was lost with P/O Ken Graham on 8 February. (*Cliff Rudland archives*)

S/L John Munro at a snowy RAF Exeter, early 1941. (*Munro Family archives*)

P6976 in a field at Cannington near Bridgwater, Somerset, after Sgt Skellon ran out of fuel on a cross country exercise. (*Author*)

Above left: Austin 7 'Far better performance than a Whirlwind' cartoon given to John Munro on leaving the squadron. (*Munro Family archives*)

Above right: Sgt Robert Skellon. *(Dorothy Skellon archives)*

March 1941

March provided three more combats, all Ju.88s, but at a grievous cost; two of the squadron's most aggressive pilots were severely injured in remarkably similar accidents. The first of these contacts saw P/O Kitchener and P/O Thornton-Brown intercept a Ju.88 twenty miles south of the Lizard, and after a long stern chase, Thornton-Brown fired 156 rounds from 200 yards and saw hits on the fuselage before the bomber disappeared into cloud. The same pair found another Ju.88 on 5 March, just south of the Scillies. This time Thornton-Brown got lost in cloud while turning to attack, but Kitchener fired all 240 rounds of his ammunition and observed damage to the bomber's port wing. When last seen it was making for home just twenty feet above the water.

A few days later on the 11th, P/O Herbert Horatio Kitchener DFM tangled with yet another Ju.88, he recalls:

> The weather on the 11 was so bad that the squadron was released early in the morning although two of us were required to remain at Readiness in case there was a flap. F/L Crooks and I volunteered. It was pouring with rain all morning, but around 1530 the ops Room rang through to say that a bandit (Raid 105) was flying along the south coast and if we thought the weather was clear enough would one of us go up and take a look. Dave (Crooks) said 'what about it' and I replied, 'I'll go.' I took off in P6985 into poor visibility with solid cloud at just a few hundred feet

P/O Herbert Kitchener DFM.
(*Lilian Macdonald archives*)

and was told to patrol near St Ives but if I thought the weather was too bad, to return and not fly out to sea. As I could not see much, I returned to St Eval after almost an hour of instrument flying. As I taxied to dispersal, I saw Dave taking off, so asked for my aircraft to be quickly re-fuelled and waited in the crew room. Not long after, ops telephoned to say they had lost contact with him and would I go up again. I took off and flew south over Cornwall then proceeded to patrol over the coast at 22,000 feet until the Controller informed me that the Bandit was coming towards me from the west just out to sea. I looked in the direction indicated, and there it was, but as I had had no contact with Dave, I thought it might have been him so climbed to 24,000 feet to give myself time as the unidentified aircraft flew beneath me. The Whirlwind was very unstable at that height and not nice to fly or manoeuvre. As I turned and looked down, I saw the black crosses on the wings and thought it was either a 110 or 88 so I commenced a dive onto his tail but although I was going very fast and had the height advantage, I only gained slowly. He was headed for France and a thick bank of cloud just off the coast, and although I was flying at full throttle I realised that he would reach the cloud before I could close to a decent range. Remembering my previous encounter with thick cloud I opened fire with a short burst and saw pieces fly off the fuselage, but noticed a burst of tracer and heard a thud on my port side and glycol began streaming from the engine. By now, we had entered the cloud and I lost sight of him so turned for home shutting the port engine down as I did so. The weather between 20,000 and 15,000 feet was lovely, but as I descended through 12,000 feet it began to change, and below 10,000 feet, it was bad. I made landfall near Falmouth where I received another shock. I had been concentrating on my navigation so much that I had not noticed the temperature of the starboard engine. It usually read 130 degrees but was more than 200 degrees and it sounded very rough. I realised I would not make St Eval and did not want to risk crossing Dartmoor on one engine, so remembering a recent lecture by the air sea rescue boys, I undid my straps and prepared to bail out. Just as I was about to transmit a 'Mayday' the thought struck me that the Germans would be listening and as I did not want to admit defeat, I changed my mind. Predannack near Falmouth was unfinished, but it had one runway in operation. In fact we had about a dozen ground crew there with fuel for when we operated off the south coast so I turned towards it, forgetting to re-do my straps. The starboard engine was spluttering badly by now and the temperature was 'off the clock' but I kept on a heading for that sole runway at just above stalling speed. I informed the Controller of my intention, and as the aerodrome came into view, I unsuccessfully attempted to re-start the port engine. As I crossed the boundary at about ten feet with the wheels and flaps down, the starboard engine cut, the aircraft stalled and crashed. I don't remember much after that, but apparently I crashed near a gang of workmen and they pulled me from the wreckage just seconds before the aircraft blew up. I was rushed to hospital with a fractured skull and elbow and remained there for some six months.[13]

Three days later the other half of the squadron's most successful duo, P/O Patrick Glynn Thornton-Brown, also crashed. During a patrol over the Lizard with Sgt Mason, his starboard engine failed, quickly followed by his R/T and Wireless. He descended through thick cloud and managed to find Portreath, but then flew around for twenty minutes attempting to burn off excess fuel before attempting to land. Unfortunately, as he crossed the boundary with undercarriage and flaps down the port engine cut, *P6988 HE-J* stalled and crashed. He was seriously injured and only returned to flying duties in 1943.

P6985 HE-J was lost on 11 March. *(Author)*

Construction equipment, such as this steam roller, posed a hazard to aircraft running off the runway. (*Chris Thomas archives*)

Cliff Rudland remembers one incident that took place at St Eval during this period:

> One of the Bowsers was parked behind S/L Donaldson's office, and we would help ourselves to some fuel for our cars. It was surprising the performance you got from a clapped out old motor with 100-octane, the engines didn't last too long though. Unfortunately, whoever was on lookout missed the CO approaching because he caught us. He said, 'Christ, what are you lot doing?' There was a short pause, and then he added, 'I'm CO, I'm first.'[14]

On the nights of 12 and 14 March, St Eval was bombed and at least nine Whirlwinds damaged, as a result, the aircraft were dispersed to Portreath at night, and the on 18 March the squadron moved there permanently. The station was still under construction, and was described by the ORB as, 'without form or void'. A house in Portreath village served as the officers' mess; holiday chalets on the cliff top as the sergeants' mess, and unfinished Nissen huts on the aerodrome accommodated the ground crews. These were damp, with no running water, no lighting, and no sanitation. To compound the problems, the operations Room remained at St Eval, and on several occasions all phone lines between Portreath and St Eval failed and communications were only possible by W/T. The pilots on readiness sat huddled over oil stoves in the Watch Office, and whilst the three runways were good, the surfaces at the sides were still under construction, which resulted in a number of accidents, the worst of which occurred when Sgt Lawson overshot a landing in *P6991* and collided with a motor roller. The Board of Enquiry found that he had, 'landed with too much speed, and had put too great a reliance on his brakes'.

April 1941

April was marked by a succession of tragedies resulting in the loss of F/L Crooks DFC, F/O Howe and P/O Milligan, whilst the operational flying consisted mainly of convoy patrols from Portreath and Mullion, in fact so many were flown from the latter on 3 April that the aerodrome's petrol supply was exhausted. On the whole these patrols were routine and uneventful, but there was occasional action as was evidenced by P/O Ferdinand and Sgt King who engaged a Ju.88 of KG54, which was attacking a ship in convoy *Sapper* off Falmouth. Ferdinand fired two bursts at the bomber before it escaped into cloud with no visible signs of damage.

S/L Donaldson and F/L Crooks were scrambled from Mullion on 1 April to patrol base. When they were over Land's End they were informed of an incoming raid approaching Portreath at 8,000 feet and were vectored towards it. Donaldson identified a Dornier Do.217 and commenced an attack, at which point Crooks was slightly behind him, but after calling the 'Tally Ho' he lost sight of his colleague. He opened fire at 250 yards when he saw the black crosses on the fuselage, and as the bomber turned away in a shallow dive he fired two more bursts whilst closing to 50 yards. After the last burst, several pieces flew off both engines, which began emitting black and white smoke before the bomber half rolled and dived into cloud. Donaldson followed and broke through into the clear at 500 feet over the coast facing out to sea. He turned around and saw a column of smoke rising from a crashed aircraft which he assumed was the Dornier. Unfortunately it was from the wreckage of Whirlwind *P6989*. F/L David Andrew Cummings Crooks, who had received a DFC flying Fairey Battles with 266 Squadron in France, died when *HE-J* crashed near Helston on Goonhilly Downs, Cornwall. S/L Donaldson did not see return fire, but the wreckage had several 7.9-mm bullet holes in it which would point to F/L Crooks being shot down by the Dornier.

Not every scramble resulted in the interception of an enemy aircraft, more often than not the 'plot' disappeared from the radar and the Whirlwinds were recalled, or, as happened on more than one occasion the 'bandit' turned out to be a friendly Coastal Command aircraft. It was somewhat unusual therefore that when P/O Tooth and F/O Howe intercepted two Heinkel He.111s south of the Lizard and clearly damaged both of them, neither pilot submitted a claim. The two I/KG27 aircraft jettisoned their bombs and dived to within a few feet of the sea making the interception extremely difficult. A claim was eventually submitted to Fighter Command by the Adjutant in May but it was denied, being too long after the event.

The squadron left Portreath on the 10 and moved to RAF Filton, where it had formed on the 1 October 1939, causing the ORB to comment that, 'The facilities were far superior to those of Portreath, with proper fighter pens, permanent hangars and brick built accommodation. Since then the operational flying has been limited to convoy patrols in the Bristol Channel.'

Personnel movements saw Sgts Herbert John Blackshaw and Joseph William Ernest Holmes report for flying duties in place of P/O Donald William Lintern and Sgt James Edwards Sainsbury who were posted, as was P/O Geoffrey Hugh Hadley, the Adjutant, who was replaced by P/O Charles Stanley Fleet.

One weakness in the design of the Whirlwind came to the fore in April. The stern frame was a light alloy casting to which the tail wheel and its hydraulic retraction jack

F/L David Andrew Cummings Crooks DFC was lost on 1 April. (*Kevin Meldrum archives*)

Lance Lowes (centre) was an engine fitter. (*Lance Lowes archives*)

were attached, but it was prone to cracking when subjected to heavy landings and to replace it entailed the removal of the whole tail unit. At one point there were five tail-less Whirlwinds sat at Filton awaiting repair, but the problem existed for several more months until a new steel frame was designed by Westland engineers Hugh Saint and Eric Sibley, who also devised a quick method of installing it without removing the tail.

There were two very similar accidents during the latter half of the month, both fatal. On 20 April F/O Bernard Howe had visited friends at RAF Wittering and, as was customary, on departing he 'beat up' the aerodrome. Eyewitnesses said he dived from 5,000 feet, crossed the boundary at twenty feet and high speed, then half way across the aerodrome pulled two slightly inclined upward rolls. As he completed the second however, something fell away from *P6992*, which immediately went into a spin and crashed in the grounds of nearby Burghley House, bursting into flames on impact. He was buried in Wittering (All Saints) Churchyard with Full Military Honours, the squadron being represented by S/L Donaldson and F/L Pugh.

The second accident occurred on the final day of the month when S/L Donaldson, P/O Milligan and Sgt Rudland flew to RAF Harwell for a Fighter Affiliation Exercise with three Wellingtons of 15 OTU. They were to carry out stern attacks on a section of three bombers at 4,000 feet whilst they were tracked by the trainee Air Gunners. The first three attacks took place according to plan, but Milligan appeared to misjudge the closing speed on his fourth and in an effort to avoid a collision pulled into a sharp climbing turn to port. As he did, something was seen to fall away from the aircraft, then seconds later the port wing folded back; the tail unit broke away and the remainder of the aircraft – *P7008* – tumbled to earth and crashed half a mile east of Aldermaston. P/O George Stanley Milligan, a veteran of the Norwegian Expeditions, did not bale out.

Following these accidents and another involving Sgt Rudland in *P6974* (although he landed safely), all aerobatics and violent manoeuvres were restricted pending the results of an investigation. *P7008* had a little over six hours air time and her remains were taken to Farnborough for examination by the Accidents Investigation Branch. They found that as P/O Milligan pulled up to avoid a collision, she entered a high speed stall which caused the outer slats to open. The slat mounting had not been designed for such stress and broke away fatally damaging the front spar; this in turn weakened the wing structure which collapsed. The tail unit came off under centrifugal force as the wreckage spun to earth and did not contribute to the accident. It was clear however that both this accident and that of F/O Howe were the result of a high speed stall which subsequent tests at A&AEE Boscombe Down on *P6997* confirmed. The Handley Page slats were constructed of duralumin with two aluminium alloy formers which carried the lugs for the track attachment. Operated by aerodynamic forces, there had been several accidents attributed to these lugs shearing and slats coming adrift during high speed manoeuvres, the slats were therefore bolted shut, and whilst take-off, approach and landing speeds were unaffected, the pilots reported that the aircraft was much more pleasant to fly at speeds at which the slats were previously open.

P/O Donald Vine, P/O George Milligan, P/O David Stein and P/O Roy Ferdinand, RAF Drem, early November 1940. (*Tom Eeles archives*)

May 1941

During May the squadron flew eighty-one convoy patrols and twenty-two other patrols, a total of 210 sorties, but made no contact with the enemy. The training also continued, led enthusiastically by S/L Donaldson, who after one formation flight wrote in his logbook, 'This was the first time anywhere that twelve Whirlwinds were airborne together.' He also flew a Spitfire Mk.II in a comparison test with F/L Pugh in a Whirlwind; the results showed the Spit to be 10 mph slower than the Whirlwind at 3,000 feet.

The compliment of the squadron was strengthened in May when eight pilots reported for flying duties, P/Os Humphrey St John Coghlan, and Norman James Freeman, W/O Geoffrey Higson Wylde, F/S Anthony Victor Albertini, and Sgts Frank Oswald Dimblebee, Harry Garthwaite, Reginald Gunn Pascoe, and John James Walker. Five were posted out however – Freeman, Wylde, Sgt Glyn Barrow Foden, Sgt Robert Burton Skellon and Sgt Walter David Waddington. On landing following his first solo, Freeman swung off the runway and tipped *P6982* on her nose, causing substantial damage. He was thought to be 'unfit for fighters' whilst Skellon was 'not suitable for Whirlwinds' and Foden was re-mustered to ground duties. Cliff Rudland remembered that Waddington 'was rarely seen without his .38 Smith & Wesson revolver and it was rumoured he even wore it in bed.'[15]

Some accidents were unavoidable; others were a result of over enthusiasm or lack of judgement, and two incidents on 29 April exemplified this. The first involved P/O

Sgt Walter Waddington with .38 Smith and Wesson revolver and Sgt Dennis Mason with a Morris 10, at RAF Portreath. (*Cliff Rudland archives*)

Sgt Don Tebbit wrote off *P7006* on 29 May. (*Author*)

Coghlan and *P6979*. As he landed at Filton, one of the main wheels burst which locked up the wheel and caused an uncontrollable ground loop, following which the undercarriage collapsed. Coghlan was absolved of blame; unfortunately the same could not be said of Sgt Tebbit who wrote off *P7006* whilst on a training flight. He collided with a balloon cable, and crash-landed two miles north of Chepstow where *P7006* burnt out after possibly trying to fly under the old Sharpness Bridge. S/L Donaldson placed him under open arrest and grounded him pending an enquiry, but as there were no eyewitnesses, the charges were dropped and he returned to flying duties, but the incident severely delayed his future promotion.

June 1941

The accelerated wartime training programme all too frequently also led to accidents such as the one which occurred on 11 June. P/O Rudland led Sgt Pascoe on a formation flying exercise, but forty-five minutes into the flight, as they approached Usk, the latter announced that his port engine had failed. Rudland told him to apply full power on the starboard engine and full opposite rudder and assured him he would be able to return to base safely, but instead Pascoe decided to make a forced landing. Eyewitnesses stated that the aircraft *(L6845)* came down under control near Llandenny with one engine smoking and the undercarriage lowered, but just before touchdown she clipped a large tree, lost her tail and cart wheeled across a field shedding wings and engines in the process, and eventually came to rest in a small stream. Pascoe was thrown clear but died a short time later from internal injuries. Apparently when the wreckage was removed much time was spent searching for his revolver. The engines were sent to Rolls-Royce for examination, and their report stated that the port engine had failed due to a shortage of oil, causing the 'big ends' of Nos. 3 and 4 to seize and break, which in turn caused the connecting rod bolts to stretch and fracture. The oil tanks had been topped up prior to the flight, but due to crash damage, they were unable to determine the cause of the oil shortage.

A Board of Enquiry concluded that Pascoe's inexperience on type, just sixteen hours, was a major factor to the accident, he had undershot his landing in an impossible field and lowered the undercarriage prior to gliding in to land. A more experienced pilot would have returned on one engine. Reginald Gunn Pascoe had only been with the squadron for a month, but the ORB noted, 'He was already well liked by his comrades.'

The squadron was still coming to terms with the loss of Sgt Pascoe when on the following day Roy Frederick Ferdinand was killed as *P7045* spun in from fifty feet on approach to Filton. He was seen to make several steep turns during a low, slow approach and at first it was thought it may have been due to a slat failure causing asymmetric lift but investigation of the wreckage showed the slats to be locked shut and that the accident would have occurred even if they had not been. The ORB noted, 'He had become one of the real characters of the squadron, and his death is deeply regretted and mourned by all who knew him.'

Sgt Holmes came close to being a casualty twice in the same day. As he landed at Filton following an aerobatic practice in *P7000*, the rudder bar slipped out of his reach. The aircraft then veered off the runway and was brought to an abrupt halt when it collided

Above left: Sgt Reginald Pascoe was lost on 11 June. (*Della Payne archives*)

Above right: F/O Roy Ferdinand was lost on 12 June. (*Author*)

Sgt Carl Long was posted on 12 June. (*Carl Long archives*)

with a piece of farm machinery. The conclusion was that the rudder bar was not been locked and as it was hidden from view beneath the instrument panel, instructions were issued to check it was locked by giving it a swift kick. Later in the day, on a convoy patrol off Barry, in *P7005*, he approached too close to shore, and flew into the cable of a barrage balloon which was hidden in cloud. Luckily there was no serious damage and he returned to base.

F/S Robert Arthur Brackley and Sgts Thomas Hunter and Geoffrey Buckwell arrived for flying duties to replace P/O Albert Tooth, Sgt Carl Arthur Long and Sgt Donald Frank Jellicoe Tebbit. The latter due to his crash in May, although he returned in October 1942 to complete his tour.

Warhead

Intelligence reports indicated that I and II/JG.2 and part of III/JG.26 were based at Maupertus aerodrome with seventy Me.109s, and that III/JG.2 was at Querqueville aerodrome with thirty more. So, on Saturday 14 June, the Whirlwinds finally commenced offensive operations when S/L Donaldson, F/L Pugh, P/O Mason and Sgt Rudland flew operation 'Warhead No. 1'. Donaldson and Rudland were met by intense flak over Maupertus as they attacked tarpaulin covered dispersal pens, reporting later that they

F/O Joe Hughes, P/O George Milligan, P/O Cliff Rudland, Sgt Herbert Blackshaw, Sgt Don Tebbit, and F/S Cecil King, at RAF Filton. The houses were used as billets. (*Cliff Rudland archives*)

saw their shells exploding in the pens, but could not determine results. Pugh and Mason found Querqueville covered by a thick morning mist and were forced to return.' Not an auspicious beginning, but a beginning nevertheless.

The only other incident of note during the month involved F/O Stein, F/S Blackshaw and Sgts Jowitt, King, Rudland, and Walker who were scrambled and given several vectors onto 'an enemy aircraft with a fighter behind it.' They intercepted a twin engine aircraft identified as a Junkers Ju.88 with a Defiant on its tail and Stein led the section into the attack. Seconds before opening fire however he recognised the machine as a Blenheim and shouted a warning over the R/T. All broke away except King, who fired a two-second burst at the bomber, luckily he missed.

July 1941

The Squadron led a nomadic existence during July, making excursions to Exeter Ibsley, Middle Wallop and Portreath to relieve squadrons taking part in offensive operations over France. In addition, seven interception patrols and forty-seven convoy patrols were flown but no contact was made with the enemy. Between the detachments, experiments were carried out testing the efficiency of the Whirlwind's cannons against tanks. Two pilots reported for flying duties, Sgts Jack Maddocks and John Eutychus Meredith; they replaced Sgts Harry Garthwaite and Graham Lewis Lawson.

August 1941: 'The Whirlwind Proves Itself'[16] – Warhead Continued

The Warhead operations begun in June continued during the first week of August. The first, Warhead No. 2, was a simultaneous attack on Querqueville and Maupertus aerodromes. S/L Donaldson and F/L Hughes crossed the French coast east of Cap de la Hague and flew to Querqueville where they attacked an aircraft that was being refuelled by the hangars. The ORB described it as a 'good beat up of the aerodrome' and as they returned over the Baie de Nacqueville, they also sank a dinghy. F/L Pugh and P/O Mason abandoned their attack on Maupertus and strafed an E-Boat they found half a mile off Cherbourg Harbour, leaving it smoking fiercely amidships and sinking. Warhead No. 3 was again a double-header. S/L Donaldson and Sgt Holmes attacked Ju.87s and Me.109s at Maupertus, leaving several burning, and then as they withdrew strafed lorries on the coast road destroying at least two. At the same time F/L Hughes and Sgt Jowitt attacked a wireless station near Querqueville.

P/O Mason, P/O Coghlan, Sgt Rudland, and Sgt Brackley set out on Warhead No. 4 to attack Maupertus but according to the ORB, 'Their navigation seems to have left something to be desired and, not to put too fine a point on it; they do not know where they got to. They flew out on a course of 184 degrees but there is considerable disagreement as to which part of the French coast they struck. Some say Cap de la Hague, while others say Pointe de Barfleur. At any rate, they did not find the aerodrome and after orbiting for a short time in search of a target, P/O Mason gave the order to return.' Five miles off the French coast he attacked an E-Boat leaving it sinking whilst the others knocked chunks off a nearby lighthouse. They returned on 257 degrees and made landfall at Portland, which suggests they had been near Pointe de Barfleur not Cap de la Hague.

As if the squadron needed it, Warheads 5 and 6 resulted in the 'complete vindication of the Whirlwind as an offensive aircraft.' With the failure of Warhead No. 1, S/L Donaldson, P/O Coghlan, Sgt Rudland and F/S Albertini flew Warhead No. 5. This time they reached Maupertus where Donaldson strafed a line of Me.109s and Ju.87s which were 'well and truly shot up' whilst Rudland dived down to 100 feet and fired a two second burst at a Me.109 just as it left the ground, seeing it catch fire and crash.[17] Coghlan and Albertini also went down the line of Me.109s damaging several and as the four withdrew they left several columns of thick black smoke rising from the burning aircraft. Rudland stated that Maupertus 'had all the appearance of being a very well pranged aerodrome.' Back out over the Channel Donaldson attacked two 3,000 ton tankers five miles off Cherbourg scoring hits on the bridge of one and leaving it smoking. These vessels became the target for Warhead No. 6 by S/L Donaldson, Sgt Rudland, P/O Mason and F/S Brackley, but the ORB noted, 'This time the Hun was on his toes, and five miles off the French coast between Querqueville and Cap de la Hague they were met by three Me.109s followed by twelve to twenty more. A terrific dogfight developed between 1,500 feet and sea level, and although outnumbered five-to-one they more than held their own.' Donaldson noted that, 'Everywhere one looked there were 109s on Whirlwinds tails!' He saw Mason being chased by two, so pulled in behind and fired a half second burst at one from 200 yards. It did a half roll and dived away but he followed and his second burst ripped a panel off its wing. This was followed by a puff of white smoke, indicating a hit in the radiator but he then lost it whilst taking avoiding action from the attentions of several of its colleagues. Brackley heard Rudland call over the R/T 'there are two 109s on my tail' and saw a Whirlwind to his right being chased by two fighters. The first crossed his sights too quickly but he fired a two and a half second burst at the second which flew right through his stream of shells and dropped like a stone into the sea. As this was happening however a 109 got on his tail, but Rudland, who had evaded his own pursuer, turned back through 180 degrees and saw Brackley coming towards him followed by a 109. He opened fire at 300 yards and broke away five feet above it as they passed and saw his shells strike just behind the cockpit, but as he pulled around he could only see Brackley. S/L Howell, leading the escorting Spitfires, saw the 109 go straight into the sea, and confirmed Rudland's second victory of the day. The Whirlwinds gradually withdrew from the mêlée and returned home where Donaldson's and Rudland's machines were found to be riddled with bullet holes. Brackley had a more eventful return trip. Shortly after leaving the combat his starboard engine began running rough and emitting white smoke. He shut it down, flew the final sixty miles on the port engine and headed for the first available aerodrome, RAF Hurn. On final approach however his port fuel tank, which had been hit in combat, ran dry, the engine stopped, and the aircraft stalled and crashed. The lack of interconnection between fuel tanks was a factor in the crash, as the starboard tank held fuel for thirty minutes more flying. *P6983* was the first aircraft to 'land' on the new runway at RAF Hurn and the ORB noted of the Warhead operations, 'One fallacy was exploded, namely that the Whirlwind is no match for a Messerschmitt Me.109.'

The squadron moved from Filton to RAF Charmy Down on 7 August prompting the ORB to note, 'a station now in a very similar state to that in which we found at Portreath, more need not be said.'

Cliff Rudland claimed two kills on 6 August, seen here with *P6991 HE-R*. (*Cliff Rudland archives*)

Operation 77

Cliff Rudland remembers flying a series of endurance tests with S/L Donaldson during the first week of the month: 'We escorted the squadron Hurricane to Suffolk and back on several occasions.'[18] Fourteen aircraft were ordered to RAF Martlesham Heath on 11 August where the reason for the endurance tests became apparent – Operation No. 77 was an attack on two power stations near Cologne, the Goldenberg Plant at Knapsack and the Fortuna Plant at Quadrath by fifty-four Blenheims of 2 Group. S/L Donaldson, F/L Hughes, F/L Pugh, F/O Coghlan, F/O Stein, P/O Mason, P/O Rudland, F/S Albertini, Sgt Blackshaw, Sgt Buckwell, Sgt Jowitt and Sgt King were to provide close escort as far as Antwerp. 'We took off, all twelve of us, in line abreast and rendezvoused with the bombers and Spitfires over Orford Ness.' The Blenheims flew at fifty feet in two boxes, with six of the Whirlwinds at the same height between the two boxes and six up sun of them. As the formation crossed the Dutch coast the Whirlwinds climbed to 1,000 feet and weaved above the bombers, but seven minutes later, near Doel, four miles north-west of Antwerp, they reached the limit of their endurance and turned back[19] They followed the course of the Scheldt, six aircraft flying at fifty feet while the other six weaved above them at 500 feet. Near Walcheren they attacked six flak barges, sinking one and damaging two. Pugh also damaged another barge north west of Walcheren. No enemy fighters were seen but flak was experienced from several points and the ORB noted, 'on the outward journey, F/O Stein observed some soldiers run out of a house, and shoot at him with rifles. He marked the position on his map saying "I'll deal with you later, when I have more time." On the return journey, he and Sgt King searched diligently for the spot but were unable to find it.' The Blenheims successfully bombed their targets, but at a cost of twelve aircraft and the squadron later received a telegram from Air-Vice Marshal Orlebar,[20] AOC 10 Group thanking them for their part in the operation.

> Very many thanks for your courageous support today. You will be glad to hear that the two great Power Stations of the Rhur, Knapsack and Quadrath with an output totalling nearly a million Kilowatts were completely destroyed and described by one of the bombing leaders as 'fucked up' for the rest of the war. Would be glad if you would convey the thanks of leaders and crews of 2 Group to S/L Donaldson and 263 Squadron, W/C Herbert Percy, S/L Forbes and 66 Squadron, S/L Darwin and 152 Squadron and S/L Stevens and 234 Squadron. Well done – Orlebar.

Lannion and Maupertus

During the second half of August, the squadron was involved in a series of five attacks on the aerodromes at Lannion and Maupertus. The first of these saw four Whirlwinds make a feint at Maupertus at 15,000 feet with the intention of enticing German fighters into the air and allowing the Spitfire and Hurricane escort to deal with them. The ORB noted however that, 'The Hun was not playing.' S/L Donaldson, F/L Pugh, P/O Rudland, and F/S Albertini flew the second attack from Predannack against Lannion accompanied by seven Spitfires of 66 Squadron. They made landfall at Ile Grande, but were then intercepted and chased fifty miles out to sea by several Me.109s. The third attack was a simultaneous strike on both aerodromes. Only three aircraft were available to attack Lannion, but F/L Pugh, F/L Hughes, and F/O Coghlan, escorted by 66 Squadron, had a field day. Pugh attacked two Ju.88s parked between Hangars, seeing explosions and fires in both; Coghlan attacked two more, again observing smoke and flames, whilst Hughes attacked a solitary Ju.88 in the southern dispersal area and also saw it start to burn. The ORB noted, 'An admirable escort was provided by 66 Squadron who damaged four Ju.88s. Not a bad three minutes work, five Ju.88s destroyed and four damaged.' A POW report on 4 October confirmed the claims, though two of the aircraft destroyed were Do.217s.

The strike against Maupertus was also successful. P/O Rudland, P/O Mason, F/S Brackley and Sgt Meredith escorted by the Spitfires of 234 Squadron destroyed seven Ju.87s and a Ju.88. Unfortunately, the penultimate attack on Lannion failed due to an incorrect wind being forecast which saw the formation make landfall too far east; whilst the squadron's role in the final attack on Lannion was minor. They formed part of the Predannack Wing which provided withdrawal cover for Blenheims that had bombed the aerodrome on *'Operation Gudgeon IV.'*

On 21 August, S/L Donaldson was awarded the Distinguished Flying Cross, and promoted to Wing Commander Flying, Colerne, to command a Whirlwind Wing. F/L Pugh replaced him, but W/C Donaldson flew several more sorties with the squadron, which almost proved to be his undoing. He also noted in his logbook that the first month of offensive operations had been an unqualified success, and the Whirlwind had 'proved itself at last'.

F/L Tom Pugh became the fourth Whirlwind CO. (*Tom Eeles archives*)

September 1941

September saw an influx of eighteen pilots, due to the imminent formation of 137 Squadron. They were F/O Colin Anthony Gordon Clark, P/Os John Michael Bryan, Philip Harvey, Ormond John Horace Hoskins, John Clifford Lawton, George William Martin, and Geoffrey Berrington Wames, Sgts James Patrick Coyne RCAF, Ralph Otto Gustaf Häggberg, John Frederick Luing, Hugh Leo O'Neill, Maurice John Peskett, Derrick Ellis Prior, John Joseph Robinson, Kenneth Charles Ridley, Basil Lionel Robertson, John Anthony William Sandy, and Douglas Francis Small. In addition, F/O Arthur Hereward Ormerod, who had been Squadron Adjutant since July 1940, was replaced by P/O Andrew Sigfrid Wordsworth, and P/O Rudland received the DFC.

The first offensive sorties of the month took place on the fourth under the guise of 'Operation Gudgeon VI' when twelve Whirlwinds provided close escort for six Blenheims detailed to bomb the SS *Solmglint*, a 10,000-ton whale oil ship, in Cherbourg Harbour. The Whirlwinds rendezvoused with the bombers at 8,000 feet over Warmwell and took up station with four aircraft in line astern on each side of the bombers and 500 feet above, two aircraft to the rear and 500 feet above, and two aircraft weaving 500 feet above the whole formation. Top cover was provided by the Spitfires of 302 Squadron. They were not intercepted until the Blenheims were on their bombing run, but at that point several combats took place almost simultaneously.

A single Me.109 dived on the formation, but F/O Stein turned into its attack and fired at it from 600 yards damaging it; two more approached the bombers but S/L Pugh and P/O Rudland turned towards them and they made off, whilst P/O Mason, who was one of the 'weavers', observed two more approaching from astern. He turned into them and fired a half second burst at one causing it to break away but the other got on his tail and followed him in a dive to sea and for thirty miles out over the Channel. It eventually turned back but not before scoring numerous hits and the pilot, Feldwebel Phillip of JG2, later claimed to have shot him down. Sgt Holmes, the second 'weaver', was attacked by three 109s but avoided their combined fire. Over the harbour two 109s attacked Sgt Buckwell, who, it was thought, did not see them. His starboard engine caught fire and he baled out of *P7042* some five miles off Cherbourg. The 109s were attacked by a section of 302 Squadron and both were claimed destroyed, but neither was in fact hit. As the formation withdrew, the *Solmglint* was ablaze, and more importantly an armed trawler was seen putting out from Cherbourg Harbour to rescue Geoffrey Buckwell. (See Chapter 13)

Ten Whirlwinds acted as anti-flak escort to twelve Blenheims on a shipping strike against a convoy on the 8th. Unfortunately, P/O Rudland was forced to turn back with engine trouble and owing to a misunderstanding he was followed by Sgts Holmes and Hunter. The remainder of the formation continued and found two convoys near Guernsey – the first comprised a tug and four barges; the second, eight tugs and several small vessels. S/L Pugh, P/O Coghlan and P/O Mason attacked a 400-ton vessel in the second convoy, leaving it 'burning along the whole length of its deck', whilst Sgt King attacked two tugs in the same convoy, leaving one of them sinking. F/L Hughes, P/O Mason, F/S Brackley, Sgt Blackshaw and Sgt Walker attacked a tug in the first convoy, 'doing considerable damage'. The Whirlwinds then returned to base, Pugh and Coghlan with the bombers, the remainder singly and in pairs.

F/L Cliff Rudland and W/C Arthur Donaldson outside Buckingham Palace after receiving the DFC and DFC and AFC respectively. (*Cliff Rudland archives*)

F/L Joe Hughes, P/O Cliff Rudland, and P/O Dennis Mason. (*Cliff Rudland archives*)

A Gestapo HQ near Quinéville was the objective of a Mandolin on the tenth by P/O Mason and F/O Stein. They crossed the Channel at twenty feet and flew down the French coast to the Iles St Marcouf, but as they crossed the coast, visibility dropped to 1,000 yards and although they searched between Lestré and Montebourg they were unable to identify the target. In the hope of finding a secondary target they made for St Vaast de la Hogue to search for E-Boats, but east of Lestré they found a Bofors gun position and a battery of four machine guns. Mason led them up to cloud base (1,200 feet), stall turned and dived down on the guns. Stein followed him in the dive waiting for him to pull up before opening fire himself, but Mason dived straight into the ground. His aircraft (*P7001*) did not catch fire, but disintegrated on impact and finished on her back in shallow water. Stein delivered three attacks on the Bofors gun then silenced the machine gun battery with his remaining ammunition, before flying four circuits of the crashed aircraft, but could see no signs of life. He returned to base to report the death of Dennis William Mason. The ORB noted that, 'His loss was keenly felt by the whole squadron.'

Between the operational sorties and convoy patrols, training continued, and so too did the inevitable accidents, five during the month of September. Sgt Jowitt was involved in two, the first in *P7013* when the starboard engine failed; he landed heavily and the port wingtip struck the ground. The Board of Enquiry noted that, 'The Whirlwind will fly perfectly well on one engine if the speed is kept above 150 mph. The pilot allowed the speed to drop

Sgt Douglas St John Jowitt was involved in two accidents during September. (*John LaGette archives*)

below this, and consequently made the approach in a semi-stalled position.' The second accident, in *P7035*, occurred when the tail wheel would not lower due to faulty hydraulics; the stern frame and rudder were badly damaged, but he was not blamed. Sgt Prior, *P6983*, stalled on approach and landed heavily following the failure of his starboard engine and Sgt Sandy *P7005* had a tyre burst on landing causing the aircraft to swing off the runway. The result in both cases was that the undercarriage collapsed. The worst accident of the month occurred on the fifteenth, however, when Sgt Meredith overshot his landing in *P6996* and, although he attempted to take off again, clipped *P7039* which was parked near the runway, then crashed into a Nissen Hut where the aircraft caught fire. Meredith was uninjured but an unfortunate airman who was in the hut suffered severe though not fatal injuries. *P7039* required a new tail and starboard outer wing but *P6996* was written off.

Following intelligence reports of Ju.88s based at Morlaix aerodrome, a Mandolin on 28 September aimed to catch them on the ground. W/C Donaldson, S/L Pugh, Sgt Dimblebee and Sgt King, escorted by eleven Spitfires of 313 Squadron, crossed the French coast over Plouescat. From there they flew to Taule, and then climbed to 500 feet as they approached Morlaix. Unfortunately, the aerodrome was devoid of the promised bombers, and the only aircraft visible was a single Me.109 near a blister hangar. Pugh fired a two second burst at it and saw hits on the wings and fuselage, then continued across the aerodrome, being struck several times by flak as he did so; Dimblebee and King also attacked the Me.109, but Donaldson's attack was rather more eventful. The following account was written by him whilst convalescing.

> I am Wing Commander Flying for the Colerne Sector of 10 Group. My chief job should be to lead a Wing of Whirlwind Fighters that is two Squadrons, 263 and 137. As the latter Squadron has only just formed I have had no opportunity, as yet, to lead the Wing, so I have been in the habit of keeping

Sgt John Meredith, Sgt Herbert Blackshaw, and P/O Les Currie. (*Cliff Rudland archives*)

> myself interested by joining 263 Squadron on some of their numerous 'beat-ups' of aerodromes etc in the Cherbourg-Brest area. On this occasion, we flew from Charmy Down to Predannack in Cornwall to operate from there. The CO of the squadron was to lead one section, and I was to lead the other in an attack on Morlaix Aerodrome, which is west of Lannion. There were supposed to be about sixteen Hun aircraft on the ground and we were to have 313 (Czech) Squadron as close escort. The distance from Predannack is about 120 miles, and we all flew at sea level to avoid being picked up by Hun RDF. We hit the French coast about ten miles west of Morlaix and eventually picked up the aerodrome. Unfortunately the sixteen Hun aircraft which were reported must have flown away, because all I saw was one 109 with no prop, which led me to believe it was a dummy; and a petrol bowser. I can remember thinking that the flak was more intense than ever before, but it does not worry one. One feels that it will only bounce off if it does hit you. I was weaving frantically and I climbed to 300 feet to attack an AA post, I silenced the gunners, and then I attacked the 'phoney' 109. This attack did not seem to catch it alight as usual, so I realised it was a dummy and concentrated on the petrol bowser. I remember I was rather too close to deliver a good attack, so I pushed the stick forward to get my sight lowered on to it. Of course both engines stalled or rather cut momentarily through lack of fuel. I again remember thinking that the intense flak was getting uncomfortably close, when suddenly one hit me. I felt this one because it was in the fuselage. Then there was a colossal bang and I briefly lost consciousness.

Three heavy calibre shells, probably 40 mm, hit *P7044*. Unsurprisingly, none bounced off. The first struck near the tail, destroying the tail wheel; the second struck mid-fuselage, destroying the actuating gears and rudder control cables, but the third shell caused all the trouble. Six inches lower and it would have killed him instantly, instead it exploded against the top of the canopy sending slivers of Perspex down into the cockpit, shredding his leather flying helmet and wounding him in his head, hands, and legs.

Press photo showing the damage to Donaldson's leather helmet. (*Author*)

It was a funny feeling, rather like a severe 'blackout', I could not see, although I do remember, I think, seeing the ground coming up at me. But I couldn't think for a bit, I remember, all in a flash of course, thinking 'Christ I'm hit' and my one thought was not of death but rather of the threat of being a prisoner of war. I can remember opening the throttle and pulling the stick back. I can remember too that the aircraft did not respond particularly well. The next thing I remember was gradually coming to. Here again my sense recovered before my sight, and when I could see, I noticed that I was out to sea about a mile, meaning that I had travelled three to four miles at about 300 mph whilst unconscious. My head felt ghastly, and then I felt my arm and hand go all wet, the sort of feeling one imagines a child to have when he wets his bed. I saw that my left hand was covered in blood and the right one was a bit bloody too. I felt the blood dropping on my trousers. My head felt awful. I could not see too well and the noise in my ears was terrific. I decided that nothing was worse than being a prisoner of war, and as both engines were going, I made for home. It was some seconds before I noticed I was steering about north-east instead of north-west. I opened the throttles fully and I tried to climb, but the controls felt all wrong, all 'sloppy'. I climbed gradually and I next noticed that the blood had stopped on my hand but my arm felt very wet. I climbed to about 6,000 feet because I was certain I should have to jump by parachute. I can remember feeling my head, and noticing that my helmet was cut in two and I felt blood too. It hurt one too much to turn round and look to see if I was being chased and anyhow I did not care. I remembered that it was good thing to turn on the oxygen, which I did but it did not work. I noticed that my wireless did not work either. I was glad to see that another Whirlwind [S/L Pugh] was with me in open formation. He saw I was hit and was following me home.

Unbeknown to him, there were also several Spitfires weaving around the two Whirlwinds.

Halfway across the Channel I opened the hood because I felt so stuffy and wanted air. I noticed it only opened a little before it jammed. When I landed I had to take off my parachute off to get

Cartoon given to W/C Donaldson shortly after the event. (*Donaldson Family archives*)

> out of the gap, so I doubt if I could have jumped even if I had made up my mind. [The canopy could not be jettisoned; it was opened and closed by turning a handle on the starboard side of the cockpit.] Every few seconds I felt very faint and sick, several times I nearly jumped but then pulled myself together in time. The airspeed was showing 260 mph but I thought it might be wrong, about 120 mph was my estimate. I later found out the airspeed was in fact correct. Eventually I saw the English coast and I felt much better I almost wanted to scream with delight. I thought the aeroplane was too badly damaged to land, so I climbed to 3,000 feet, recognised the Lizard and stalled her. That seemed all right so I lost height. Once again, at 500 feet, I nearly gave up, but I was too low to jump so I pulled myself together. I did not feel like concentrating on a good landing, and I did not care if I landed downwind. Actually, I landed across wind without even knowing it. The tail wheel was shot up so the aircraft pulled up pretty quickly. I got out feeling very groggy and swore to myself because there was no ambulance. I walked around in a daze for a while and then felt very weak, so I sat down on the runway until the ambulance arrived. My head was now thumping heavily, the top felt rather sore and the singing in my ears was terrific. I could barely hear the ambulance men I was so deaf. I longed for a cigarette, which I was given. I was then taken to Sick Quarters at Portreath.

After a month in hospital he was sent to the RAF Officers Hospital in Torquay on 28 October to convalesce, but within a week he was back in harness when he ferried *P7112* from Charmy Down to Portreath. The Whirlwind Wing never materialised and as a new role was not immediately available, he kept busy flying Whirlwinds, but apart from one scramble in December he flew no further operations.

In the late afternoon of 29 September, the squadron was ordered to undertake Mandolin Operation 77 as a matter of urgency as many Ju.88s had been reported on Lannion aerodrome. F/O Coghlan, P/O Warnes, Sgt Hunter, and Sgt Maddocks were escorted at zero feet across the Channel by Spitfire IIas of 313 Squadron, but the Spitfires

F/S Joe Holmes, Sgt Thomas Hunter, F/S John Walker, Sgt Frank Dimblebee. (*Dimblebee Family archives*)

refused to cross the French coast, alleging an operational order to that effect, and the four Whirlwinds pressed on alone through the gathering darkness. Coghlan led them across the aerodrome through an intense flak barrage, and destroyed a Ju.88 near a hangar, but he later noted that he could see nothing of the others due to the gloom. Warnes noted that the darkness and tracer made it difficult to see anything, but he did fire at dispersal pens and a gun post, whilst Hunter and Maddocks attacked the hangars. Coghlan toppled his gyro whilst dodging the flak and coupled with the incorrect wind given at the hurried briefing he made landfall at the Scillies. All four ran short of fuel on their return. Coghlan's engines cut out 500-yards from the end of the runway but he force landed *P6998* in a field with little damage. When Warnes arrived over Predannack he was forced to orbit for twelve minutes waiting for the runway lights to be switched on and was on the verge of abandoning his aircraft when a chance light came on and he landed with three gallons of petrol left. Maddocks landed safely at Portreath but Thomas Hunter, *P7009*, informed the controller that he was five miles from the coast and was going to bale out as his engines were failing due to lack of fuel. One minute later he said he would not bail out until he was over the coast but nothing further was heard from him. The Exeter Observer Corps reported a parachute going into the sea five miles south-west of the Eddystone Light, but despite an extensive air sea rescue search no trace of him was found. His body washed ashore at Poldhu Cove near Mullion on the 10 October, and his death was felt more than most due to the senselessness of the operation and the lack of adequate preparation; just thirty minutes briefing was all that was possible. It was later learned that a large number of Ju.88s left Lannion thirty minutes before the attack, had they still have been on the ground, the rushed dusk operation would have been justified.

October 1941

Eight RCAF Sergeant Pilots reported for flying duties at the beginning of the month: Edger Brearley, John Robert Brennan, Donald Gill, Irving Farmer Kennedy, William Albert Lovell, John Edward McClure, Harvey Donald Muirhead, and Richard Irl Reed. Lovell and Reed were actually American citizens. Also arriving was Battle of Britain veteran F/L Guy Marsland. The second Whirlwind Squadron, No. 137, was formed at the end of September and, at the beginning of October, thirteen pilots were posted to it. They did not have far to travel, however – just across the aerodrome. They were P/Os John Michael Bryan, John Clifford Lawton, and George William Martin, Sgts James Robert Brennan. Ralph Otto Gustaf Häggberg, John Frederick Luing, Jack Maddocks, John Edward McClure RCAF, Hugh Leo O'Neill, Maurice John Peskett, Basil Lionel Robertson, John Anthony William Sandy, and Douglas Francis Small. At the same time, Engineering Officer P/O John Charles Garland was replaced by F/O Alfred Arthur Hay. As a consequence of the personnel movements, the month was quiet from an operational point of view; there were two scrambles, two convoy patrols and two Rhubarbs against Morlaix airfield. The ORB noted that the code word 'Rhubarb' had replaced 'Mandolin' at the beginning of the month to denote a small scale unescorted fighter attack upon enemy territory or shipping. There was also good news. Firstly, Geoff Buckwell, who had been shot down off Cherbourg on 4 September, was reported as a POW, and, secondly, S/L Pugh and F/L Coghlan were awarded the Distinguished Flying Cross.

P/O Harvey brought Whirlwind *P7013* in to a spectacular landing on the first of the month when the port engine cut, the port wing stalled and the undercarriage collapsed as the aircraft hit the ground. He was uninjured but a Board of Enquiry found that, 'Due to inexperience, he had opened the throttle too quickly.'

P/O Ormonde John Horace Hoskins was killed in a flying accident on the ninth. During a formation practice near Bath, he was involved in a collision with F/L Coghlan, but whilst the latter baled out and landed in Weston High Street (on the West side of Bath) and *P6999* crashed at Kelston, Hoskins appeared to have regained control of *P6968 HE-H* despite extensive damage to the tail and circled down from 7,000 feet. Eyewitnesses stated that at the last moment he pulled up to avoid several houses, stalled and spun into a railway weighbridge at Saltford. He had been with the squadron for less than a month but 'was already well liked for his good humour and cheerful personality.'

On the twelfth, Sgt Coyne flew his first solo in a Whirlwind. His experience was similar to every other novice:

> It was scary to fly for those first few flights. There was no two-seat version for dual instruction, no way of learning how to manage an aircraft with two engines, taxi it or become familiar with any odd characteristics. Much later we did get an Oxford, but only for twin-engine ground handling. The landing speed was in excess of 25 mph beyond that of the Hurricane on which I trained. My

Six of the RCAF pilots posted to the squadron at the beginning of October – Bill Lovell, Eddie Brearley, John McClure, John Mitchener, Bob Brennan, and Hap Kennedy. (*Hap Kennedy archives*)

Above left: Sgt Douglas Small, P/O George Martin and P/O Philip Harvey. (*Cliff Rudland archives*)

Above right: P/O Ormonde Hoskins was lost in *P6968 HE-H* on 9 October. (*Gordon Hoskins archives*) recollection is that we didn't even have a manual. Visibility from the cockpit was excellent and in my view, even better than the Mk.IV Mossie I flew later. The bubble canopy, which wound back on a single crank system for normal opening, was great. We were each allocated to an experienced Sergeant pilot on the squadron who became our tutor with a show and tell approach. From him we were expected to learn how to fly the Whirlwind. We also learned other useful things by going over to the maintenance hangar and inspecting the emergency systems, armament and such things. On 12 October the Flight Commander asked my tutor if I was ready to fly the aeroplane. My tutor assured him that I was, and he told me to get my parachute and sign out *P7003*. After sitting in the cockpit for what seemed like an hour but was probably about ten minutes, and being vigorously grilled by the Flight Commander, he suddenly slapped me on the shoulder and told me to 'Get it into the air.' As I sat in the cockpit I knew very little about this curiously unconventional aeroplane and all I could think of was how to get the damned thing into the air and more importantly, get it back down again. My mind still retained and half believed many of the strange rumours we had heard in the previous few weeks at OTU that it was hard to fly; that it was a killer; that it could not fly on one if you lost an engine on take-off and would proceed to roll upside down; that it had been seen to take-off, roll inverted and climb out of sight. Another story had it that, on a nose over, the four cannon which were mounted virtually in your lap would break loose and separate the top half of your body from the bottom half, and a whole host of others both good and bad. I also had the 'pukka-gen' from my tutor and I had been primed with all of the procedures necessary to get me out of me out of scrapes. But I only half-believed him when he said it was a great machine to fly. My ultimate concern had to do with the unconventional but very advanced features of the aircraft. Unlike the Spit and Hurricane which had monstrous cooling radiators hanging down in the slipstream, the Whirlwind had the rads in the wings which reduced drag, but while it was very clean-looking, this feature made the engines prone to overheating on the ground, so a quick take-off – as soon as you started the engine – was essential, and I had a long way to taxi.

Jimmy Coyne RCAF, seen here in 1943. (*Bill Watkins archives*)

There were two engines to deal with, and I wasn't completely familiar with the RAF's system of hand brakes. I had to taxi this twin-engine, marginally-cooled thing with a scant supply of air pressure. It was certainly a daunting picture. I was more than somewhat worried but told myself I had already coped with 794 flying hours and I should be able to put one more hour in safely. As I checked to see that everything was clear, my two ground crew – who knew it was my first solo – gave big grins and violent thumbs-up signals and I started the engines. Quickly now before the radiators boil. Check the hydraulic pressure. Check flaps down and up. Pressure back up. Set maximum cooling flap. Check coolant and oil temperatures. Set +2 boost. Check props for pitch change. Open up to +5. Check all four magnetos. Taxi out; prime the exactors. Run-up at +9 at 3,000 revs on each engine; complete the cockpit check and quickly taxi onto the runway and open up. The take-off is remarkably quick and little if any differential throttle was needed. The tail came up very quickly and the large rudder kept the aircraft straight down the runway. One hundred yards up, I checked three-in-the-green [all three wheels up and locked]. Roll the coupe top closed. The Whirlwind was the first fighter to have a retractable tail wheel as well as a single-piece canopy that wound back and forth on rack-and-pinion rails. These were nice features. So now we're in the air, pull the boost and revs back and climb away at 180 mph. I level off and cruise at 240. Remember, it will fly on one engine at 140 mph. Temperatures OK so close coolant flaps. Now, try a few gentle turns and climbs and dives, then a little steeper, 'Wow this thing really moves and climbs like a bat out of hell.' I throttle back one engine, add a little boost to the other and with a touch of rudder trim it flies hands off. I sit back relax and enjoy. Pretty soon realisation comes that maybe, just maybe, I'll be able to cope with this machine until I can convince the CO to post me to a Spitfire squadron. Okay, now it's time to land. Join the circuit downwind, throttle back to 150 mph, prime the exactors, lower undercarriage, set the cooling flaps, turn in, props fully fine, slow down a little, flaps fully down and hold at 125 mph. Come in over the fence at no less than 110 mph and drop onto the runway at 100-105 mph. Quite a difference from the Hurricane, although those monstrous Fowler flaps sure slow things down. Flaps up to max cooling and quickly taxi to the hard-stand. One year and two days after being sworn in, I had finally flown a real fighter on a real fighter squadron. The comment in my diary was very brief, 'These things come in really fast.'

The night before we new RCAF pilots were to have a formal interview with the CO, we decided en masse to tell him we did not wish to fly twins and to demand a posting to a Canadian single-engine fighter unit. The next morning, needless to say, he tore off great strips from our hides and threatened us with dire penalties, court martial and other unpleasantness. He firmly stated that we would all fly the Whirlwind and he guaranteed that we would grow to love it, and then dismissed us. As we waited for transport to take us back to the field, wondering what our fate was to be, the CO's Whirlwind appeared. He dived down on us and pulled up into a series of upward rolls then treated us to a fantastic series of aerobatics at low level the likes of which I was never again to see. We thought maybe it won't be so bad having to fly this strange aeroplane.[21]

With just over four hours experience on Whirlwinds, Sgt Brearley took part in a training flight on the 24. He recalled the events later:

I took off on a battle climb to 25,000 feet in *P6995* and climbed steadily with the flaps in the cooling position. Faint glycol fumes were noticeable between 10,000 and 23,000 feet but at 24,000 feet they increased in intensity with the coolant temperature at 90 degrees. I immediately ceased to climb and put the machine in a gentle dive. At 20,000 feet I closed the flaps and increased the

Sgt Don Gill RCAF, Sgt Bas Abrams, and Sgt Eddie Brearley RCAF. (*Hap Kennedy archives*)

> angle of glide; on reaching 15,000 feet the coolant temperature of the starboard engine suddenly rose to 140 degrees and the oil temperature to 100 degrees. I immediately throttled back the engine and found the airscrew pitch control lever was fixed in the forward position although the pitch was fully coarse. I continued to glide down with the starboard engine temperature remaining unchanged. The fumes increased and on the way down I informed 'Manikin' I was about to make a single engine landing at his base [Colerne]. More fumes filled the cockpit when I opened the hood whilst in the circuit. My approach was good but as I touched down, flames enveloped the starboard engine. With no brakes or engine control I was unable to check the swing to the right, and the undercarriage was stressed. I came to a standstill in front of the watch office. By now the starboard engine was blazing fiercely and it was very hot in the cockpit as I switched off and jumped out, dragging my parachute after me. The fire tender was on the spot as soon as I came to rest but at least three minutes elapsed before the hoses were in operation.

The cause of the fumes was a loose coolant cap, and on its return from Westland, he had a Maple Leaf motif painted below the cockpit.

Morlaix aerodrome was the target for Rhubarbs 33 and 35 during the final two days of the month. F/S Brackley and Sgt King flew Rhubarb 33 against Morlaix aerodrome. They crossed the Channel in rainstorms and on reaching the aerodrome fired at six to eight dull black camouflaged Ju.88s parked in the western dispersal area, although neither pilot was able to observe the results. Sgt King collided with a tall mast in the centre of the dispersal area, causing damage to the port wing coolant tank which immediately began to leak glycol forcing him to shut the engine down. He joined up with F/S Brackley just off the coast who escorted him back across the Channel.

Rhubarb 35 on the 30 by F/O Stein *P7015* and Sgt Ridley *P6994* failed to locate the aerodrome and they were forced to make two circuits over the town of Morlaix before they identified it. Sgt Ridley saw no aircraft on the aerodrome, but described the area as 'so well camouflaged, that it would have been easy to miss them!' He did see one unidentified aircraft in a Bessoneau type hangar which he attacked, but while firing he heard and felt a 'woof' and something struck his starboard main plane. He pulled up sharply and saw F/O Stein nearby with one engine on fire and climbing as if preparing to bail out. He then lost him in cloud as he headed for the coast with oil and glycol streaming from his own starboard engine. As he crossed the Channel he was able to climb to 400 feet before the glycol temperature reached 150 degrees, the oil pressure reached zero, and he was forced to shut it down. He transmitted a 'Maidez' but managed to reach Predannack where he overshot his landing and stopped in the barbed wire perimeter fence. Unfortunately, F/O David Stein did not return and was listed as missing. The ORB noted that, 'His loss to the squadron was inestimably great, as a pilot, humourist or friend.' He had in fact crashed in flames at Kerdiny near the aerodrome and although his body was seen in the wreckage he has no known grave.

November 1941

After the comparative quiet of October, November saw a revival of offensive operations, but 'The 6th was, it is hoped, the culmination of a run of bad luck. The Adjutant, F/L Fleet, injured his leg falling off a bus; Sgt Albertini was hit by a stray pellet during clay-pigeon shooting and it is feared that he will lose the sight of his right eye; in any case the services of an able and aggressive pilot are lost to the squadron for several months. Finally, Sgt John Robinson, who had been detailed to his first war flight with Sgt Blackshaw acting as Section Leader for the first time, was lost.' In addition, F/L Humphrey St John Coghlan was posted as Commanding Officer 137 Squadron on the 2 November following the loss of their CO, S/L John Sample DFC. The ORB noted, 'He leaves many friends in 263 Squadron and takes with him the good wishes of all.'

F/S Anthony Victor Albertini, a Battle of Britain veteran, was transferred to 137 Squadron on the sixth, though on paper only as he was in hospital following his accident on the shooting range. Four pilots arrived for flying duties: P/Os Norman Vincent Crabtree RCAF (an American) and Vivian Lester Currie from 137 Squadron, Sgts Basil Courtney Abrams and Walter Roylance Wright from OTU; the Adjutant, F/L Charles Stanley Fleet, was replaced by F/L Eugene Charles Owens, known to all as 'The Bish'.

Sgt Robinson was lost on Rhubarb 56, an attack on the road and railway network west of Maupertus. Led by Sgt Blackshaw they crossed the English Channel at sea level and made landfall near Cap Levy. From there they flew southeast to St Pierre-Eglise at 200 feet, but only saw two farm carts and a few soldiers. After flying to within half a mile of Barfleur, they turned southeast and followed a road and railway running south, but again found no targets so they headed north again for Barfleur then north-east out to sea. At this point Blackshaw saw two Me.109s orbiting about a mile inland, and, although they did not seem to have observed the Whirlwinds, he called Robinson with the warning 'rats to port' and confirmed that he was in no trouble and that he had forty gallons of petrol left for each engine. After Blackshaw had called 'rats', Robinson, who had been weaving slightly behind and above him, began weaving more vigorously. He appeared on both sides of Sgt Blackshaw but on crossing from port to starboard for the second time he failed to reappear. Blackshaw pulled round and completed two orbits but could see no trace of him. He did not think the two Me.109s had followed them and it seemed likely that Robinson had dipped his wingtip into the sea and gone in at very high speed. However, post-war research suggests that he was shot down by Oberfeldwebel Magnus Brunkhorst of 9/JG2, who claimed a Whirlwind in this area at this time. An air sea rescue search was mounted as far as Cherbourg, but no trace of Sgt John Joseph Robinson or Whirlwind *P6970* was found and the ORB noted, 'He was a quiet and efficient person, and his loss is recorded with very great regret.' One of the ASR pilots was P/O Tooth who had left the squadron in June and was with air sea rescue Warmwell.

Distillery Targets

At the beginning of November, the squadron was allocated new targets on the Cotentin Peninsula in the shape of several distilleries. In view of the pilots' propensity for alcohol consumption it was perhaps rather ironic. The first attempt to reconnoitre them was on 7 November, when F/S Brackley and Sgt Walker took off for Target 216 at Courseulles, but Brackley returned early with engine trouble and Walker was unable to find the target. P/O Warnes, Sgt Blackshaw and Sgt King crossed the Channel to Cap de la Hague where King turned towards Target 305 at Hyenville. Near Douville, Blackshaw turned towards Target 206 at Cérences, leaving Warnes to continue alone to Target 207 at Bréhal. Neither Warnes nor Blackshaw found their targets, but King had more luck, as his combat report shows.

Above left: Sgt Antony Albertini, seen whilst an Air Gunner with 600 Squadron, was posted on 6 November. (*Albertini Family archives*)

Above right: F/L Humphrey St John Coghlan was posted to command 137 Squadron on 2 November . (*Mike Coghlan archives*)

F/L Eugene 'The Bish' Owens, reported for duty as Adjutant on 26 November. (*Bill Watkins archives*)

> I was Red 3 of five Whirlwinds ordered to reconnoitre distillery targets on the Cherbourg Peninsula, and to attack any other targets seen. I took off from Warmwell to reconnoitre target 205 at Hyenville. I followed Red 1 [Warnes] at zero feet to three miles west of Grimouville, where I left him to search for my target. I flew up the river from Heugueville to Hyenville where I observed two goods trains, then recognised the target, and acting on instructions did not fire at it. I turned north to attack the goods engines, but at this moment I saw two Me.109s on my starboard beam at the same height. One enemy aircraft turned to attack me and fired at extreme range. I turned at zero feet to starboard and climbed towards to cloud cover, eventually reaching 5,000 feet. My Whirlwind out-climbed the Me.109s. I then flew northwards on a zigzag course for about ten minutes. Cloud cover now diminished and I could see that my position was about three miles west of Cap de la Hague. At this moment I again saw two Me.109s on my starboard beam about 300 feet above me. I was now flying at 3,000 feet. Both the enemy aircraft turned to port diving to a beam attack on the starboard side. I dived slightly and turned to starboard keeping underneath them, then, as one of the enemy aircraft turned to starboard again, I was able to pull up pull up and fire a one and a half second burst at him from 150 yards, using full deflection. [King expended just fourteen rounds from each cannon.] There was an explosion like a ball of flame at the back of the cockpit and it went into a very steep dive with black smoke and flames pouring from it. I claimed this enemy aircraft as destroyed. The other enemy then broke off the combat, flying towards Cap de la Hague. I flew back to Warmwell at 3,000 feet. My aircraft was undamaged.

P/O Warnes set course for Warmwell from Cap de la Hague, but just off the coast saw a conical cloud of black smoke. He flew towards it expecting to see a ship, but there was nothing and he concluded that an aircraft had crashed there. As he circled he was bounced by two Me.109Es, but turned underneath them and saw their fire go into the sea before he evaded and returned to base. The operation had been hastily prepared and its

Sgt Cecil 'Rex' King. (*Bill Watkins archives*)

failure was responsible for the setting up of a permanent briefing room at Charmy Down, allowing intelligence data to be on continuous display.

Rhubarb 61 on 11 November saw eight aircraft cross the Channel in formation before they split up and headed for separate targets. S/L Pugh and Sgt Blackshaw attacked Target 206, Cérences, a tall red brick building with two rows of windows and adjoining chimney north of the town. Both pilots fired at the building and Blackshaw reported an orange flash inside. Pugh destroyed a locomotive outside the distillery. F/L Warnes and P/O Harvey were assigned Target 207, Bréhal. They left the formation three miles east of Coutances but became separated in cloud. Harvey was unable to locate the target and returned to Warmwell without firing his guns but Warnes attacked a tall square building with many windows by a river at Hyenville although he considered it to be more like a watermill than a distillery. Sgt King and Sgt Ridley were assigned Target 205 at Hyenville, but despite an extensive search could not locate it. Finally, P/O Holmes and Sgt Prior were assigned Target 216 at Courseulles. They set course from St Catherine's Point on the Isle of Wight, but fifteen miles from the French coast were intercepted by a Me.109E. As they turned into the attack, the 109 broke off, 'climbed like a rocket and disappeared into cloud.' They resumed their course but could not locate the target.

On the 17 the ORB noted, 'it was hoped that the squadron could finally destroy the distillery targets allotted to them, but despite heavy rain and the poor visibility at Warmwell, the three sections involved found no cloud over the Cherbourg Peninsula, and were forced to return.' The only incident occurred as Sgt Dimblebee landed. He swung off the runway and collided with Spitfire Vb *AD294* of 118 Squadron, seriously damaging the Spitfire, his own Whirlwind, *P6987 HE-L,* and his reputation.

Poor weather in December severely restricted flying although several exercises were flown in connection to a new type of predicted searchlight. Unfortunately, during one of these in *P7044*, Sgt Derrick Ellis Prior was killed. He was seen to emerge from thick cloud in a vertical dive, and crash in a marsh near Coleford, Gloucestershire. Popular for his sense of humour and excellent spirit, it was thought he lost control in cloud or the aircraft iced up.

F/L Guy Marsland (to 137), F/S Robert Arthur Brackley and Sgt Frank Oswald Dimblebee were posted during the month and replaced by P/O Stuart James Lovell and Sgt Robert Alex McFadgen RCAF, and a move to Charmy Down caused the ORB to comment that it, 'brought to an end the squadron's connection with Filton which had existed on and off, always in the most friendly fashion, since our first formation there on October 2 1939.' The officers were comfortably, even luxuriously, billeted at Cold Ashton Manor House. Sergeants and other ranks found Charmy Down, and especially their quarters at Dingle Dell, exceedingly cold and muddy but it was always a cheerful and happy station. Almost everyone in the squadron had 'friends in Bath' – indeed the hospitality of the Bathonians to the squadron was the best found anywhere. One such person was a local butcher – Tom Dingle – he 'adopted' the squadron and would regularly visit Charmy with extra meat rations.

Stuart Lovell moved his wife into lodgings near the aerodrome, and the couple frequently hosted parties. At one of the more memorable ones Cliff Rudland recalls, 'there was a shortage of glasses, but the pilots of 263 were nothing if not resourceful – we drank our beer out of flower vases. We finally gave up around four in the morning, and most of us slept on the floor. Joe Holmes was the lucky one, he got the sofa.'[22]

Sgt Frank Dimblebee damaged *P6987 HE-L* in a collision with a Spitfire on 17 November. (*Dimblebee Family archives*)

Sgt Donald Gill RCAF, Sgt Irving Kennedy RCAF, Sgt John Walker, F/S Antony Albertini, Sgt Derrick Prior, Sgt Joseph Holmes, seen on the award promotion of Tony Albertini to Flight Sergeant, October 1941. (*Author*)

January 1942

Snow and fog were frequent during January, and there were several days in which the whole station laboured with pick, shovel, brush and snowplough to clear the runways, though the pilots found this operational inactivity extremely tedious. There were four accidents during the first few weeks of the New Year. *P7038* was mysteriously destroyed by fire. The official report stated that it was probably caused by a faulty heater although it had been inspected by the manufacturer – Aladdin Industries – and appeared to be in order. An unknown person was seen on the port side of cockpit when aircraft was on fire and may have been involved – sabotage perhaps. The second accident, on the fifth, involved Sgt Wright and *P7105*. As he landed he failed to fully close the starboard throttle, the port wing dropped and the wingtip touched the ground. Then the stern frame of *P7110* collapsed whilst taxiing. The final accident was caused by the cold weather. As Sgt Abrams taxied to take-off his tail wheel ran too close to the edge of the perimeter track which had been damaged by frost and collapsed, as did the tail wheel of *P7056*.

Personnel changes saw F/O John Peyto Shrubb Slatter, P/O Stewart Gordon Brannigan RNZAF, Sgts Colin Douglas Bell RAAF, Peter Ewing RAAF, and Peter Alastair Jardine report for flying duties, whilst Sgt Edger Brearley was attached to AFDU Duxford, and Sgt John Eutychus Meredith left for RAF Cranage and a Navigation Course. Finally, F/O Walter Pollock Weir, the squadron Medical Officer, left for RAF Goxhill and was replaced by Clifford William Douglas Cole.

The squadron moved to RAF Colerne towards the end of the month, causing the

P7038 was destroyed by a suspicious fire. *(Author)*

F/L Clifford Cole, Medical Officer, and F/O Andrew Wordsworth, Intelligence Officer. (*Cliff Rudland archives*)

ORB to note, 'The maintenance echelon is already there and there will undoubtedly be a gain in efficiency in rejoining it. Colerne is a Bullshit Station, very sticky. The officers were billeted in comfortable Ashwick Hall, and Sergeant Pilots were in a mess in which it appeared as though strait jackets were needed for 263 and 417 [the other Squadron on the aerodrome] to conform to the rules and regulations.'

February 1942

During February the squadron flew the highest number of hours in 10 Group, 458 on 419 sorties, and the ORB noted, 'The large number of scrambles may be accounted for partly by many friendly aircraft and partly by the renewed interest shown by the Hun in shipping in the Western Approaches.' Convoy patrols began and at first everyone was excited by them. They continued (on and off, but mainly on) for six months and three days, during which time the squadron became 'the World's No. 1 [for] convoy jobs'. Pilots averaged 100 hours on them and altogether some 1,600 convoy hours were flown and about one and a half million tons of shipping was safely escorted between Aberystwyth, Porthcawl, Lundy and Ilfracombe. (A pair of Whirlwinds would orbit over the ships at 1,000 to 1,500 feet to discourage the low flying Ju.88s, which according to Cliff Rudland was 'a dangerous pastime due to the propensity of British ships of whatever sort to fire at any aircraft which came within range, regardless of whose side it was on. Fire first, ask questions later, was the Navy motto.')[23]

> The enemy was not seen, although there is no doubt that Ju.88s of 1/121 and 3/121 sniffing around the Western Approaches often saw the Whirlwinds and sheared off. These Ju.88s appeared like rather irregular clockwork every day between Land's End, Carnsore Point (Eire) and Holyhead, and every day the squadron and others in the Fairwood Common Sector would scramble after them from one to five times. Enormous trouble was taken to catch the enemy aircraft, plots were recorded tabulated and analysed and, an operation called 'Pigstick' was devised. This involved sweeping large areas of the Western Approaches in very wide echelon, two miles between the sections of which the aircraft were 1/2 mile apart, and in R/T silence. The last was important because the plots showed that the enemy aircraft picked up, or had relayed to them, our vectors and took suitable action. But it should be understood that the Hun did not approach the coast unless he had cloud cover and normally flew at zero feet, only pulling up for a minute or two to get a wider view (it was then that he was plotted) and that interception was attempted over considerable distances, thirty to eighty miles from the coast of Wales. Saltee Isles patrols were also instigated following reports of Luftwaffe floatplanes operating from these Islands off the southern coast of Eire, and became a regular occurrence during the following months. However, during the six months and three days spent at Fairwood Common and Angle, pilots of the squadron while on defensive patrol, did not so much as obtain a visual of an enemy aircraft. It should equally be remembered that during that time only two ships were sunk in the Western Approaches.

When the squadron moved to Fairwood Common on 10 February, it 'took to the air in sixteen Whirlwinds, the Hurricane, Magister and Oxford, and it is believed to have been the largest number of Whirlwinds airborne at any one time' but when the unfamiliar aircraft appeared over Fairwood they caused a panic, with many ground crews heading for the air-raid shelters believing they were under attack.

> The squadron was soon keeping time with the high pressure swing of the Fairwood Common way. All ranks found it a station in which flying was regarded as of paramount importance, and one in which the sense of belonging as fostered in many interesting, unorthodox and successful ways. It is generally regarded as the happiest station at which the squadron has been. On the first day, 'Batchy'[24] helped an erk out by swinging the prop of the Tiger Moth. The Squadron would like to remark on the co-operation between Fairwood Station Officers and the squadron, which takes many forms, but is most evident in all flying matters. The Fairwood runways with their multivariate slopes and borders of treacherous ground necessitated a complex system of Flying Control, a system that is not always without friction.

The runways were soon considered 'bad medicine' for Whirlwinds, constructed as they were on a hilly marsh, and despite the addition of hundreds of tons of industrial shale, the runways and taxi-tracks undulated alarmingly, not only up and down, but also from side to side. They actually rippled as an aircraft moved along them and were described as like looking along a corkscrew. Running off them could be disastrous, the first of several accidents occurred on the thirteenth when F/S Coyne touched down in *P7108* and swung off the runway in a crosswind. He recalled:

> The wheels sank into soft ground and the forward momentum flipped the aircraft over onto her back. No sooner had the aircraft come to rest than a gang of airmen appeared and lifted up the tail. I pulled the pin on my Sutton harness and landed on my head. Crawling out from under, I vented my anger by giving the aircraft a kick, thereby sustaining my only injury, a broken toe, which kept me off flying for a couple of days.[25]

S/L Thomas Patrick Pugh DFC was posted as S/L Tactics 82 Group Headquarters on the twelfth and was replaced by S/L Robert Sinkler Woodward DFC who came from 137 Squadron. The ORB praised S/L Pugh: 'He led the squadron in many operational sorties and was a noted protagonist of the Whirlwind low level attacks. He takes the best wishes of the Officers and men with him to his new appointment.' He had few opportunities to test his low-level attack theories – which were later proved to be correct. Two other pilots reported for flying duties, F/O Donald Bruce Ogilvie, a Battle of Britain veteran, who had spent some time as a service test pilot with Westland, and P/O Christopher Peter van Zeller.

Between the twelfth and twenty-first of the month, eight aircraft developed serious engine trouble and except for convoy patrols and scrambles, the squadron was grounded. The defect was traced to the three-way union and the ORB noted, 'Very bad visibility, but the convoy was found and patrolled. P/O Holmes was flying at one hundred feet near the convoy, some twenty-five miles south of St Govan's Head. Without any warning from his instruments, his starboard engine exploded, caught fire and disintegrated. He lost height to within inches of the sea but managed to climb to four hundred feet, pulling the fire extinguisher knob, which had good effect upon the flaming engine. Unable to gain

RAF Colerne 10 February 1942 prior to S/L Pugh leaving for 82 Group. *Front row*: F/S Jimmy Coyne, F/S Harvey Muirhead, Sgt Ken Ridley, P/O Johnny Walker, Sgt Douglas Small, F/O Stuart Lovell, F/S Bill Lovell. *Second row*: F/S Eddie Brearley. P/O Joe Holmes, P/O Norman Crabtree, S/L Tom Pugh DFC, G/C Harvey (Station CO); F/O Geoff Warnes, F/O 'Bish' Owens, P/O Philip Harvey, P/O Herbert Blackshaw. Third row: P/O Alfred Hay (EO), Sgt Peter Ewing, P/O Les Currie, P/O Stuart Brannigan, F/S Cecil King, Sgt Don Gill, Sgt Colin Bell. *Back row*: F/S Richard Reed, Sgt Basil Abrams, F/S Hap Kennedy, F/S Peter Jardine, Sgt Roy Wright. The dog is ASO Ranee. (*Hap Kennedy archives*)

'A' Flight ground crews. (*Purkis Family archives*)

more height to bale out, he fell back to fifty feet, but surmounted the cliffs by using full flaps.' The first aerodrome he came to was Carew Cherton a small grass training base. 'He gained four hundred feet by using full flap again and after pulling the emergency knob for the landing gear, made a successful landing. Two bucketfuls of smouldering engine parts fell out when the cowlings were taken off; the rest of the engine had disappeared. The Peregrine had scored again by being twins.' There was not enough remaining to say for certain, but the failure had the hallmarks of a three-way union failure. Rolls-Royce quickly manufactured stronger unions and aircraft on both Squadrons and at the Maintenance Units were modified by 4 March.

March 1942

March brought two milestones for the squadron. On the first there was the presentation of a crest granted by His Majesty the King under AMO N.227/1942. The crest, devised by the Chester Herald, and sponsored by the Royal Norwegian Government, consisted of the Lion of Scotland rampant holding in its forepaws the Blue Cross of Norway, thereby commemorating the squadron's exploits in the first and second North Western (Norway) Expeditions of 1940 and the period of re-fitting with Whirlwinds which was spent in Scotland. The Motto was *Ex Ungue, Leonem* ('the lion is known by his claws).

> AVM Augustus Orlebar CBE AFC presented the Crest to S/L Woodward in front of the squadron who were paraded outside the Watch Office. He spoke to F/S Goss BEM, one of several veterans of the Norwegian Expedition still with the squadron, and commemorated the major events in the squadron's history. It was chosen to re-equip with Whirlwinds, because it was at that time the crack Squadron of Fighter Command; but events showed that height had become a major factor and this the Whirlwind lacked. Nevertheless, Whirlwinds of the squadron had been markedly successful in the offensive operations of 1941. G/C Atcherley OBE AFC and W/C Donaldson AFC DFC were both present at the ceremony. The former was Air Attaché in Norway; commanded the Bardufoss Wing in which 263 Squadron operated; was the Station Commander of Drem and Fairwood Common. W/C Donaldson's connections with the squadron are well known.

Known only as the 'cannon fighter' in official circles, it was 17 December 1940 before the Whirlwind was mentioned during a speech in the House of Commons. But the aircraft had been described in detail by a French aeronautical journal in 1939, whilst *The Aeroplane* had prepared recognition charts for the RAF, but were prevented from publishing photographs. The secrecy was somewhat lost on the Luftwaffe – it knew of the Whirlwind shortly after her maiden flight in 1938! On Friday 20 March, the Air Ministry belatedly removed the aircraft from the Official Secrets List. A team of photographers and journalists arrived during the day, and 'The pilots threw themselves into press interviews with gusto; lines were shot by all and sundry.' F/L Rudland flew several low level high speed passes and aerobatics for the cameras in *P7120*, and photos were taken outside 'A' Flight dispersal hut, whilst the pilots were having a well-earned cup of tea. The newspapers broke the news of the existence of the Whirlwind to the British public over the following few days.

The squadron flew twenty-eight sweeps of the Smalls-Carnsore-Saltee area and four evening patrols off Linney Head during the month, but despite the presence of thirty-six Ju.88, He.111s and He.115s in the Brest area, no contact was made. On the 28 F/L Warnes and P/O Crabtree flew an air sea rescue Search for a pilot of 402 Squadron who had ditched south of Tenby. Unfortunately the pilot, F/S Lloyd Elliott, was not found, the incident proving the advantages of two engines as the ORB noted, 'The cutting of one Whirlwind engine is almost a routine occurrence, so much so that only the spectacular cases are recorded.'

Personnel movements saw four pilots posted, P/Os Stewart Gordon Brannigan RNZAF and Stuart James Lovell (he returned later to complete his tour), and Sgts Colin Douglas Bell RAAF and Peter Ewing RAAF. The squadron also lost the services of Sgt Peter Jardine, who made a very heavy landing in Whirlwind *P7039*, causing both tyres to burst and the aircraft turn over onto her back. He suffered a fractured spine and was in RAF Wroughton Hospital until April. *P7039* was sent to Westland but was deemed uneconomical to repair and written off. Finally, S/L Jackson, Maintenance Officer of Fighter Command, visited P/O Hay, the Engineering Officer to congratulate him on the high standard of maintenance and serviceability following the three-way oil union problem.

S/L Robert Woodward DFC, P/O Philip Harvey, Sgt John Walker, F/S Cecil King, F/L Geoff Warnes (on wing), P/O Les Currie, P/O Herbert Blackshaw, Sgt John Meredith, Sgt Harvey Muirhead RCAF and Sgt Ken Ridley watch Cliff Rudland's demonstration flight. (*Jane Renton archives*)

Seated: Sgt Bas Abrams, P/O John Walker, F/S Harvey Muirhead RCAF, F/S Cecil King, Sgt Ken Ridley, Sgt John Meredith. *Standing*: P/O Herbert Blackshaw, S/L Robert Woodward DFC, F/L Geoff Warnes, P/O Norman Crabtree RCAF, P/O Joe Holmes, F/L 'Bish' Owens (Adjutant), F/L Cliff Rudland, P/O Andrew Wordsworth (IO), P/O Alfred Hay (EO), P/O Philip Harvey, and P/O Les Currie enjoying a cup of tea outside 'A' Flight Dispersal Hut. (*Cliff Rudland archives*)

P/O Philip Harvey, S/L Robert Woodward DFC, Sgt Cecil King, P/O Christopher van Zeller, and Sgt Jimmy Coyne at Fairwood Common. Note the Gas Patch next to the roundel on the wing of *P7105 HE-N*, S/L Woodward's aircraft. (*Cliff Rudland archives*)

April 1942

During April the squadron flew a total of 659 hours, sixty-six of them on 8 April alone, a record for the squadron with Gladiators or Whirlwinds. In addition, the contents of fifty-five ammunition boxes (10,536 rounds) were fired. 222 convoy patrol sorties, involving 270 hours were entirely uneventful, causing the ORB to note, 'The recent run of convoy patrols began to tell on the nerves of the perpetual drunks of 263. The boys got to know Swansea, the Mumbles and Langland Bay Hotel.' Many of the sorties to the local pubs were in the squadron's old Riley, which had a Guinness label as a tax disc and ran on petrol 'liberated' from the re-fuelling bowsers.[26]

Two accidents were caused by a 50 mph crosswind on the first. It caught P/O Holmes at the end of his landing run, *P7100* ground-looped and damaged a wingtip. P/O Harvey was not so fortunate. As he touched down, F/O Wordsworth was heard to remark, 'That was a wizard landing' but then the crosswind caught him, *P7112* swerved off the runway, bounced, turned over and disintegrated, but 'Tim was levered out upside-down from the remains of his cockpit, with just a bruised elbow.' Two weeks later Harvey crashed again, this time whilst trying to land *P7100* out of wind. The aircraft swung on touchdown and his attempt to correct caused a tyre to burst. The official report stated that the Whirlwind had a tendency to weathercock but that P/O Harvey tended to overcorrect on crosswind landings and he should undertake further training. Other accidents during April saw Sgt Abrams collide with a dispersal bay in *P7041* when he taxied too fast with a following wind and the brakes failed to stop him. Sgt Meredith also had two encounters with the accident gremlins. The starboard wheel of *P7035* would not lower on approach despite all emergency procedures and as he touched down the undercarriage collapsed. Although no fault was found in the system, he was absolved of blame. On 16 April, he ferried *P7117* to the servicing echelon at Fairwood for a new oil cooler, but at the end of the landing run the port wing rose and the starboard wingtip touched the ground. He was recommended for a transfer following several landing accidents, for, whilst it was possible, the Whirlwind was not easy to land on three-points without a wing dropping due to the steep angle of incidence when on its wheels (almost beyond critical angle of stall), and a wheeled landing was always recommended.

During their off-duty hours, 'Both flights became fanatical gardeners, which left the environs of both flights extensively gardened and fenced, but it was a bad time when bandit sheep ate A Flight's wallflowers.' The sheep at Fairwood were a major problem; periodically they would break through a fence and 'raid' the aerodrome. Cliff Rudland recalled one day, as Geoff Warnes was on final approach, a particularly troublesome sheep strayed across his line forcing him to go round again. After finally landing, he taxied to the dispersal hut, disappeared inside and emerged with a shotgun, with which he despatched the recalcitrant sheep. 'We pilots dined on mutton that night.'[27]

The squadron moved to RAF Angle, Fairwood Common's satellite on 18 April. The contents of the Armoury was transported by train but, as it passed through Llanelli, the wooden truck next to the engine was seen to be on fire. It was quickly moved in to a siding where the exploding Verey lights gave an excellent display, but the fire was extinguished by the fire-brigade before the ammunition exploded. Of the new station, the ORB noted, 'just the same work as at Fairwood, but the convoys were nearer home. Angle is ten miles

P7112 after being caught in a crosswind whilst landing. P/O Philip Harvey emerged unscathed. *(Author)*

Battle of Britain veteran F/O Donald Ogilvie was posted to 137 Squadron on 20 April. (*Ogilvie Family archives*)

from the nearest town, Pembroke, an enlarged but uninteresting village. Desolation and lack of "popsies". Things became frightful.' Personnel changes saw P/O Stewart Gordon Brannigan return from a month's sojourn with 2 Delivery Flight/286 Squadron, and Battle of Britain veteran F/O Donald Bruce Ogilvie leave for 137 Squadron.

May 1942

The squadron flew 818 hours 35 minutes, of which 536 hours were on 321 convoy patrols. This was a record for the squadron and amongst the highest recorded without accidents in Fighter Command. The ORB noted, 'Besides flying a great many hours, the pilots have occupied themselves in "binding", playing poker, shooting rocks and rabbits, dancing and sailing.' They also patrolled Portreath to Falmouth during a visit by the King and Queen.

P/O Stuart James Lovell returned to the fold in May, whilst P/O Stewart Gordon Brannigan RNZAF and Sgt Robert Alex McFadgen RCAF left. F/O Alfred Arthur Hay BEM, the Engineering Officer, who had been with 263 since 1 October 1941, was replaced by P/O Oswald Ash and finally, F/L Clifford William Douglas Cole, the MO, was also posted. He was, 'A popular member of the squadron, and showed a great interest in all flying matters.' His successor was F/O Eric Comissiong Eadie. P/O Eddie Brearley was also temporarily unavailable to the squadron when he slipped as he alighted from *P7089* and fractured his jaw on the wing.

P/O Philip Harvey, Sgt Cecil King, P/O Stewart Brannigan RNZAF, Sgt Ken Ridley, and Sgt Jimmy Coyne. (*Cliff Rudland archives*)

Sgt Robert McFadgen RCAF. (*Hap Kennedy archives*)

263 Sailing Club

RAF Angle was so remote that there was little to occupy the off duty pilots until F/O Wordsworth chartered two twelve-foot sailing dinghies from the Pembroke Yacht Club. They were towed across to Angle by the barge *Mary Jane* and were carpentered, painted, rigged and varnished. S/L Clover, Station Commander, became Commodore of the '263 Sailing Club' and generously presented it with £2, and many happy hours were spent on the water. During the month the officers of the squadron were entertained on board HM Destroyer *Brocklesby*, which was based at Milford Haven. Her Captain, Lt Cdr Ash DSO, had led a Flotilla of MTBs against the *Scharnhorst* and *Gneisenau* during the 'Channel Dash' in February. F/L Rudland, P/O Holmes, P/O Currie and P/O Crabtree were the first to visit. Apparently the four returned very late in a thick mist, although whether this was atmospheric or alcoholic was not recorded! S/L Woodward's visit was more eventful however. With his wife Virginia, he accompanied F/O Wordsworth in one of the dinghies, but the Intelligence Officer's masterly handling resulted in the vessel capsizing. They managed to cling to the upturned hull until they were rescued by a launch from the *Brocklesby*. This does not appear to be an isolated incident: at one point they organised a race, during which 'B' Flight managed to capsize.

When on thirty minutes notice, the pilots would relax on the nearby beach. If there was an emergency the station Magister would take off over them and fire a red flare, thus starting a mad scramble up the cliffs back to the aerodrome. The ORB noted, 'Great Fun; better fun when the WAAFS arrived.' Dances were held in the officers' mess, a large house known as 'The Hall' and, 'although the great distance to other human habitants prevented there being a superfluity of young ladies, a good time was had by all.' At one

The '263 Sailing Club'. *In boat*: F/L Herbert Blackshaw, F/L Cliff Rudland. *Seated*: F/O Andrew Wordsworth Intelligence Officer. *Standing*: F/L William Cole Medical Officer, P/O Christopher van Zeller. (*Cliff Rudland archives*)

party, Cliff Rudland remembers 'helping to hold Stuart Lovell up so that he could make footmarks on the ceiling. Stu was an outstanding party type, a real character, game for a party.' Although a party-goer, Stu Lovell was married and preferred to spend time with his wife Alicia who was staying nearby, as did S/L Woodward, whose wife Virginia stayed in the same hotel near the airfield. The rabble rousing was usually led by Geoff Warnes who was 'leader of the gang.' It was also around this time that Cliff managed to overturn 'A' Flight's Standard van.[28]

On 21 May, P/O Walker and Sgt Reed set another record for the Whirlwind. They were scrambled and vectored to The Smalls and back several times, before being vectored towards Dublin. P/O Walker's R/T failed as they neared the Irish coast, so Reed took the lead and a Beaufighter of 125 Squadron relayed a vector to him as the section flew out of R/T range of the Humbry Repeater. They saw nothing in 10/10 cloud and were recalled, but with insufficient fuel to return to Angle they flew east until they crossed the Welsh coast at the tip of the Lleyn Peninsula, where the weather became worse. With empty fuel tanks, they landed on the tiny cliff-top grass aerodrome of Hells Mouth, near Pwllheli where P/O Walker saw 67 gallons put into his starboard tank: its capacity was 67 gallons! The flight of two hours was the longest made in a Whirlwind at that time.

June 1942

The squadron flew over 695 hours, of which 489 were on 300 convoy patrols. The month saw the resumption of offensive operations and the first accident in 1,236 hours flying time.

Ramrod 19, on the fifth, was an attack on Lannion and Morlaix aerodromes. Red Section, S/L Woodward, P/O Blackshaw, P/O Coyne and F/S Muirhead escorted by 234 Squadron, headed for Lannion where Woodward and Coyne strafed five Ju.88s lined up in front of the watch tower, but thought they were dummies; Blackshaw attacked a Ju.88 being serviced in a hangar. It had a dark sea blue underside, prompting the ORB to suggest, 'that the squadron has at last seen and damaged an aircraft of 3/123 which it has lately so often chased' and Muirhead scored hits on two blister hangars. Blue Section – F/L Warnes, P/O Crabtree, P/O Holmes and P/O Kennedy – made landfall too far west, and, with the element of surprise lost, returned to base.

Nine months after joining the squadron, P/O Irving Farmer Kennedy finally convinced the CO to post him to single engine fighters; fellow Canadian Sgt John Davidson Mitchner was also posted, as an instructor. He had been with the squadron since October 1941 but had only flown seven hours due to being admitted to hospital with diabetes and was not operational. The third pilot to be posted was Sgt John Eutychus Meredith, whilst P/O Norman Latham and Sgt Curtis reported for flying duties.

Tuesday 23 June saw the end of the longest accident free period in the squadron's history when the tail of *P7110* was damaged on landing. F/L Warnes was the unfortunate pilot. The ORB noted 'It was a record which will be difficult to emulate, as between 30 April and 23 May, 1,236 hours fifty minutes were flown without mishap.' The accident was traced to hydraulic failure of the tail wheel. Although he used the emergency air bottle to blow the wheel down, it did not work. The ORB did not mention that the accident

Cliff Rudland the morning after crashing 'A' Flight's standard van. (*Cliff Rudland archives*)

Mickey Mouse on the nose of a Whirlwind at RAF Fairwood Common, early 1942. The squadron Hurricane and S/L Woodward's *P7105 HE-N* can be seen in the background. (*Cliff Rudland archives*)

F/S Hap Kennedy RCAF was posted 14 June. (*Author*)

Sgt John Mitchner RCAF was posted 29 June. (*Joan Foster archives*)

occurred at Brough near Hull, however. Warnes had arranged to meet some naval friends at the airfield and had been given permission by S/L Woodward to take *P7110*. Luckily there was little damage as an inquiry would have asked why he was on such a visit in an operational machine – the flight was entered in official records as an endurance test.

July 1942

'A' Flight was detached to Portreath in July, whilst 'B' Flight held down, virtually unaided, the whole operational commitment of Fairwood Common Sector. 'A' Flight, doing the same for the Portreath sector, enjoyed the change of being at Portreath but had to work hard all day at more convoy patrols

The ORB noted, 'A combined Rhubarb of the Landivisiau area on the twenty-third caused considerable damage to road and rail transport, but it was difficult to reconcile this with the loss of two of our most experienced pilots, P/O Les Currie and P/O Johnny Walker. They were in different ways extremely competent and most popular members of the squadron.' Twelve Whirlwinds left Predannack and rendezvoused with twenty-four Spitfire Vbs of 130 and 234 Squadron over the Lizard, then crossed the Channel at sea-level and the French coast near Plouescat. As they approached Landernau, the Whirlwinds split into six sections, each escorted by two Spitfires.

Red Section (S/L Woodward and P/O Coyne) attacked Landivisiau Station and, as they crossed out over the Baie de Morlaix, also attacked a lightship tender and a trawler; Blue Section (F/S King and P/O Currie) attacked a lorry on the Landivisiau-Morlaix road; Yellow Section (P/O Walker and Sgt Abrams) attacked a lorry and a signal box near St Tregonnec and a train in Belair Station; Green Section (F/L Warnes and P/O Stuart Lovell) attacked huts, wireless masts and a camouflaged lorry between Landivisiau and Landernau; White section (F/L Rudland and P/O Harvey) attacked a distillery north of Landivisiau; and Black Section (P/O Holmes and Sgt Wright) attacked the same huts as Green Section, and the distillery attacked by White section.

The individual sections re-crossed the coast unscathed but struggled to reform. Red, White and Black Sections formed up on S/L Woodward, but Blue and Yellow Sections became separated. F/S King joined Green Section, and shortly afterwards noticed P/O Currie, *P7035*, in the distance with four other aircraft. S/L Woodward also saw a single Whirlwind with four Me.109s on its tail and turned back to intercept, but as he did so the Whirlwind dived into the sea in flames. P/O Vivian Lester Currie did not return. Ten minutes from the English coast S/L Woodward saw another single Whirlwind with its starboard wing on fire, being attacked by three Me.109s. P/O John James Walker, *P7060*, did not return either, both were shot down by Unteroffizer Freidrich Steinmüller of 11/JG2.

F/L William Davie of RAE arrived, to gain experience on the Whirlwind prior to playing a major role in the next chapter of her operational career. Three other pilots also reported for flying duties: F/S James Ian Simpson, Sgts Maxwell Tylney Cotton RAAF and Francis Leslie Hicks RAAF, whilst P/O Norman Latham and Sgt Curtis were posted after just a month.

Above left: Sgt John Walker was lost on 23 July. (*Author*)

Above right: P/O Les Currie was lost on 23 July. (*Cliff Rudland archives*)

August 1942: The Whirlibomber is Born

On Wednesday 12 August, instructions were received from HQ Fighter Command stating that all Whirlwinds were to carry two 250lb bombs. The fitting of bombs was first suggested by S/L Pugh DFC, in September 1941, but was rejected because fighter bombers were in their infancy and the 'Hurribomber' had yet to go into action. F/L Rudland carried out test flights in *P7057* with 250lb and 500lb bombs and reported:

> Generally speaking, I found the performance not greatly impaired by the addition of bombs or racks, with the exception of the maximum speed which at sea level was reduced from 312 mph to about 280 mph. This latter speed is hardly affected by the presence or absence of bombs in the racks. With 500lb bombs the aircraft climbed to 15,000 feet in 16½ minutes. When diving at 310 mph indicated there is a disconcerting aileron flutter which became apparent at slower speeds nearer the ground on occasions. With two 500lb bombs the take off was approximately 125 yards greater and landing 100 yards greater.

Following the tests he requested a transfer to fighters, stating, 'If I had wanted to drop bombs I would have flown a Lancaster.'[29] The official trials took place at A&AEE Farnborough on *P6997* during October 1942; some of the testing was carried out by

F/L Cliff Rudland: 'If I had wanted to drop bombs I would have flown a Lancaster.' (*Cliff Rudland archives*)

F/L Davie who had been briefly attached to the squadron in July. His report echoed F/L Rudland's findings

Having been at Angle since April and in the Fairwood Common Sector since February, during which the operational hours flown were consistently the highest in the Group, the squadron moved to Colerne on the fifteenth to enable 3055 Servicing Echelon to fit bomb racks. Of Angle, the ORB noted, 'though there were compensations in the country sports of shooting, sailing and bathing, it was too remote for such a long stay to be continuously enjoyable.'

Three pilots left on attachments during this period, P/O Philip Harvey for Liaison duties with the USAAF, Sgt Francis Leslie Hicks RAAF to AAEE, Boscombe Down, to help test the Whirlibomber, and Sgt Douglas Francis Small to 2 Delivery Flight. At the same time, Sgt David John Williams reported for flying duties and F/S Peter Alastair Jardine returned following his crash in February.

September 1942: Whirlibomber ops Commence

September brought a move from Colerne to Group Practice Camp at Warmwell to work up on the Whirlibomber, but as 263 was the only fighter-bomber squadron in 10 Group, when enemy shipping was reported in the Channel Islands area, four aircraft were ordered to attack it. S/L Woodward, F/L Blackshaw, F/L Warnes, and P/O Brearley staged through Bolt Head and were escorted by the Exeter Wing, but the ORB noted, 'this was the first operation on which Whirlwinds were fitted with bombs, it was a pity therefore that no shipping was found.' They did not have to wait long for another opportunity. On the ninth, the same four, escorted by Spitfires of 118 and 66 Squadrons, found four armed trawlers between Cap de la Hague and Alderney. Following immediately behind the anti-flak Spitfires, S/L Woodward and F/L Warnes attacked one ship, and F/L Blackshaw and P/O Brearley a second; when the rear support Spitfires arrived six minutes later only two ships were left afloat. These were the first bombs dropped 'in anger' and the squadron initially claimed the vessels as 1,000 tons each, but on 27 October, Fighter Command reduced the tonnage to 500 tons. Even this was an overestimation, the vessels were in fact the *Henca* of 305 tons, which capsized and sank in seven minutes, and *V207* of the 2 Vorpostenflotille. The first month's operations with Whirlibombers had been a success, vindicating S/L Tom Pugh's theories.

At the beginning of the month, P/O Cecil Percy King was awarded the Distinguished Flying Medal and F/L Clifford Percival Rudland DFC was granted his wish when he was posted to 19 Squadron. The ORB noted, 'He was the second pilot to be awarded the DFC for work done with Whirlwind aircraft and the squadron was extremely sorry to lose him.' Of P/O Joe Holmes, who left for 137 Squadron, it commented 'Of steady and good temper, he was a fine athlete and good companion, and will be missed.' F/S Harvey Donald Muirhead RCAF also left, whilst F/L Arthur Norman William Johnstone DFC and Sgt John Gray Macaulay arrived for flying duties, the former as a supernumerary. Finally, P/O Norman Vincent Crabtree, P/O William Albert Lovell, and F/S Richard Irl Reed, American citizens who had joined the RCAF prior to America's entry into the war, were Honourably discharged from the RCAF on taking up appointments with the USAAF 94th 'Hat in the Ring' Fighter Squadron, at Ibsley, to fly P-38 Lightnings.

After completing the armament practice camp, the squadron was officially transferred to Warmwell and the ORB noted, 'The dispersal was at this period in a marquee to the south of the aerodrome. Fortunately the weather was fine and warm, but the marquee blew down on the twentieth.' The squadron established itself in the Knighton Wood headquarters and dispersals, as these were evacuated by 175 Squadron, a set-up which proved quite the most comfortable and commodious which the squadron had enjoyed in its three year history. 3055 Servicing Echelon was two hundred yards away from the dispersals. Warmwell brought interesting operational flights other than bombing. Standby cockpit readiness was sometimes assumed to relieve other squadrons, or if Zeals was non-operational. Air sea rescue searches off Cherbourg were found to be more adventurous than those off the Saltees. Moreover, armed shipping recces of the Channel Island-Barfleur area became a day-to-day occurrence.

On the twenty-first, P/O King led Sgt Peter Alastair Jardine on a sector reconnaissance and cloud flying exercise, but they were recalled forty minutes after take-off due to deteriorating weather. As they approached Warmwell at 1,500 feet, they flew into thick cloud and became separated; whilst King landed safely, Jardine and *P7003* were seen by several soldiers to crash. He had been a Lieutenant in the South African Air Force before transferring to the RAF and joined the squadron in January 1942, but following the accident in March when he fractured his back, he was in RAF Wroughton Hospital

P/O William Lovell was discharged from the RCAF and joined the USAAF on 29 September. (*Jane Renton archives*)

Above left: W/O Harvey Muirhead RCAF was posted on 28 September. (*Cliff Rudland archives*)

Above right: P/O Norman Crabtree was discharged from the RCAF and joined the USAAF on 29 September. (*Jane Renton archives*)

'A' Flight. *Standing*: F/S Ken Ridley, P/O Max Cotton RAAF, F/S Cecil King, F/O Herbert Blackshaw. *Kneeling*: P/O Christopher van Zeller, and P/O Jimmy Coyne. (*Jane Renton archives*)

Sgt Peter Jardine was lost on 21 September. (*Author*)

until April. The ORB noted, 'of a quiet good humoured disposition and very well liked'. He was laid to rest in Warmwell Village Churchyard on 26 September with full military honours.

October 1942

There were several social functions during the month. Westland organised a dance at the Boden Social Club in Chard, which was commended for its 'first class organization, plenty to eat and drink and lovely partners.' The squadron also 'learned with much pleasure that the Bellows Club has added to its gift of eight Whirlwinds, another most generous gift – £100. It appears that this gift reciprocated the autographed Greetings Card, which was sent to the Bellows Club, together with photos of the squadron's aircraft and pilots. £40 was spent on an excellent beer-up, social and dance.' On the thirty-first,

F/O Harvey, P/O Brearley, F/S Ridley, and Sgt Wright flew a Rhubarb to the rail triangle north-west of the La Haye du Puits. The ORB noted, 'This operation was well planned and successfully executed and the railway line in the target area was probably destroyed in two or three places.' Referring to this operation, the BBC's news bulletin on 1 November stated, 'Whirlwind aircraft, without seeing any enemy fighters, penetrated the Cherbourg Peninsula and bombed an important railway junction, destroying a goods engine.'

Not all operations were successful, but unlike a shipping reconnaissance on the eighth, most at least left the ground. S/L Woodward and F/O Harvey took off and began to orbit Warmwell, but F/L Johnstone attempted to take off in course pitch and ran out of runway. He throttled back to avoid dispersed aircraft and ended up in the trees of Knighton Wood. He was uninjured, but *P7014 HE-T* was damaged beyond repair and the operation was abandoned.

Seven pilots arrived for flying duties during the month, three from 137 Squadron, two from OTU and two from detachments. P/Os Donald Burton McPhail and Dattatraya Anant Samant, and F/S John McGowan Barclay arrived from 137; P/O Arthur Henry Lee-

P/O Christopher van Zeller. (*Jane Renton archives*)

White and Sgt Sayana Puram Duraiswamy Thyagarajan from OTU, whilst F/S Francis Lesley Hicks returned from attachment to A&AEE, Boscombe Down, and F/S Donald Frank Jellicoe Tebbit from 10 Group Flight. The only pilot leaving the squadron was P/O Christopher Peter van Zeller, who was described by the ORB as, 'A quiet but reliable pilot.'

November 1942

F/L Arthur Norman William Johnstone DFC was posted in November, and it was only the second month during 1942 that was free from accidents of any kind, but the squadron did suffer an operational loss during Rhubarb 99 on the seventh when the Valognes-Vaudreville-Montebourg rail triangle was the target for P/O Abrams, P/O Coyne, P/O Gill, and Sgt Cotton. They crossed the French coast in good weather but this turned rapidly to heavy rain and the pilots could only see properly through their side panels. They continued, however, and Coyne and Cotton damaged a locomotive near Montebourg with cannon fire whilst Gill and Abrams bombed the tracks but became separated in the poor visibility. Unfortunately, P/O Donald Ross Gill, *P7043 HE-A*, did not return. The ORB noted, 'He is missing in circumstances which only guesswork can provide any clue. He was efficient, hard working and of great integrity, and will be greatly missed.' He flew into high ground in the poor visibility, and was buried in the military cemetery at Cherbourg.

The first all Whirlwind Roadstead was flown on the nineteenth when S/L Woodward, F/O Coyne, F/O Harvey and Sgt Cotton flew Whirlibombers, and F/L Warnes, F/O Brearley, W/O McPhail, and F/S Wright flew the Anti-Flak Whirlwinds (bomb racks removed), but the torpedo boats reported off Le Havre-Cherbourg were not found.

P7043 HE-A and P/O Don Gill RCAF were lost on 7 November. (*Chris Thomas archives*)

S/L Alcott, S/L Geoff Warnes, and P/O Stuart Lovell. (*Jane Renton archives*)

Beaufort photographic aircraft. (*Jane Renton archives*)

The Air Ministry authorised British Movietone News to record the squadron's activities during the month, ostensibly for South American (Bellows Club) consumption. S/L Alcott of 10 Group acted as Liaison Officer but the Beaufort photographic aircraft did not arrive on time, and permission was eventually withdrawn. The cameramen therefore took footage of the Whirlwinds and squadron personnel from the back of 'A' Flight's van and also of F/L Warnes, F/O Lovell, F/S Abrams, and F/S Wright who flew low attacks and formations. The Photographic Beaufort from PRU Benson eventually arrived – in February 1943 – and air-to-air film was taken off Lyme Bay.

December 1942

Roadstead 45, on Monday 7 December, was a day of 'triumph and tragedy' when a shipping strike was flown against a convoy off Jersey. Anti-Flak Spitfires of 66 Squadron flew line abreast ahead of eight Whirlibombers in echelon starboard, and they were covered from above and behind by Spitfires of 118 Squadron. This formation had been developed in Malta, and the ORB thought this was the first occasion on which it had been used in Britain. They found a convoy off Baie de St Brelade Jersey. S/L Woodward and Sgt Williams attacked an 800 ton merchant vessel, but Woodward's aircraft, *P7105 HE-N*, was hit by flak seconds before he released his bombs and both engines streamed glycol. Williams scored direct hits on the stern of the vessel setting it on fire, then saw Woodward's aircraft ditch about 400 yards past the convoy and a quarter of a mile off shore. F/O Harvey attacked a 1,000 ton Dutch coaster; his first bomb exploded in the water but the second went through the deck, and probably blew her bottom out. P/O King also attacked this vessel, but did not bomb. His usual aircraft, which was being serviced, had the bomb release button on the throttle lever, whilst *P7057* had hers next to the camera gun button on the control column: with the target in his sights, he pushed the wrong button! W/O McPhail and P/O Lovell headed for a Seiner-type merchant vessel, but the former was seen to fly through spray sent up from a heavy flak burst and crash into the sea at full speed. His aircraft, *P6987*, disintegrated on impact. P/O Lovell scored direct hits. F/S Yates did not bomb. Like P/O King, he was not flying his usual aircraft, whose release button needed just a slight depression to release the bombs. That on *P6986* needed to be pushed all the way. He then had to slide away from the Seiner-type merchant vessel to avoid his leader's bomb bursts but attacked a barge towed by a tug, with cannon.

The squadron claimed an 800 ton merchant vessel as probably sunk; a 1,000 ton Dutch coaster and a Seiner-type merchant vessel as damaged, and a barge as probably damaged. A Reconnaissance Spitfire later found only one merchant vessel afloat escorted by four armed trawlers, although the actual results were two ships sunk, two barges sunk and one ship badly damaged. The ORB noted that, 'Both P/O King and F/S Yates were extremely chastened to learn that they had not released their bombs, especially when the causes were revealed.' It also expressed the hope that S/L Woodward was a POW.

S/L Robert Sinkler Woodward DFC did not escape from *P7105* as was initially hoped and the ORB noted something of his record, 'The months of May to November without accidents; the full and effective programme of operational training, as well as the intense convoy activity of the spring of 1942; the development of the Whirlibomber, and finally the offensive activity of the past three months. In operations, S/L Woodward's keenness both in persuading Group to lay them on and in his own leadership and his own exploits were both gallant and successful.' His wife Virginia lived near the station, strictly against regulations, and apparently knew he had not returned even before she was told.

W/O Donald Burton McPhail was described by the ORB as being 'of sober habits, and very well liked. An excellent amateur photographer, his productions were in great demand, and he was officer in charge of squadron photographic records.'

F/L Warnes was promoted to command the squadron on 9 December. Initially rejected for aircrew due to defective eyesight, he was commissioned in the RAFVR in April 1940, and served as an Equipment Officer in France. He later attended a refresher course then became a flying instructor but the local MO noticed he always wore glasses and ordered him to take a sight test. Prior to doing so, however, he purchased contact lenses and memorised the eye chart! Having passed, he was posted to 56 OTU, then 263 Squadron in September 1941. The officers of the squadron celebrated the double event of his promotion and his forthcoming marriage in a party at Stafford House.

Cliff Rudland recalled that during off duty nights they had an ingenious method of obtaining free beer. They would visit a pub and whilst the others chatted to the locals, Warnes would stand alone at the end of the bar. During the conversation they would point to Warnes and say, 'That man over there is impervious to pain. He can stick a pin in his eye and not feel it.' The conversation was then expertly manoeuvred to the point where a challenge was laid down. If he managed this feat, would the locals buy a round of drinks. 'In those days very few people knew of contact lenses, and we got pissed many times on that caper!' Another story was that every morning he would take a cold bath and his batman would bring him a cigar and a pint of beer as he did so.[30]

14 December saw the first air combat since March 1941, and the first Whirlwind combat with a Focke-Wulf Fw.190, when F/O Coyne and Sgt Cotton were bounced by a brace of 190s of 10/JG.2 off St Aldhelm's Head. During a dogfight between 4,000 feet and sea level, both Whirlwind pilots scored hits and Coyne claimed one damaged.

F/L Donald Bruce Ogilvie returned following liaison duties with the USAAF, and the ORB noted that, 'This is F/L Ogilvie's second tour of operations. He fought in the Battle of Britain with 601 Squadron, and has taken part in a great many offensive operations.' It also noted, that 'Christmas was celebrated with traditional unstinted festivity and good cheer and it was perhaps lucky that the weather was non-operational on Boxing Day.

January 1943

With the coming of 1943, the Whirlwind was showing her age, and but for the teething troubles experienced with the Typhoon, the squadron would have re-equipped with these aircraft early in 1943. As it was, they struggled on for a further twelve months with the redoubtable Whirlwind. Despite this, however, not one pilot had a bad word for her; most simply said she was 'a gentleman's aircraft'.

During the month, 123 hours were flown, of which forty-one were operational, and it was the third month in succession to be entirely free from accidents. The lack of flying

Above left: S/L Robert Woodward DFC was lost on 7 December. (*John LaGette archives*)

Above right: W/O Donald McPhail RCAF was lost on 7 December. (*Jane Renton archives*)

F/L Geoff Warnes and F/L Joe Holmes. (*Cliff Rudland archives*)

Sgt Tommy Taylor, the Link Trainer, at Lulworth Cove. (*Bill Watkins archives*)

gave time for a good deal of ground training, all pilots learnt daily inspections and re-arming, both cannon and bombs. There were lectures on evasion and a number of films dealing with tactics, ship recognition and the like, and full use was made of the link trainer, which was under the command of Sgt 'Tommy' Thomas. S/L Warnes attended an Army Co-Op Course at Old Sarum; P/O Dattatraya Anant 'Sammy' Samant was posted, and F/O Cyril Brooking Thornton and W/O Kevin Patrick O'Dowd arrived from 535 Squadron.

During the month, F/O Brearley, P/O Lee-White, F/S Ridley, and Sgt Cotton were detached to Predannack to harass minesweepers expected off Ile Vierge. They flew several times but returned to Warmwell on the twenty-fouth without having seen the 'entirely elusive, if not illusionary, minesweepers.'

February 1943

Five Rhubarbs, six Night Offensive operations and the commencement of dive bombing attacks occupied 'A' Flight during the month, whilst 'B' Flight was based at Fairwood Common for defensive duties.

On the twelfth, F/O Harvey and Sgt Williams flew Rhubarb 164, a successful attack on trains in a siding at Pont Bail near La Haye du Puits. Unfortunately, Sgt David John Williams was hit by flak during the attack and was forced to ditch *P7052* four miles off Cap de Carteret on the return flight. F/O Harvey orbited and saw him organising his dinghy but was forced to leave when his fuel ran low. As soon as he landed, he took off again as navigator in an air sea rescue Walrus to continue the search, but failed to find his colleague in very rough seas.

A second loss occurred on the nineteenth, during 'Exercise Longford.' F/O Harvey, F/O King, F/S Hicks, and Sgt Macaulay were briefed to beat up mechanised transport of the Armoured Brigade of Guards, south of Chiseldon, Wiltshire. Hicks was the last to attack, but as he completed his strafing run the port wing tip of *P7062 HE-L* clipped a tree, she went into a violent horizontal spin and crashed. The Board of Inquiry found that the accident was caused by his misjudgement of the 'sink' at the bottom of the dive but examination of the starboard engine suggested a 'big end' failure occurred which would have resulted in sudden asymmetrical power that contributed to, if not caused the crash, but this appears not to have been taken into account. F/S Francis Lesley Hicks RAAF had joined the squadron in July 1942, but was attached to A&AEE Boscombe Down between August and October 1942, where he took part in the testing of the Whirlibomber.

There was almost a third loss when Sgt Macaulay's starboard engine, aboard *P6991*, cut during take-off. He avoided several high tension cables before crash-landing in a field west of the aerodrome. The accident was witnessed by Air Vice-Marshal Dickson, AOC 10 Group, and the ORB noted, 'The AOC directs that Sgt Macaulay be commended for putting up a creditable performance when his starboard engine cut when taking off.'

Other personnel movements saw squadron old boy F/L Joseph William Ernest Holmes return from 137 Squadron as 'B' Flight Commander, to replace F/L Donald Bruce Ogilvie who was posted. P/O Lee-White left for Liaison Duties with the USAAF and F/S John

P7062 HE-L was lost with F/S Frank Hicks RAAF on 19 February. (*Jane Renton archives*)

Above left: Sgt Dai Williams was lost on 13 February. (*Bill Watkins archives*)

Above right: F/S Frank Hicks RAAF was lost on 19 February. (*Jane Renton archives*)

McGowan Barclay returned to 137 Squadron, whilst F/O Cyril Brooking Thornton and W/O Kevin Patrick O'Dowd were posted after less than a month with the squadron. There were also eight new arrivals from OTU – P/O Paul Thomas Richard Mercer, and Sgts Norman Peter Blacklock, Harold Medd Proctor, John Barrie Purkis, John Thould, William Edwin Watkins, and George Albert Wood. The last three were close friends and known as 'The Three Mustgetbeers'. The final new arrival was a Martinet Target tug aircraft that according to the ORB 'Had a useful turn of speed, which improves the resemblance of operational conditions.' Finally, S/L Warnes and F/L Blackshaw were awarded the DFC.

During January, S/L Warnes had experimented with dropping parachute containers loaded with 120lb of sandbags, with a view to using the aircraft for re supply missions. His report read, 'There was no difficulty attaching them to the bomb racks and the container did not interfere with the flap. A rather longer run than usual was necessary for the take-off, but the machine handled as usual in the air and the stalling speed was the same as when carrying 2 x 250lb bombs. The containers were dropped from 500 feet, the parachute opening practically instantaneously, and there was no difficulty in dropping the containers in a very small space.' A successful live trial took place on 8 February, at Netheravon, but unfortunately nothing came of the experiments.

On the twentieth, 'A' Flight, the orderly room, and the intelligence and medical sections moved to RAF Harrowbeer near Yelverton, south Devon. 'B' Flight remained detached at Fairwood Common, and 3055 Echelon remained at Warmwell. The ORB noted, 'Conditions which, whilst no doubt are not unreasonably described as "on Active Service" are very much less comfortable than the particularly good facilities of dispersal and messing which the squadron enjoyed at Warmwell.'

The final three days of the month saw the commencement of dive bombing attacks. The ORB noted, 'Soon after he took over command of the squadron, S/L Warnes suggested to Group authorities that the squadron might practice and use a form of dive bombing, so that it might take part in Circus operations. Practices were carried out, and the operations of these three days were laid on. Judgement about their absolute success, whether in the form of damage to aerodrome installations and or morale at Maupertus, or in the bringing to battle of enemy fighters, must evidently be the concern of higher authorities. However, let it be recorded here that these operations were intensively enjoyed by all who took part in them.' In all three, the Whirlibombers dived at 45 degrees from around 15,000 to 5,000 feet, and the escorting Spitfires, who dived with them, found it difficult to keep up. The attacks were the squadron's contribution to Circus operations flown in conjunction with strikes on the Brest U-boat pens by the US 8th Air Force. Of the third mission – Circus 17 – the ORB noted, 'This was 'B' Flight's first dive bombing attack. It was successful, as buildings were seen to 'open up like flowers'. Unfortunately, the USAAF dropped 155 tons of bombs short of the pens.

March 1943

The squadron was still divided between Harrowbeer, Fairwood Common, and Warmwell but as it was the only fighter-bomber Squadron in 10 Group, both flights returned to

Above left: Sgt Harold Proctor reported for flying duties 25 February. (*Bill Watkins archives*)

Above right: 'The Three Mustgetbeers': Sgt George Wood, Sgt John Thould, and Sgt Bill Watkins reported for flying duties 24 February. (*Bill Watkins archives*)

'A' Flight ground crews. (*Purkis Family archives*)

Warmwell on the fourteenth for Circus 18, a dive bomb attack on Maupertus. Bombs were seen to burst on the aerodrome, perimeter and dispersal areas causing the ORB to note, 'The success of these operations is hard to estimate, but they seem to have been excellent.'

Another record was set on the nineteenth, when S/L Warnes, F/L Blackshaw, F/L Holmes, F/O Brearley, F/O Coyne, F/O Harvey, F/O King, P/O Abrams, P/O Yates, W/O Tebbit, F/S Wright, and Sgt Simpson flew Roadstead 53. The ORB noted, 'These twelve Whirlibombers were the greatest number ever to become airborne for an operation. It was a pity therefore that the large convoy which had been reported south of Guernsey could not be located in thick haze.' Between 20 and 23 March, nine pilots – S/L Warnes, F/L Blackshaw, F/L Holmes, F/O Brearley, F/O Harvey, F/O King, P/O Abrams, F/S Wright, and Sgt Simpson – flew Night Rhubarbs, two against Morlaix viaduct, the other against Ponthou viaduct. During the attacks on Morlaix viaduct, they claimed six direct hits, whilst most were forced to bomb through heavy flak and were unable to observe results and several pilots were forced to return early with mechanical trouble. Similar results were obtained against the Ponthou Viaduct and congratulations were received from AOC 10 Group, but this could not hide the fact that the age of the aircraft was beginning to show. Despite the unceasing efforts of the ground crews the number of technical faults was beginning to affect serviceability.

The final operational sorties of the month took place on the twenty-sixth and caused the ORB to note, 'Four Rhubarb operations, of which two found no useful target, one was very successful, and one brilliantly successful.' F/O Brearley and Sgt Simpson were the pair who found no cloud cover; F/S Wright and W/O Tebbit mistook Cap Flamanville for Cap Carteret and so searched too far north. F/O Coyne and P/O Yates attacked and damaged the Ouistreham lock gates, but as they climbed away F/O Coyne's aircraft, *P7108*, was hit by a 40-mm shell just behind the cockpit. The radio took the full force of the impact, one of the oxygen bottles exploded and ripped a three-foot hole in the fuselage skin, but no serious damage was done and he returned safely to base. Finally, P/O Abrams and F/O Lee-White attacked a transformer station near St Lo. Both scored cannon strikes which caused clouds of blue sparks, before Abrams' bombs disintegrated the whole transformer unit.

Two pilots reported for duty in March – Sgts Hoare and Ramamurthy, whilst F/S Ridley was detached to 1 SLAIS, RAF Milfield, and Sgt Turner was posted to RAF Colerne. The ORB noted, 'Sgt Turner had been with the squadron since 16 March 1940, and was thus one of its oldest members. As Orderly Room Sergeant he came as near as absolute perfection as is given to human beings in the RAF. He will be very greatly missed by all ranks, as a friend and councillor.'

April 1943

April proved to be the most dramatic month in the history of the squadron since its return from Norway. Between the thirteenth and the nineteenth there were seventy offensive sorties, which wreaked considerable damage on the enemy, but five pilots and aircraft were lost in the process. A further three pilots were posted: F/O Stuart James

Hope Farm, near Morton Station, provided the sergeant's billets at RAF Warmwell. (*Bill Watkins archives*)

Sgt Roy Wright and *HE-Q* in a Knighton Wood dispersal pen at RAF Warmwell. (*Chris Thomas archives*)

F/S Ken Ridley was detached to 1 S.L.A.I.S. on 20 March. (*Jane Renton archives*)

Lovell, F/S Roy Wright, and P/O Jocelyn Ivan Yates.

The first successful operation of the month took place on the thirteenth, when ten aircraft dive bombed Brest/Guipavas aerodrome during Circus 22. They noted that the target was indifferently camouflaged, outlined by a newly made perimeter track, and bursts were seen in the dispersal areas, on the watch office, and a hangar near it.

An unusual incident occurred on 14 April when F/O Harvey and F/O Lee-White, took off from Predannack on a shipping recce. Twenty miles south of Start Point they flew over a partly submerged Lancaster with her crew in a dinghy nearby. They immediately abandoned their mission and began to orbit the bomber whilst transmitting for a 'fix' until two ASR Beaufighters and an air sea rescue launch arrived and the crew were rescued. The previous night Bomber Command had attacked Spezia in Italy and one of the aircraft involved was Lancaster B.I *W4318 PM-C* of 103 Squadron flown by Sgt Johnny Stoneman and crew. They successfully bombed the target, but during the return flight the R/T failed, so when they ran out of fuel they were unable to inform anyone of their position. Unusually the aircraft did not sink, if it had, the low flying Whirlibombers may have missed the small dinghy and her crew. Unfortunately, one of the launches attempted to tow the Lancaster to port but got too close and accidently severed her tail resulting in the bomber sinking.

Later the same day, F/O Harvey, P/O Abrams, Sgt Macaulay, Sgt Simpson, and Sgt Thyagarajan flew Roadstead 57 in search of shipping in the Lannilis estuary, escorted by Spitfire Vb.s of 65 Squadron. The formation flew into the Baie de Brest, and just off Pointe St Mathieu, Harvey, Simpson, and Thyagarajan sank one of three ships they found, an 800 ton Dredger with a crane in the bows. She was in fact the 474 ton *Emile Allard*, which was hit by two bombs and sank in minutes. The other two vessels, trawlers, were claimed Cat 4. Sgt John Macaulay, *P7010*, attacked a small ship nearby but nothing further was seen of him although he was heard to say over the R/T that he had engine trouble and 'I'm going down now, I am going to land.' The ORB expressed the hope that he had crash-landed on the Brest Peninsula, but it was not to be. He was shot down by Leutnant Wilhelm Godt of 8/JG.2.

In a similar operation to the Chameleon Patrols of January 1941, F/O Coyne, F/O Lovell, P/O Cotton and Sgt Thyagarajan flew an Armed Dusk Reconnaissance on 16 April 1943 in search of E-Boats believed to leave Cherbourg at last light for the Cornish coast. Unfortunately, the result was the same, they saw nothing. Eight aircraft also took off to attack industrial targets in the Caen Mondeville area. S/L Warnes returned early due to a faulty compass, but F/O Harvey, F/O King, F/O Lee-White, P/O Abrams, and Sgt Simpson successfully attacked their targets. On his return, Lee-White was shot up by an armed trawler north of Ouistreham, which hit his starboard engine nacelle, bursting the tyre and damaging the flap; F/O King also saw this vessel, and F/L Blackshaw bombed it but missed. Unfortunately, F/O Edgar Brearley, *P6995*, did not return. The ORB noted, 'he had been with the squadron for nineteen months, and was so competent a pilot and likeable a person, that to write briefly of him scarcely does him justice.' An intercepted Vichy radio report stated that a Canadian aircraft had been shot down by flak while attacking a train at St Lo and the pilot was killed. As F/O Brearley's personnel aircraft carried a crest of Maple Leaves it was initially thought this might have been him. However, his body was washed ashore at Swanage on 20 May and he was buried in Warmwell village churchyard with full military honours.

The following night, 'Nine aircraft sought out targets in almost the whole seaward

Sgt John Macaulay was lost in *P7010* on 14 April. (*Bill Watkins archives*)

and landward area within the squadron's range from Warmwell.' F/L Blackshaw and P/O Cotton returned with engine trouble; S/L Warnes, F/O Coyne, and F/O Lee-White found no targets, but nothing was heard from either F/O Philip Harvey, *P7090*, or P/O Basil Courtney Abrams, *P7099*, after they left Warmwell. During briefing, Harvey had shown an interest in the armed trawler off Ouistreham, which was thought to have shot down a Beaufighter and F/O Brearley, and damaged F/O Lee-White the previous night. It was assumed that both pilots had also been shot down by it. F/O Cecil Percy King, *P7117 HE-H*, searched for trains between Isigny and St Lo but did not return either, it was thought that he was shot down by flak over Airel.

The loss of four pilots was a grievous blow, causing the ORB to record:

> It is not possible to set down here what we felt about them. 'Rex' King was the oldest member of the squadron in terms of service, almost twenty-nine months. 'Bas' Abrams and 'Tim' Harvey had been with us for seventeen and nineteen months respectively. Harvey was a person of rare charm and goodness, whilst Abrams and King were good friends and companions of the rest of the squadron. Along with Eddie Brearley, they were the backbone of the squadron and were typical of the varied origins of the pilots. They came from Canada, Eire, British Guiana, and South Africa.

The squadron received word on the 1 May that Philip Harvey had been awarded the DFC.

The next operation, Roadstead 59, on 27 April, saw S/L Warnes, F/L Blackshaw, F/O Lee-White, P/O Cotton, W/O Tebbit, and Sgt Simpson, escorted by the Ibsley Wing,

Above left: F/O Eddie Brearley RCAF was lost on 16 April. (*Hap Kennedy archives*)

Above right: F/O Philip Harvey was lost on 18 April. (*Cliff Rudland archives*)

P/O Basil Abrams and F/O Cecil King DFM were lost on 18 April. (*Moira Fletcher*)

attack a convoy of nine vessels off St Helier. A large armed trawler led a 1,500 ton merchant vessel, heavily laden barges, a Motor barge, a 100 ton converted Yacht and an E-Boat which was towing barges. Following immediately behind the anti-flak Spitfires, who attacked the first six ships, Warnes, Blackshaw and Cotton sank the 1,500 ton merchant vessel; Lee-White damaged the armed trawler but returned with his starboard tail-plane bent upwards by the blast of his bombs and Tebbit probably sank the motor barge. Simpson attacked the converted yacht, which was blown 30 degrees off course by the explosion of his bombs, and was probably sunk. He then went on to damage the E-Boat with cannon fire. The only vessels not attacked were the barges, and the ORB noted, 'This was without doubt the most successful of all the squadron's operations to date.'

The final operations of April saw S/L Warnes, F/L Blackshaw, F/O Lee-White, P/O Cotton, W/O Tebbit, and Sgt Simpson fly to Exeter for Roadstead 60, an attack on a convoy near Les Sept Iles, which had been mauled by HMS *Goathland* and HMS *Albrighton* during the previous night. S/L Warnes took W/O Tebbit's aircraft when his own refused to start whilst Lee-White was forced to abandon the mission due to faulty exactors. Twenty-four Spitfires of the Exeter Wing escorted the remaining Whirlibombers to the convoy, which consisted of six M-class minesweepers and armed trawlers led by a Destroyer with a further M-class minesweeper bringing up the rear. There was intense flak during the attack despite the concentrated attacks of the anti-flak Spitfires, but Warnes and Blackshaw probably sank the rearmost minesweeper whilst Simpson damaged an 800 ton armed trawler and Cotton a minesweeper, but in return, flak tore an 18 inch hole in the starboard wing of his aircraft – *P6981.* Roadstead 62, later in the day, failed to locate the depleted convoy, but a congratulatory signal was received from AOC 10 Group on Roadsteads 59 and 60 which read, 'For S/L Warnes from AOC. Hearty congratulations on your shows of yesterday and today. I realise full well your present difficulties over aircraft and pilots.' The six pilots involved were the only ones operational for shipping attacks and so also flew Roadstead 63 on 29 April, when they found a patrol boat escorting several fishing vessels off Isigny. Only S/L Warnes attacked, his bombs struck the vessel amidships and she blew up.

May 1943

At the beginning of May, Sgt John Thould was detached to the Air Crew Refresher Course at Brighton following the first accident ascribed to carelessness for ten months. As he came into land in a strong gusty wind, he held off at thirty feet, and wrote off *P7057* in the subsequent heavy landing. A mix of youthful exuberance and deadly ordnance was the catalyst for another serious accident when several pilots gathered at the shooting range to loose off a few rounds from their revolvers. Unfortunately, F/S Simpson was accidentally shot in the stomach by Sgt Thould. He was rushed to Bovington Hospital where he made a complete recovery, but John Thould, who had just returned from his refresher course, was posted to RAF Warmwell for target towing duties. Following a month 'in the wilderness he returned a very chastened and reformed character.' Never operational on Whirlwinds, he later served with distinction on Typhoons.

P/O Max Cotton flew *P6981* over 180 miles back to Base with this 18 inch hole in the starboard wing. *(Jane Renton archives)*

Apart from the war against the Germans, the squadron had its own internal conflict, between its resident Indian pilots. To keep some semblance of peace, Sgt Thyagarajan, a Hindu, and Sgt Ramamurthy, a Muslim, were separated in to 'A' and 'B' Flights respectively, and both were posted to 286 Squadron in May, although Thyagarajan returned in January 1944. Quite how 286 handled the pair is not known.

Three pilots also reported for flying duties, Sgts Fred Green, William Whittaker Heaton, and Graham Natt Smith RAAF. Despite these additions, the number of operational pilots was low and 'The CO obtained a directive from Group that the squadron was to maintain thirty minutes available by day and night with as many pilots and aircraft as possible.'

Four Roadsteads during May searched for minesweepers off Bréhat, but found only the Casquetes and the French fishing fleet. Roadstead 67, against the 4,000 ton *Solmglint* berthed in the Basin Napoleon in Cherbourg Docks, was more successful, in the sense that they were able to bomb. S/L Warnes, F/L Blackshaw, F/L Holmes, F/O Coyne, F/O Lee-White, P/O Mercer, F/S Simpson, and Sgt Ridley were escorted by the Ibsley Wing and attacked out of the glaring yellow sunset, which appeared to confuse the flak gunners. The ORB noted that, 'The Whirlibombers secured a good pattern of bombing without seeing a direct hit. This it was felt would have been a remarkably lucky shot. Two explosions were seen fifty yards away from her; one in the Basin Charles X and another in the Petite Rade near the Quai Liemet.'

Sgt John Thould, carrying a 250lb bomb. Seconds after the photo was taken he collapsed under its weight. (*Bill Watkins archives*)

Above left: Sgt Sayana Thyagarajan was posed on 25 May. (*Bill Watkins archives*)

Above right: Sgt O. Ramamurthy was posted on 25 May. (*Bill Watkins archives*)

F/S James Simpson and Sgt Graham Smith RAAF. (*Bill Watkins archives*)

F/S Fred Green, F/S Bill Watkins, F/S Peter Cooper, F/S Tommy Handley, and F/S William Heaton. Those in Mae Wests were on 15 minutes Readiness. (*Revd George Wood archives*)

Lord Trenchard visited the squadron on the fifteenth, and that night F/O Lee-White found an eight ship convoy off Cap Barfleur and probably sank a 2,500 ton merchant vessel. S/L Warnes and F/S Simpson were unable to find the ships whilst F/L Holmes bombed one but did not see the results. F/L Herbert John Blackshaw DFC was heard to say over the R/T that he was 'OK' and was tracked as he re-crossed the English coast near RAF Exeter, which he orbited without lights and R/T, before flying to Harrowbeer, where he orbited again then returned to Exeter where he crashed. Although he abandoned his aircraft, *P7094 HE-T*, a few seconds before it crashed, his parachute did not have time to fully deploy. An investigation of the wreckage revealed little other than the bombs were not on board. He had been airborne for two hours and twelve minutes, twelve minutes longer than the maximum operational flight time of a Whirlwind. It was thought he had probably been concussed by flak or by the explosion of his bombs. The ORB paid tribute to him, 'The loss of "Blackie" as a friend, leader and councillor in every matter concerned with the squadron's activities was extremely severe. A careful and clever pilot, he was shrewd, witty, and gentle as a person.' He was laid to rest in Warmwell churchyard.

An armed shipping reconnaissance by S/L Warnes, F/L Coyne, F/O Lee-White, and F/S Ridley on 16 May, escorted by 504 Squadron was abandoned west of the Casquetes when they were attacked by two Fw.190s from NAG.13. Lee-White and Coyne each fired a burst at the enemy fighters, and the ORB noted, 'this was the second Fw.190 damaged by Coyne, and the third damaged by Whirlibombers.' Post-war research suggests neither 190 was actually hit however.

'The most successful and spectacular of the squadron's night operations' was how the ORB recorded Night Roadstead 2 on 21 May. The target was a 4,000 ton merchant vessel escorted by four armed trawlers between Cap de la Hague and Cherbourg. S/L Warnes found the convoy, and following his attack on the merchant vessel, gave a running commentary which was later broadcast by the BBC. F/L Holmes and P/O Cotton finished off the merchant vessel although Cotton was hit by flak and his aircraft, *P7108*, was so riddled by splinters she was described as 'looking like a pepper box.' He made a good landing after four attempts, but with his rudder partly jammed and no hydraulics, he had to use the emergency air bottle to lower the wheels and flaps. F/L Coyne found only the bows of the merchant vessel visible so attacked and sank one of the trawlers. Last on scene was F/O Lee-White. Flak pierced the coolant system of his starboard engine as he attacked, causing a fire that highlighted him to the flak gunners, but he bombed from mast height, then pulled up, orbited Querqueville at 1,500 feet and informed Warmwell of his intention to bail out. The fire abated, however, and he returned to Warmwell, where, according to the ORB, 'He appeared over the aerodrome like "Jehovah to the Israelites in a flickering fire" which took hold again as he landed, but the fire crew extinguished it before it reached the fuel tank.' George Wood remembers, 'The Intelligence Officer, F/O Wordsworth, like his namesake, waxed lyrical in his report, likening Lee-White to Elijah in reverse [2 Kings 2 v. 11] and "Elijah went up to heaven in a whirlwind"'[31]

At the beginning of May the ORB commented, 'It had been evident since the middle of April, that it was no longer possible to obtain from Westland's or from the Maintenance Units, replacements for more than one or two of the Whirlwind's which were written off in operations, or which were u/s during major inspections. It was inevitable that the

F/L Herbert Blackshaw DFC was lost on 15 May. (*Cliff Rudland archives*)

P7094 HE-T seen with F/S Jimmy Coyne in the cockpit, was lost with F/L Blackshaw on 15 May. (*James Coyne archives*)

F/O Arthur Lee-White RCAF. (*Bill Watkins archives*)

Standing: F/S Robert Beaumont, F/O Robert Tuff RAAF, F/L David Ross, F/O Peter Green (Medical Officer). *On Whirlwind*: F/S John Purkis, F/S Peter Cooper, F/S George Williams. (*Purkis Family archives*)

squadron would soon re-equip with new aircraft, although which type was a matter of great debate.' Thus when a cipher was received on 28 May which 'Ordered the immediate re-equipment with an unexpected type of aircraft' it was received with more feigned than real enthusiasm. The aircraft involved although not mentioned, was either the Vultee Vengeance dive bomber or the Hurricane IV.[32] The cipher was immediately cancelled, however, and the ORB continued, 'The squadron would be receiving fourteen Whirlibombers from 137 when they re-equipped with Hurricanes. Thus to the great satisfaction of this unit, which flew the first Whirlwinds in July 1940, first used Whirlwinds in defensive and offensive operations in 1941, and flew the first Whirlibomber operations in September 1942, will also have the privilege of using, as profitably as we may reasonably hope, the last two dozen Whirlwinds that remain.'

S/L Warnes, F/L Coyne, F/O Lee-White, P/O Cotton, W/O Tebbit, and F/S Ridley found a large convoy off Barfleur on Roadstead 71, but the ORB noted, 'There were fifteen ships there, the French fishing fleet again' and, as an afterthought, 'They were not attacked.' Finally an uneventful armed shipping recce on 30 May saw the four hundredth Whirlibomber sortie.

June 1943

'June brought nineteen days of rain, wind, low cloud and sea fog with sunny intervals; however, the same nineteen days brought high honours and far reaching changes to the squadron.' The high honours were the award of no less than four DFCs and a DSO. The latter, to S/L Warnes DFC, was the second awarded for work accomplished entirely with 263 Squadron; the first was awarded posthumously to S/L 'Baldy' Donaldson in July 1940. The DFCs went to F/L Coyne RCAF, F/L Holmes, F/O Lee-White RCAF, and P/O Cotton RAAF. It was not just the aircrew who received honours, F/S R. A. Hollamby, I/C 'A' Flight ground crews, and F/S H. O. J. Watts, I/C Armament Section, were mentioned in despatches. The far reaching changes saw four experienced Whirlwind men reach the end of their tours. F/Ls James Patrick Coyne DFC, Joseph William Ernest Holmes DFC, F/O Arthur Henry Lee-White DFC, and P/O Kenneth Charles Ridley DFC DFM, who had flown 439 Whirlwind ops between them. The ORB noted of Coyne, 'He took part in nearly all of the squadron's operational work and by his gallantry and leadership earned the award of the DFC.' F/L Eric Comissiong Eadie, the squadron MO, was also posted and a party was held at the Golden Lion in Weymouth, given by the decorated officers. 'It was a magnificent party magnificently enjoyed.' Eleven pilots also reported for flying duties: P/O Robert Bruce Tuff RAAF, and Sgts Robert Charles Beaumont, Peter Frederick Cooper, Iain David MacDonald Dunlop, Leonard Scott Gray, William Anthony Handley, Richard John Hughes, Leonard James Knott, Denis Charles Todd, and George Williams from OTU, and F/L John Edward McClure RCAF from 137 Squadron, as 'B' Flight Commander.

Due to the recent awards, the squadron had exhausted its stock of medal ribbon, so F/O Lee-White was ordered to take two ground crew to Ibsley on the fourteenth in the Oxford (*T1063*) and whilst there collect more ribbon. They were awaiting take-off clearance when 616 Squadron returned from a sweep, but, as it landed, one of the Spitfire VIs left

'B' Flight seen on 13 June following the awards to Cotton, Lee-White and Holmes. *Back row*: F/O Paul Mercer, W/O Don Tebbit, P/O Max Cotton DFC RAAF, F/O Arthur Lee-White DFC, F/O Joe Holmes DFC, F/S Graham Smith RAAF, Sgt George Wood, Sgt Fred Green. *Front row*: Sgt Bill Heaton, Sgt Len Knott, Sgt Bill Watkins. (*Revd George Wood archives*)

F/S Iain Dunlop, P/O Norman Blacklock, F/O Jimmy Coyne DFC RCAF, Sgt Len Gray (*Len Gray archives*)

the runway and collided with *T1063*. The prop severed the Oxford's wooden fuselage just behind the cockpit, narrowly missing F/O Lee-White and his two passengers. The ORB noted, '*T1063*, an old and useful chariot that has hitherto proved inviolable was replaced by a newer and faster Oxford [*T1058*]'.

An armed shipping recce at first light on 15 June, by F/O Lee-White, P/O Cotton, P/O Ridley, and Sgt Wood, found five ships north east of Sark. Two M-class minesweepers abeam of each other sixty yards apart, 150 yards behind them were two two-funnel warships possibly *Geleitboote*, whilst an armed trawler was 700 yards astern of the others. The eight Anti-Flak Spitfires of 616 Squadron attacked the two M-class minesweepers, losing one of their number in the process. F/O Lee-White and Sgt Wood attacked one of the minesweepers from below mast height, but as they were using eleven-second delay bombs for the first time did not see them explode. Cotton and Ridley attacked the 775 ton armed trawler, *M483*, which had a 105-mm gun on her stern, a 37-mm gun on her bow and seven 20-mm anti-aircraft guns on her decks – a formidable target. Seconds after releasing his bombs, P/O Cotton, *P7000*, received a direct hit from flak, burst into flames as he passed over her, then dived into the sea about 100 yards from his victim, disintegrating on impact. Three Spitfire pilots reported that Ridley's bombs hit the stern, and *M483* sank so quickly there was no time to launch her lifeboats. Less than fifteen minutes after first sighting the convoy, the remaining aircraft reformed and returned to base having sunk *M483* and seriously damaged the four other vessels, but at a grievous cost. George Wood remembers, 'This was my first op, my baptism of fire. I was hit in the tail as I passed over the ship but didn't wait around to see if she sank.'[33] The ORB paid P/O Maxwell Tylney Cotton DFC RAAF a fitting tribute, 'From the first, he proved to have an extraordinary flare for accurate bombing. Both in practice and in action, he rarely missed a direct hit. As a pilot and leader, his matter of fact calmness before, during and after operations made him invaluable to the squadron. As a person, his courtesy and frank and open nature and constant good humour endeared him to all who knew him.'

The squadron was still absorbing the loss of Max Cotton when news was received that it was also to lose S/L Warnes DSO DFC, who was to be posted to 10 Group for Sector Gunnery Duties. He had flown more than 135 operational Whirlwind sorties and the ORB noted, 'S/L Warnes had commanded the squadron since December 1942. During that time the work of the squadron was largely of his creation. Briefly, he was a strict disciplinarian who combined a fierce and forthright manner with personnel kindness; a commander who never left the least doubt about what he wanted and who consistently obtained these qualities because he himself consistently displayed them. He himself did more than he required of others. As a tactician, S/L Warnes may have some place in the history of the war, as the creator of medium level dive bombing by fighter-bombers, and his notes on shipping attacks have been adopted as a Fighter Command Tactical Memorandum' (*see Chapter 12*). Of his replacement, S/L Ernest Reginald Baker DFC, the ORB continued 'He comes to the squadron on his third tour of operations. He has fought and flown in aircraft of many designations in almost every theatre of the war, other than the Far East. It is felt that the squadron has again been most fortunate in his appointment.' His first tour was on Sunderland Flying Boats during which he was awarded the DFC for destroying two U-Boats and damaging a third.

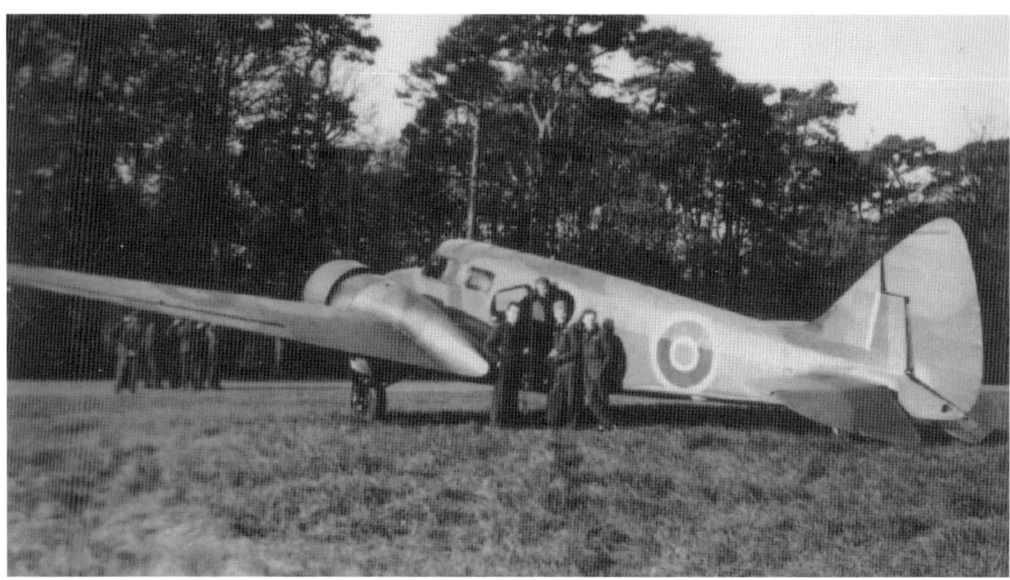

Oxford *T1063*, 'an old and useful chariot', was wrecked on 14 June when she was hit by a Spitfire of 616 Squadron . (*John Purkis archives*)

P/O Max Cotton DFC RAAF was lost on 15 June. (*Jane Renton archives*)

Bill Watkins remembered that Warnes was known amongst the pilots, although never to his face, as 'the Blind Ace' and 'When following him home from an operation we always knew when he was taking his contacts out. His wings would waggle and he would career all over the sky and on landing he would be wearing glasses.'[34] As mentioned previously, stories of Geoff Warnes are legendary. He was probably the first operational pilot to wear contact lenses and one of his 'tests' for new pilots joining the squadron was to buy them a pint in the local. During the conversation, he would lean over the bar and adjust his eye-lid whereupon the lens would pop out, and drop into his pint. If the new recruit continued the conversation without making comment, he was 'in'. Another 'tradition' he started was the Friday night session at the Golden Lion, attendance at which was compulsory. Sgt Proctor missed one session for a date with a WAAF and the following day was ordered to report to the CO. He was convinced that he had a valid excuse, but was told that women were never, under any circumstances, to interfere with the squadron night out! Another custom was for the pilots of 263 and 257 to descend on Weymouth

25 July 1943. The arrival of S/L Baker DFC. *Front row*: Sgt George Williams, Sgt Bill Watkins, Sgt James Simpson, Sgt Harold Proctor. *Second row*: W/O Don Tebbit, F/O Eric Holman, F/O David Ross, F/O Peter Green, F/S Williams (B Flt Chiefy), F/L Jimmy Coyne DFC RCAF, S/L Reg Baker DFC, F/L John McClure DFC RCAF, F/L Eugene Owens (Adjutant), F/O Douglas Mogg, F/O Oswald Ash (Engineering Officer), F/O Andrew Wordsworth (Intelligence Officer). *Third row*: Sgt Kelly (g/c), Sgt 'Pongo' Cole (g/c), Sgt Richard Hughes, P/O Ken Funnell, F/O Robert Hunter, Sgt George Wood, Whirly, Sgt Bob Beaumont, Sgt Iain Dunlop, Sgt Armstrong (g/c), F/S Reg Harvey (A Flt Chiefy), F/S Denis Todd, Sgt Rogers (g/c). *Back row*: Sgt Tommy Handley, Sgt Peter Cooper. (*Bill Watkins archives*)

F/S Bill Watkins and *P6997 HE-R*. (*Bill Watkins archives*)

Above left and right: The result of S/L Warnes having 'one over the eight' at the Golden Lion. This accident occurred on the night of 12 February 1943 in West Stafford near Warmwell. (*Jane Renton archives*)

The Golden Lion, Weymouth, the squadron pub. (*Purkis Family archives*)

on Friday nights for sausage, eggs and chips at the Ritz Café, and afterwards they met up with their girlfriends to go dancing.

Len Gray remembers:

Occasionally after a particularly merry evening in the mess or at some hostelry in Weymouth or Dorchester, the CO would decree that we required some practice in formation flying. This involved vics of up to twelve aircraft in tight formation at about 1,000 feet. On one such occasion there was considerable turbulence. The CO pressed on undaunted and things got very dodgy but somehow we got through the exercise and landed safely. I was later informed that I had almost had my tail chopped off. I had not been aware of this fortunately as I was too busy to use my rear view mirror![35]

On 19 June, ten Whirlwinds and the Magister moved to Zeals, which was described as, 'a place in very beautiful country and a station which has been without a flying Unit since 1942. The squadron will remain for three weeks for intensive training, and will be non-operational, as it now consists very largely of new pilots.' After making a successful landing following his first Whirlwind solo in *P7013*, one of these new pilots, Sgt Richard Hughes, selected 'wheels up' instead of 'flaps up' causing considerable damage to both the aircraft and his reputation. The Board of Enquiry noted that, 'He did not check the lever before pulling it' but he was not blamed for the accident, however, as the locking nut on the lever failed to work correctly. Another incident occurred during an Army Co-operation Exercise. Sgt Watkins clipped a tree with his starboard wingtip when he pressed his attack too low. He managed to put his aircraft, *P7110*, down safely at Stoney Cross in the New Forest. Two months later he was to collide with another tree whilst taxiing at Warmwell, damaging a wingtip of *P7096*.

'Tommy' Handley recalled:

My brother was an engineer and before the war and was approached by Westland's to design and manufacture a machine that would make retractable tail wheels for the Whirlwind. Westland's were delighted with the prototype and ordered half a dozen more which meant plenty of work for my brother's factory. During the last week of June all of 137's aircraft [five] came to us at 263 except one which was undergoing an engine change, thus 263 was again the only Whirlwind Squadron. When the last aircraft was ready the opportunity came for me to have a weekend at home in Romford with my parents and then go on to Southend to collect the aeroplane and fly it back to Warmwell. I saw my brother whilst at home and arranged to overfly his factory after picking the aircraft up. I duly went to Southend, picked up the aeroplane then flew down the Southend arterial route and picked out his factory. I then proceeded to give it a really good beating up. In the evening when my brother went to his Home Guard meeting in the village pub he was surprised to hear about 'that little bugger this morning nearly took my chimney pots off' so he didn't let on it was his brother.[36]

F/S Tommy Handley and *P6997 HE-R*. (*Tommy Handley archives*)

July 1943

In addition to the eleven pilots in June, ten more arrived in July: F/L David George Ross as a supernumerary, F/L Lamont Maroy Parsons, F/Os Eric John Holman, Robert Charles Hunter, Douglas Edwin George Mogg, Vincent Kenneth Moody, Stanley Joseph Shewell, and Douglas Wallis Sturgeon, P/O Kenneth James Forrester Funnell, and Sgt C. B. Foes, but Parsons, Moody, Shewell and Foes, were posted back out within days. Finally, F/O Peter Roland Green reported for duty as Medical Officer and there were two awards to add to those of the previous month when P/O Ken Ridley DFM (posted to AFDU in June) and F/L John McClure RCAF received the DFC in recognition of their work on Whirlwinds.

Sgt Leonard James Knott was badly injured in a crash on the thirteenth. 'I was approaching Warmwell when the starboard engine failed, I attempted a crash-landing but remember nothing more.'[37] *P7110 HE-C* stalled and crashed in a field near the watch office, disintegrating on impact and catching fire. Luckily, the cockpit section remained intact and he was pulled from the wreckage and rushed to Bovington (Army) Hospital where he regained consciousness the following day. He was later moved to the East Grinstead Hospital, where he was treated by Dr. Archibald McIndoe, and became a member of the Guinea Pig Club.

An armed shipping reconnaissance off Alderney by four Whirlibombers escorted by the Ibsley Wing was intercepted by a single Fw.190 near Portland. It sheared off before attacking, but in a moment's confusion, Sgt Wood identified one of the escorting Spitfires as the enemy. He wrote in his logbook, '2-3 second burst at Spit V. Missed him.' S/L Baker added, 'Rotten Shooting.'

P7110 HE-C following Len Knott's crash landing on 13 July. *(Len Knott archives)*

Maintenance. (*Jane Renton archives*)

Sgt Richard Hughes, Sgt John Purkis, Sgt Harold Proctor, Sgt Robert Beaumont, Sgt Len Gray, and F/S Ken Ridley. (*Bill Watkins archives*)

The reputation of the Peregrine engine, whether deserved or not, was well known in the RAF, as highlighted by the following anecdote from Tony Poole who was serving at Elmdon Aerodrome in the summer 1943:

> I was on duty in the tin hut that served as Flying Control. From above came a very unusual engine sound. I dashed outside and was just in time to see an aircraft disappear over the boundary at 1,500 feet. The distinctive high tail plane of a Whirlwind was visible and from both engines came an ominous trail of black smoke. Knowing that the Peregrine units were prone to throwing rods, I deemed this to be an emergency. Elmdon had no radio facility but it did have a direct phone link to Honiley, the nearest airfield with ground-to-air and station-to-station radio. I gave them a report of what I had seen. At the end of my watch, I gave Honiley a call to find out what had happened. The reply was, 'No incident reported, no Whirlwind missing from operational units, suggest you take "more water with it".' Was this the end of the story? Not quite. Elmdon, autumn 1944, we had our first landing of a Gloster Meteor and straight away I noted the distinctive high tail plane and the two massive engine pods that trailed black smoke – however on this occasion I didn't bother to ring Honiley and warn them of a Whirlwind in distress.[38]

August 1943

The first day of August was fine and sunny, but a 50 mph cross wind caught Sgt Cooper as he landed in *P6981*. The aircraft bounced, dropped a wing, cart wheeled twice, and caught fire. Luckily he was uninjured and the fire was quickly extinguished. He was involved in another more humorous incident a few days later. On the squadron, the recognised cure for a hangover was a few minutes of pure oxygen, so after a particularly heavy night at the Golden Lion he arrived at dispersal feeling under the weather, walked out to the nearest aircraft, climbed in and plugged into the oxygen supply. He returned to the dispersal hut after ten minutes to announce that the effects of the alcohol had gone and he felt fine, until one of the ground crew pointed out that the oxygen supply in the aircraft he had chosen was empty![39]

S/L Baker laid on a low-level shipping strike into Cherbourg harbour on the fifth when it was reported that *Solmglint* was due to put to sea. He called for three volunteers for this suicidal mission, and to a man, the whole squadron volunteered, but the operation was cancelled by the Air Ministry. In June 1944, the 10,000 ton whale oil ship was used as a blockship in Cherbourg, she had not left port in three years.

Massacre at L'Aber Wrac'h

Roadstead 74, on 11 August, was described by the ORB as 'the squadron's most uniformly successful operation.' S/L Baker, F/L Ross, P/O Blacklock and Sgt Proctor (Red Section), and F/L McClure, P/O Tebbit, Sgt Purkis and Sgt Wood (Blue Section) left Predannack escorted by the Polish Portreath Wing. The target was eight E-Boats in the L'Aber Wrac'h estuary. The formation crossed the Channel at sea level and the Spitfires led them straight into the mouth of the estuary where they found two E-Boats moored at the pier at Landéda with an armed trawler nearby and five E-Boats anchored in mid-stream. Queen Mary was in the ops room as the attack went in, and was treated to a barrage of swear words in Polish accents, for which the senior officers present apologised! The Spitfires attacked from 800 feet and the Whirlibombers bombed as the last cannon shells exploded. Baker led Red Section along the pier, where they left one E-Boat engulfed in flames and sank a second, the armed trawler was also 'blown to bits'. Blue Section attacked three vessels in

Sgt Peter Cooper had a lucky escape on 1 August. (*Bill Watkins archives*)

P6981 following Sgt Cooper's crash landing on 1 August. (*Chris Thomas archives*)

mid-stream, and were 'greatly impressed by the red, orange, and green explosions on one of the E-Boats caused by high explosive of German origin.' Flak was light from the ships but intense from the shore although only one aircraft was hit, and a pall of smoke rose to 1,000 feet over the estuary as they withdrew. John McClure noted, 'we caught them with their pants down, the crews were still trying to wrench the tarpaulins from their guns as the bombs went down, others were seen diving overboard, and some were seen rushing up and down the deck with doubtful purpose.' The vessels were from the 4 and 5 S-Boat Flotillas; S.121 was sunk, S.117 and four other boats were heavily damaged, only S.110 escaped intact.

In common with most squadrons, 263 had a several mascots, and when F/O Doug Sturgeon arrived, he was given the task of looking after them. He recalls:

> There were about nine altogether, and S/L Baker inspected them every Wednesday. There was one mongrel in particular who was a real character – Cpl Glycol, so named because as a pup he drank from a puddle of the coolant that had leaked from an engine. The ground crews took lunch in two shifts, and when the flight sergeant would shout 'early lunch', Glycol was the first in the truck that took them to the mess. He would then wait there for the second sitting, thus getting

Who said war was hell? The original photo was signed 'Love Kay xxx'. (*Tommy Handley archives*)

two meals. After the war, I went back to Warmwell and in a local pub got chatting with a farmer. I said I had flown from the aerodrome and had looked after the mascots but often wondered what happened to them when we left. He said they were all adopted by local families and as he had originally given 'Glycol' to the squadron, he had him back. He went on to say that each morning he would disappear for the day, only returning at nightfall. Intrigued, the farmer followed him. 'Glycol' went to the aerodrome and sat in the same spot every day, in front of the dispersal hut, as if waiting for his friends to return. This went on for a few years, and then one night he did not return. The next day the farmer found him curled up in his usual spot having died in his sleep.[40]

Escape Exercise

On Saturday 14 August, twenty pilots dressed in civilian clothing assembled outside one of the dispersal huts where they posed for photos before being taken in closed lorries to various points five miles from Warmwell for an evasion exercise. The objective was to return without being apprehended by the Home Guard, police, or RAF Regiment, who were also participating. Being resourceful chaps, they soon entered into the spirit of the exercise and employed various means to aid their return. F/O Mogg, P/O Blacklock, and Sgt Heaton took an empty taxi they found in Puddletown, abandoned it near the aerodrome and entered the camp through Knighton Wood; Sgts Dunlop, Todd, and Watkins disguised themselves as platelayers and walked along the nearby railway before entering the camp; F/S Simpson and Sgts Gray, Green, Proctor, and Wood also made successful returns. F/O's Hunter and Funnell reached Weymouth where F/O Hunter entered the Burndon Hotel and took a naval officer's uniform whilst its owner was otherwise engaged with his girlfriend. They drove back to Warmwell in the officer's car, and were saluted at the gate before driving through unchecked. Unfortunately, the Navy took a dim view of his actions and he was sent on a 'corrective course' to appease them!

P/O Tebbit turned up at the dispersal hut with Cpl Glycol, and then teamed up with his room-mate F/O Sturgeon. When the latter asked why he had brought the dog he smiled and said wait and see. After they were dropped off, Tebbit said to the dog, 'early lunch' and according to Doug Sturgeon, 'the dog took off across the fields with us in tow, heading for the aerodrome.' Near the aerodrome, in Morton, they came across the baker's van, which delivered into the camp each day. As the driver was not around they 'borrowed' it, drove up to the main gate, and were waved straight through without being checked.

The police quickly apprehended P/O Holman, whilst P/O Tuff and Sgt Purkis were caught trying to get through the barbed wire on the perimeter of the aerodrome. According to the diary 'it was too near teatime to select a safer entry.' F/S Smith was chased across several fields and a river before he was apprehended. Unfortunately as he had entered a little too far into the spirit of the exercise and hit a policeman during the chase, he was locked in a cell overnight, before being returned to Warmwell the following morning.[41]

S/L Baker destroyed an E-Boat off Jersey on the night of 14 August, and then found a Heinkel He.111 north of Guernsey. He closed slowly from below and fired a short burst from 200 yards dead astern, the bombers port engine caught fire and a second burst sent it crashing into the sea, prompting the ORB to describe his sortie as, 'Quite simply the most remarkable individual achievement up to the present time by any member of this squadron since the return from Norway in 1940.' Sgt Beaumont 'drew attention to himself' on 15 August when he flew an armed shipping reconnaissance to the Barfleur-

Escape Exercise, 14 August. *Back row*: P/O Don Tebbit, P/O Doug Sturgeon, Sgt Bill Heaton, F/O Douglas Mogg, P/O Norman Blacklock, F/S James Simpson, Sgt Fred Green, F/O Robert Tuff RAAF, Sgt Len Gray, Sgt George Wood, Sgt Iain Dunlop. *Front row*: Sgt Bill Watkins, Sgt Harold Proctor, F/S Graham Smith RAAF, F/O John Holman, Sgt John Purkis. (*Bill Watkins archives*)

Escape Exercise, 14 August. F/O Ken Funnell and F/O Bob Hunter. *DWK33* was Hunter's, *JT5927* was the Navy's. (*Bill Watkins archives*)

Escape Exercise, 14 August. Cpl Glycol, W/O Don Tebbit, and F/O Doug Sturgeon. (*Bill Watkins archives*)

Grandcamp-Cap de la Hague area. He initially mistook the Cherbourg forts for ships, but as he dived down to investigate, he found a 350 ton coaster towing four heavily laden barges just north of the harbour. He bombed the coaster from dead astern whilst under fire 'from every gun in the harbour' and reported that his hood was partially open during the attack and he could hear the flak exploding even above the noise of the engines and slipstream! The ORB noted, 'What makes this sortie all the more remarkable is that it was the first time that a Whirlwind had "bearded the Cherbourg flak at low level" it was also Sgt Beaumont's first offensive night patrol.' The diary added, 'Through force of circumstances he could not stay to see the results.' His next sortie was a shipping reconnaissance in *P6986* which ended in a spectacular landing, described as 'thrilling', when 'he was forced to blow the wheels and flaps down with the emergency air bottle due to a hydraulic failure. As he settled onto his approach his port engine cut out, and unable to maintain height he jettisoned his bombs 'safe' west of Knighton Wood before landing. 'Some time was spent searching for the bombs the next day. One section of the search party failed to locate them but did locate the New Inn! Len Gray also had problems. 'It was a dark night and I landed about six feet too high.'[42] The tail casting of *P7055* was fractured and she was out of commission for six weeks.

According to the ORB, 'Fourteen aircraft were a fine sight in formation with their lights burning in the still clear twilight before dawn on the way to Predannack for 10 Group Ramrod 74. The ground crews had worked all night: and the complete repainting at night of a Whirlwind is worth a special mention.' It was a pity therefore that the operation on 17

F/S Joe Hanmore, Armament Section, seen in front of his lorry 'Esther II', in Normandy, 1944. It was named after his wife. 'Esther I' was blown up just after landing in France. (*Joe Hanmore archives*)

Maintenance in a Knighton Wood dispersal pen RAF Warmwell. (*Bill Watkins archives*)

August involving five squadrons was abandoned off the French coast due to 10/10 cloud. They returned to Warmwell from Predannack individually, in thick cloud. Len Gray made the trip at low level. 'I suddenly saw lighter cloud ahead, pulled up and just missed the chalk cliffs.'[43]

The final operational sorties of August were shipping recces of the Cherbourg area by S/L Baker and F/L Ross. Baker was engaged by flak from a trawler a mile off Cherbourg, but to position for his attack he had to turn inside Cherbourg harbour where he was caught by searchlights and flak. Nonetheless he saw a large explosion on the stern of the ship and left her sinking, her guns silent. Ross found no trace of her an hour later on his reconnaissance.

Correct formation flying was of absolute importance in dive bombing whilst rapid and precise changes of formation were vital in low level bombing of ships. With this in mind, the squadron flew numerous practices during the month. On one, 'George Williams lost his scalp – his line on landing was "I had a hard time extracting the COs tail from my cannons."' On another, 'Sgt Williams tried to lead from out on the wing, much to the CO's displeasure.'

September 1943

During September, the squadron flew operations from Manston and Predannack, the most south-easterly and south-westerly aerodromes of England.

Operation Starkey

Fourteen Whirlibombers flew to Manston on 7 September to take part in Operation Starkey a large-scale mock invasion of the Pas de Calais. The objectives were to bring the Luftwaffe to battle, and to test the overall German reaction to what hopefully appeared to be a full-scale invasion. The squadron's contribution was three attacks against naval guns and heavy flak positions at Hardelot, in order to safeguard ships of the amphibious exercise, Exercise Menagerie, which were to make a feint at Boulogne on 9 September. To avoid confusion, identification markings were applied to all Allied aircraft, the nose of each Whirlwind was painted white whilst the underside of the wings outboard of the engines were painted black with two white bands. The ORB noted, 'This is the squadron's first detachment to 11 Group since the Knapsack Raid of 12 August 1941.' During the flight to Manston, S/L Baker lost his airspeed indicator but by formatting on Sgt Todd, he landed safely.

The first attack, on the eighth, was escorted by Typhoons. Halfway across the Channel, however, S/L Baker's port engine and F/L Ross' R/T failed, but as they pulled out of formation they were mistakenly followed by Sgts Beaumont, Purkis, and Todd. F/L McClure led the remaining aircraft, P/O Heaton, F/S Cooper and Sgts Proctor, Watkins, Wood, and Williams, onto the target, although the results of the attack were not observed. The second attack 'went well from start to finish.' Twelve aircraft bombed in dives from 14,000 feet to 3,500 feet, and all bombs were observed to burst within 150 yards of the target, whilst a third attack, on 9 September, was escorted by 609 Squadron's Typhoons, and the ORB noted that their pilots were 'somewhat shocked by the steepness of the Whirlibombers dive.' S/L Baker's bombs hung up, and F/L Ross had a constant speed unit fail, but the attack was deemed a success. On their return, the aircraft were re-fuelled and re-armed for an attack against St Omer aerodrome and actually taxied out to take off before the operation was cancelled.

The ORB noted, 'These three days at Manston under the auspices of "Operation Starkey" were greatly enjoyed by all who took part. Whatever the results, there should also be added on the credit side the roaring good spirits ("excellent morale" is the official phrase)

The nose of each Whirlwind was painted white whilst the underside of the wings outboard of the engines were painted black with two white bands. (*Bill Watkins archives*)

Operation Starkey. *Back row*: F/O Robert Tuff RAAF, P/O Paul Mercer, F/S Robert Beaumont, Sgt George Wood, Sgt John Purkis, F/L John McClure DFC RCAF, S/L Reg Baker DFC, F/L David Ross, Sgt Peter Cooper, F/L Andrew Wordsworth (IO). *Front row*: Sgt Denis Todd, P/O Norman Blacklock, Sgt Bill Watkins, Sgt George Williams, Sgt Tommy Handley. (*Bill Watkins archives*)

F/L John McClure RCAF DFC and S/L Reg Baker DFC. (*Bill Watkins archives*)

which were engendered in the pilots of this squadron by the privilege of playing a part in the drama of the preparation and execution of this operation. One gun was destroyed and another rendered unserviceable for eight hours.' On their return to Warmwell, S/L Baker capped a frustrating few days when his aircraft, *P7096*, hit a ridge, which ripped off the port oleo and wheel and damaged both wingtips. He accepted responsibility, saying that the 'Ridge was bad but not bad enough to have caused the accident by itself; it was partly due to a heavy landing.' The diary entry on the tenth noted, 'The afternoon was spent in removing the zebra stripes bestowed on us for yesterday's operation. The removal degenerated into a fair scale water fight and everyone got very wet.'

'Chatanooga Choo-Choo'

The next major operation involved fourteen Whirlwinds staging through Bolt Head on 17 September for 'Chatanooga Choo-Choo'. Devised by S/L Baker and 10 Group Intelligence, the intention was to sever the main Rennes-Brest railway line between Lamballe and Morlaix, and thereby 'bottle up' trains on the night and cause further rail movements to be diverted along a single track loop line that would be vulnerable to long-range Mosquitoes the following night. The pilots were briefed to cross the Channel at 2,500 feet, penetrate enemy territory at the point nearest to their target, and bomb their targets as an absolute priority. The ORB noted with satisfaction that, 'These orders were successfully carried out. Our aircraft met neither searchlights nor flak and all took off from Bolt Head under the direction of F/L Connolly (FCO Warmwell) and landed back at Exeter.' This was the largest night operation undertaken by the squadron, and apart from F/L McClure who returned early with engine trouble, all pilots hit their target. S/L Baker, P/O Blacklock and F/S Proctor bombed Ponthou viaduct; F/S Purkis and F/S Smith the line southwest of Morlaix; F/L Ross and F/S Beaumont saw their bombs explode in cuttings near Lamballe; P/O Simpson hit the line west of Plouaret; F/O Mercer the line east of Plouvara; and P/O Heaton the line in Bois de Manlany. An hour after the first eleven, F/O Holman and Sgt Watkins took off on Ranger sorties to attack trains held up by the initial attacks. They found targets near Plouaret, and the squadron heard later that as a result of P/O Simpson's attack, a locomotive and train ran into a hole in the embankment near Lamballe as did the one sent to rescue it. Bad weather the following night prevented the follow-up by Mosquitoes.

The diary also commented, 'The CO, who supports a nifty crop of whiskers Mk.I (upper lip for the use of), has ordered all the squadron to grow moustaches, causing considerable comment and rebellious remarks from young "shavers" whose face minus fungus is costing them a pint all round as a fine.' It also noted, of the numerous air sea firing exercises, 'So much lead was put into the sea that it is thought the National Salvage Commission will send a diver to collect the stray bullets. These will probably be made into frying pans.'

During the month, all the sergeant pilots received their 'crowns' and promotion to Flight Sergeant, whilst S/L Baker received a Bar to his DFC and P/O Simpson received the DFM for his work with the squadron. F/L Frederick Donald Snalam reported for flying duties as a supernumerary; F/O Leonard Arthur Unwin, P/O Alexander Barr, and W/O Alton James Ryan arrived from OTU, and F/S Richard John Hughes was posted, as was Engineering Officer F/O Oswald Ash, who was replaced by P/O Rheon Thomas Parry, who the diary likened to Oliver Cromwell.

Ramrod 85, an attack on Morlaix aerodrome took place on 23 September. F/L McClure led F/L Ross, P/O Heaton, F/Ss Dunlop, Gray, Green, Heaton, Proctor, and Wood from Bolt Head, escorted by 610 Squadron. They commenced their attack at 14,000 feet in heavy, accurate flak, but George Wood's aircraft (*P7113*) blew up just as he released his bombs, causing one of the Spitfire pilots to comment, 'It was just like a flower opening up.' Iain Dunlop remembered, 'It was my first operational sortie and I was George's No. 2. I followed him into the dive and one second he was there the next he just blew up and I remember thinking to myself, bloody hell, this is a dangerous job.'[44] S/L Baker wrote in his diary, 'One of my boys was killed on a job this morning; he blew up over the target. He would not have known what hit him – I suppose that is some consolation.' The ORB noted, 'A skilful and gallant pilot. Light-hearted in his manner and handsome, he was very like the popular notion of a fighter pilot. He was twenty-one.'

Bill Watkins remembered. 'Reggie Baker decided one day that we needed cheering up, so he ordered George to take his aircraft, *P7113*, and beat up the aerodrome. As this was against the rules, we went out to watch thinking that it was the CO, so imagine our surprise when Reggie himself came out to watch the display! After that, George was allowed to fly Reggie's aircraft whenever he wasn't there. It had his call sign 'Lochinvar' painted below the windscreen and it was this aircraft George was flying when he was shot down over Morlaix airfield.'[45] 'Tommy' Handley and George looked similar, and were often mistaken for each other. Tommy recalled, 'That night I walked into the mess and someone said to me "Good God, I thought you were dead."'[46] (*See Chapter 14*).

F/S Iain Dunlop: 'Bloody hell, this is a dangerous job.' (*Iain Dunlop archives*)

A Ramrod to Lannion aerodrome on 25 September was abandoned due to 10/10 cloud over the target, and the bombs were jettisoned just off the French coast on the way home. Seconds after F/S Green (*P7040*) released his, there was an explosion, and a spout of water hit his starboard engine, forcing him to shut it down. The bombs probably detonated a mine. At de-briefing he commented: 'Circled the target – No flak – No fighters – No secret weapons, not even bows and arrows!'

October 1943

During a shipping recce on the night of 9 October, P/O Heaton was shot up by a convoy off Cap de la Hague, and a shipping strike of seven aircraft was quickly organised. Despite a thick haze, which prevented him from seeing the vessels until he was 100 yards away, S/L Baker bombed one and saw two explosions. He then orbited the target but came under attack by flak from Alderney, Cap de la Hague and the ship, which he thought was a 2,500 ton Sperrbrecher and far too dangerous an opponent in the poor visibility. He therefore ordered the remaining pilots back to base, but due to thick fog over Warmwell they were diverted to Tangmere. During the return P/O Simpson (*P7047*) reported his starboard engine had failed and his port engine was overheating and losing power. He jettisoned his bombs over the sea and made a low approach but struck an anti-landing post one hundred yards from the runway and crashed. As a result of this accident, a chance light was placed at the end of the runway and all obstructions removed. P/O James Ian Simpson DFM was, next to S/L Baker, the squadron's most experienced pilot and the ORB noted, 'He was very well liked and is a loss both as a pilot and a friend.'

Sgt James Simpson DFM was lost on 9 October. (*Jane Renton archives*)

Operation Chuffa-Prang

Operation Chuffa-Prang, flown on 17 October 1943, was devised by S/L Baker to disorganise railway communications across the Cherbourg Peninsula, and was similar to Operation Chattanooga Choo Choo. Baker blew up an ammunition train south east of Valognes, the explosion of large yellow flames and vivid white and green flashes was visible to the others over twenty miles away. F/L Ross, F/S Cooper, and F/S Todd damaged the bridge over the River Vire near Isigny, whilst F/O Mercer damaged a locomotive on the bridge over the River Seulles near Bayeux. Unfortunately, F/S Dunlop was unable to find his target and F/S Williams was unable to start his engines. F/O Blacklock damaged two trains in Airel station and a small motor launch north of Ile Marcouf, whilst F/S Beaumont, F/S Green, F/O Holman, and P/O Proctor disintegrated rail tracks at various locations. The ORB noted of the night's activities, 'It is quite likely that the success of this operation was not confined to the damage listed above. During a Rhubarb twelve hours later by Typhoons, seven locomotives were found between Lestré and Sottevast – a concentration which may have been caused by this operation.'

The diary recorded the night's events somewhat differently:

> During the night operation Chuffa-Prang took place, and can be assumed a success. The CO blew up an ammunition train whilst Cooper, Ross and Todd bombed a rail bridge. Beaumont maintains he dropped his bombs on a ladies waiting room in a wayside station, and from what Proctor says, it is clear he bombed a laundry, although he will not admit it and maintains it was a factory. Purkis and Dunlop had less exciting trips. Purkis found no trains and aimed his bombs at the line. Dunlop had bad luck to find nothing and swears there are no railways on the Peninsula! If this were so, the rest of us must have been bombing Scotch mist, although Proctor's might have been steam from the laundry! In addition to his trains, Blacklock also had a crack at an unbelievably small sea borne craft for which no explanation can be found. It must have been either the lighthouse keeper going for his six monthly rest or a garbage launch. On the way back, Beaumont spent time vainly pursuing a star, thinking it was Purkis on fire! Is this what flak does for one?

Two Rhubarbs on 19 October resulted in two of the remaining Whirlwinds being damaged. P/O Proctor and F/S Dunlop attacked locomotives west of Ecausseville on the first, but as they banked away from the attack, Dunlop's starboard wing was hit by a 37-mm shell that jammed the ailerons and he crash-landed back at Warmwell where *P7055* was further damaged. P/O Blacklock and F/S Beaumont destroyed a locomotive near Neuilly, but on their return to Warmwell they encountered a 45 mph crosswind which caught Blacklock (*P7046*), causing him to overshoot and retract his undercarriage to avoid running over the perimeter and into a gravel pit. He was concussed in the ensuing accident. The ORB noted, 'Watching this landing was the shakiest thing the writer has ever seen.' The Board of Enquiry showed no sympathy however, and stated it was an error of judgment.

On 22 October a signal was received from HQ Fighter Command forbidding Whirlwinds from carrying bombs on Rhubarb operations. No explanation was given, but S/L Baker obtained permission for two final Rhubarbs. F/L Ross and F/O Holman returned due to bad weather from the first, but P/O Tebbit and F/S Gray attacked the rail bridge over the River Vire south of Isigny. They observed three bursts near the eastern end of the bridge and in the water underneath it. The fourth was not seen to explode, but dislodged a girder under the bridge.

John Purkis (the scribe) and Bob Beaumont (the artist), were the keepers of the unofficial diary and were busy during the month. Firstly they noted that, 'The quack suddenly gets the bright idea to inoculate a few people, so numbers in the flight gradually dwindle as one by one the pilots succumbed to the dreaded needle.' The order was in preparation for the forthcoming invasion of Europe. Next, 'The CO provided the squadron with a new mascot, an Irish Wolfhound known either as Tristan, Tiny, or Joe. He seems amiable, being the strong silent type who does not say much but thinks a lot. Chief custodian of the hound is "Uncle" Bill Holman.' Finally, 'The "Forestry Commission" worked hard stocking up for winter. Ably led by "Friar" Len Gray, his Merry Men sawed and sawed with a will, and many logs rent asunder.' They did not have it all their own way however, Len Gray recalled getting his own back, 'Bob Beaumont was dozing in an armchair with his feet up so to liven things up I slipped a Verey cartridge into the stove, and soon the inevitable happened, the cartridge exploded with a loud bang and red smoke quickly filled the room. Bob got such a start that he tipped over backwards and ended up on the floor. You can imagine what he said on collecting his scattered wits; he was not complimentary to Scots in general and me in particular. He did not survive the war, I heard he got married in 1944 but was killed not long after. He was a very talented artist and was allowed to decorate several Whirlwinds.'[47]

Some more of Bob Beaumont's nose art: 'Golden Lion', named after the Squadron's pub. (*Bill Watkins archives*)

F/S Robert Beaumont with 'Gremlin' nose art. A talented artist, he decorated the nose of several Whirlwinds. (*Bill Watkins archives*)

Unknown, F/S Denis Todd, F/O Gerry Racine RCAF, P/O Don Tebbit, Sgt Harold Proctor, Capt. Hargreaves (Army Liaison Officer), P/O Sandy Barr. (*Denis Todd archives*)

Personnel changes saw F/O John Thomas Lilleystone, F/O Gerry Geoffrey Racine, and P/O Dugald Andrew Carmichael report for flying duties, whilst P/O Robert Tuff was detached to 1 SLAIS at RAF Milfield and F/L John Edward McClure DFC was rested.

MV *Münsterland*

Intelligence sources suggested at the beginning of the month that the 6,400 ton *MV Münsterland*, a blockade runner carrying a cargo of rubber, wolframite, and nickel large enough to supply two divisions for two years, was about to attempt a run through the Channel. This resulted in numerous uneventful reconnaissances in the Les Sept Iles–Ile Bréhat–Ile de Batz area, from both Warmwell and Predannack looking for her.

A recce of the Cherbourg shipping lanes by six Whirlibombers on 24 October caused the ORB to note, 'The squadron conducted its own anti-flak [six Whirlwinds with bomb racks removed], as had often been suggested in the past. The *Münsterland* was not found between Casquetes and Barfleur, only a clinker-built sailing boat with a single mast off Querqueville. It is thought that this will be the last time in the history of the world in which twelve Whirlwinds were airborne together.' It is a pity therefore that it was uneventful, but as they returned, a PRU Spitfire found the *Münsterland* alongside the *Digue du Homet* in Cherbourg's inner harbour. She was to remain the squadron's prime target for several weeks, but Roadstead 79, on 24 October, was the first and most costly attack against her.

Roadstead 79 provided another first for the squadron – a low-level attack on Cherbourg harbour. S/L Baker, F/O Mercer, P/O Proctor, and F/S Williams (Red Section) led F/L Ross, F/S Beaumont, F/S Cooper, and F/S Gray (Blue Section) across the Channel at sea level protected by Spitfires and Typhoons. They flew between the outer moles at fifty feet and into the harbour where they found the *Münsterland* tied up at Digue du Homet; a small merchant vessel, an armed trawler and M-class minesweepers were also discovered. Baker, Beaumont, Mercer and Proctor bombed the *Münsterland* from mast height, and then strafed the minesweepers whilst Ross and Gray attacked the merchant vessel, and Cooper and Williams damaged the trawler. Typhoons of 257 Squadron saw fires on either side of *Münsterland*'s funnel, whilst those of 266 Squadron reported that the ship was 'well ablaze with smoke and flames visible for ten miles.' The ORB noted, 'It is difficult to give a picture of the flak without seeming to exaggerate. There were over a hundred guns on the shore and on the nine ships. Continuous gun flashes came from every part of the harbour and the air filled with tracer and black puffs.' Bob Beaumont commented, 'It was like a horizontal hail storm, with the hail stones painted red.' Although every Whirlibomber was hit by flak, they all flew out over the back of the harbour, but the starboard engine of F/S Gray's *P6979 HE-G* was smoking badly and he glided down from 150 feet about three miles southeast of Cherbourg where it was thought he made a forced landing. F/O Mercer announced that he had been hit by flak although he thought he could make it back to base, but whilst the rest of the formation dropped to zero feet to cross the coast near St Vaast, he remained at 200 feet and was again hit by flak. The aircraft, *P6986 HE-Q*, dived into the sea 200 yards off shore and disintegrated. Over the target, F/L Ross' aircraft, *P6974 HE-X*, was severely hit in the nose and starboard wing by explosive shells. He had difficulty keeping a straight course and the starboard wing stalled at 180 mph, forcing him to make a belly landing at Warmwell at that speed. Not surprisingly, the aircraft was

Flak damage to *P6974 HE-X*. F/L David Ross crash-landed her at 180 mph. (*Bill Watkins archives*)

F/L David Ross. (*Bill Watkins archives*)

Flak damage to Sgt Peter Cooper's *P6973. (Bill Watkins archives)*

Survivors of the 24 October *Münsterland* op: F/S Peter Cooper, F/S Robert Beaumont, S/L Reg Baker DFC, F/L David Ross, F/S Harold Proctor, and F/S George Williams. (*Bill Watkins archives*)

written off, and the Diary noted, 'The Flight Commander pranged most spectacularly, fortunately only in a Mk.I Chair of Ancient Vintage. No injuries resulted except to the onlookers who suffered considerable pain by laughter!' The starboard undercarriage of Cooper's *P6973* collapsed on landing and S/L Baker was bruised on the shoulder when his canopy was shattered by flak. The *Münsterland* was severely damaged and was moved to Dry Dock 5 for repairs.

F/O Paul Thomas Richard Mercer was described by the ORB as, 'a skilful and gallant pilot, and very well liked as a person.' He had married S/O Anderson just a week before being shot down. Leonard Scott Gray was on his thirteenth operational sortie and the ORB expressed the hope he had crash-landed safely, as indeed he had (*see Chapter 15*). Unfortunately this operation reduced the number of available Whirlwinds to fourteen, and the ORB noted, 'Thus the re-equipment of the squadron with some other type of aircraft, which has been expected consistently during the past two or perhaps three years – has become inevitable in the not too distant future. It is felt that the low-level attacks in Cherbourg's inner harbour by 263 and 183 Squadrons, deserve to be remembered among the many exploits of true gallantry in this bloody war.'

Although *Münsterland* was in dry dock, she was still a viable target, and Ramrod 96 on the 28 October 1943 brought another first for the squadron – the use of 500lb bombs in dive bombing. Escorted by a mixed force of Spitfires and Typhoons, S/L Baker, F/L Ross, F/O Mogg, and F/Ss Beaumont, Handley, Proctor, Purkis, and Watkins crossed the French coast at 13,000 feet and attacked in 70 degree dives. Although all bombs fell within 500 yards of the Basin Napoleon, starting fires amongst oil tanks, there were no hits on

P6997 HE-R is prepared for a sortie at Warmwell. Her pilot, F/O Douglas Sturgeon, is on the far right. Third from right is F/S Bill Watkins. (*Bill Watkins archives*)

the ship itself. The penultimate operation, Ramrod 99, was flown on 30 October by just seven aircraft, there being no more serviceable. Ten miles south of Lulworth, F/L Snalam lost a bomb and returned to base, but S/L Baker, F/O Holman, P/O Heaton, and F/Ss Dunlop, Green, and Proctor escorted by twelve Spitfire Vcs of 610 Squadron continued. S/L Baker started the dive too early, pulled back up to 12,000 feet, and then dived almost vertically, and a cluster of bombs hit warehouses and the dry dock area. The ORB noted that, 'they achieved quite good results, in the sense that it would have been lucky if the vessel had received a direct hit.' It also noted that, 'The Hun now has dive bombing weighed up. His heavy flak was intense and accurate at 12,000 feet and during the dive from 9,000 to 7,000 feet. S/L Baker therefore led on down to 5,000 feet. This and the early dive appear to have led to only one Whirlwind being slightly damaged by flak.' The final attack of the *Münsterland* campaign took place on the 5 November when S/L Baker, F/L Ross, F/O Holman, and F/Ss Beaumont, Watkins, Cooper, and Todd flew Ramrod 100 Part 3, but 10/10 cloud over the target thwarted them.

November 1943

November was a microcosm of the squadron's history during the previous fifteen months and proved to be a fitting climax for the Whirlibomber. Eighty-eight offensive sorties were flown, mostly low level shipping attacks by day and night. There were a number of shipping recces, uneventful except for the routine flak from the Channel Islands and Cap de la Hague. The function of the squadron at Warmwell was primarily that of a central Channel stop, to prevent the use of the coastal waters from Ile Bréhat to Isigny to the enemy. The presence at varying hours of light and darkness of armed Whirlibombers and the absence of enemy shipping in these waters is a testament to the squadron's success.

The squadron was informed that George Wood, believed killed on 23 September, arrived in Plymouth on 31 October, the squadron's first evader. Len Gray, who was missing on 24 October, was reported as a POW, whilst other personnel movements saw P/O Robert Bruce Tuff return from detachment at 1 SLAIS, and P/O Dugald Andrew Carmichael leave on posting.

The diary noted, 'New idea for night operations. On dark nights Ye Olde Albacore is to be sent out on their crawl around the shipping lanes carrying flares. On sighting a convoy (or probably the Casquetes) base is contacted and the ever-faithful "Joes" (us) are vectored onto the find. On approaching the target, the leading Whirlwind type howls "OK Joe drop your bloody candles!" (or something similar) and low and behold, (to coin a phrase), the stooging Albacore showers bags of light on the subject and consequently draws all the flak (good show) we then sink the Casquetes.' It also stated that F/S Beaumont drew attention to himself by flying a long shipping reconnaissance south of Ile D'Ouessant, 'He reckons he has some Bay of Biscay in his blood after his long patrol, and 'The "Order of the Irremovable Finger" was bestowed on him for his unerring faith in his ability to make landfall by smell and his utter scorn for ETA.'

Denis Todd recalled an incident which occurred on 18 November:

All of the pilots were summoned to S/L Baker's office, and when we were all assembled he locked

Above left: F/S Reg Harvey 'A' Flight Chiefy. (*Bill Watkins archives*)

Above right: F/O Robert Tuff RAAF returned from a detachment to 1 S.L.A.I.S. on 3 November. (*Bill Watkins archives*)

> the door, swore us all to secrecy, and solemnly informed us of his plan to sink the *Münsterland*. Dave Ross and Iain Dunlop were to fly over Cherbourg at 2,000 feet with their lights on as decoys, whilst he would sneak in at low level and bomb the vessel. Almost as an afterthought, he added that he did not expect to come back. Dave and Iain went rather pale, but never said a word. I was to fly a weather reconnaissance prior to the attack, and was to send the message, 'The oranges are sweet' if conditions were good, or 'The oranges are sour' if they were not. The weather over the target was actually clear blue sky, but my message was 'The oranges are sweet, but rapidly turning sour' and we heard nothing more of it – much to the relief of Dave and Iain! I did not tell anyone until some considerable time later when both Reg and Dave had left the squadron. They were both subsequently killed.[48]

On 19 November, the squadron lost the services of F/O John Holman. He had flown F/O Green, the Medical Officer, and Cpl Hamer, one of the ground crew, to Biggin Hill in the Oxford, but as they touched down the aircraft swung violently in a cross-wind and headed towards parked Typhoons. He attempted to take off again but clipped the prop of a Typhoon which tore off the Oxford's port flap and, although he kept her airborne, he was unable to climb and they crashed into the motor transport store. The three were pulled from the wreckage badly injured.

The Ibsley Wing escorted S/L Baker, F/L Ross, F/O Tuff, F/O Mogg, F/O Unwin, P/O Tebbit, F/S Dunlop, and F/S Williams on three dive bombing sorties over the 25 and 26

Above left: F/S Denis Todd, 'The oranges are sweet but rapidly turning sour'. (*Denis Todd archives*)

Above right: F/O Norman Blacklock flew the last ever Whirlwind sortie. (*John Purkis collection*)

November. Ramrods 106 and 108 were on Cherbourg Docks, nicknamed the 'Haven of Peace' by the diary, and every aircraft suffered flak damage. Ramrod 109 attacked a target southwest of Cherbourg at Martinvast which was protected by eight heavy flak positions, and again all eight Whirlibombers involved were damaged. No hint was given as to the target in the ORB, but it was a V-weapons site.

'Operation Hanwich', on the twenty-ninth, was planned to intercept minesweepers or mine destroying Ju.52s thought to be operating off Cherbourg. Unfortunately, S/L Baker, F/O Mogg, F/L Snalam, and F/O Blacklock found only violent rainstorms and 10/10 cloud, and when Norman Blacklock and *P7102* touched down at Warmwell on their return, they brought to an end not only the final operational sorties of the month, but also the operational career of the Westland Whirlwind. The squadron was to re-equip with Typhoons.

December 1943

> Our new Typhoons have arrived, with their shiny new paint and fittings they rather make the ole faithful Whirlies look a trifle shabby. The latter have given stout service and the squadron have been very proud to fly them.

So read the diary entry for 1 December. Two days later, it noted:

> Truly an amazing day, the whole squadron looking forward to a huge dinner and piss up given by the Directors of Westland's. With the boys all on 'twitch' we get the gratifying news of the CO's promotion to Wing Commander, and his posting (this not so good). This gives the weak willed 'smooth' types grounds for a luncheon piss up. However, the sergeants being 'rougher' have a dinner booze (same meal).

Westland gave a party to all members of the squadron and a number of faithful adherents of 3055 Echelon. The party consisted of an excellent dinner at the Manor Hotel, Yeovil, followed by a dance in the Assembly Rooms. This marked the end of the squadron's official relations with Westland, a liaison which has constantly been maintained with good will and personal friendship. In one of the speeches at the dinner, S/L Baker paid tribute to the Whirlwind, drawing on the material found in the ORB: 'The writer would like here to state plainly that all the pilots who flew Whirlwinds in operations against the enemy had absolute confidence in and affection for their aircraft. It is worth noting that all of the Whirlwinds built were known to the squadron and the echelon by their individual numbers, and the particular idiosyncrasies and excellences of each were noted and respected.'[49] The diary commented, 'It is incredible that so many blacks could be put up by so few to so many.' It continued on the following morning:

> 'Awake for morn into the bowl of night; has flung the stone that put the stars to flight' or at least that's how the poet put it, but on this particular morn it would take the odd boulder or two to make the stars fly for the 'black putters up' of last night's piss up. Greenish googly faces peering into the CO's Office were cheerfully informed of a Squadron Balbo over Westlands. Three lines of (incredibly crooked) Whirlwinds staggered over Yeovil. If the worthy workers were not impressed, the staff of the Watch Office had their full quota of entertainment by a talk over the R/T from S/L Baker entitled 'Words not in the English Dictionary,' or 'Pull your fingers out you bastards.' Operations at night were confined to trips to the Officers Mess where stories of very ancient vintage were told over a gill or two.

When the squadron moved from Warmwell to Ibsley on 5 December, it did so with just four serviceable Whirlwinds. Led by F/L Ross, the four did a final fly past over Warmwell then headed for their new base just a few miles away where they landed in quick succession just fifty yards apart. They were met by their new commanding officer – none other than Geoff Warnes. RAF Ibsley was described as grim and the ORB noted, 'Living conditions for both officers and sergeants were very much less comfortable than at Warmwell, but liberty runs to Bournemouth and the St Leonards Hotel compensated for the poor state of the messes.'

W/C Ernest Reginald Baker DFC*, who had been with the squadron for six months, was flown to Aston Down by F/O Unwin in the Oxford for a Fighter Leaders Course, unfortunately on his return F/O Unwin lost his way near Poole in haze and poor light and force landed in gathering darkness near North Maltravers.

Eventually six Whirlwinds were available to maintain night readiness during the moon period but no operations were ordered and, as of the 19 December, the squadron became

263 Squadron. *Back row*: LAC Munday, LAC Skinner, AC Oxford, LAC Priest, Sgt Johnston, Cpl Bradford, Unknown, LAC May, AC Armour, LAC Longshaw, LAC Japp, AC Anderson, LAC Marshall, Unknown, Unknown, LAC Sullivan, LAC Day, LAC Whitcome, Unknown, Cpl Lawrence, LAC Bennett. *Third row*: Sgt Kelly, F/S Handle, Unknown, LAC Stephens, Unknown, Cpl Hurn, Sgt Coope, LAC Davies, LAC Jones, LAC Duffin, Cpl Frobisher, LAC Robinson, LAC Derrick, LAC Lewas, Cpl Hatfield, LAC Johnson, LAC Oliver, LAC Greenhough, Cpl Burgess, Cpl Butler, Cpl Whitemoss, Cpl Nash, Sgt Rogers. *Seated*: F/S Williams, F/O Robert Hunter, F/S Bill Watkins, F/O Robert Tuff RAAF, F/L Wannop, P/O Andrew Wordsworth (IO), F/L Frederick Snalam, F/L David Ross, S/L Reg Baker DFC*, F/L Eugene Owens (Adjutant), P/O Don Tebbit, P/O Norman Blacklock, Capt Hargreaves (Army Liaison Officer), F/O Douglas Mogg, F/O Len Unwin RCAF, F/S Fred Green, F/S Reg Harvey (A Flt Chiefy). *Front row*: F/S George Williams, F/S Alton Ryan RCAF, F/S Graham Smith RAAF, F/S Tommy Handley, F/S Denis Todd, F/S Harold Proctor, F/S Robert Beaumont, F/S Peter Cooper, P/O Alexander Barr RCAF, F/O Gerry Racine RCAF, Sgt Hall, F/S Joe Hanmore (Armourer). (*Joe Hanmore archives*)

F/S John Shellard. (*John Shellard archives*)

non-operational when the surviving aircraft were put up for disposal. Over the following two months they were flown to 18 MU at Dumfries for storage. All were eventually reduced to produce in July 1944 by Airwork.

In 1940, a sixteen-year-old John Shellard had been on a LDV exercise when they were 'buzzed' by several 263 Squadron Whirlwinds. Three years later he joined the very same squadron as it began working up on Typhoons.

> Geoff Warnes sent me on leave as he was too busy to see me. Later, when we moved to Beaulieu, there was a solitary Whirlwind. I asked if I could fly it. Geoff Warnes snapped 'NO' at me and walked away. Later someone told me that he had accused them of 'putting me up to it' as they knew how touchy he was about losing his Whirlwinds. The whole squadron was disappointed at losing their beloved aircraft, and morale took a dip due to the poor reputation of the Typhoon, which was proved correct when we lost three pilots in February 1944 due to fuel feed problems.[50]

The final word must go to George Wood. He returned to the squadron as it converted to Typhoons, and was asked to fly the last remaining Whirlwind to Westland:

> All I can say about *P7092* is that a W/O engineer will be turning in his grave, for he spent five days trying to discover why the port engine belched blue smoke which I discovered soon after take-off. Eventually he found the problem, a small speck of carbon in the carburettor. He did explain in detail, but it was all Greek to me. He then pleaded with me not to beat up the airfield or do a slow roll, etc. Just to 'Get the bloody aircraft safely to Yeovil.' When I got there, I couldn't enter the circuit, as the Fleet Air Arm were doing circuits and bumps at half my speed, and no one had alerted them I was on my way. Eventually, after buzzing the control tower, they pulled their fingers out and gave me clearance to land by calling off the circuits and bumps. I landed it all in one piece, much to my relief (remember I had not flown for over three months, so was a bit rusty) and the patient, painstaking work of the W/O was rewarded.

And so the Whirlwind, Britain's first cannon-armed single seat fighter, passed into history. No. 263 Squadron continued its tradition, serving with distinction in 2 Tactical Air Force with the Typhoon until the end of the war in Europe.

3
No. 137 Squadron: Do Right, Fear Nought

No. 137 Squadron was formed on 1 April 1918 at RAF Shawbury, on de Havilland DH.9s, but the cessation of hostilities prevented a planned move to France and it was disbanded on 4 July 1919.

September 1941

The opening lines of the 137 ORB noted:

> This new squadron was ordered to be formed at Colerne on 20 September 1941 under Fighter Command Signal Q109 of 12 September 1941 to be equipped with Whirlwind Mk.I aircraft. S/L John Sample DFC was posted to command on the date of formation. The site of formation was however subsequently changed from Colerne to the satellite aerodrome of Charmy Down, as the squadron was to replace 125 Squadron, and in short time the personnel began to arrive. F/L Joseph Grantley Hughes, F/L Colin Anthony Gordon Clark and Sgt Douglas St John Jowitt were posted in from 263 Squadron with effect from 22 September 1941 and orders were sent out to various Maintenance Units for the delivery of eighteen operationally equipped aircraft, and this number was held on charge by the squadron as at 30 September 1941.

October 1941

When F/L Philip Hogan arrived as Adjutant, P/O Leslie William Barnett as Intelligence Officer, P/O Dennis Lionel Patrick Moore as Engineering Officer, and P/O Richard Barnett Clayton as Medical Officer the squadron was well on the way to full status, which was finally achieved with the arrival of eighteen pilots: F/O Alexander Torrance, P/Os John Michael Bryan, Norman Vincent Crabtree, Vivian Lester Currie, John Clifford Lawton, and George William Martin, F/Ss Joseph Laurier De Houx, RCAF and Charles Eldred Mercer RCAF, and Sgts John Robert Brennan RCAF, Ralph Otto Gustaf Häggberg, John Frederick Luing, Jack Maddocks, John Edward McClure RCAF, Maurice John Peskett, Hugh Leo O'Neill, James Rebbetoy RCAF, Basil Lionel Robertson, and John Anthony William Sandy. Most did not have far to travel, just moving across the airfield from 263 Squadron.

Intensive training occupied the first three weeks of October, with aircraft being flown to Sand Bay for air firing tests, and Filton for maintenance and inspections, and the

S/L John Sample DFC (*seated centre*), seen here the day after shooting down a Do.17Z-2 with 504 Squadron. (*Alan White archives*)

Above left: F/L Joseph Grantley Hughes. (*Cliff Rudland archives*)

Above right: F/L Richard Clayton. (*Alec Torrance archives*) honour of damaging the first aircraft went to Sgt Peskett, who had an engine failure in *P7063* due to a petrol leak but unfortunately stalled to high on landing and crashed. Despite the setbacks, one Flight declared operational with eight pilots and twelve aircraft on 20 October and the first operational sorties were flown on Friday 24 when S/L Sample, in *P7053*, F/O Clark, in *P7050*, and Sgt Häggberg, *P7094*, as reserve, flew to Predannack. Once refuelled, Sample and Clark took off on a Mandolin to railway sidings at Landernau near Brest, where trains of fuel tankers had been reported. They found the target area, but the tankers were not there so S/L Sample attacked and damaged several coal trucks and F/O Clark attacked a large locomotive, leaving it enveloped in steam. Two days later, F/L Hughes and Sgt Robertson flew a similar operation to the Landivisiau goods yards where they damaged a train, but F/L Hughes (*P7096*) burst his tail wheel on landing back at Predannack, and Sgt Peskett, who was acting as reserve, later flew it back to Charmy following repairs.

During the morning of 28 October, Sgt Brennan was carrying out practice single engine landings in *P7057* when one engine failed on approach to Colerne and he was forced to land with the undercarriage retracted; then in the afternoon, S/L Sample led Sgt Luing and Sgt Peskett on a training exercise just south of Bath. They carried out several formation manoeuvres before Luing broke away to carry out astern attacks. He closed to seventy yards on the first run before breaking away to make a second. Exactly what happened next is not certain, but as he turned in to make his second attack he saw one of the other aircraft falling away out of control. What is known is that the aircraft had suffered serious damage to the fin and wing and spun down out of control, losing the tail unit as it did so. Eyewitnesses stated that the pilot took a long time to evacuate the aircraft, and only did so when he was too low for his parachute to fully deploy. S/L Sample's aircraft struck Sgt Peskett's from below suggesting he may have throttled back and inadvertently drifted upwards as he searched behind for Sgt Luing. *P7053* crashed onto a cowshed on Manor Farm, English Coombe, and caught fire whilst Sgt Peskett managed to return to base. The damage to both sets of undercarriage doors and the central bulge of the Fowler flap, suggested his starboard propeller had hit the tail of his leader's aircraft as the two collided. *P7058* was flown, with her undercarriage down, to Filton for repair, whilst Sgt Maurice Peskett was posted. He had had a traumatic month: the accident on the third in *P7063* was deemed to be an error of judgement on his part – he had just eighteen hours on the Whirlwind – and following the death of S/L Sample was posted away before he lost all confidence. John Sample DFC was laid to rest in his family plot at Bothal (St Andrews) Churchyard, Northumberland, on 3 November. The service was conducted by the Bishop of Lindisfarne.

The squadron was still absorbing the loss of S/L Sample when F/O Clark (*P7091*) and Sgt Jowitt flew a 'Mandolin' to the Landernau railway yards. They attacked several goods trains, destroying at least one, and as they left the target area there were several columns of black smoke rising into the sky. Shortly after re-crossing the French coast, Sgt Jowitt overtook F/O Clark, who was flying on one engine – the other had been hit by flak – and called him up on the R/T but was unable to understand the reply, so he climbed to 1,500 feet and weaved around him until his petrol ran short and he was forced to head for Predannack. As he neared the coast, however, he heard Clark transmit a 'Maidez' and inform the controller that he would have to bail out. Sgt Robertson took off from

F/O Colin Clark was lost on the Squadron's first Operation on 30 October. (*Author*)

Predannack to escort an air sea rescue Lysander to search for F/O Clark and dropped a dinghy close to him, but he made no attempt to get into it. He was picked up by a Destroyer some twenty-six miles south of Lizard Point, but unfortunately died a short time later and his body was taken to the Royal Naval Hospital at Stonehouse in Plymouth. Colin Anthony Gordon Clark had been a journalist in South Africa before the war and served with the Fighter interception Unit during the Battle of Britain before being posted to the squadron.

November 1941–January 1942

Following the loss of S/L Sample and F/O Clark, the squadron was made non-operational at the beginning of November and an Oxford trainer was delivered to give the pilots more twin-engine experience. S/L Humphrey St John Coghlan DFC was also posted in from 263 Squadron as CO and moved the squadron to Coltishall. The ORB noted, 'Maintenance conditions at Coltishall are excellent, and with the arrival of spares, the squadron found itself in a satisfactory position, and assumed its operational responsibilities on 9 November 1941.' The weather during November prevented much flying, but convoy and Yarmouth patrols, which continued over the following six months, were carried out and although these patrols were interspersed with scrambles, by and large there was little to report.

During the period the squadron was still in a state of flux. Flight Commander F/L Joseph Grantley Hughes was posted to Central Flying School and replaced by F/O Robert Sinkler Woodward DFC; F/S Anthony Victor Albertini was transferred in from 263, but on paper only as he had been admitted to Bath Military Hospital on 6 November with a

Ye Olde Oxford. (*Terry Smith archives*)

S/L Humphrey St John Coghlan DFC. (*Mike Coghlan archives*)

shotgun wound following an accident on the clay pigeon range. He subsequently lost the sight in the eye and was posted to ground duties in early December when the squadron re-located, yet again, to RAF Matlaske.

On 10 December, 137 encountered its first enemy aircraft in the air when Sgt Maddocks intercepted a Ju.88. However, it escaped in cloud before he could open fire. Twenty-two uneventful scrambles and 105 routine Yarmouth patrols were flown as was one unusual task which saw P/O Martin, F/S Robertson, Sgt Brennan and Sgt McClure guide two tugs to a sinking steamer in the North Sea. It was towed back to port under the 'watchful eye of the Whirlwinds'. The only other incident of note saw the starboard engine of *P7094* cut out as Sgt O'Neill approached Matlaske on return from a convoy patrol. He crashed half a mile from the runway, but whilst the aircraft was badly damaged he received only scratches.

At the beginning of January, F/S Robertson and Sgt Sandy intercepted a Ju.88 east of Cromer, but it disappeared in cloud before they could close. The squadron then devised a plan to intercept these Ju.88s as they approached the English coast – two aircraft patrolled low, three miles off the coast, and two more twenty miles out to sea at 10,000 feet. Unfortunately, although this was attempted on several occasions, it did not result in an interception. Frequent heavy snowfalls and cold weather had a serious effect on flying during the month, and probably caused two serious accidents. The first involved P/O

Above left: F/O Robert Woodward DFC arrived as 'B' Flight Commander on 7 November. (*John LaGette archives*)

Above right: F/S Antony Albertini was posted in from 263 Squadron. (*Albertini Family archives*)

P/O Paul LaGette and *P7092* seen on 11 January. (*John LaGette archives*)

P/O Les Barnett (Intelligence Officer), F/O Frederick Furber, F/S Art Brunet RCAF, F/O Eddie Musgrave RAAF, P/O John Lawton, and Sgt Des Roberts RNZAF. (*Mike Coghlan archives*)

LaGette, who had just become airborne on a training sortie, when his aircraft, *P7092*, dropped a wing, struck the ground and crashed. P/O LaGette walked away uninjured, and although the cause of the accident could not be determined, it was probably due to icing. The second accident was more serious. Sgt Jack Maddocks (*P7062*) overshot his landing in poor visibility returning from a Yarmouth patrol and crashed. He sustained serious injuries which kept him in hospital for several months, and he did not return to the squadron.

F/L Guy Marsland, P/O Charles Wilbert DeShane RCAF, P/O Edward Lancelot Musgrave RAAF, P/O Dattatraya Anant Samant, P/O John Edward van Schaick, W/O Donald Burton McPhail RCAF, F/S Robert Elmer Douglas Wright, Sgt Joel Hilton Ashton RCAF, Sgt Arthur Gaston Brunet RCAF, and Sgt Francis Gordon Waldron reported for flying duties whilst P/O Geoffrey Wallis arrived as Engineering Officer. S/L Coghlan also flew a series of tests on 29 January that would shape the squadron's future role when he test fired the cannon at night and reported that, 'There was no blinding flash and he considered the Whirlwind was suitable for night flying and firing.'

February 1942

February was the blackest month in the squadron's history: four pilots were lost on operations, and the Peregrine engines developed problems with the three-way oil union, which grounded all aircraft for several days, although Rolls-Royce rapidly delivered new, strengthened unions, and all aircraft were quickly serviceable again.

Personnel movements saw F/L Robert Sinkler Woodward DFC promoted to Squadron Leader and posted to command 263 Squadron. He was replaced by another Battle of Britain veteran, F/L Leonard Harold Bartlett, whilst F/L Guy Marsland was posted to the Far East. Frequent and heavy sleet and snow showers prevented all but operational

RAF Manston, February 1942: P/O Dattatraya 'Sammy' Samant, F/O Richard 'Doc' Clayton, F/S Arthur 'Art' Brunet RCAF, F/S John 'Mac' McClure RCAF, P/O Charles 'Pat' DeShane RCAF, P/O George 'Gus' Martin, P/O Robert 'Bob' Wright RCAF, P/O Douglas 'Gorgeous' Jowitt, P/O Paul 'Jeep' LaGette RCAF, S/L Humphrey 'Humpers' Coghlan DFC, F/L Robert 'Woodie' Woodward DFC, P/O John 'Gladys' Lawton, P/O Ralph 'Haggie' Häggberg, W/O Charles 'Merce' Mercer RCAF, Sgt Francis 'Jack' Waldron, P/O John 'Sandy' Sandy, P/O Geoffrey 'Why' Wallis, Sgt Joel 'Hilt' Ashton RCAF, P/O Edward 'Ed' Musgrave RAAF, P/O Alex 'Scottie' Torrance, and W/O Basil 'Robbie' Robertson. (*Alex Torrance archives*)

flying and on several occasions the pilots helped the ground crews clear a runway before any flying could take place. The cold weather may have been a contributory factor when the port engine of *P7097* failed on take-off. The aircraft stalled and crashed in a field two miles east of Coltishall but F/S Rebbetoy walked away from the wreckage unhurt. The lack of flying, however, gave the pilots the opportunity to inspect a captured He.111 and Ju.88 up close.

P/O Martin and F/S McClure were on patrol off Yarmouth on 1 February when they were vectored on to a 'black painted Dornier', but although Martin fired eighty-five rounds at it and reported damage, it escaped in cloud. F/L Woodward and F/S Robertson had a similar experience on 5 February whilst escorting convoy 'Casing' off Mablethorpe. They saw the splashes from bombs exploding in the sea before Robertson spotted a Dornier Do.217 above them. He pulled up steeply and fired a four second burst, before it disappeared in snow clouds. He followed for five minutes before it emerged and turned towards him, and thinking that that the bomber pilot had realised that he was out of ammunition and was going to attack, he took evasive action, and lost contact. He saw no damage, so made no claim.

Operation Fuller

Thursday 12 February began routinely enough, but turned out to be the worst day in the squadron's history. P/O Häggberg, P/O DeHoux, W/O Robertson and F/S Mercer, all of Yellow Section, were recalled from training flights and quickly briefed to provide escort to five ships of the 16 and 21 Destroyer Flotillas in the Channel. Incredibly, they were not informed of the reason – the presence of the German battle cruisers *Scharnhorst* and *Gneisenau*, along with the *Prinz Eugen*, and their escorts, who had broken out of Brest the previous night. Consequently, when they caught sight of several naval vessels through a hole in the clouds some twenty miles off the Belgian coast they assumed them to be friendly. P/O Ralph Otto Gustaf Häggberg, in *P7093 SF-A*, led the four down to investigate, but at 1,000 feet and 3,000 yards from the ships they were attacked by twenty yellow nosed Me.109s of III/JG.2 and a wild dogfight ensued. P/O Häggberg was not seen again. W/O Robertson was attacked by a Me.109F; F/S Mercer – his wingman – pulled in behind it and later reported that although he had the 109F in his sights his cannon would not fire. He himself was then attacked from astern by a 109, presumably the wingman of the first, but P/O DeHoux attacked this although again without result. At 1,500 yards from the ships, the flak batteries opened fired and to avoid them F/S Mercer turned to starboard as W/O Robertson turned to port. Mercer then saw a 109 going down in a steep dive at 1,000 feet, with heavy black smoke coming from it but whether it had been hit by one of his colleagues or by flak he could not tell. He was then attacked by two enemy aircraft and lost sight of W/O Basil Lionel Robertson, *P7107*, as he avoided orange, red and pale blue tracer fire. When they broke off the engagement he dived to sea level, turned towards home and landed at Ipswich where he was able to inspect the damage to *P7055* – the port tyre had been punctured, there were bullet holes in the port nacelle, through a propeller blade, the starboard fuel tank and the wings. P/O DeHoux, *P7012*, turned in behind a 109 that was attacking F/S Mercer and opened fire from 350 yards with three bursts, but observed no results. During this combat he saw a Whirlwind in a slight dive trailing white smoke with a Me.109 behind it, but did not have time to see who it was.

Having expended all his ammunition he dived to sea level and returned to base. He later remarked that he was not chased and that the enemy aircraft did not appear to want to leave the vicinity of the convoy. P/O George William Martin, *P7106 SF-D*, and P/O John Anthony William Sandy, *P7050*, were shot down by Me.109s. They took off, with P/O LaGette to attack the screen of E-Boats, but whilst he returned to base with engine trouble the others appear to have attacked the *Gneisenau*. Only P/O Bryan and Sgt Ashton, who escorted several Royal Navy destroyers, failed to contact the enemy.

German claims exactly match the number of aircraft lost. Oberleutnant Egon Mayer, Unteroffizer Willi Reuschling, Feldwebel Hans Stolz, and Hauptman Hans 'Assi' Hahn claimed one Whirlwind each. *Scharnhorst* was damaged by an air dropped mine later in the day, but both ships reached Kiel where *Gneisenau* took a direct hit during a bombing raid and never sailed again. *Scharnhorst* was sunk off North Cape by the Navy on 26 December 1943.

Above left: P/O Ralph Häggberg was lost on 12 February. (*John LaGette archives*)

Above right: W/O Basil Robertson was lost on 12 February. (*Author*)

Above left: P/O George Martin was lost on 12 February. (*Author*)

Above right: P/O John Sandy was lost on 12 February. (*John LaGette archives*)

F/S Charles Mercer flew *P7055* during the Channel Dash Op. (*Chris Thomas archive*)

17 February 1942. *Front row*: Groundcrew, F/S James Rebbetoy RCAF, Groundcrew, Cpl Phil Robson, Groundcrew, Groundcrew, Groundcrew, Groundcrew. *Standing*: F/S John Barclay, F/S Hugh O'Neill, F/S Tom Sutherland, Groundcrew, Groundcrew, Groundcrew, P/O Les Barnett (Intelligence Officer), F/L Len Bartlett, S/L Humphrey St John Coghlan DFC, F/L Guy Marsland, F/O John Bryan, F/O Eddie Musgrave, P/O Dattatraya Samant (on Whirlwind), Groundcrew. (*Mike Coghlan archives*)

March–April 1942

Both flights were detached to RAF Snailwell for Army Co-operation Exercises – 'A' Flight in March, 'B' Flight in April – to practise formation flying, map reading, air-to-air camera gun, low-level attacks on Army transport, Tac-R, and ground attack. F/L Bartlett also took several Army types up in a Master from the Target Towing Flight to give them an idea of how objects appeared from the air. The squadron's operational commitment was undertaken by the flight at Matlaske, but only one uneventful scramble and one air sea rescue patrol were called for.

Despite the lack of flying the squadron did sustain a fatality. On 9 March, P/O Charles Wilbert DeShane RCAF was detailed to carry out an air to ground camera gun exercise in *P7036 SF-X*. He was seen by eyewitnesses to engage in a low-level dogfight with Spitfires, but following an extremely tight turn the aircraft went into a spin at 3,000 feet and crashed on Whitehorse Common, North Walsham.

Six pilots reported for flying duties, adding to the multi-national composition of the squadron. F/O Donald Bruce Ogilvie and W/O Robert Leslie Smith DFM were English; P/O Frederick Michael Furber was Rhodesian; 2nd Lt Neville Austin Freeman was South African; Sgt Desmond Arthur Roberts RNZAF was a Kiwi, and Sgt John Harvey Curry RCAF was American, although he was posted out within a few weeks. Also leaving was P/O John Clifford Lawton.

P6982 SF-P. (Chris Thomas archives)

Sgt Charles DeShane RCAF, F/S James Rebbetoy RCAF, Sgt Joseph DeHoux RCAF, P/O John Lawton, Sgt Charles Mercer RCAF, Sgt Hilt Ashton RCAF, and F/S Art Brunet RCAF. (*Alex Torrance archives*)

F/O Donald Ogilvie, F/S Don McPhail RCAF, and P/O Douglas St J. Jowitt. (*Andrew Ogilvie archives*)

P/O Frederick Furber reported for flying duties on 3 March. (*Alex Torrance archives*)

Sgt Des Roberts RNZAF 'knocking them back'. (*Terry Smith archives*)

Sgt John Curry RCAF and *P6983. (Alex Torrance archives)*

There were three accidents at Snailwell in early April. The first saw Sgt Roberts break the tail wheel of *P7048* when he taxied over an unfinished drain; P/O Bryan returned from an Army co-op exercise with several hundred feet of high tension cable wrapped around the fin of *P7122*, and was admonished for descending below 200 feet – and the third involved P/O Furber, who was forced to crash-land *P7005* when an internal glycol leak caused the starboard engine to catch fire.

May 1942

On Monday 4 May, P/O Wright took off to carry out dog-fighting practice with a colleague who was forced to return with engine trouble. Ten minutes after take-off, *P7103 SF-O* suffered catastrophic structural failure whilst recovering from a dive and plunged into grassland about one mile north of Aylesbury in Norfolk, giving him no chance to escape. The wreckage was spread over the ground for a distance of about 312 yards. The main parts of the aircraft, which were found separately, comprised the tail unit with part of the fuselage and pilot's cockpit, centre section, flaps, and the two main planes. There was no fire either in the air or after the crash.

The wreckage was taken to RAE Farnborough and the official report stated that the aircraft had separated along a riveted joint line between the main plane and fuselage just behind the cockpit. The most likely sequence of events was that as P/O Wright pulled back on the stick to recover from the dive, the heavy tail-down loading caused the cockpit joint to fail. The wings and heavy engines were rapidly twisted to a negative incidence; the fuselage forced the flaps down as it twisted upwards which caused the wings to fail under the sudden downward pressure. The separate parts then fell to earth.

P/O Robert Wright RCAF and *P7119 SF-S*. (*Alex Torrance archives*)

Calculations indicated that there was insufficient reserve strength in the riveted joint, but the accident was assumed to be an isolated incident so no special modifications were thought necessary, although both squadrons were advised to closely inspect the joint on all aircraft. However, there were similarities to the crash of *P7008*, which killed P/O Milligan, of 263 Squadron, on 30 April 1941. Most aircraft that crash-landed also broke along the same joint line. The ORB noted of P/O Robert Elmer Douglas Wright, 'His quiet, unassuming manner made him popular with everyone'. He was laid to rest in Scottow Cemetery, near RAF Coltishall, on 7 May 1942.

There were several encounters with the enemy during the month, but only two resulted in interceptions; the other three saw the enemy aircraft disappear into cloud before the Whirlwinds could close. The first contact came on 15 May when F/S Brennan and F/S Brunet left Matlaske to patrol a convoy off Lowestoft. Whilst flying at 300 feet, three miles east of the convoy, they saw an unidentified aircraft flying south-east three miles away, which turned away and increased its speed as they headed towards it. When they were about a mile away from the 'bogey' it started a steep climbing turn for dense cloud at which point it was identified it as a Ju.88. F/S Brennan (*P7111*) fired five bursts from 800 yards closing to 600, observed a large red flash above the upper gun turret and several pieces fly off, but his aircraft was then hit by return fire and one engine put out of action. F/S Brunet only managed one burst and didn't see any strikes but the Ju.88 was claimed as damaged.

The final interception of the month was confused and ended in tragedy. F/S Brennan and P/O LaGette were on an Outer Channel patrol on 27 May when they sighted an enemy aircraft two miles away at 800 feet, and as they turned towards it, F/S Brennan identified it as a Ju.88. P/O LaGette made a beam attack from 600 yards, then F/S Brennan opened fire from 200 yards and the machine fell into the sea twenty miles off Cromer. F/S Brennan, whose R/T was weak, then told P/O LaGette to return to base (to the west), but he himself turned east and when informed of this he replied, 'everything under control' so P/O LaGette returned to base. Nothing further was heard from F/S John Robert Brennan RCAF. The squadron sent aircraft out to search for him, but without success, and it later emerged that a Coastal Command Blenheim was last plotted at the same time at the scene of the combat. It was presumed at the time that the Ju.88 shot down the Blenheim before being dealt with by the Whirlwinds, but post-war research shows that it was more likely that they shot down Blenheim *V5568* of 1401 Meteorological Flight, Bircham Newton, and that F/S Brennan realised his mistake, broke away and headed for the Dutch coast where he attacked the steel factories at Ijmuiden before being shot down by flak near Velsen in *P7122*.

Three accidents occurred at the end of the month: the tail wheel of *P7046* collapsed as P/O Bryan touched down, then as P/O Jowitt arrived over the aerodrome at 800 feet after an early morning patrol, his port engine caught fire and his Whirlwind went into a spin. Unable to correct it, he baled out, landing safely near the officers' mess whereupon he gathered up his parachute and casually strolled into the mess just in time for breakfast. *P7118* crashed in a water meadow on Binty Farm, Itteringham, near Sheringham. Finally, F/S Brunet had just made a perfect three-point landing when he hit a bump and bounced, and as the tail wheel touched down, again it collapsed.

Above left: Cpl Reg Hine of 137 Medical section. (*Reg Hine archives*)

Above right: F/S John Robert Brennan RCAF was lost on 27 May. (*Terry Smith archives*)

P/O Mike Bryan and P/O Douglas St John Jowitt both had accidents in May. (*John LaGette archives*)

Itteringham Mill, Officers' Quarters at RAF Matlaske. (*Alex Torrance archives*)

June 1942

Non-operational flying in June involved four Army co-operation exercises – Falcon, Trout, Walton and West Match – during which the squadron beat up concentrations of troops and tanks, and flew air firing and affiliations with Wellingtons and Stirlings. Personnel changes saw Sgts John McGowan Barclay, Alfred Edward Brown and Robert Woodhouse arrive for flying duties and F/O Donald Bruce Ogilvie leave for liaison duties with the 94th FG USAAF flying P-38s.

F/S Ashton and W/O Mercer intercepted a Do.217, twenty miles east of Cromer on the 20. F/S Ashton fired two bursts but observed no results, whilst W/O Mercer made three attacks, firing all his ammunition, and saw numerous hits. They followed it for twenty miles, noting that its speed was only 150 mph, but were then forced to return to base when their fuel ran low. W/O Mercer claimed it as damaged, but the 3/KG2 machine failed to make it home, thus becoming the squadron's first 'kill.' However, as with 263 Squadron, this was not realised at the time and another victory was celebrated as the first.

During a shipping reconnaissance along the Dutch coast, on 26 June, P/O Bryan and Sgt O'Neill intercepted a Ju.88 but although they both fired at it, no results were observed before it escaped in cloud. The same night, Sgt Waldron obtained strikes on a Do.217 before it escaped in the dark. The final interception of the month took place on the 27 when F/S Brunet and P/O Musgrave left Matlaske to patrol convoy 'Pilot.' Twenty minutes into their flight, they saw a Ju.88 one and a half miles away, at 100 feet, and gave chase, but

Sgt Hilt Ashton RCAF was involved in the Squadron's first victory on 20 June. (*Rick Ashton archives*)

P7101 SF-A after F/L Bartlett collided with Lysander *N1269*. (*Len Bartlett archives*)

although they were flying at 300 mph they could not overtake it, and when F/S Brunet's engines began overheating he fired from 1,000 yards before breaking off. P/O Musgrave continued the chase alone, and fifteen minutes after the first sighting, fired two bursts from 800 yards without result before the enemy escaped in cloud.

There were two accidents towards the end of the month. On 27 June, P/O Furber held off too high in *P7049* when returning from a convoy patrol and both props were damaged in the resulting heavy landing. Then, on 30 June, the squadron lost *P7101 SF-A* when F/L Bartlett ran into Lysander *N1269* of 1489 Flight as he landed. P/O McClure noted in his logbook that there was almost another loss when he 'took three of the ground staff on leave in Oxford *AS873*. Halfway through the flight the starboard engine cowling ripped loose and we almost pranged. The aircraft flicked into a dive that took two of us to pull out of at tree top height. Started at 3,000 feet!'

Throughout their lives, the two squadrons were constantly defending the Whirlwind, and a report written by S/L Coghlan in June 1942 was no exception. It concluded, 'Whirlwinds have a quite undeservedly poor reputation among uninformed RAF personnel. While some points could have been better, they are nevertheless doing a good, steady, and essential job of work.'

July 1942

July saw numerous air sea rescue patrols which resulted in a dinghy and its occupants being found ninety miles off shore, and a badly damaged Wellington escorted home over the North Sea. The squadron also participated in Exercise 'Limpet' where they 'beat up' tanks, motor transport and troops building a pontoon bridge. The operational flying brought five interceptions and two victories.

The first of the interceptions took place on the sixth when F/L Bartlett and Sgt Roberts were scrambled and vectored out to sea where they found a Ju.88 forty miles off the coast. On sighting the Whirlwinds, it climbed towards 10/10 cloud, and, although F/L Bartlett (*P7111*) fired all of his ammunition as it did so, observing many strikes on its underside, it disappeared into the cloud before Sgt Roberts could get close enough to open fire, and despite the damage it regained its base at Creil near Paris.

W/O Smith and Sgt Waldron were one of nine sections that patrolled a convoy off Yarmouth during 23 July. Shortly after take-off Sgt Waldron's suppressor failed and he lost all lights, his R/T and gun sight, but he stayed with his No. 1. After twenty-five minutes, W/O Smith was informed of an unidentified aircraft approaching at sea level. His combat report noted:

> I opened to +4lbs boost with Sgt Waldron 300 yards behind and began the chase at 280 mph at 300 feet. As the enemy did not attempt to dodge into the cloud I realised he could not have seen us and decided to stalk him by climbing to 400 feet in the base of the cloud. Sgt Waldron stayed with me at the same height. I ducked below the cloud every thirty seconds but even though we were closing quite rapidly he made no attempt to get into the 10/10 cloud, which would have given him ample cover from us. After stalking for eight minutes we were a mile behind and I judged his speed to be 200 mph so decided another minute in cloud would bring us in range for a quick

F/O John Luing, F/L Len Bartlett, P/O Mike Bryan, F/S James Rebbetoy RCAF, P/O Dattatraya Samant, and W/O Art Brunet. (*Mike Coghlan archives*)

'Pop' Smith's kite, RAF Matlaske, August 1942 – W/O Robert Smith's *P7035 SF-X*. (*Terry Smith archives*)

> squirt before he pulled into cloud. We emerged from cloud 500 yards astern and identified the aircraft as a Ju.88. I fired a one second burst from 400 yards the same time as the 88 pulled to starboard and up into cloud with black smoke emitting from its port engine.

Sgt Waldron's report added:

> I was flying to starboard of W/O Smith, and as he turned away to port I continued for thirty seconds on my original course and the enemy aircraft dived out of cloud 250 yards in front of me. I gave a burst at full deflection, and then pulled around after him. Black smoke came from both engines as he accelerated into cloud at 400 feet. I followed and gave another burst.

W/O Smith caught the bomber again in a gap in the cloud, firing a one second burst from 250 yards then broke off the attack and returned to base to claim it as damaged.

Saturday 25 was a Red Letter Day for the squadron when P/O McClure (*P7104 SF-V*) and W/O Smith (*P7012*) shot down a Ju.88 from 3(F)/122, the squadron's first confirmed 'kill'. In his combat report, W/O Smith stated:

> I was Black 2 detailed to patrol six miles east of convoy 'Pilot'. As pre-arranged with P/O McClure, I was in line astern at zero feet with P/O McClure above at 2,000 feet. While flying northwest six miles east of Smith's Knoll I saw an aircraft one mile away flying in the opposite direction at sea level. I immediately told P/O McClure, and as the aircraft, which I identified as a Ju.88, turned east, I opened up fully and turned to starboard, putting myself in line astern. I was now within 500 yards doing 280 IAS and, as I did not appear to be gaining I fired a burst from 10 degrees starboard astern and 100 feet above, seeing bursts in the sea just below the tail. I could see P/O McClure diving on his port beam and as he was easily overtaking the Ju.88 I edged off to starboard withholding my fire. I saw P/O McClure slightly overshoot and turn away to port with glycol pouring from his starboard engine. Just previously, I had noticed the Ju.88 firing at P/O McClure from the dorsal gun position at approx. 250 yards. In the meantime, I had climbed to 200 feet keeping 400 yards behind. I closed in to draw fire and opened fire from 250 yards observing strikes and pieces falling off the starboard engine, I used up all my ammunition, closing to 200 yards. I throttled back as I saw P/O McClure coming in again on the port side. I pressed my camera gun button from 300 yards taking film of P/O McClure closing on Ju.88 to fifty yards. I saw his strikes on the fuselage, which burst into flames. A few seconds later, the starboard engine caught fire and the enemy aircraft pulled up to fifty feet and dived straight into the sea. I saw pieces of wreckage on the water, but no survivors. I took photos of wreckage then escorted P/O McClure back to base.

The bomber was Ju.88A-5 *8H+KL* of 3(F) Aufklärungsgruppe 33, flown by Unteroffizer Hans Schorn and crew, all of whom perished.

F/S Rebbetoy (*P7058 SF-G*) and Sgt O'Neill (*P7005 SF-H*) obtained the squadron's third victory on 29 July, another aircraft from 3(F)/122, this time it was Ju.88D-1 *F6+EL*. They took off from Matlaske to patrol convoy 'Ribald'. Fifteen miles north east of Happisburgh with F/S Rebbetoy at 1,500 feet and Sgt O'Neill at 200 feet, they sighted an enemy aircraft, the black crosses were outlined in white and it was camouflaged blackish green underneath and sea green above. F/S Rebbetoy informed Sgt O'Neill of the aircraft and

P7104 SF-V showing the victory marking. (*John McClure archives*)

Mac's Kite RAF Matlaske, 14 August 1942, *P7104 SF-V* flown by F/O John McClure RCAF. (*Terry Smith archives*)

Sgt Robert Woodhouse, Sgt Aubrey Smith, F/S John Barclay, W/O Don McPhail RCAF, Sgt Des Roberts RNZAF, Sgt Edward Brown, W/O Art Brunet RCAF, Sgt Hilt Ashton RCAF at Matlaske 1942. (*Rick Ashton archives*)

P/O Paul LaGette was posted on 31 July. (*John LaGette archives*)

identified it as a Ju.88 which was climbing and turning away from them. F/S Rebbetoy gave it a burst from 250 yards but saw no results before he broke away to starboard and Sgt O'Neill, who had climbed to 3,000 feet, gave it a two second burst observing strikes on the nose. He broke away and the enemy aircraft dived down to 2,000 feet turned to starboard and started to climb up again. The Whirlwinds followed. F/S Rebbetoy fired a second burst from 100 yards range and 30 degrees starboard astern seeing flashes on the starboard engine and fuselage and as the enemy aircraft turned to port he broke away underneath it as Sgt O'Neill fired two bursts from 250 yards and 30 degrees to port. F/S Rebbetoy saw tracer just skimming underneath the Ju.88 which continued to climb steeply and he gave it a two second burst from 100 yards dead astern, closing to 50 yards, finishing his ammunition and seeing strikes underneath the starboard engine. The bomber then dived steeply with white smoke pouring from its starboard engine and levelled off at sea level. Sgt O'Neill finished his ammunition in a final burst but continued firing his cine gun and the section followed the bomber for fifteen miles. It jettisoned its bombs, and as Rebbetoy told the controller to send out another section, flames appeared under its starboard wing, it then hit the sea and burst into flames. A yellow dinghy was seen but there was no survivors. The Ju88, flown by Unteroffizer Rudolf Pilz and crew, came down twenty-five miles north east of Happisburgh.

Sgt Aubrey Cartwright Smith arrived for flying duties during the month, whilst P/O Paul Milton LaGette, an American who had travelled to Canada and joined the RCAF before the US entered the war, was posted, as was Medical Officer F/L Richard Barnett Clayton who was replaced by P/O Robert Smollet Flynn.

August 1942

The first eleven days of August were spent at Drem, under the auspices of Exercise 'Dryshod'. The ORB noted that 'the change of scenery was appreciated by the squadron and turned out to be a welcome rest for everyone as owing to unfavourable weather, very few sorties were made.'

Sgt O'Neil saw a Ju.88 on the eighteenth whilst searching for a dinghy thirty miles east of Yarmouth. He reported it to P/O Luing then began the chase. The bomber's dorsal turret opened fire at 600 yards but Sgt O'Neil closed to 300 yards before firing, and observed strikes forward of the top turret. P/O Luing also attacked, but the Ju.88 escaped in cloud.

The nineteenth saw the ill-fated Commando attack on Dieppe, 'Operation Jubilee', and whilst not directly involved, the squadron flew six scrambles, two convoy patrols, one air sea rescue patrol, one escort, and one Outer Channel patrol in a supporting role, resulting in two interceptions. P/O Bryan and Sgt Roberts flew one of the scrambles, and were vectored onto a Dornier Do.217 fifty miles off Happisburgh. Sgt Roberts opened fire from 250 yards, knocking pieces off it then P/O Bryan attacked observing strikes on the underside of the fuselage and port engine, and more pieces falling away. He finished his ammunition in two further bursts from dead astern, observing strikes on the fuselage near the cockpit before he broke away and Sgt Roberts attacked again with three more bursts from 200 yards. As he broke away, smoke began streaming behind the bomber

F/S Hugh O'Neill, seen here with the Squadron's tame Spitfire *V SF-Z* shared the destruction of a Ju.88 on 29 July. *(Terry Smith archives)*

and four of the crew baled out from 1,500 feet before it stalled and dived into sea in flames. Dornier Do.217E-4 *F8+BN* of 5/KG40 flown by Oberleutnant Wolf and crew came down forty miles northeast of the Happisburgh Light. An air sea rescue Walrus picked up Oberleutnant Wolf, the only survivor, who insisted he had been shot down by Beaufighters.

F/L van Schaick and Sgt Brown flew a patrol of the Outer Swept Channel between Cross Sands and Smiths Knoll, with F/L van Schaick at 1,000 feet and Sgt Brown at sea level. Near the end of the patrol line Sgt Brown sighted a Ju.88 coming towards him. He informed F/L van Schaick who turned to intercept, but his starboard engine cut and he lost sight of Sgt Brown. Unfortunately he could not contact him either as Sgt Brown's R/T had been hit by return fire, so he searched the area without success before returning to base. Sgt Brown in the meantime had observed black boost smoke come from the bombers engines as it began to pull away from him so he opened fire with a one second burst seeing his shells hitting the sea behind it. The bomber was weaving violently but he finished his ammunition in four bursts, observing strikes and smoke coming from starboard engine, then followed it for a while before returning to base to claim it as damaged. A later patrol by P/O DeHoux and Sgt Barclay saw a large patch of oil on the sea in the same area which may have been from this aircraft.

On 20 August, F/L Bartlett and Sgt Barclay flew another patrol of the Outer Swept Channel, F/L Bartlett at 2,000 feet and Sgt Barclay at sea level. Twelve miles north of Smith's Knoll, the latter sighted a Junkers Ju.88 and closed to 500 yards. He fired three bursts, seeing a piece fall off, but then lost it in 10/10 cloud. F/L Bartlett, who had

Clockwise from bottom left: /O Douglas Jowitt, F/O Eddie Musgrave RAAF, P/O Charles Mercer RCAF, P/O Robert 'Pop' Smith DFM, P/O Des Roberts RNZAF, Mrs Pop Smith, F/S James Rebbetoy RCAF, Sgt Francis Waldron, F/S Robert Woodhouse, F/S Edward Brown, W/O Don McPhail RCAF, P/O John McClure RCAF. In the centre: F/S Art Brunet RCAF. (*Terry Smith archives*)

retained his height, saw the bomber as it emerged from the cloud and gave chase, but it dropped back into cloud again and disappeared, allowing Sgt Barclay to claim it only as damaged.

On 23 August, 'The squadron heard with regret that it was moving to Snailwell, a satellite of Duxford. It also learnt with dismay that its main role would be night flying.' Four aircraft flew to Duxford on 25 August for night operations, where F/L van Schaick discovered that he had been a member of all three squadrons on the Station: 266, 609 and 137.

September 1942

The sole operation in September was a Rodeo to Lille escorted by twenty-four Spitfires of 485 and 411 Squadrons. S/L Coghlan, F/L Bartlett, F/L van Schaick, 2nd Lt Freeman, P/Os Bryan, Furber, McClure, DeHoux, Musgrave, Mercer, and Brunet, and F/S Rebbetoy took off with the intention of making a feint at Lille, hoping that enemy aircraft would come up and be dealt with by the Spitfires and Typhoon escort. Thirty miles off Oostende, they climbed to 12,000 feet, crossed the coast between Blankenberghe and Oostende, and flew to Diksmuide then out over Nieuwpoort, but the Luftwaffe did not rise to the bait.

Above left: F/L Leonard Bartlett was posted to Command 253 Squadron on 16 September. (*Len Bartlett archives*)

Above right: S/L John Wray arrived as a supernumerary on 20 September. (*John Wray archives*)

Sgt Tom Sutherland arrived for flying duties on 1 September, seen here with 'SF-U' 'Hazel' named after Sgt Aubrey Smith's future wife. (*Terry Smith archives*)

Best man F/L Robert Woodward DFC and groom S/L Humphrey Coghlan DFC. (*Mike Coghlan archives*)

P/O Joseph DeHoux RCAF, P/O Frederick Furber, P/O John McClure RCAF and 2nd Lt Neville Freeman SAAF at S/L Coghlan's wedding. (*Mike Coghlan archives*)

Orders were also received in September posting the squadron to Manston, which put it 'back in the thick of the action.' The order also stipulated that 250lb bombs were to be fitted to the Whirlwind. At the same time 'A' Flight Commander, F/L Leonard Harold Bartlett, was posted as Officer Commanding 253 Squadron. The ORB noted that, 'The squadron was sorry to lose him as he was very popular with all ranks, and a very efficient Flight Commander.' His place was taken by F/L Joseph William Ernest Holmes from 263 Squadron. Two other pilots reported for flying duties during the month: S/L John Basil Wray as supernumerary, and Sgt Thomas Arthur Sutherland. The main news of the month, however, was that S/L Coghlan was married in London to Marie Lacoste. Robert Woodward was best man, Alex Torrance was an usher, and several pilots also attended the ceremony.

October 1942: Whirlibomber Operations:

It was an inauspicious start to the month for P/O Dattatraya Anant Samant and Sgt John McGowan Barclay, *P7037*, when they were caught in a strong crosswind on landing and crashed through the boundary fence. Although neither was injured, the accidents resulted in their being posted to 263 Squadron within a week, as was P/O Donald Burton McPhail whilst Sgts Edmund Alexander Bolster and Gerald Oscar Harrington Walker reported for flying duties. Adjutant, F/L Philip Lewis Hogan, who had helped re-form the squadron, in October 1941, was also posted and replaced by P/O Norman Emery Freeman.

By now the Whirlwind was beginning to show her age, for when P/O McClure and W/O Brunet intercepted a Fw.190 sea level off Margate, they noted that although they were doing 300 mph, the enemy aircraft pulled away very easily. A change of role however brought her a new lease of life

Anti-shipping patrols during the first three weeks of the month resulted in little to report, but the addition of bomb racks resulted in the Whirlibomber being a much more potent weapon in the squadron's 'Channel Stop' role. F/O Bryan and Sgt Sutherland flew the squadron's first Whirlibomber sorties, on 21 October 1942, under the auspices of a new type of operation – an armed shipping recce. They searched between Sangette and Gravelines but found no shipping so bombed a beached wreck on the French coast instead.

First Rhubarb Operations

On 28 October, the squadron was informed that its Whirlibombers were to be employed on Rhubarbs over enemy territory. Unfortunately, the first sorties, on 31 October, proved to be nothing short of disastrous. F/L van Schaick, *P7064*, with Sgt Waldron, *P7109 SF-N* (Blue Section), and P/O Jowitt, *P7115*, with P/O Furber, *P7102* (Green Section), left the English coast at Dungeness and crossed the French coast between Plage St Gabriel and Plage St Cecily. Blue Section was to attack a hutted camp near Etaples and Green Section a similar target three miles to the north.

Green Section was unable to locate their target but encountered intense flak whilst searching for it. P/O Furber's aircraft was hit, and he saw P/O Jowitt's aircraft streaming a trail of petrol from the starboard engine so they abandoned the mission and turned for home. After crossing out over the French coast he called a 'Mayday' for P/O Jowitt, and heard him say he was baling out, but then lost him in cloud. P/O Jowitt did not return. Neither did Blue Section.

F/L van Schaick, Blue 1, later noted:

> A large amount of Bofors and small arms fire was experienced and I fired a short burst at two Bofors gun positions between the coast and north-west of the target, silencing both of them. I saw two or three persons walking about in the target camp and fired a short burst and dropped my bombs from 200 feet. On looking back, I saw two palls of smoke rising from the centre of the camp. After seeing Sgt Waldron coming in to bomb behind me, I lost all contact with him. Before bombing, my aircraft was hit by a cannon shell in the port engine, which went u/s. On leaving the target, I flew into a valley and fired the rest of my ammo at a stationary goods train without an engine, observing strikes. On breaking away, my aircraft was shot through the tail and I flew through some overhead wires. Flying on one engine, I headed out to sea and when just off shore was struck in the starboard engine by flak. I tried to climb in order to Mayday and bale out, but the elevator control was missing. I lost speed and my aircraft hit the water. It floated for about thirty seconds and I jumped into the sea. After about five hours in the dinghy I was picked up by a Walrus of 277 Squadron when about five miles out to sea between Le Touquet and Boulogne and taken to Hawkinge.

It was not the first time he had taken a dip in the Channel – the first occasion was on 21 July 1941 when he was shot down whilst flying Spitfire *W3372* with 609 Squadron.

This brief combat report, given on his return to the squadron the following day, holds yet another remarkable story. Whilst on a shipping reconnaissance to Dieppe, a 91 Squadron Spitfire, flown by Sgt Round, spotted him eight miles west of Cap Gris Nez. A 277 Squadron Lysander was scrambled, but unfortunately was vectored to the wrong area, although he was found shortly afterwards by Walrus *W3076* flown by P/O Hilton and F/S Seales and escorted by three Spitfires.

By this time, not only had he drifted close to shore, but also into the middle of a minefield. Undaunted, P/O Hilton landed crosswind between the rows of mines. He overshot the dinghy and had to turn around and taxi back between the mines with only four foot clearance on each side. As they approached the dinghy, F/S Seales threw a line to F/L van Schaick and he was hauled into the Walrus. The take-off was no less exciting. P/O Hilton 'bounced' the Walrus over six mines before finally reaching flying speed and climbing away. F/L van Schaick was taken to Hawkinge Hospital for the night suffering from mild exposure.

P/O Hilton was awarded the DFC for this and several other rescues, whilst F/L van Schaick was taken off operations, having flown sixty operational sorties. News was received on 9 November that Sgt Francis Gordon Waldron was a Prisoner of War, but unfortunately, P/O Douglas St John Jowitt was never found.

Sgt John 'Tich' Barclay, the squadron comic. (*Terry Smith archives*)

One of Tich's many! *P7037* SF-J, 5 October, after going through the boundary fence. (*Terry Smith archives*)

W/O Art Brunet RCAF. (*Terry Smith archives*)

P/O Frederick Furber, seen with the Squadron Spitfire, was the only one to return from the first Rhubarb Operation on 28 October . (*Alex Torrance archives*)

Above left: F/L John van Schaick DFM ditched returning from the Squadron's first Rhubarb Operation on 28 October. (*Len Bartlett archives*)

Above right: Sgt Francis Waldron failed to return from the Squadron's first Rhubarb Operation on 28 October and was reported as a POW. (*John LaGette archives*)

Below right: F/O Douglas St John Jowitt was missing after the Squadron's first Rhubarb Operation on 28 October. (*Vic Bingham archives*)

November 1942

Apart from routine convoy patrols and abandoned Rhubarbs, there were just three operations during November. F/O Bryan and W/O Brunet flew the first, a Rhubarb on the sixth, but seconds after take-off Brunet's port engine seized, forcing him to jettison his bombs and make an emergency landing.

P/O McClure and 2nd Lt Freeman staged through Ford for the second, an attack on a hutted camp at Bolbec, but when they became separated in cloud, P/O McClure bombed a viaduct in Mirville, then strafed two long huts, one of which caught fire. 2nd Lt Freeman followed a railway and bombed a road bridge over the line between Bolbec and Yvetot. Finally, P/O Mercer and P/O DeHoux flew night time Rhubarbs in search of locomotives near Lille, but found nothing. P/O Mercer saw an aircraft preparing to land on Longuenesse aerodrome but, as he approached, it switched off its lights, as did the aerodrome and he came under attack from intense flak so broke away and bombed a transformer station north of Watten instead. P/O DeHoux bombed a railway yard north of Bourbourgville but did not observe results due to poor visibility.

November saw W/O Alexander Ivan Doig report for flying duties whilst F/O Gordon Edmund William Priest arrived as Adjutant to replace F/O Norman Emery Freeman, who had occupied the role since the beginning of October.

December 1942

F/L John Edward van Schaick DFM was rested following an eventful tour and replaced as 'B' Flight Commander by F/L Alex Torrance, and the squadron flew a variety of operations – Intruders, armed shipping reconnaissances, a Roadstead and numerous Rhubarbs. In addition, there were two encounters with the deadly 'Butcher Bird' – the Focke-Wulf Fw.190.

The first Rhubarbs took place on the tenth. F/O Bryan and F/S Roberts returned from the Belgian coast due to insufficient cloud whilst S/L Coghlan, with P/O DeHoux, and P/O R. L. Smith DFM, with W/O Ashton, took off to attack a train of petrol wagons due to arrive at Doullens from Amiens but owing to thick cloud en route they became separated. All crossed the French coast near Berck sur Mer but could not reach the target area due to low cloud covering the hill tops and so attacked targets of opportunity. S/L Coghlan bombed covered dispersal bays on Crécy-en-Ponthieu aerodrome whilst P/O DeHoux bombed a group of houses from which light flak was coming. P/O Smith bombed a long building with two chimneys next to Auxi-le-Château station, whilst W/O Ashton dropped his bombs on the station. The ORB noted, 'All our aircraft returned with damage.'

On 15 December, P/O Robert Smith took Whirlwind *P6976* up from Manston on a night flying test, and at 1,000 feet, 500 yards south of Ramsgate harbour, observed what he took to be snowflakes in the air, but was most probably a flare dropped by an Albacore of 841 Squadron. He flew towards it to investigate, but as he did so he saw four aircraft about five miles away approaching Ramsgate in echelon starboard, so pulled up into cloud. After a few seconds he emerged to see four enemy aircraft, which he identified as greenish

Above left: F/L Alex Torrance and F/L John McClure RCAF, Flight Commanders. (*Alec Torrance archives*)

Above right: P/O Robert Smith DFM, 'Either a remarkable pilot or a remarkable line'. (*Alex Torrance archives*)

grey camouflaged Fw.190s, at 300 feet, one mile away orbiting in line astern 200 yards apart and two miles south east of Ramsgate. He dived on the rear Fw.190, but as he did so the towns defences opened fire. He heard strikes on his port wing and a few seconds later smelt petrol and saw a thin trail of white vapour coming from his port engine. The flak caused the enemy aircraft to jink, however, and the No. 4 straggled some 400 yards behind the rest. He attacked it from 20 degrees port astern and 500 yards, closing to 250 yards with six one-second bursts, seeing hits on the tail and starboard wing close to the root. The enemy aircraft made no attempt to evade and black smoke started to stream out from under the fuselage, but he was forced to throttle back to avoid overtaking it, and last saw it losing height and heading south east. In the meantime, the three remaining 190s had turned, and he now became the hunted. One attacked him from the port beam and he put down full flap just as he took hits on the elevator, which jammed the control column, leaving him no fore and aft control. He turned into the attack and saw six streams of white tracer coming from the enemy aircraft, which closed to fifty yards and skidded underneath him; as it did so he dived, trying to force it into the sea. By now his port fuel tank was very low on petrol so as he was heading towards land, he decided to withdraw from the fight. He pulled the flaps up, opened up to +9 boost, and with two 190s rapidly closing in from astern, headed for Ramsgate. A mile off shore the ground defences opened up again forcing the enemy aircraft to break off their attack, but he had trouble controlling his damaged aircraft, and only just managed to keep it out of the sea by using the elevator trimmers and full flap to jump the cliffs, barely missing houses on the shoreline in the process. His port engine was spluttering due to lack of fuel as he made his approach to Manston, but he landed safely with the help of the elevator trimming tab. On inspection, the tail plane, elevators, rudder, port rear fuel tank and starboard propeller had been damaged by a combination of friendly flak, cannon shells and machine gun fire. Someone at Fighter Command HQ did not quite believe his version of events, and wrote on the report, 'Either a very remarkable pilot or a very remarkable line.'

The second encounter with the 'Butcher Bird' took place on 19 December, over the Goodwin Sands, and involved F/O Bryan and P/O Rebbetoy who were on patrol over Pegwell Bay. P/O Rebbetoy's combat report stated:

> F/O Bryan made a head on attack at the starboard enemy aircraft and I made a head on attack on the port enemy aircraft firing a one second burst from 300 yards, but did not observe any hits. I broke to port and the enemy aircraft to starboard. I then saw F/O Bryan in the middle of the enemy aircraft in a steep turn. I turned in to attack and they turned to attack me head on. We closed rapidly and as one pulled up to avoid a collision I gave him a ½-second burst, observing hits all along the bottom of the fuselage. He passed over my head missing me by about fifteen feet. I turned to port and saw the enemy aircraft at about 200 yards and attacked him from 70 degrees starboard astern firing a 1½-second burst and observing strikes all along the fuselage. Black smoke started to pour from the engine and both enemy aircraft made for home at a slow speed. Before we turned back I saw one enemy aircraft with black smoke still pouring out going down in a 45 degrees dive on its side from 400 feet. I claim one Fw.190 as probably destroyed, shared with F/O Bryan.

P7011 SF-U. (Chris Thomas archives)

W/O Brunet flew a Roadstead on 20 December, during which he damaged a trawler moored to the Zeebrugge Mole, whilst Intruder sorties by S/L Wray, S/L Coghlan, F/L Torrance, F/Os Bryan, DeHoux, Furber, and Musgrave, and P/Os McClure, Mercer, and Rebbetoy destroyed locomotives in Gent marshalling yards and Roulers station, damaged bridges near Calais and Courtrai and destroyed an ammunition dump at Forêt d'Houthoulst.

The final few days of the month highlighted not only the highly dangerous nature of operations, but also the robustness of the Whirlwind. An example of the first occurred when P/O McClure and F/S Woodhouse took off to attack a clothing factory at Auchy-les-Hesdins. Unable to locate it, they attacked an engine drawing twelve goods trucks near Crecy-en-Ponthieu aerodrome from opposite sides, dropping their bombs from fifty feet. One burst on the engine, the other three all around it and the train was seen to topple over. F/S Woodhouse was caught in the blast of P/O McClure's bombs and was thrown 100 feet upwards, fortunately with no damage to the aircraft or himself. An example of the second occurred as Sgt Sutherland and F/O Musgrave searched for trains in the Abbeville area. Sgt Sutherland was severely hit by flak in both engines as he released his bombs, and the port power plant seized during his return flight. He overshot his landing at Lympne and crashed; the port engine caught fire and although the crash tender quickly put the flames out, *P6998* was badly damaged.

The final Rhubarbs of the month, on the twenty-eighth, were forced to turn back off the French coast due to the weather, and when F/O DeHoux landed, he brought the operational flying for 1942 to an end.

January 1943

The squadron gained another victory during January, but also lost two pilots. In addition, S/L Wray was detached on liaison duties to the USAAF, P/O Frederick Michael Furber was posted, and F/O John Fredrick Luing returned to the fold after a four month detachment with the USAAF. Several tests were also undertaken to ascertain if the Whirlibomber could carry two 500lb bombs, and whilst these proved satisfactory, the heavier bombs over-stressed the wings and were rarely used. The weather also interfered with operations, forcing several Rhubarbs to be abandoned at the enemy coast. The only section to achieve any success was P/O R. L. Smith and Sgt A. C. Smith, who attempted to attack a clothing factory at Auchy-les-Hesdins, but cloud cover dissipated over the target area and they were forced to search for alternative targets. A railway bridge over the river Authie near Mont de la Motte, and a stationary goods train with twenty trucks in a station near Conchil-le-Temple were damaged by their bombs.

The second half of January was more productive as, between the sixteenth and nineteenth, seven Night Intruder operations were flown resulting in the destruction of several railway trucks by S/L Coghlan. P/O Rebbetoy bombed a passenger train outside Calais, reported to be bringing 'Huns' back from leave. Several coaches were derailed, and raked from end to end twice with cannon; F/O Bryan flew two sorties, on the first he destroyed a locomotive and several trucks in the Ypres area, whilst on the second

'Smithy Boys', possibly *P7102 SF-Q* was flown by F/S Aubrey Smith (seen here) and W/O Robert Smith DFM. (*Terry Smith archives*)

Syd Fairmain, fitter to Aubrey Smith 22 July 1942 to 10 April 1944 in Aubrey Smith's battledress at Manston. (*Terry Smith archives*)

he attacked a passenger train on the Brugge-Gent line with one bomb, derailing the locomotive and two coaches which he then strafed. As he was doing this he saw a goods train approaching from the opposite direction so dropped his second bomb on this before finishing his ammunition in a strafing run, observing strikes on several trucks and the engine. Finally, F/O Musgrave bombed a train leaving the locomotive on its side enveloped in clouds of steam. F/O Luing ran over a ridge on take-off in *P7051*; the aircraft became airborne prematurely, stalled, hit the ground, then cart wheeled and caught fire. He was uninjured, but the fire 'cooked' the bombs, which exploded, causing P/O John McClure to note in his logbook, 'Boy did he run.' A few days later, he noted of an Air to Ground Firing Exercise, 'Sgt Brown took a chunk out of my starboard wing. Landed OK. Close formation!'

Five Rhubarbs were flown on 23 January, resulting in the destruction of a six locomotives and many trucks. F/O Bryan and Sgt Walker claimed three of the engines and several trucks; S/L Coghlan and F/O Musgrave damaged a further three. The remaining two sections were not so lucky, however. Following the destruction of a locomotive, P/O McClure and W/O Doig *P7054* became separated over Poperinghe as they avoided intense flak. Unfortunately, W/O Alexander Ivan Doig did not return. He crash-landed at Roesbrugge-Haringe and was on the run for four days before being captured near Cambrai. The squadron received word that he was a POW on 8 February.

The final section, 2nd Lt Freeman and Sgt Brown, *P7095 SF-H*, attacked a goods train north of Doullens from which they experienced return fire. After the attack they climbed into cloud, but became separated. Sgt Brown contacted 2nd Lt Freeman on the R/T and told him he was OK, although he had been hit in the port engine, but nothing further was heard from him and he did not return. After he went missing, the squadron waited in vain for news that he was a POW. Post-war, when allied personnel were moved to official war cemeteries, the body of a 'Sgt Manston' was exhumed from the edge of Amiens aerodrome. As no pilot by that name had been lost, further investigations proved it was Alfred Edward Brown, buried more than forty miles from where he crash-landed. Manston was the aerodrome he had taken off from. He was still in his uniform and had 'escape' money in his pockets; the only things missing were his dog-tags. Photographs of *P7095* show bullet holes in her port nacelle and on the port side of the fuselage, and although this is consistent with the damage reported by him over the R/T, there is no sign of blood and the straps of his harness were hung over the side of the cockpit showing that he was unhurt when he vacated her. It is possible he died of internal injuries, but as he was so far from the crash site, there may be more sinister connotations. His death will probably remain a mystery however.[1] Notification of his commission and promotion to Pilot Officer came through shortly after he took off on his last flight.

During the last few days of the month, F/L Priest, the Adjutant, was taken up in the 'Maggie' by P/O Rebbetoy, but the ORB noted that whilst, 'The latter enjoyed himself with aerobatics, the Adjutant did not have quite the same amount of pleasure. After witnessing the flight, the Intelligence Officer decided it was best to have one foot on the ground, and changed his mind, cancelling his trip.'

F/O Musgrave found enough cloud cover on 28 January to penetrate as far as Thielt where he bombed a goods train, leaving the locomotive enveloped in steam, but he was then intercepted by two Fw.190s, the leader of which fired two bursts from 300 yards. He

F/O John Luing, 'Boy did he run.' (*Alex Torrance archives*)

P7095 SF-H following F/S Ted Brown's crash landing near Doullens on 23 January. (*John Wray archives*)

L8280, the Squadron's Magister. (*Terry Smith archives*)

avoided the six streams of yellow tracer, then throttled back and put down full flap which caused the Fw.190 to overshoot and pull up into cloud. As it reappeared, he gave it a short burst at 300 yards, but did not see the results as it disappeared into the cloud again. His fire was accurate, however, as Fw.190A-4 '*Black 2*', from 8/JG26, crashed, killing her pilot, Unteroffizer Heinrich Wälter.

February 1943

F/L Joseph William Ernest Holmes DFC left for 263 Squadron, and F/S John McGowan Barclay and Sgt Albert Witham arrived for flying duties during the month, whilst F/O Eddie Musgrave and P/O Robert Leslie Smith DFM received the Distinguished Flying Cross. Unsuitable weather restricted operational flying to a minimum, but the sorties that did take place resulted not only in the damage of one of Germany's commerce raiders, but also in the loss of two pilots.

A large ship was reported to be attempting to pass through the Straits of Dover during the first half of the month, so when it was detected on radar on the tenth, the squadron was ordered to sink it despite weather conditions that would normally have kept them on the ground. F/O Musgrave was the only one vectored onto it by Swingate Control, south-west of Boulogne, but due to poor visibility he did not see her until he was half a mile away, however he did see two escorts ahead of it; two behind it and a fifth about half a mile to seaward. He decided to attack from landward and found a 'V' shaped sand bar on the coast which he used to pinpoint the ship. As he turned back out to sea, however, he was illuminated by three searchlights and forced to take evasive action. He returned to his pinpoint a second time, only to be caught by the searchlights again. On his third attempt, he climbed to cloud base and as the searchlights were exposed, he dived through

F/L Joe Holmes was posted back to 263 Squadron on 16 February. (*Mike Coghlan archives*)

Eddie's Gong: F/O John Hadow, P/O Hilt Ashton RCAF, P/O Des Roberts RNZAF, F/L Mike Bryan, F/O Eddie Musgrave DFC RAAF, P/O Norbury Dugdale, W/O Art Brunet RCAF. *Crouching*: Sgt Robert Woodhouse, Lynn the mascot. (*Terry Smith archives*)

the beams to sea level then headed for the ship whilst taking violent evasive action due to intense flak. He levelled off and released his bombs from 100 feet before passing over the centre of the ship. The flak followed him, a 20-mm shell ripped a large hole in his starboard elevator and two pieces of shrapnel passed through the Perspex of his cockpit coupé, but the ORB noted, 'This merchant vessel of 5,000 tons is claimed Cat 3. Reports from the Naval Authorities indicate that it stopped for 1½ hours, and was possibly towed to Boulogne Harbour, where it stopped all night, getting just inside the mole next morning where it was sighted by Spitfires of 91 Squadron. Naval opinion is that unless the ship was heavily damaged and possibly in danger of sinking it would have been admitted to Boulogne harbour at once, without waiting for daylight.' The merchantman was in fact the commerce raider *Togo*, and although she limped back to Kiel via Dunkirk, she was so badly damaged that she was never fully repaired and finished the war as a Night Fighter direction ship.

A record number of sorties were flown on the night of 19 February – fourteen – but as P/O Charles Eldred Mercer took off in *P7119* he crashed into 2nd Lt Neville Austin Freeman who was just taxiing out onto the flare-path in *P7114*. Both machines immediately caught fire and two of the bombs exploded just as rescuers were nearing the wreckage, fortunately no further injuries were sustained. Cpl Phil Robson was an armourer, 'I rushed to the scene on a bomb tractor, and was about thirty-yards away

Above left: P/O Charles Mercer was lost on 19 February. (*Alec Torrance archives*)

Above right: 2nd Lt Neville Freeman SAAF was lost on 19 February. (*Mike Coghlan archives*)

when the bombs went off. They were already dead however.'[2] Of the remaining pilots, F/L Bryan destroyed three locomotives near Roulers, F/O DeHoux damaged a fourth near Watten whilst F/O Musgrave bombed a fifth near Furnes but was unable to observe results due to flak and searchlights. W/O Ashton and P/O R. L. Smith did not penetrate enemy territory, the former due to fog in the Berck area, the latter with Exactor trouble. F/S O'Neill and Sgt Sutherland carried out uneventful shipping patrols off the French and Belgian coasts whilst F/L Torrance destroyed a barge near Nieuwpoort, and then found three merchant vessels near Dunkerque. He climbed and gave a 'fix' whereupon F/O Luing and Sgt Walker were ordered to attack them. The former bombed one of the escort vessels, the latter a 2,000 ton vessel. Both claimed near misses despite intense flak. F/O DeHoux and F/O McClure attacked another convoy off Calais, obtaining near misses on an E-Boat and 2,000 ton merchant vessel respectively. S/L Coghlan flew two sorties; he returned from the first with a faulty R/T, and he found no targets on the second.

March 1943

Personnel movements saw no less than six pilots report for flying duties: S/L Patrick Henry Lee as a supernumerary, F/O John Tapscott Davidson, F/O John Maude Hadow, P/O Gordon Stanley Chalmers, P/O Norbury Dugdale, and W/O William Malia. F/L Mike Bryan also received a DFC for 'his good work with the squadron.'

The squadron kept up the pressure on the German transport system during March, but the losses also continued. As in February, many Rhubarbs were laid on only to be cancelled as weather conditions on 'the other side' were not suitable. Six aircraft took off on 2 March to attack targets in the Roulers–Neufchâtel area, and F/L Bryan's bag of locomotives grew to twenty as he destroyed another north of Roulers; P/O Rebbetoy damaged a power-driven barge on the Canal de la Colone, and F/S Roberts bombed two bridges and cannoned a lock gate without seeing results. S/L Coghlan, W/O Brunet and Sgt Walker flew to the Neufchâtel area but were forced to return when they found the cloud was down to the hilltops. W/O Brunet was asked for a vector to base by Sgt Walker when they became separated in cloud but, as he neared the English coast, he heard Sgt Walker give a 'Mayday', which was not picked up by the ground stations. Unfortunately, Sgt Gerald Oscar Harrington Walker and *P7005* did not return, and despite extensive searches, he was not found. He actually came down near Neufchâtel, and was quickly taken prisoner although he feigned amnesia when being questioned so as not to give away any details to the enemy.

Eight Whirlwinds were airborne during the afternoon of 3 March to practice formation flying in preparation for twenty journalists and photographers who were due on 4 and 5 March to 'write up' 137 Squadron. The ORB noted that, 'the journalists duly arrived, and many stories of noble deeds were told, to appear in various stages of distortion in the papers during the following few days. Four aircraft from each flight carried out a formation flight, and F/O McClure flew a low level "beat up" of the aerodrome.' More photos were taken on the 5 when F/L Bryan 'beat-up' the aerodrome and several group photos and a series of posed shots by the ground crews were also taken.

On 11 March, a shipping attack by F/O McClure, Sgt A. C. Smith, Sgt Barclay and, Sgt

W/O William Malia, P/O Gordon Chalmers, F/O John Hadow, and F/O John Davidson at Manston in March. (*Terry Smith archives*)

F/L Mike Bryan in *P7121 SF-C* showing an impressive tally of kills. (*Terry Smith archives*)

Sgt Gerald Walker was lost on 2 March and became a POW. (*Chris Goldring archives*)

Press Day 5 March 1943: F/S Hilt Ashton RCAF, F/S James Rebbetoy RCAF, Sgt Albert Witham, P/O Robert Smith DFM, F/S Des Roberts RNZAF, F/O Eddie Musgrave RAAF, F/S John Barclay, W/O Art Brunet RCAF, F/L John Bryan, P/O Joseph DeHoux RCAF, F/S Aubrey Smith, F/O John McClure DFC RCAF, W/O Tom Sutherland, F/O John Hadow, S/L Humphrey St John Coghlan DFC, Sgt Edmund Bolster, F/S Hugh O'Neill, Sgt Robert Woodhouse, and P/O Norbury Dugdale. (*Mike Coghlan archives*)

Press Day, 5 March 1943: Ground crews arming a Whirlwind. (*Mike Coghlan archives*)

Press Day 5 March 1943: Armourers, Cpl Phil Robson (*centre*). (*Phil Robson archives*)

Above left: Press Day, 5 March 1943: Armourer Cpl Phil Robson. *(Phil Robson archives)*

Above right: P/O Les Barnett (Intelligence Officer) and Sgt Aubrey Smith at Matlaske. (*Terry Smith archives*)

Bolster escorted by seven Spitfire IXs of 64 Squadron flew at sea level from Marck to Nieuwpoort, where the target turned out to be about twenty fishing vessels. Then on 13 March, W/O Ashton bombed the last of four minesweepers in line astern a mile offshore of Cap Gris Nez and Calais in a dive from 1,500 feet to 100 feet, seeing a flash and spray close to the ship. On making a second run over the target, light flak was experienced from the other three ships, but not from the one attacked. Sgt Barclay was vectored by Swingate control in the Gris Nez area without sighting a target and was recalled, whilst Sgt A. C. Smith damaged a 1,000 ton ship and claimed it Cat III.

Practice dive bombing during the morning of 14 March was in preparation for an attack on Abbeville aerodrome in the afternoon. S/L Coghlan DFC, F/L Bryan DFC, W/O Brunet, F/O Musgrave DFC, P/O Rebbetoy and F/O DeHoux were escorted by Spitfire Vbs of 350 and 453 Squadrons, as close cover, and Spitfire IXs of 64 and 122 Squadrons, as top cover. They crossed the Channel at sea level and the French coast at Cayeux at 13,000 feet. Twelve 250lb bombs were released in 15,000 to 7,000 feet dives, and bursts were seen in the north east side of the aerodrome, a very successful show.

A similar operation to Abbeville was laid on for 24 March, but the formation of six Whirlwinds and thirty-six Spitfires was forced to return from the French coast due to unsuitable weather over France. On 25 March, the ORB noted that, 'S/L Coghlan went to London to dine with His Majesty the King.' Whilst he was away F/L Bryan led F/L

F/O John Davidson 'piled up' *P7104 SF-V* on 30 March. (*Wendy Douglas archives*)

Torrance, F/O McClure, F/O Luing, P/O R. L. Smith and Sgt A. C. Smith to attack the Abbeville Marshalling Yards on Ramrod 46, escorted by Typhoons of 609 Squadron and two squadrons of Hornchurch Spitfires. They bombed the target in dives from 12,500 to 7,000 feet despite heavy flak, and all sixteen 500lb bombs were observed to burst in the target area.

The most successful sorties of the month, however, occurred when F/O DeHoux and P/O Rebbetoy crossed the French coast at Gravelines on a Rhubarb, then split up. DeHoux bombed three barges on a canal near Merville, damaging all three, whilst Rebbetoy bombed a goods train between Bailleul and Armentières, blowing the engine off the rails and disintegrating the first trucks. He next attacked a locomotive between Armentières and Lille with cannon, seeing steam from its sides and coal blown up to 200 feet in the air, whilst his final targets were two barges on a canal near Lille which he damaged.

The final incident of the month took place when the port engine of *P7104 SF-V* failed as F/O Davidson approached to land on 30 March. The ORB noted that although he piled up his aircraft, 'This was not his fault, but was caused by one of the numerous bumps in the aerodrome surface.'

April 1943

During April, the squadron carried out several shipping reconnaissances between the Hook of Holland and Boulogne, escorted by the Typhoons of 198 Squadron, but the ORB noted that 'shipping was conspicuous by its absence.' In fact, the only incident took place on 4 April when eight aircraft, escorted by nine Typhoons, searched for minesweepers reported off Dunquerque. There was a slight fog and the surface of the sea was dead calm. John McClure recalls, 'Shortly after slipping over the coast I looked across at P/O Dugdale, he had water streaming over him as he lifted out of the water with both props bent back over the cowlings. He then slipped back and slowly settled on the surface. He slid back the canopy and got out ok.'

P/O Norbury Dugdale and *P7002* ditched five miles off Dungeness; he was picked up by an air sea rescue launch after five minutes. Whilst his colleagues noted that the ditching would have been a credit to a Sunderland, the authorities were not as generous, and he was reprimanded for flying too low.

The squadron lost an old friend on 13 March, when Magister *T9908* had an engine failure and hit anti-landing poles whilst force landing near Birchington, Kent. She had been with the squadron since 2 November 1941, and the pilot was none other than W/C Guy Gibson, who just over a month later led 617 Squadron on the Dams Raid. Magister *L8280* was received as a replacement.

The next attack was Ramrod 56, also on 13 March, by eight aircraft. They crossed the enemy coast at Blankenberghe and dropped sixteen 250lb bombs in a dive from 12,000 to 7,000 feet on Brugge Marshalling Yards. Again, all bombs were seen to burst on the target and all aircraft returned safely despite heavy flak.

On 15 April, F/O John Maude Hadow carried out practice dive bombing over the Goodwin Sands, but as he approached Manston on his return, he attempted one more

P/O Norbury Dugdale, seen here in *P7104 SF-V,* ditched his Whirlwind on 4 April. *(Terry Smith archives)*

F/O John Hadow, seen here in *P7104 SF-V*, was lost on 15 April. (*Terry Smith archives*)

dive. *P7121 SF-C* pulled out at 7,000 feet, flicked over onto her back and dived into the ground 200 yards from 'B' Flight dispersal. The ORB noted, 'He had only been with the squadron a short time, but had made himself very popular.'

There were five successful anti-shipping sorties under Swingate CHL Control. W/O Ashton and Sgt A. C. Smith were vectored on to twelve E-Boats near Le Tréport, and damaged several; F/O R. L. Smith attacked an armed trawler off Berck sur Mer in a dive from 1,500 feet, seeing a bright red flash, whilst F/O Musgrave bombed an armed trawler off Berck sur Mer, which broke in half and burned furiously for one and a half minutes before there was an explosion and the fire went out. Finally, Sgt A. C. Smith, on his second sortie, found an E-Boat off Blankenberghe. It took evasive action but his first bomb fell beside and stopped it, and his second bomb caused a large explosion, signifying its demise.

Eighteen individual sorties were flown during the moon period, and at least eleven locomotives were destroyed or damaged along with numerous rail trucks and tracks. Unfortunately, of the three Rhubarbs flown on 25 March, two were successful, but the third resulted in the loss of F/O Rebbetoy.

F/O DeHoux and Sgt Witham destroyed four and damaged nine of twenty barges near Brugge; F/O McClure and F/S Woodhouse destroyed a locomotive and sank a barge near Gent before being intercepted by a brace of Fw.190 fighters. F/S Woodhouse climbed into cloud, avoiding six streams of tracer as he did so, but F/O McClure could not reach the cloud in time, so although he was out of ammunition, he turned into his attackers who dived away, thus allowing him to escape. F/L Bryan and F/O Rebbetoy found a train with

F/O James Rebbetoy RCAF was lost on 25 April. (*Alec Torrance archives*)

W/O William Malia, seen here in *P7104 SF-V*, was posted on 10 April. (*Terry Smith archives*)

five coaches near Thielt, but as F/L Bryan commenced his attack, he recognised it as a flak train and immediately sheared off. He told F/O Rebbetoy to do the same, but the latter continued his attack, obtaining strikes on the locomotive and tender, but was hit by return fire. *P7058 SF-G* crashed inverted into an unoccupied house near Wijnendale, killing him instantly. She was still carrying her bombs, and as these did not detonate, the Germans forced local civilians to remove them the following day.

F/L Bryan returned to base to report the loss of F/O James Reginald Rebbetoy. S/L Coghlan wrote to his father:

> I should like to say that your son joined my squadron approximately a year and a half ago as a Sergeant, and from the very moment of joining the squadron had shown himself to be a very fine pilot, exceptionally keen and most efficient, and six months after his joining the squadron I was very happy to be able to recommend him for a commission, so that he could become one of my officers. Since that time he has done extremely well and was in the front line in the squadron for being recommended for a DFC, and but for his unfortunate loss he would have certainly earned this distinction. Apart from the work side he was very much beloved by the squadron and he had a personality which we will always remember.

Other personnel changes saw F/O Bernard Soulsby, Sgt Douglas Harris, and Sgt William John Evans arrive for flying duties, whilst W/O William Malia was posted after just a month with the squadron. Also leaving was F/L Gordon Edmund William Priest, who had been Adjutant since November 1942. He was replaced by F/L John Douglas Thomas.

The final operation of the month, on the twenty-ninth, was a Ramrod against Eu marshalling yards, abandoned when the escorting Spitfire wing did not appear at the rendezvous point.

May 1943

May proved to be by far the busiest month for personnel movements since the squadron formed. S/L Humphrey St John Coghlan DFC, who had been Commanding Officer since November 1941, was posted to 11 Group and was replaced by S/L John Basil Wray, who had been with the squadron as a Supernummary since September 1942, whilst F/S John Gates RAAF, F/S Clarence Neal RAAF, and Sgt Alfred William Emslie RAAF reported for flying duties, and S/L Patrick Henry Lee, F/S Hugh Leo O'Neill, and P/O Dennis Lionel Patrick Moore, the squadron Engineering Officer since its formation, were posted. F/O Robert Leslie Smith DFC DFM was rested and F/O William Frank Hayman replaced F/L John Douglas Thomas as Adjutant.

Operational flying during the moon period was intense, with attacks on aerodromes, shipping, and rail targets, resulting in much damage, but also the loss of F/O Musgrave. The opening night of the moon period, the thirteenth, saw four sorties, three of which found targets. Sgt Sutherland and F/O Musgrave attacked fifteen minesweepers south west of Gris Nez, and F/S O'Neill bombed four minesweepers west of Hardelot. F/O DeHoux was the only pilot not to find a target. On the fourteenth, F/L Bryan and F/O Musgrave were airborne with the intention of patrolling off the enemy coast at first light,

P7011 SF-U and fitters at RAF Matlaske. (*Terry Smith archives*)

hoping to find some shipping. F/L Bryan swept Dieppe-Gris Nez without success, but F/O Musgrave bombed an M-class minesweeper off Oostende seeing it swing round and stop. He then strafed it, obtaining strikes and silencing the flak. During the night of 14 May, W/O Ashton bombed a 2,000 ton merchant vessel escorted by ten flak ships off Le Touquet, seeing a flash, but F/S Woodhouse and Sgt Barclay, who saw the explosions from twelve miles away, were unable to locate it.

There were four uneventful shipping patrols between Zeebrugge and Boulogne on 15 May, but over enemy territory F/O Musgrave bombed two barges near Courtrai, then strafed the locomotive of a train drawing ten goods trucks near Torhout, leaving it a 'red mass'. F/S O'Neill destroyed a barge south of Furnes; Sgt Barclay bombed railway lines and W/O Ashton damaged three of six barges near Aire sur la Lys.

Eight sorties were flown during the night of 16 May. F/L Bryan bombed a concentration of thirty barges near Béthune and damaged the locomotive of a goods train; W/O Brunet sank one of fifteen E-Boats he found off Nieuwpoort, W/O Ashton, Sgt Barclay, and Sgt A. C. Smith bombed Amiens-Glisy, Moyencourt and Calais-Marck aerodromes respectively. F/O McClure bombed Poix aerodrome despite intense light flak and searchlights, then had trouble over Ashford with friendly searchlights and flak on his return. Only F/O DeHoux and Sgt Sutherland found no targets.

Around this period, S/L Wray attempted a daylight Rhubarb, which had to be abandoned before leaving the ground. He recalled:

> The usual procedure was to start our engines at the pre-determined time, taxi to the end of the runway and form up. We would take off together with the No. 2 slightly behind and to one side.

F/O Eddie Musgrave DFC RAAF was lost on 17 May. (*John LaGette archives*)

> On this particular day I got to the runway and waited but when I looked around my No. 2 was sat about fifty yards away. I thought this was unusual and signalled for him to close up; he waved back but didn't move. We always maintained R/T silence, hence the hand signals. Eventually he turned around and taxied back to the dispersal. I had no option but to follow, thinking he had a technical failure. After I parked up, I switched off the engine, got out of the aircraft and went over to him. 'What's the matter old chap' I said. His reply shook me slightly, 'One of your bombs fell off!' As it had not fallen far enough to arm itself there was little danger of it exploding but it must have been alarming for him to have seen it happen.

The night of 17 May saw five aircraft leave Manston to attack shipping reported in the Mardyk and Gravelines areas. F/O DeHoux, Sgt Sutherland and Sgt Witham attacked two minesweepers escorting eight loaded barges off Mardyk. F/L Bryan found three minesweepers north east of Gravelines. His bombs fell alongside one of them causing it to swing round through 90 degrees. F/O Edward Lancelot Musgrave DFC RAAF (*P7063*) took off to attack shipping in the Gravelines area, but did not return. He was plotted by the CHL station attacking ships, and was then heard to say over the radio that he was attacking again with cannon, but his plot then disappeared and it was assumed he was shot down by flak. The ORB noted, 'He was a keen and efficient pilot, very popular with the squadron.' The following night, F/L Bryan and W/O Brunet flew uneventful shipping recces from Gris Nez to Oostende. Sgt Sutherland returned with technical problems, but the remaining eight aircraft attacked their targets. W/O Brunet bombed one of seven E-Boats leaving Gravelines, leaving it stationary and listing badly; F/O DeHoux released his bombs on the leader of four minesweepers half a mile off Gravelines jetty. F/O Soulsby

Sgt Fowler and Sgt Lyatt. (*Alec Torrance archives*)

bombed the leader of five minesweepers he found two miles off Nieuwpoort despite intense flak, then fired a four second burst of cannon at one of three E-Boats north of Dunkerque. Finally, F/L Torrance bombed one of six E-Boats off Oostende, W/O Ashton attacked a minesweeper and four barges off Nieuwpoort, and Sgt Barclay bombed one of nine minesweepers he found three miles off Dunkerque. Unfortunately they were unable to observe the results. At the same time as the shipping attacks, F/O McClure and Sgt A. C. Smith crossed the enemy coast and searched for rail targets. McClure destroyed a goods trains near Courtrai whilst Smith found a convoy of large military lorries ten miles from Gent which he bombed then raked with cannon fire, destroying at least four and damaging many others.

Twelve sorties were flown during the night of 19 May, F/O DeHoux bombed Crécy-en-Ponthieu aerodrome, seeing bursts on a group of buildings whilst W/O Brunet inadvertently passed over Amiens-Glisy aerodrome at 200 feet, receiving intense light flak and being illuminated by six searchlights for his troubles. He dropped his bombs on several buildings however, seeing two explosions. F/L Bryan met a Ju.88 head on near Abbeville-Glisy aerodrome but then lost it in the dark. He too flew across the aerodrome at low level, was illuminated by two searchlights but bombed several large buildings. Sgt A. C. Smith bombed Poix aerodrome, and noted ten dispersed aircraft, but W/O Ashton arrived over Poix to find the aerodrome lighting and flare path on and an unidentified aircraft taking off. He gave it a four second burst of cannon but could not observe results before he dropped his bombs on the middle of the flare path. At the same time as the aerodrome attacks, F/L Torrance, F/O McClure, F/O Soulsby and F/S O'Neill were searching for rail targets; none were forthcoming however so they all bombed rail tracks. Sgt Sutherland damaged five barges he found south of Brugge, whilst F/O R. L. Smith and

S/L Humphrey St John Coghlan DFC was rested on 23 May. (*Mike Coghlan archives*)

S/L John Wray assumed command of the Squadron on 23 May. (*Terry Smith archives*)

P/O Roberts encountered fog near the Belgian coast and returned to base.

On 23 May, after an incredibly long tour, two years with 263 and 137 without a break, S/L Coghlan was posted to 11 Group and his place was taken by S/L Wray. The following incident was not mentioned in the ORB, but happened around this time. John Wray recalls:

> One night, we were sitting in the briefing room at Manston drinking coffee at about 0330, when I thought I heard an Oxford fly overhead. I thought this was odd because a training aircraft should not have been in our area, especially at night. Almost immediately the telephone rang and an excited Air Traffic Control WAAF said 'A Focke-Wulf Fw.190 has just landed.' We rushed out of the briefing room, just as the Fw.190 came to a halt. I jumped onto the wing and as the pilot opened the hood, he got my revolver in his ear. He was 'helped' out of the cockpit by several of my pilots and led off to the briefing room. It turned out our beacon was flashing the same letter as a beacon he was expecting to see on Cap Gris Nez, and as he was short of fuel, he landed. The aircraft was a brand new 190 of the latest mark, an absolute prize. My senior Flight Commander, Mike Bryan, was waiting to land in his Whirlwind having just returned from this German's home base. In fact, he'd been following him round the airfield for ten minutes not realising the other fellow was a Hun. Lucky for the Hun, because Mike was a mean man and would have had no compunction in shooting him down. I said I would taxi the 190 to a hangar, and was given plenty of advice to the effect that the pilot had probably set a switch, so that when I opened the throttle the aircraft would blow up. My main concern however was that I might inadvertently pull up the undercart. Anyway, with a prayer in my heart, and everybody else hurrying to a safe distance, I opened the throttle and taxied safely away. A test pilot from Farnborough collected it the following day.
>
> A few months previously, 609, the other squadron at Manston had captured an enemy aircraft in similar circumstances. Their pilot was taken to the mess, fed, and had his photo taken with their goat mascot, but when the intelligence people arrived to interrogate him they berated the CO for treating him so well and putting him at his ease. We therefore did not offer our fellow any food and locked him up until the intelligence bods came next morning. Needless to say they tore a strip off me in front of him for not treating him well. They told me later that it was part of their psychological approach to convince him they were friendly and he could trust them.[3]

The pilot, Unteroffizer Heinz Ehrhardt, and Focke-Wulf Fw.190A-4/U8 *Red 9+* of 1/SKG 10, had taken off from St Omer, and become lost. The aircraft was given RAF serial number *PM679* and sent to A&AEE Boscombe Down, then 1426 (Enemy Aircraft) Flight, for evaluation but was broken up for spares in July 1944.

June 1943

John Wray remembered:

> It was fairly obvious that our time with the Whirlwind was coming to an end, and we all looked forward to equipping with the Typhoon. I had flown them with 181 and 174 Squadrons, but none of my pilots had and as I did not want us taken out of the front line to train, I spoke to my good

> friend Bee Beaumont, CO of 609 on the other side of the aerodrome, and was very grateful when he agreed that my pilots could train with his squadron so when the time came I would be able to say to the AOC that my chaps were fully operational and could just receive our new aircraft and remain in the front line. Things did not go according to plan however.
>
> Our local pub was the Walmer Castle in Westgate, and I was in there one day in late May when the Station Equipment Officer came up and said, 'I hear you're being re-equipped with Hurricanes.' I said, 'Don't be ridiculous, we are getting Typhoons.' 'Bet you're not, I've just received the paperwork, the spares are already en-route.' I just couldn't believe it, so next day I went up to 11 Group to see the AOC and asked him what was going on. He phoned the SASO at Fighter Command, a chap called 'Cab' Calloway. I was then treated to a comical one-sided conversation that went something like, 'What? Oh, Ah, You don't say, Oh that's a shame.' He finished the call then filled me in. 'Because of the shortage of Sabre engines no more Typhoon Squadrons are being formed at the moment so you're getting the Vengeance.' I said, 'What's that?' He said it was an American dive bomber. I was crushed. What would I tell my chaps? I went back to Manston feeling very depressed, and once I told everyone, they became very depressed as well. All this happened at the same time that Biggin Hill held their famous 1,000 kill party at Grosvenor House, and anyone who had served in the Biggin Hill Wing was invited. As that included me I went along and whilst there I bumped into an old friend and ex-Battle of Britain pilot – Mike Crossley. At the end of his tour he had been despatched to America to test their aircraft to see which were suitable for RAF use. I asked him if he had flown the Vengeance, he said he had but when I asked him what it was like, there was a long pause then he said, 'Well, it dives very well.' I returned to Manston in a very much more depressed state, and sure enough, a few days later I received a signal notifying me that we were to re-equip – with the Hurricane IV.[4]

The first operational sorties of the month saw S/L Wray and F/O DeHoux, escorted by two Typhoons of 609 Squadron, badly damage two of four M class minesweepers they found off Ambleteuse, but the operational commitment during the moon period was directed at the aerodromes of Amiens-Glisy (six sorties), Coxyde-Furnes (three sorties), and Poix (nineteen sorties). These attacks resulted in bombs being dropped on hangars and runways, and were mostly without incident, although on one sortie W/O Brunet did inadvertently fly over Abbeville aerodrome at 200 feet, where he was greeted with intense accurate light flak and searchlights, and his aircraft took several hits, whilst and on another S/L Wray fired at a Fw.190, seeing strikes on its tail before it disappeared in the dark.

On Monday 21, five Whirlwinds flew to Manston for a night attack on Poix aerodrome. S/L Wray, F/L Bryan, F/O Luing and F/S Ashton observed explosions from their 500lb bombs on the runway. Sgt John McGowan Barclay could not find the target so bombed a stationary goods train near Rue instead. Unfortunately, as he approached Manston on his return, the starboard Exactor jammed in the fully open position and the engine lost power, the port engine then failed through lack of fuel, and he force-landed in a field just short of the runway. Although he walked away from the crash unhurt, *P6993 SF-A* was written off and the ORB noted, 'This proved to be an unfortunate climax to the squadron's association with the Whirlwind, as during the last week of the month the remaining aircraft were transferred to 263 Squadron and we took possession of our new Hurricane

P/O Gordon Chalmers in *SF-N*. (*Terry Smith archives*)

F/O Phillip Unwin, Gordon Chalmers, and Sgt Tom Sutherland. (*Terry Smith archives*)

Sgt Eddie Ashworth reported for flying duties on 8 June but did not fly a Whirlwind. (*Edwin Ashworth archives*)

Sgt Edmund Bolster was posted on 30 June. (*Terry Smith archives*)

Mk.IVs.'

Personnel changes saw F/O Philip Herbert Buxton Unwin, Sgt Edwin Ashworth, and Sgt John Thomas Naldrett Frost RAAF arrive, whilst out went F/L John Edward McClure RCAF, back to 263 Squadron, P/O Desmond Arthur Roberts RNZAF, Sgt Edmund Alexander Bolster, Sgt William John Evans, and F/S Robert Woodhouse. Also leaving was the squadron MO F/L Robert Smollet Flynn, who was replaced by F/O James Lawson Morgan. The squadron also moved to Southend, although the month's operational flying took place from Manston.

Despite S/L Wray's best intentions, 137 became non-operational for three weeks. The Hurricanes, although armed with two 40-mm cannon or eight rockets, were much slower than the Whirlwind and were not popular. Morale took a dip, but following six months of operations the squadron converted to the Typhoon and operated successfully as the only Typhoon squadron in the campaign against the V1 flying bombs before transferring to 2nd TAF in Europe where they were known as the 'Rocketeers.'

PART 2

THE FACTS BEHIND THE FLYING

4

Pilots of 263 & 137 Squadrons

ABRAMS Basil Courtney
Nationality: South African. *S/n:* 1377968 (Sgt), 133547 (Officer) RAFVR. *Rank:* Sergeant; Pilot Officer on 28 September 1942; Flying Officer on 28 March 1943. *Squadron:* 263. *Flight:* B. *In:* 11 November 1941 from 55 OTU. *First Whirlwind Op:* 13 February 1942. *Out:* 18 April 1943 MIA. *Hours:* 115:55 on 108 ops. *Incidents: P7056* tail wheel collapsed at Charmy Down on 25 January 1942; *P7041* caught by a tail wind and hit a dispersal bay at Fairwood Common on 2 April 1942. *Nickname:* Bas. *Remarks:* Born in 1922 and educated at Felsted School, Dunmow, he was a keen cricketer. 'An excellent pilot' he disappeared in *P7009* off Ouistreham, possibly shot down by an armed trawler (*see also* Philip Harvey) and his name appears on Panel 122 of the Runnymede Memorial.

ALBERTINI Antony Victor
Nationality: British. *S/n:* 119844 RAFVR. *Rank:* Sergeant; Flight Sergeant. *Squadron:* 263. *Flight:* B. *In:* 17 May 1941 from 600 Squadron. *First Whirlwind Op:* 26 May 1941. *Out:* 7 November 1941 to 137 Squadron. *Squadron:* 137. *Flight:* B. *In:* 7 November 1941 from 263 Squadron. *First Whirlwind Op:* Not operational. *Out:* 1 December 1941 Non Effective. *Hours:* 33:20 on 24 ops. *Incidents: P7013* hit by flak on 12 August 1941. *Nickname:* Tony. *Remarks:* Born on 29 September 1920, in Dartford, Kent, he joined 600 Squadron in 1938 as an Air Gunner, fought with them in the Battle of Britain, and damaged Blenheim *L6266* in a night landing at Catterick on 12 November 1940, then on 6 November 1941 he lost an eye in a clay pigeon shooting accident with 263 and his move to 137 was on paper only. He was one of twenty-six pilots who served with both Whirlwind Squadrons. Transferred to the Flying Control Branch as a Pilot Officer on 29 April 1942, he was Mentioned in Despatches on 8 June 1944, finished the war as a Flight Lieutenant and was posted to Prague where he teamed up with F/L Frank Dimblebee and was released in 1946. He passed away in September 1992.

ASHTON Joel Hilton
Nationality: Canadian. *S/n:* J/17890 RCAF. *Rank:* Sergeant; Flight Sergeant on 15 March 1942. *Squadron:* 137. *Flight:* A. *In:* 21 December 1941 from 57 OTU. *First Whirlwind Op:* 21 December 1941. *Out:* 30 November 1943 Rested. *Hours:* 91:30 on 78 ops: *Claims:* Do.217 of 3/KG.2 destroyed on 20 June 1942 in *P7012 SF-V* shared with W/O Mercer. *Incidents: P7012 SF-V* force landed at Matlaske on 18 June 1942. *Nickname:* Hilt. *Remarks:* He enlisted on 23 October 1940, in Toronto, flew seven ops on 137's Hurricane IVs and was awarded the DFC on 23 October 1943, but did not receive the medal until 24 June 1945.

He destroyed a Me.109 on 20 April 1945, finished the war as a Flight Lieutenant with 401 Squadron and passed away in 1996.

ASHWORTH Edwin

Nationality: British. *S/n:* 1318546 RAFVR. *Rank:* Sergeant. *Squadron:* 137. *Flight:* A. *In:* 8 June 1943 from 52 OTU. *First Whirlwind Op:* Not operational. *Out:* 4 January 1945 Rested. *Nickname:* Eddie. *Remarks:* He joined the squadron too late to fly Whirlwinds, but completed five ops on Hurricane IVs and 106 more on Typhoons. On 29 October 1944, he abandoned *MN995 SF-X* when she was hit by flak and set on fire, but despite damage to his parachute he landed safely in Allied lines. He finished the war as a Flight Lieutenant and became a Prison Officer.

BAKER Ernest Reginald DFC*

Nationality: British. *S/n:* 40660 RAF. *Rank:* Squadron Leader. *Squadron:* 263. *Flight:* Commanding Officer. *In:* 15 June 1943 from 182 Squadron. *First Whirlwind Op:* 13 July 1943. *Out:* 5 December 1943 to 146 Wing: *Awards:* Bar to DFC on 27 September 1943. *Hours:* 46:00 on 40 ops: *Claims:* Ju.88 of KG.26 destroyed on 14 August 1943 in *P7113*: *Call Sign:* Lochinvar. *Incidents: P7096* hit a ridge landing at Warmwell and port undercarriage broke off on 10 September 1943; *P7111 HE-W* exactor failure on 15 August 1943; *P6990* hit by flak on 24 October 1943; *P6983* hit by flak on 26 November 1943. *Nickname:* Reggie. *Remarks:* Born in Doncaster on 30 March 1914, he began the war flying Sunderlands with 210 Squadron and received the DFC on 22 November 1940 for sinking two U-Boats. He converted to fighters for his second tour. Awarded the DSO on 15 June 1944, he was shot down by flak whilst leading his Wing on the following day in Typhoon *MN754*. As he was crashing his pilots heard, 'Hello all Carefree and Vampire aircraft, Port 180 degrees Lochinvar Out.' Aged thirty, he is buried in Beny sur Mer Canadian War Cemetery, Calvados.

BARCLAY John McGowan

Nationality: British. *S/n:* 655794 RAFVR. *Rank:* Flight Sergeant. *Squadron:* 137. *Flight:* B. *In:* 27 June 1942 from 58 OTU. *First Whirlwind Op:* 12 October 1942. *Out:* 9 October 1942 to 263 Squadron. *Squadron:* 263. *Flight:* B. *In:* 10 October 1942 from 137 Squadron. *First Whirlwind Op:* 17 October 1942. *Out:* 16 February 1943 to 137 Squadron. *Squadron:* 137. *Flight:* A. *In:* 16 February 1943 from 263 Squadron. *First Whirlwind Op:* 23 February 1943. *Out:* 31 July 1943 KIFA. *Hours:* 38:30 on 28 ops, 231:00 total: *Claims:* Ju.88 damaged on 20 August 1942 in *P6982*. *Incidents: P7037 SF-J* hit boundary fence at Manston on 5 October 1942; *P6986* engine failure on 30 April 1942; *P7056* hit by flak on 17 June 1943; *P7111* hit by flak on 18 June 1943; *P7011 SF-U* tail wheel collapsed at Rochford on 20 June 1943; *P6993 SF-A* force landed near Manston with battle damage on 21 June 1943. *Nickname:* Titch. *Remarks:* He was one of twenty-six pilots who flew with both Whirlwind Squadrons, and was known as the 137 Squadron joker. On 21 June 1943, when he force landed *P6993 SF-A* near Manston with battle damage, it was 137's final Whirlwind sortie and final Whirlwind casualty. He converted to Hurricane IVs, but on 31 July 1943 the ORB noted, F/S Barclay was out as No. 1 to P/O Johnstone and diving from 2,000 feet in order to shake P/O Johnstone off his tail, could not pull out and hit the ground, his aircraft bursting into flames near Malden, Essex. He is buried in Brookwood Military Cemetery, Surrey, plot 25.C.9.

BARR Alexander
Nationality: Canadian. *S/n:* J/26504 RCAF. *Rank:* Pilot Officer. *Squadron:* 263. *Flight:* A: *In* 20 September 1943 from 55 OTU. *First Whirlwind Op:* 24 October 1943. *Out:* 14 October 1944 KIA. *Hours:* 2:35 on 3 ops. *Nickname:* Sandy. *Remarks:* Born in Hamilton, Ontario, of Scottish parents, he was awarded his 'Wings' in April 1942 but remained in Canada as an instructor before being posted to the UK. He was killed in *MN769 HE-B* south of Oostburg when it was struck by *R8923 HE-U* which had been shot down by flak. Aged twenty-four, he was buried in Plot 6.E.9 of the Bergen-Op-Zoom Canadian War Cemetery.

BARTLETT Leonard Harold
Nationality: British. *S/n:* 102959 RAFVR. *Rank:* Pilot Officer; Flying Officer on 11 May 1942; Flight Lieutenant on 10 December 1942. *Squadron:* 137. *Flight:* A Commander. *In:* 10 February 1942 from 59 OTU. *First Whirlwind Op:* 18 February 1942. *Out:* 16 September 1942 to 253 Squadron. *Hours:* 138:05 on 109 ops: *Claims:* Ju.88 damaged on 6 July 1942 in *P7111*. *Incidents: P7058 SF-G* tail wheel collapsed at Drem on 8 August 1942. *Nickname:* Red. *Remarks:* Born on 20 June 1916, he was an assistant buyer at Smithfield Market prior to enlisting in May 1939, and fought through the Battle of Britain with 17 Squadron sharing in the destruction of two Ju.88s. On 18 March 1941 he was shot down over Chiddingly, Sussex in Hurricane II *Z2704*, but bailed out wounded and on his recovery was posted to 137 Squadron where he was, 'Very popular with all ranks, and a very efficient Flight Commander.' He later commanded 253 Squadron; then Vis Island off Yugoslavia and finished the war with a DSO; Mentioned in Despatches; a US Legion of Merit and four enemy aircraft destroyed. He was one of the Group Captains who escorted Winston Churchill's coffin, and he retired from the RAF on 20 June 1966 and emigrated to Australia.

BEAUMONT Robert Charles
Nationality: British. *S/n:* 1301714 (Sgt); 169061 (Officer) RAFVR. *Rank:* Sergeant, Flight Sergeant on 13 January 1943; Pilot Officer on 7 December 1943. *Squadron:* 263. *Flight:* A. *In:* 1 June 1943 from 55 OTU. *First Whirlwind Op:* 20 July 1943. *Out:* 15 May 1944 to RAF Harrowbeer. *Hours:* 21:56 on 19 ops. *Incidents: P7096* crashed at Warmwell on 17 August 1943; *P7046* hit by flak on 24 October 1943. *Nickname:* Bob. *Remarks:* A talented artist, he illustrated the unofficial 'diary' and painted the nose-art on several Whirlwinds. He later flew twenty ops on Typhoons and was 'Posted to Harrowbeer on the way to marriage and non-operational flying, after a gallant and successful first tour.' He was killed when 84 GSU Typhoon *JP664* crashed into a hill at Encomb Wood near Piddletrentide, Dorset, on 18 August 1944. Aged twenty-two, he is buried in Wellingborough Doddington Road Cemetery, Northants, Block S Grave 16.

BELL Colin Douglas
Nationality: Australian. *S/n:* 741449 RAAF. *Rank:* Sergeant. *Squadron:* 263. *Flight:* A. *In:* 20 January 1942 from 61 OTU. *First Whirlwind Op:* Not operational. *Out:* 21 March 1942 to 450 Squadron. *Nickname:* Dinger. *Remarks:* Born in Sydney, he enlisted on 6 January 1941. He left 263 for the Middle East to fly Kittyhawks, and was shot down by flak off Vlissingen in 127 Squadron Spitfire XI *PL326* on 11 September 1944. Aged twenty-five, he is buried in Oostende New Communal Cemetery, Plot 9, Row 5, Grave 39.

BELL Eric Wilfred

Nationality: British. *S/n:* 77775 RAF. *Rank:* Pilot Officer. *Squadron:* 263. *Flight:* A. *In:* 27 June 1940 from 1 Airfield Construction Squadron. *First Whirlwind Op:* Not operational. *Out:* 24 July 1940 KIFA. *Remarks:* Born in Edmonton, London, he was a talented artist and worked for Lloyds Bank before enlisting on 16 April 1938, but was killed on 24 July 1940 whilst on a twin-engine conversion course at 5 OTU when Blenheim IF *L1105* suffered engine failure and crashed near Frampton Mansell, Gloucestershire. A memorial was later placed at the site. Aged twenty-three, he is buried in Brandon Hill Cemetery, Wallington, Surrey, Section P Grave 290.

BLACKLOCK Norman Peter

Nationality: British. *S/n:* 1294837 (Sgt); 147757 (Officer) RAFVR. *Rank:* Sergeant; Pilot Officer on 15 June 1943; Flying Officer on 15 December 1943. *Squadron:* 263. *Flight:* A; B. *In:* 25 February 1943 from 56 OTU. *First Whirlwind Op:* 4 August 1943. *Out:* 5 February 1944 MIA. *Hours:* 21:45 on 17 ops. *Incidents: P6971* crashed at Warmwell on 19 October 1943. *Nickname:* Blackie. *Remarks:* Born in Brentford, London. Later flew five ops on Typhoons, but failed to return in *JR251*. He was heard to say over the R/T, 'Apples are Red' indicating that he was attacking, but except for a faint 'I am going to...' nothing more was heard. He was regarded as a 'press-on type' and it is thought that he attempted to dive bomb E-Boats off Cap de la Hague, despite being on his first night operational flight in a Typhoon. Aged twenty-four, his name appears on Panel 204 of the Runnymede Memorial.

BLACKSHAW Herbert John DFC

Nationality: British. *S/n:* 1152371 (Sgt); 111980 (Officer) RAFVR. *Rank:* Sergeant; Pilot Officer on 15 November 1941; Flying Officer on 1 October 1942; Flight Lieutenant on 1 September 1942. *Squadron:* 263. *Flight:* A; B; A Commander. *In:* 1 April 1941 from 501 Squadron. *First Whirlwind Op:* 25 April 1941. *Out:* 15 May 1943 KIA: *Awards:* DFC on 17 February 1943. *Hours:* 171.35 on 148 ops. *Incidents: P7040* engine failure on 22 March 1943. *Nickname:* Blackie. *Remarks:* Born in Rickmansworth, London on 16 September 1916, he was a Company Representative before enlisting. He returned from America on the White Star *Georgic* on 18 July 1939 to join the RAF. Awarded the DFC at the same time as S/L Warnes, he was killed when *P7094 HE-T* crashed near Exeter. 'The loss of Blackie as a friend, leader and councillor in every matter concerned with the squadron's activities was extremely severe. A careful and clever pilot, he was shrewd, witty and gentle as a person.' Aged twenty-six, he is buried in Warmwell (Holy Trinity) Churchyard.

BOLSTER Edmund Alexander

Nationality: British. *S/n:* 1090706 RAFVR. *Rank:* Sergeant. *Squadron:* 137. *Flight:* A. *In:* 25 October 1942 from 55 OTU. *First Whirlwind Op:* 4 November 1942. *Out:* 30 June 1943 to 247 Squadron. *Hours:* 5:50 on 7 ops. *Nickname:* Paddy. *Remarks:* Wrote off *P7061 SF-A* when he collided with *P7102* whilst taxiing at Manston on 13 January 1943. Transferred to 247 Squadron, he accidentally shot W/O Betts on 4 July 1944. Demoted and severely reprimanded, he survived the war.

BRACKLEY Robert Arthur
Nationality: British. *S/n:* 518164 RAFVR. *Rank:* Sergeant. *Squadron:* 263. *Flight:* B. *In:* 2 June 1941 from 55 OTU. *First Whirlwind Op:* 15 June 1941. *Out:* 1 December 1941 to 2 Delivery *Flight: Whirlwind Hours:* 31:45 on 25 ops: *Claims:* Me.109 of JG.2 destroyed on 6 August 1941 in *P6983*. *Incidents: P6983 HE-H* force landed at Hurn on 6 August 1941. *Remarks:* Born in Lewes, East Sussex in 1916. Shot down in 253 Squadron Hurricane *L1655* on 18 May 1940, he then became an instructor with 55 OTU where as a passenger in Master *T8610* he was involved in a crash-landing at Pannal near Harrogate as the Unit transferred from Aston Down to Usworth. He finished the war as a Flight Lieutenant and passed away in Bedford in 1978.

BRANNIGAN Stewart Gordon
Nationality: New Zealander. *S/n:* NZ/404885 RNZAF. *Rank:* Pilot Officer. *Squadron:* 263. *Flight:* A. *In:* 13 January 1942 from 61 OTU. *Out:* 11 March 1942 to 2 Delivery Flight. *In:* 19 April 1942 from 286 Squadron. *First Whirlwind Op:* Not operational. *Out:* 5 May 1942 to 118 Squadron. *Nickname:* Brandy. *Remarks:* Born on 22 August 1918. He was possibly operational on Whirlwinds. Lost over the Channel in 501 Squadron Spitfire Vb *EP128 SD-J* on 11 August 1942 in combat with Fw.190s of 9/JG2. Aged twenty-three, his name appears on Panel 115 of the Runnymede Memorial.

BREARLEY Edgar
Nationality: Canadian. *S/n:* R/78087 (Sgt); J/15157 RCAF (Officer) RCAF. *Rank:* Flight Sergeant on 1 February 1942; Pilot Officer on 5 February 1942; Flying Officer on 24 November 1942. *Squadron:* 263. *Flight:* B. *In:* 9 October 1941 from 55 OTU. *Out:* 16 April 1943 KIA. *First Whirlwind Op:* 12 February 1942. *Hours:* 104:00 on 90 ops. *Incidents: P6995* force landed at Colerne on 24 October 1941: *P6979* damaged by flak from a Convoy off Cap de la Hague on 9th September 1942. *Remarks:* Born in England on 31 October 1916, his family emigrated to Canada in 1927. A stenographer before he enlisted on 9 October 1940. Failed to return from a night Intruder sortie in *P6995* and his body was later washed ashore near Swanage. Deputy 'B' Flight Commander, he had been with the squadron for nineteen months, and 'was so competent a pilot and likeable a person, that to write briefly of him scarcely does him justice.' Aged twenty-six, he is buried next to F/L Blackshaw in Warmwell (Holy Trinity) Churchyard.

BRENNAN John Robert
Nationality: Canadian. *S/n:* R/72637 RCAF. *Rank:* Sergeant. *Squadron:* 263. *Flight:* B. *In:* 9 October 1941 from 55 OTU. *Out:* 26 October 1941 to 137 Squadron. *First Whirlwind Op:* Not operational. *Squadron:* 137. *Flight:* B. *In:* 27 October 1941 from 263 Squadron. *First Whirlwind Op:* 23 November 1941. *Out:* 27 May 1942 KIA. *Hours:* 80:15 on 69 ops, 176:00 hours total: *Claims:* Ju.88 destroyed on 27 May 1942 in *P7122* shared with P/O LaGette. *Incidents: P7057 SF-S* engine failure and landed with the undercarriage retracted at Charmy Down on 28 October 1941: *P7111 SF-E* hit by flak on 15 May 1942. *Nickname:* Bob. *Remarks:* He was one of twenty-six pilots who served with both Whirlwind squadrons. The Ju.88 he destroyed with P/O LaGette was actually Blenheim *V5568* of 1401 Meteorological Flight, Bircham Newton, and the assumption is he realised his mistake, broke away and headed for

the Dutch coast despite being told he was headed in the wrong direction. He attacked the steel factories at Ijmuiden before *P7122* was shot down by flak near Velsen. Aged nineteen, he is buried in Bergen Op Zoom General Cemetery, Netherlands; Plot 1, Row C, Grave 3.

BRITTON Allan Walter Naylor

Nationality: British. *S/n:* 72033 RAFVR. *Rank:* Flying Officer. *Squadron:* 263. *Flight:* B. *In:* 21 April 1940 from 5 OTU. *First Whirlwind Op:* 9 December 1940. *Out:* 12 December 1940 KIFA. *Hours:* 1:00 on 1 Op, 9:00 hours total. *Remarks:* Born in Medway, Kent, in 1917, he learned to fly with the Cambridge University Air Squadron. An Honours Graduate he joined the RAFVR in November 1937, was called up in September 1939, and fought in both Norwegian campaigns. He converted to Hurricane Is then Whirlwinds, but was killed when *P6980* dived into Sand Bay, Weston-super-Mare during an air-sea firing exercise. Aged twenty-three, his name appears on Panel 5 of the Runnymede Memorial.

BROWN Alfred Edward

Nationality: British. *S/n:* 656417 (Sgt); 141474 (Officer) RAFVR. *Rank:* Sergeant; Pilot Officer on 9 January 1943. *Squadron:* 137. *Flight:* B. *In:* 27 June 1942 from 58 OTU. *First Whirlwind Op:* 12 August 1942. *Out:* 23 January 1943 MIA. *Hours:* 13:30 on 13 ops: *Claims:* Ju.88 damaged 19 August 1942 in *P6976. Remarks:* He failed to return from a Rhubarb near Doullens in *P7095 SF-H*, and at the end of the war his body was found buried near Lille aerodrome, forty miles from where he crash-landed, under the name Sgt Manston, (the aerodrome from which he took off). His dog-tags were missing and it was not certain how he died. His promotion to Pilot Officer came after his death, but was backdated to 9 January. Aged twenty-seven, he is buried in Plot 1, Avelin (Ennetières) Cemetery, Nord, France.

BRUNET Arthur Gaston

Nationality: Canadian. *S/n:* J/17907 RCAF. *Rank:* Sergeant; Flight Sergeant on 1 March 1942; Warrant Officer on 1 September 1942; Pilot Officer on 1 March 1943. *Squadron:* 137. *Flight:* A. *In:* 1 January 1942 from 59 OTU. *First Whirlwind Op:* 18 February 1942. *Out:* 16 October 1943 Rested. *Hours:* 110:05 on 100 ops. *Incidents: P7005 SF-H* tail wheel collapsed landing at Matlaske on 30 May 1942: *P6998* engine failure on take-off on 6 November 1942: *P7046* hit by flak on 12 February 1943: *P7046* hit by flak on 14 April 1943: *P7092 SF-U* hit by flak on 14 June 1943. *Nickname:* Art. *Remarks:* Born in St Thomas, Ontario, he enlisted on 19 September 1939. He damaged a Fw.190 on 24 July 1943; received the DFC 14 August 1943, and flew eight ops on Hurricane IVs before being Rested and returning to Canada on 8 November 1943.

BRYAN John Michael DFC

Nationality: British. *S/n:* 1195470 (Sgt); 102570 (Officer) RAFVR. *Rank:* Pilot Officer; Flying Officer on 1 October 1942; Flight Lieutenant on 16 February 1943. *Squadron:* 263. *Flight:* A. *In:* 13 September 1941 from 56 OTU. *First Whirlwind Op:* Not operational on Whirlwinds. *Out:* 1 October 1941 Posted. *Squadron:* 137. *Flight:* B; A Commander. *In:* 1 October 1941 from 263 Squadron. *First Whirlwind Op:* 15 November 1941. *Out:* 31 August 1943 Posted: *Awards:* DFC on 12 March 1943. *Hours:* 182:30 on 165 ops: *Claims:* Do.217E-4 *F8+BN* of 5/KG40 destroyed on 19 August 1942 in *P7121* shared with Sgt Roberts; Fw.190 probably destroyed on 19 December 1942 in *P7114* shared with P/O Rebbetoy. *Incidents: P7046* tail wheel collapsed at Matlaske on 27 February 1942: *P7046* tail wheel collapsed at Matlaske on 29 May: *P7105* damaged on 15 November 1941: *P7058 SF-G* crashed at Coltishall on 24 March 1942: *P7122* damaged 9 April 1942: *P7121 SF-C* crashed at Matlaske on 24 May 1942. *Remarks:* Born in South Norwood in 1922, he enlisted in 1940, and was one of twenty-four pilots who served with both Whirlwind Squadrons. He later flew seven operational sorties on Hurricane IVs and his keenness and efficiency had a lot to do with the excellent results obtained by the Squadron. Awarded the DFC and Bar for his constant good work with the squadron, he was promoted to command 198 Squadron, but as W/C Flying 136 Wing, he was shot down in Typhoon *MN415* near Falaise on 10 June 1944. Aged twenty-one, he is buried in Plot VII.G.5 of Bretteville-sur-Laize Canadian War Cemetery, Calvados, France.

BRYANT Robert Francis
Nationality: British. *S/n:* Fleet Air Arm. *Rank:* Sub-Lieutenant. *Squadron:* 263. *Flight:* A. *In:* 1 July 1940 from Fleet Air Arm. *First Whirlwind Op:* Not operational. *Out:* 10 July 1940 to 219 Squadron. *Remarks:* With 263 for nine days, he went to 219 then 245 Squadron before returning to the Fleet Air Arm in November 1940 to fly Fulmers with 805 Squadron. As a Lieutenant Commander he took command of 808 Squadron in June 1945 and led them in strikes against Sumatran airfields and providing cover for the occupation of Malaya after VJ-Day. He retired from the Navy in 1951.

BUCKWELL Geoffrey Leighton
Nationality: British. *S/n:* 1254477 RAFVR. *Rank:* Sergeant. *Squadron:* 263. *Flight:* B. *In:* 10 June 1941 from 52 OTU: *Whirlwind Hours:* 17:36 on 15 ops. *Out:* 4 September 1941 POW. *First Whirlwind Op:* 24 June 1941. *Remarks:* Born 29 January 1921, in Strait Settlement, Malaya, he grew up in England. Shot down in *P7042* by Oblt. Siegfried Schnell, his 50 victim, and became a POW in Lamsdorf, Poland. He emigrated to Australia post-war, became a Doctor and passed away on 2 May 2002, in Victoria. (*See Chapter 13*)

CARMICHAEL Dugald Andrew
Nationality: British. *S/n:* 129718 RAFVR. *Rank:* Flying Officer. *Squadron:* 263. *Flight:* B. *In:* 31 October 1943 from RAF Uxbridge. *First Whirlwind Op:* Not operational. *Out:* 5 November 1943 Posted. *Remarks:* With 263 for five days, he survived the war and was demobbed in October 1946.

CHALMERS Gordon Stanley
Nationality: British. *S/n:* 131146 RAFVR. *Rank:* Pilot Officer; Flying Officer on 30 April 1943. *Squadron:* 137. *Flight:* B. *In:* 12 March 1943 from 59 OTU. *First Whirlwind Op:* 29 May 1943. *Out:* 30 April 1944 to 198 Squadron. *Hours:* 2:30 on 3 ops. *Remarks:* Born on 21 November 1921 in Glasgow, he flew thirteen ops on the Hurricane IVs and fifteen on Typhoons before being posted to 198 Squadron. Posted to 263 as a Flight Lieutenant in 1944 then back to 198 Squadron where he was hit by flak in Typhoon *MN344* on 8 February 1945, he crash-landed on fire at B.86 Helmond. Mentioned in Despatches on 1 January 1946, he finished the war as a Flight Lieutenant and was promoted to Squadron Leader on 15 October 1954. He passed away in 2009.

CHARLTON John

Nationality: British. *S/n:* 153011 RAFVR. *Rank:* Flight Sergeant. *Squadron:* 263. *Flight:* A. *In:* 1 December 1943 from 55 OTU. *First Whirlwind Op:* Not operational. *Out:* 24 June 1944 KIA. *Nickname:* Charlie. *Remarks:* Shot down by flak over St Malo harbour in Typhoon *MN296* on his thirteenth operational sortie. Aged twenty-two, he is buried in Row G, Plot 15, Dinard British Cemetery Ille-et-Vilaine, St Malo France.

CLARK Colin Anthony Gordon

Nationality: South African. *S/n:* 42192 RAF. *Rank:* Flying Officer. *Squadron:* 263. *Flight:* B CO. *In:* 13 September 1941 from FIU. *First Whirlwind Op:* Not operational. *Out:* 20 September 1941 to 137 Squadron. *Squadron:* 137. *Flight:* A Commander. *In:* 22 September 1941 from 263 Squadron. *First Whirlwind Op:* 24 October 1941. *Out:* 30 October 1941 KIA. *Hours:* 4:45 on 4 ops. *Nickname:* Nobby. *Remarks:* A journalist before the war in South Africa, he joined 266 Squadron in October 1939, and the Fighter interception Unit on 25 June 1940. He was flying Blenheim *L6805* as a target aircraft for an AI-equipped Boston, on 13 October 1940, when an engine failure forced him to crash-land near Lancing College. The aircraft was written off but he was unhurt. He was one of twenty-six pilots who served with both Whirlwind Squadrons, and flew *P7091* on 137's first operation, but was forced to ditch in the Channel during the return flight and although rescued by a Destroyer, he died on board. Aged twenty-eight, he was buried in Geldeston (St Michael) Churchyard, Norfolk on 5 November 1941.

COGHLAN Humphrey St John DFC

Nationality: British. *S/n:* 90117 RAFVR. *Rank:* Pilot Officer; Flying Officer on 7 June 1941; Flight Lieutenant on 1 October 1941; Squadron Leader on 11 November 1941. *Squadron:* 263. *Flight:* B; B Commander. *In:* 16 May 1941 from 600 Squadron. *First Whirlwind Op:* 22 May 1941. *Out:* 2 November 1941 to 137 Squadron. *Squadron:* 137. *Flight:* Commanding Officer. *In:* 2 November 1941 from 263 Squadron. *First Whirlwind Op:* 4 November 1941. *Out:* 23 May 1943 to 11 Group HQ. *Hours:* 108:15 on 96 ops: *Awards:* DFC on 8 October 1941; Mentioned in Despatches on 1 January 1943. *Incidents: P6979* starboard tyre burst, ground looped and the undercarriage collapsed on 29 May 1941; *P6999* abandoned over Bath on 9 October 1941: *P7096* overshot landing and hit the boundary fence at Horsham St Faith on 14 February 1942: *P6998* crashed at Predannack on 29 September 1941: *P7111* hit by flak on 4 April 1943: *P7111* engine failure on 8 May 1943. *Nickname:* Humpers. *Remarks:* Born 18 April 1915, he joined the RAF in 1934 but resigned his Commission on 23 April 1937 when he joined the Auxiliary Air Force Reserve of Officers. He was one of twenty-six pilots who served with both Whirlwind Squadrons. On 14 February 1942, he overshot landing at Horsham St Faith in *P7096* and hit the boundary fence. This was fortuitous, however, as he met his future wife whilst there and they were married on 17 September 1942; Robert Woodward was his best man. Post-war, he was head of the Coghlan Iron & Steel Co. and he passed away in July 1988.

COOPER Peter Frederick

Nationality: British. *S/n:* 1477083 RAFVR. *Rank:* Sergeant; Flight Sergeant on 7 August 1943. *Squadron:* 263. *Flight:* A; B. *In:* 17 June 1943 from 59 OTU. *First Whirlwind Op:*

31 August 1943. *Out:* 22 December 1944 Rested. *Hours:* 9:25 on 8 ops. *Incidents: P6973* undercarriage collapsed, flak damage at Warmwell on 24 October 1943. *Remarks:* Born on 23 October 1921 in Blackpool. Crashed on landing at Warmwell on 1 August 1943, in *P6981,* due to a strong crosswind. The aircraft bounced, cart wheeled twice, lost both engines and wings and was written off – he walked away unhurt. Described as 'high, wide and handsome' he flew eighty-three ops on Typhoons and was Rested as a Flying Officer. He passed away in Lancaster in August 1986.

COTTON Maxwell Tylney DFC

Nationality: Australian. *S/n:* 408204 RAAF. *Rank:* Sergeant; Pilot Officer on 29 December 1942. *Squadron:* 263. *Flight:* A. *In:* 30 July 1942 from 87 Squadron. *First Whirlwind Op:* 10 October 1942. *Out:* 15 June 1943 MIA: *Awards:* DFC on 13 June 1943. *Hours:* 60:20 on 47 ops: *Claims:* Fw.190 of 10/JG.2 damaged on 14 December 1942 in *P7052. Incidents: P7108* hit by flak on 27 April 1943; *P7108* hit by flak on 21 May 1943; *P6981* hit by flak on 28 April 1943; *P7089* hit by flak on 23 May 1943. *Nickname:* Max. *Remarks:* Born on 2 May 1921, in Tasmania, he enlisted on 25 April 1941, in Hobart. 'A quiet modest Aussie, from the first, he proved himself to have an extraordinary flair for accurate bombing. Both in practice and in action he rarely missed a direct hit. As a pilot and leader, his matter-of-factness, calmness before, during and after an operation made him invaluable to the squadron. As a person his courtesy, frank and open nature and constant good humour endeared him to all who knew him.' He was shot down and killed attacking a convoy off Sark in *P7000.* Aged twenty-two, his name appears on Panel 190 of the Runnymede Memorial.

COYNE James Patrick DFC

Nationality: Canadian. *S/n:* J/15233 RCAF. *Rank:* Sergeant; Flight Sergeant on 1 December 1941; Pilot Officer on 26 February 1942; Flying Officer on 24 November 1942; Flight Lieutenant on 20 May 1943. *Squadron:* 263. *Flight:* A; A Commander. *In:* 1 September 1941 from 55 OTU. *First Whirlwind Op:* 12 December 1941. *Out:* 20 June 1943 Rested: *Awards:* DFC on 2 June 1943. *Hours:* 174:15 on 137 ops: *Claims:* Fw.190 of 10/JG.2 damaged on 14 December 1942 in *P7057*; Fw.190 of NAG.13 damaged on 16 May 1943 in *P7110 HE-E. Incidents: P7108* swung off the runway at Fairwood Common and turned over on 14 February 1942; *P7108* hit by flak on 26 March 1943. *Nickname:* Curly. *Remarks:* Born near God's Lake, Manitoba, on 23 October 1920, he enlisted on 10 October 1940, received his 'Wings' on 10 June 1941, and was posted to the UK and 55 OTU the following month. He became 'A' Flight Commander on 20 May 1943, and his DFC, although effective from 1 June 1943, was only presented by the King on the 8 February 1944. He was posted as President of the RCAF Aircrew Reselection Board in Warrington before returning to Canada on rest, but he was back in the UK in 1944 as a Squadron Leader for a tour with 418 Squadron on Mosquitoes. He remained in the post-war RCAF and served in staff positions until his retirement in 1965, when he became a teacher. During training, he appeared as an 'extra' in the 1942 James Cagney film *Captains of the Clouds* and knew John Gillespie, the author of 'High Flight': 'Maggy was one place ahead of me on our Wings Parade.' He passed away in February 2013.

CRABTREE Norman Vincent

Nationality: American. *S/n:* J/107779 RCAF. *Rank:* Pilot Officer. *Squadron:* 137. *Flight:* B. *In:* 1 October 1941 from 55 OTU. *First Whirlwind Op:* Not operational. *Out:* 2 November 1941 to 263 Squadron. *Squadron:* 263. *Flight:* B. *In.* 2 November 1941 from 137 Squadron. *First Whirlwind Op:* 30 December 1941. *Out:* 29 September 1942 to 8 USAAF. *Hours:* 103.00 on 90 ops. *Remarks:* He joined the RCAF prior to America's entry into the war and was one of twenty-six pilots who served with both Whirlwind Squadrons. Discharged from the RCAF to join the 94th 'Hat in the Ring' Fighter Squadron, 1st Fighter Group US 8th Air Force flying P-38s, by 10 November 1944 he was a Major in the 9th Air Force in France when he wrote off a Piper L4-B.

CROOKS David Alexander Cummins DFC

Nationality: Canadian. *S/n:* 40678 RAF. *Rank:* Pilot Officer; Flying Officer on 3 September 1940; Flight Lieutenant on 2 January 1941. *Squadron:* 263. *Flight:* A; A Commander. *In:* 20 August 1940 from 266 Squadron. *First Whirlwind Op:* 8 December 1940. *Out:* 1 April 1941 KIA. *Hours:* 43:15 on 49 ops. *Incidents: P6986* damaged on 23 February 1941. *Remarks:* Born in Toronto, on 17 January 1913, he was appointed as a Pilot Officer on 7 May 1938. During the Battle of France he flew Fairey Battles with 266 Squadron and was awarded the DFC on 25 June 1940, cited with his crew Sgt Thomas Clifford Davies and LAC William Reginald John Green (both awarded DFM). As 'A' Flight Commander with 263 he was shot down in *P6989 HE-C* by a Dornier Do.215 near Helston, Cornwall. Aged twenty-eight, he is buried in Illogan (St Illogan) Churchyard, Cornwall, Row 1 Plot 1.

CURRIE Vivian Lester

Nationality: British. *S/n:* 106035 RAFVR. *Rank:* Pilot Officer. *Squadron:* 137. *Flight:* B. *In:* 1 October 1941 from 55 OTU. *First Whirlwind Op:* Not operational. *Out:* 2 November 1941 to 263 Squadron. *Squadron:* 263. *Flight:* A. *In:* 2 November 1941 from 137 Squadron. *First Whirlwind Op:* 12 January 1941. *Out:* 23 July 1942 MIA. *Hours:* 61:10 on 58 ops. *Incidents: P7002* heavy landing at Colerne on 13 December 1941; *P7004* burst a tyre and undercarriage collapsed at Fairwood Common on 14 March 1942. *Nickname:* Paddy. *Remarks:* Born in Newhaven, Sussex, he was one of twenty-six pilots who served with both Whirlwind Squadrons. He was shot down into the sea off Ile de Batz in *P7035* by Unteroffizer Freidrich Steinmüller of 11/JG2. Aged twenty-two, his name appears on Panel 69 of the Runnymede Memorial. Following his death, his brother Clifford joined the Navy.

CURRY John Harvey

Nationality: American. *S/n:* C/2645 RCAF. *Rank:* Flying Officer. *Squadron:* 137. *Flight:* B. *In:* 1 March 1942 from 58 OTU. *First Whirlwind Op:* Not operational. *Out:* 30 April 1942 to 601 Squadron. *Nickname:* Crash. *Remarks:* Born in Dallas, on 12 August 1915, he was a 'barnstormer' during the 1930s and joined the RCAF in August 1940 and flew with 118 Squadron in Nova Scotia before being posted to the UK. After leaving 137 Squadron he was posted to 610 then 601 Squadron in Malta and the Western Desert where he gained seven victories and a DFC on 1 February 1943. He was shot down by flak over Italy as CO of 80 Squadron on 2 March 1944, but returned after two months and was Rested to Canada where he became a test pilot, and was awarded an OBE on 1 September 1944. Post-war, he worked in the aerospace industry and with NASA on the Apollo programme, finally retiring in 1970. He passed away in March 2008.

CURTIS
Nationality: British. *S/n:* RAFVR. *Rank:* Sergeant. *Squadron:* 263: *Flt:* A *In:* 24 June 1942 from 59 OTU. *Out:* 1 July 1942 Posted Overseas. *First Whirlwind Op:* Not operational. *Remarks:* With 263 for seven days.

DAVIDSON John Tapscott
Nationality: British. *S/n:* 114577 RAFVR. *Rank:* Flying Officer. *Squadron:* 137. *Flight:* B. *In:* 12 March 1943 from 59 OTU. *First Whirlwind Op:* 3 April 1943. *Out:* 14 August 1943 MIA. *Hours:* 3:30 on 3 ops *Incidents: P7104 SF-V* port engine failed and 'piled up on landing' caused by one of the numerous bumps in the aerodrome surface (RAF Manston) on 30 March 1943. *Nickname:* Dave. *Remarks:* Born in March 1915, in Liverpool. He converted to Hurricane IVs and flew five ops, but was shot down ten miles off North Foreland in *KZ578* by a 'friendly' night-fighter. Aged twenty-eight, his name appears on Panel 124 of the Runnymede Memorial.

DAVIE William Bow Douglas Symington
Nationality: British. *S/n:* 72481 RAFVR. *Rank:* Flight Lieutenant. *Squadron:* 263. *Flight:* A. *In:* 7 July 1942 from RAE. *First Whirlwind Op:* 10 July 1942. *Out:* 14 July 1942 to RAE. *Hours:* 1:00 on 1 Op. *Remarks:* Born in Whitecraigs, Renfreshire on 22 January 1918. He undertook the flight testing of Whirlibomber *P6994* at RAE. He later received the AFC but was killed on 4 January 1944 as a Squadron Leader. Aged twenty-five, he is buried in Old Monkland Cemetery, Coatbridge, Lanarkshire, Section B, Grave 6.

DeHOUX Joseph Laurier
Nationality: Canadian. *S/n:* R/69546 (Sgt); J/15145 (Officer) RCAF. *Rank:* Sergeant; Pilot Officer on 1 October 1942; Flying Officer on 1 October 1942; Flight Lieutenant on 1 September 1943. *Squadron:* 137. *Flight:* A. *In:* 1 October 1941 from 56 OTU. *First Whirlwind Op:* 21 January 1942. *Out:* 2 September 1943 KIA: *Awards:* DFC on 1 August 1943. *Hours:* 93:15 on 88 ops: *Incident: P7055 SF-U* hit by flak on 6 June 1943. *Nickname:* Hooks. *Remarks:* Born in Quebec, he enlisted on 22 June 1940 and later flew seven operational sorties on Hurricane IVs, but was lost to flak on 2 September 1943, in *HX698*, on 'Operation Twitch', the Hansweert Dock Gates Raid. He had been with the Squadron for almost two years and news of his promotion to Flight Lieutenant with command of 'A' Flight was only known after he went missing. 'His loss is deeply felt by everybody.' Aged twenty-three, he is buried in Flushing (Vlissingen) Cemetery, Netherlands, Plot 7 Row G. His brother Joseph was killed on 24 February 1944 with 419 Squadron.

DeSHANE Charles Wilbert
Nationality: Canadian. *S/n:* R/75662 (Sgt); J/15148 (Officer) RCAF. *Rank:* Sergeant; Pilot Officer on 15 January 1942. *Squadron:* 137. *Flight:* B. *In:* 21 December 1941 from 57 OTU. *First Whirlwind Op:* 14 January 1942. *Out:* 9 March 1942 KIFA. *Hours:* 15:45 on 12 ops, 46:00 total. *Nickname:* Pat. *Remarks:* Employed by the Royal Bank of Canada before the war, he enlisted in October 1940, and arrived at 57 OTU in August 1941. He was killed

when *P7036 SF-X* crashed during a dogfight with a Spitfire over Whitehorse Common, North Walsham. Aged twenty, he is buried in Scottow Cemetery, Grave 264.

DIMBLEBEE Frank Oswald
Nationality: British. *S/n:* 937693 RAFVR. *Rank:* Sergeant. *Squadron:* 263. *Flight:* B. *In:* 15 May 1941 from 504 Squadron. *First Whirlwind Op:* 4 July 1941. *Out:* 3 December 1941 to Target Towing Flight, Warmwell. *Hours:* 11:20 on 11 ops. *Incidents: P7046* undercarriage collapsed on 21 August 1941; *P7011 HE-H* hit by flak on 28 September 1941; *P7041* tail wheel would not lower on 3 November 1941; *P6987* hit Spitfire Vb *AD294* of 118 Squadron on 17 November 1941. *Nickname:* Dim. *Remarks:* Born on 1 August 1916, in Market Harborough. Posted to the Target Towing Flight, Warmwell then 273 Squadron where he received a DFC on 30 July 1943. The citation read:

> This pilot is engaged on air/sea rescue operations. He has displayed skill and daring throughout, often effecting rescues far from his base and well within sight of the enemy's coastline and fighter aircraft. On other occasions he has brought his aircraft down onto rough and dangerous seas to accomplish his purpose. F/L Dimblebee has been instrumental in picking up thirty-four of his comrades He has displayed great ability and keenness and has contributed to the efficiency of his flight which has been responsible for picking up one-hundred personnel. During an earlier period of his operational career he destroyed an enemy aircraft and petrol bowser in the course of a low flying attack.

Despite being an air sea rescue pilot, he could not swim! Post-war he was Assistant Air Attaché in Prague where he teamed up with Anthony Albertini, and retired in 1949 to run a chain of successful Hotels. He passed away in Malta in 1988.

DOIG Alexander Ivan
Nationality: British. *S/n:* 565057 RAFVR. *Rank:* Warrant Officer. *Squadron:* 137. *Flight:* B. *In:* 29 November 1942 from 55 OTU. *First Whirlwind Op:* 9 December 1941. *Out:* 23 January 1943 POW. *Hours:* 0:45 on 2 ops. *Remarks:* Missing in *P7054* near Poperinge, he was on the run for four days before being captured, and was reported as a POW on 8 February 1943. He was held in Westertimke (Tarnstedt), Poland.

DONALDSON Arthur Hay DFC AFC
Nationality: British. *S/n:* 34150 RAF. *Rank:* Squadron Leader; Wing Commander on 21 August 1941. *Squadron:* 263. *Flight:* Commanding Officer. *In:* 18 February 1941 from 242 Squadron. *First Whirlwind Op:* 1 May 1941. *Out:* 21 August 1941 W/C Flying RAF Colerne: *Awards:* AFC on 1 July 1941; DFC on 21 August 1941. *Hours:* 64:05 on 52 ops 182:45 total: *Claims:* Do.215 damaged on 1 April 1941 in *P6998*; Me.109 of JG.2 damaged on 6 August 1941 in *P7001. Incidents: P7001* hit by flak on 14 June 1941; *P7001* hit by flak on 6 August 1941; *P7044* hit by flak on 28 September 1941. *Remarks:* Born on 9 January 1915, in Weymouth, he was the cousin of Douglas Bader and learnt to fly at 5 FTS Sealand. From 1936-40 he was an instructor at CFS, then served under Douglas Bader on 242 Squadron before taking Command of 263. On 28 September 1941, he was injured over Morlaix aerodrome when *P7044* was hit by flak and the canopy shattered rendering him temporarily unconscious and for years after he would scratch his head and pull out a

sliver of Perspex. As W/C Flying, Colerne, he was to have led a Wing of Whirlwinds but this never materialised, and he was posted to Malta where he led the first fighter Wing formed on the island. Injured in a dogfight when a cannon shell removed two fingers of his left hand, he was posted back to the UK but was one of only two survivors when their Liberator crashed in bad weather landing at Gibraltar – the other was George 'Screwball' Buerling. He commanded RAF Ibsley and was instrumental in the successful campaign against the V2 launch sites in Holland, and his final wartime posting in Rangoon was cut short by malaria. Post-war he was SASO 2 TAF and Deputy Director Air Defence at the Air Ministry and retired as a Group Captain in March 1959 having flown more than a hundred types of aircraft, but he considered the Whirlwind to be the best. He then ran a village shop and post office in Melbury Osmond and passed away on 5 October 1980.

DOWNER Alan Richard
Nationality: British. *S/n:* 80820 RAFVR. *Rank:* Pilot Officer. *Squadron:* 263: *Flt:* B. *In:* 23 June 1940 from 5 OTU. *Out:* 20 July 1940 KIFA. *First Whirlwind Op:* Not operational. *Remarks:* Born in Edmonton, London in 1918. He crashed force landing Hurricane *P2917*, 1½ miles south-west of Tranent, East Lothian. Taken to the Military Hospital at Murrayfield, Edinburgh, he later died from his injuries. Aged twenty-two, he is buried in New Southgate Cemetery Section AC, Grave 950.

DUGDALE Norbury
Nationality: British. *S/n:* 131147 RAFVR. *Rank:* Flying Officer. *Squadron:* 137: *Flt:* B. *In:* 3 March 1943 from 59 OTU. *First Whirlwind Op:* 4 April 1943. *Out:* 22 May 1943 to 611 Squadron. *Hours:* 0:25 on 1Op, 35:00 total. *Remarks:* Born in West Derby, Liverpool. On 4 April 1943, his props touched the sea and he ditched *P7002 SF-W* five miles off Dungeness. Rescued after five minutes by an ASR Launch, his colleagues commented that the ditching would have been a credit to a Sunderland but the authorities did not agree and he was reprimanded. He remained in the post-war RAF as a Flight Lieutenant but resigned his commission on 3 August 1946.

DUNLOP Iain David Macdonald
Nationality: British. *S/n:* 1320671 RAFVR. *Rank:* Sergeant. *Squadron:* 263. *Flight:* A. *In:* 16 June 1943 from 59 OTU. *First Whirlwind Op:* 29 August 1943. *Out:* 30 October 1944 Rested. *Hours:* 12:25 in 11 ops, 73:30 total. *Incidents: P7046* damaged on 14 August 1943; *P7055* hit by flak on 19 October 1943; *P7108* hit by flak on 30 October 1943; *P7098* was damaged on 7 November 1943; *P6971* hit by flak on 26 November 1943. *Nickname:* Dun. *Remarks:* Born in Glasgow, on 7 May 1923. On 24 September 1943, he noted, 'It was my first operational sortie and I followed George (Wood) into the dive. One second he was there the next he just blew up and I remember thinking to myself, Bloody Hell this is a dangerous job.' He flew sixty-seven ops on Typhoons but on 23 June 1944 he was hit by flak in and ditched thirty-five miles from Bolt Head, and was rescued by an ASR Walrus after thirty minutes in his dinghy. 'Dauntless Dunlop was the first 263 pilot rescued by air sea rescue. He finished the war as a Flying Officer and Link Trainer instructor and joined AerLingus where he flew their first Boeing 747 Jumbo. He passed away in January 1992.

EELES Henry

Nationality: British. *S/n:* 26177 RAF. *Rank:* Squadron Leader. *Squadron:* 263. *Flight:* Commanding Officer. *In:* 6 July 1940 from Air Ministry. *First Whirlwind Op:* 7 December 1940. *Out:* 16 December 1940 to RAF Drem. *Hours:* 1.00 on 1 Op. *Incidents: P6070* broke tail wheel on landing at West Freugh on 12 August 1940; *Nickname:* Harry. *Remarks:* Born on 12 May 1910, and educated at Harrow, he entered the RAF College, Cranwell in January 1929. His first Squadron was No. 41, in December 1930, and by 1 October 1932 he was PA to the AOC Middle East. He returned to the UK on the 11 February 1934, to the Air Armament School, and on the 19 January 1935 became Armaments Officer for 5 FTS. His next posting was as ADC to ACM Sir Cyril Newell Chief of the Air Staff from 1 September 1937, before becoming the first Whirlwind CO in July 1940. He delivered the first Whirlwind to the Squadron, and although not shown in the 263 Squadron ORB, he flew the statutory sortie to be eligible for the Battle of Britain clasp. He turned it down as he had only flown from Scotland and not southern England where the fighting took place and had not fired a shot in anger. He left 263 to command RAF Drem, then Colerne, where he used a Whirlwind as his personal aircraft, and was later posted as Head of Organisation Branch HQ Fighter Command then Deputy SASO Fighter Command. His post-war career began at the School of Air-Land Warfare, then, in April 1951, he became Assistant to the Deputy Supreme Commander (Air) NATO and, in August 1952, Commandant of the RAF College. Mentioned in Despatches twice, on 1 January 1943, and again later in the war, he received a CBE on 8 June 1944, the King Häakon VII Freedom Medal on 18 April 1947, and a CB on 31 May 1956. He retired as an Air Commodore on 29 January 1959 and passed away in July 1992.

EMSLIE Alfred William

Nationality: Australian. *S/n:* 414130 RAAF. *Rank:* Flight Sergeant. *Squadron:* 137. *Flight:* B. *In:* 19 May 1943 from 55 OTU. *Out:* 9 July 1944 to RAF Manston. *First Whirlwind Op:* Not operational. *Nickname:* Blue. *Remarks:* Born on 26 April 1921, in Irvine Bank, Queensland, he enlisted on 16 August 1941. On 29 April 1944 Typhoon *MN180 HE-Q* crashed near RAF Predannack; on 6 July Typhoon *MN468* crashed at Manston and on 8 July 1944, Typhoon *MN556* turned over on landing. He lost an eye and was posted to ground duties on 6 February 1945. Demobbed as a Warrant Officer on 24 July 1946 with 600 flying hours. He passed away on 19 July 1999.

EVANS William John

Nationality: British. *S/n:* 1382057 RAFVR. *Rank:* Sergeant. *Squadron:* 137. *Flight:* A. *In:* 1 April 1943 from 58 OTU. *First Whirlwind Op:* 29 May 1943. *Out:* 30 June 1943 to RAF Southend. *Hours:* 0:55 on 1 Op. *Remarks:* He later served with 609 Squadron, and received a DFM.

EWING Peter Alexander

Nationality: Australian. *S/n:* 403326 RAAF. *Rank:* Sergeant. *Squadron:* 263. *Flight:* A. *In:* 20 January 1942 from 61 OTU. *First Whirlwind Op:* Not operational. *Out:* 21 March 1942 to 450 Squadron. *Remarks:* Born on 25 March 1916, in Walcha, New South Wales. He left 263 for the Middle East to fly Kittyhawks, but on 15 September 1942, during a dogfight near El Alamein, a cannon shell exploded on his wing severing the control wires and he collided with a Me.109. He baled out, was captured and spent the rest of the war as a POW in Lamsdorf, Poland. Post-war he returned to Australia and passed away in 1975.

FENEMORE Stanley Allen
Nationality: British. *S/n:* 745110 RAFVR. *Rank:* Sergeant. *Squadron:* 263. *Flight:* B. *In:* 23 June 1940 from 5 OTU. *First Whirlwind Op:* Not operational. *Out:* 9 July 1940 to 219 Squadron. *Remarks:* Born in Liverpool in 1920. On 15 October 1940, he was shot down in combat with Bf.109s over Redhill in Hurricane *V6722* of 501 Squadron, and crashed at Postern Gate Farm, Godstone. Aged twenty, he is buried in Liverpool (Allerton) Cemetery, Section 2, Grave 218. A bench has been named in his honour in South Godstone near where he crashed.

FERDINAND Roy Frederick
Nationality: British. *S/n:* 80817 RAFVR. *Rank:* Pilot Officer; Flying Officer on 9 June 1941. *Squadron:* 263. *Flight:* B. *In:* 23 June 1940 from 6 OTU. *First Whirlwind Op:* 11 February 1941. *Out:* 12 June 1941 KIFA. *Hours:* 65:00 on 57 ops, 103:00 total: *Claims:* Ju.88 of KG.54 damaged on 7 April 1941 in *P6996. Nickname:* Ferdie. *Remarks:* Born in West Ham, on 10 May 1920, he worked in the Audit Office at Marylebone Council, and received his 'Wings' at 6 FTS on 4 April 1940. He flew twenty-eight ops on Hurricanes then converted to Whirlwinds, but died when *P7045* crashed on approach to Filton. Aged twenty-one, he was one of the characters of the squadron and is buried in Plot 912 Section O of Chesham Bois Burial Ground.

FODEN Glynn Barrow
Nationality: British. *S/n:* RAFVR. *Rank:* Sergeant. *Squadron:* 263. *Flight:* A. *In:* 25 January 1941 from 56 OTU. *First Whirlwind Op:* Not operational. *Out:* 29 May 1941. *Nickname:* Dick. *Remarks:* Born in Leicester, on 22 April 1919, he was a bank clerk and gained his Aero Club Certificate on 30 May 1939 and was with 263 for four months before being re-mustered as an Aircraftsman.

FOES C. B.
Nationality: British. *S/n:* RAFVR. *Rank:* Sergeant. *Squadron:* 263. *Flight:* B. *In:* 1 July 1943 from 53 OTU. *First Whirlwind Op:* Not operational. *Out:* 10 July 1943 to 66 Squadron. *Remarks:* He was with 263 for nine days.

FREEMAN Neville Austin
Nationality: South African. *S/n:* 19862 SAAF. *Rank:* 2nd Lieutenant. *Squadron:* 137. *Flight:* B. *In:* 1 April 1942 from 57 OTU. *First Whirlwind Op:* 20 May 1942. *Out:* 18 February 1943 KIFA. *Hours:* 43:30 on 45 ops, 213:00 total. *Incidents: P7104 SF-V* damaged on 12 July 1942; *P7119* engine failure on 17 January 1943. *Nickname:* Lemmie. *Remarks:* Born in Cape Town, in 1922, he was killed at Manston in *P7114* when it was hit by P/O Charles Mercer in *P7119 SF-W*. Aged twenty-one, he is buried in Margate Cemetery, Plot 16196, Section 50, next to his colleague. (*See also* Charles Mercer.)

FREEMAN Norman James

Nationality: British. *S/n:* 62685 RAFVR. *Rank:* Pilot Officer. *Squadron:* 263. *Flight:* A. *In:* 13 May 1941 from 57 OTU. *First Whirlwind Op:* Not operational. *Out:* 29 May 1941 to 504 Squadron. *Hours:* 2:00 total. *Remarks:* After his first solo, *P6982* tipped on her nose, leading to his posting. He was Mentioned in Despatches on 8 June 1944.

FROST John Thomas Naldrett

Nationality: British. *S/n:* 412514 RAAF. *Rank:* Pilot Officer. *Squadron:* 137. *Flight:* B. *In:* 1 June 1943 from 52 OTU. *First Whirlwind Op:* Not operational. *Out:* 20 August 1944 KIA. *Nickname:* Jack. *Remarks:* Born on 5 August 1922, in Walthamstow, England, his family emigrated to Australia and he enlisted on 19 July 1941, in Sydney. Inevitably known as 'Jack', he flew six ops on Hurricane IVs and fifty on Typhoons but was shot down by flak near Vimoutiers in *MN719 HE-J*. Aged twenty-two, he is buried in St Desir War Cemetery, Calvados, France, Grave VI.F.8.

FUNNELL Kenneth James Forrester

Nationality: British. *S/n:* 150141 RAFVR. *Rank:* Pilot Officer; Flying Officer on 23 July 1943. *Squadron:* 263. *Flight:* B/A. *In:* 16 July 1943 from 55 OTU. *First Whirlwind Op:* 24 October 1942. *Out:* 24 December 1943 KIFA. *Hours:* 2:30 on 2 ops. *Remarks:* Born in 1922, in Romford, Essex. He was killed when Typhoon *JR203* spun into the ground during practice dog fighting near Wimborne, Dorset. Aged twenty-one, he is buried in Plot 2076 at Ilford Cemetery.

FURBER Frederick Michael

Nationality: Rhodesian. *S/n:* SR/80203 RAFVR. *Rank:* Pilot Officer; Flying Officer on 16 September 1942. *Squadron:* 137. *Flight:* B. *In:* 3 March 1942 from 57 OTU. *First Whirlwind Op:* 28 April 1942. *Out:* 5 January 1943 to 266 Squadron. *Hours:* 58:50 on 54 ops. *Incidents: P7005 SF-H* force landed near East Wretham on 11 April 1942; *P7049* damaged props landing at Matlaske on 27 June 1942; *P7095 SF-H* damaged on 18 August 1942; *P7102 SF-P* hit by flak on 31 October 1942; *P7119 SF-S* hit by flak on 23 December 1942. *Nickname:* Rhodey. *Remarks:* With 266 Squadron, he was hit by flak on 9 July 1943 and ditched Typhoon *R8804 UO-J* off St Brieuc to become a POW being held at Sagan and Belaria in Poland. He transferred to the Southern Rhodesia Forces as a Flight Lieutenant on 17 July 1945.

GARNIER Jacques DFC

Nationality: French. *S/n:* 30.655 Free French Forces. *Rank:* Lieutenant. *Squadron:* 263. *Flight:* A. *In:* 17 February 1941 from 56 OTU. *First Whirlwind Op:* Not operational. *Out:* 20 February 1941 to 238 Squadron. *Remarks:* Real name Jean Gabrielli, he was with 263 for three days. Posted as Missing in 32 Squadron Hurricane *Z4990* on 11 July 1941.

GARTHWAITE Harry

Nationality: British. *S/n:* 748236 RAFVR. *Rank:* Sergeant. *Squadron:* 263. *Flight:* B. *In:* 27 May 1941 from 56 OTU. *First Whirlwind Op:* 27 May 1941. *Out:* 9 July 1941 to 54 OTU. *Hours:* 15:15 on 13 ops. *Remarks:* With 263 for six weeks, he finished the war as a Flight Lieutenant and was Mentioned in Despatches on 1 January 1946.

GATES John
Nationality: Australian. *S/n:* 409401 RAAF. *Rank:* Flight Sergeant. *Squadron:* 137. *Flight:* A. *In:* 25 May 1943 from 59 OTU. *Out:* 5 December 1944 POW. *First Whirlwind Op:* Not operational. *Hours:* 2:00. *Nickname:* Johnnie. *Remarks:* Born on 13 September 1922, in Orange, New South Wales, he enlisted on 15 August 1941. Crashed in Hurricane IV *KX190* at 56 OTU then flew six ops on Hurricane IVs and ninety-five on Typhoons but abandoned a flak damaged *MN546 SF-G* on 5 December 1944 near Dinslaken to become a POW in Lambinowice. He returned at the end of the war and was discharged as a Flying Officer on 14 December 1945.

GILL Donald Ross
Nationality: Canadian. *S/n:* J/15111 RCAF. *Rank:* Sergeant; Pilot Officer on 5 January 1942; Flying Officer on 28 June 1942. *Squadron:* 263. *Flight:* B. *In:* 9 October 1941 from 55 OTU. *First Whirlwind Op:* 11 January 1942. *Out:* 7 November 1942 KIA. *Hours:* 79:25 on 61 ops. *Remarks:* Hit high ground in poor visibility in *P7043 HE-A*. 'Efficient, hard working and of great integrity' aged twenty-seven, he is buried in Cherbourg Old Communal Cemetery, Plot 6, Row D, Grave 5

GRAHAM Kenneth Alfred George
Nationality: British. *S/n:* 78737 RAFVR. *Rank:* Pilot Officer. *Squadron:* 263. *Flight:* A. *In:* 14 October 1940 from 600 Squadron. *First Whirlwind Op:* 23 January 1941. *Out:* 8 February 1941 MIA. *Hours:* 3:25 on 4 ops: *Claims:* Ar.196 of 5./Ku.Fl.Gr.196 destroyed on 8 February 1941, in *P6969 HE-V*. *Remarks:* Born in East Ham, London in 1921, he fought with 600 and 111 Squadrons during the Battle of Britain but failed to return in *P6969 HE-V* after downing an Ar.196 off Dodman Point, which was deemed to be the Whirlwinds first 'kill' although that honour actually fell to P/O David Stein. Aged twenty, his name appears on Panel 32 of the Runnymede Memorial.

GRAY Leonard Scott
Nationality: British. *S/n:* 1340994 RAFVR. *Rank:* Sergeant; Flight Sergeant on 13 September 1943. *Squadron:* 263. *Flight:* A. *In:* 1 June 1943 from 55 OTU. *First Whirlwind Op:* 12 July 1943. *Out:* 24 October 1943 POW. *Hours:* 15:10 on 13 ops, 102:15 total. *Incidents: P7005* tail damaged on 15 August 1943. *Nickname:* Jock. *Remarks:* Born in 1921, in Monifeith near Dundee, he was a trainee gardener prior to joining the RAF in 1941. During training in Lancaster, California he once had tea with James Cagney on the set of '*Yankee Doodle Dandy*' and returned to the UK on the *Queen Mary*. Hit by flak in the starboard engine during the low-level attack on the *M/V Münsterland* in Cherbourg Harbour he crash-landed *P6979 HE-G* south-east of the town to become a POW. He described prison camp (Stalag IVB at Mühlburg-am-Elbe, Upper Saxony) as 'Like Butlins – but without the fun,' and feels 'I didn't really do enough after all the training.' Released from active service on 22 December 1945, he later gained a degree in Agriculture at Edinburgh University and worked at the Scottish Crops Research Institute and the Agricultural Training Board. He was also a member of MENSA. His good friend Bill Reid VC was Best Man at his wedding. He passed away in February 2012. (*See Chapter 15*).

GREEN Fred

Nationality: British. *S/n:* 1238815 (Sgt); 160670 (Officer) RAFVR. *Rank:* Sergeant; Flight Sergeant on 13 September 1943; Pilot Officer on 30 October 1943. *Squadron:* 263. *Flight:* A. *In:* 25 May 1943 from 55 OTU. *First Whirlwind Op.* 23 July 1943. *Out:* 22 December 1944 Rested. *Hours:* 23:50 on 20 ops. *Nickname:* Ginger. *Remarks:* He joined the Lancashire Constabulary on 26 February 1938 as Constable *2044* and the RAF on 28 July 1941 under the Police and Firemen (War Service) Act of 1939. On 25 September 1943 he jettisoned his bombs 'safe' into the Channel, but seconds later an explosion sent up a spout of water that damaged the starboard engine of *P7040*, the bombs had detonated a mine. He flew eighty-five sorties on Typhoons, sharing in the destruction of a Do.217 on 18 April 1944 with F/L Rutter, F/O Purkis and W/O Handley, and finished the war as a Flight Lieutenant. Mentioned in Dispatches on 15 August 1945, he briefly rejoined the police force.

HADOW John Maude

Nationality: British. *S/n:* 122121 RAFVR. *Rank:* Flying Officer. *Squadron:* 137. *Flight:* A. *In:* 1 March 1943 from 55 OTU. *First Whirlwind Op:* 1 April 1943. *Out:* 15 April 1943 KIFA. *Hours:* 3:45 on 3 ops, 36:00 total. *Remarks:* Schooled at Repton, Derbyshire, he joined the RAF in June 1941 but was killed when *P7121 SF-C* dived into the ground two hundred yards from 'B' Flight dispersal at Manston. He had only been with the squadron a short time, but was very popular. Aged twenty, he was buried on 19 April 1943, in Plot 16195, Section 50 of Margate Cemetery.

HÄGGBERG Ralph Otto Gustaf

Nationality: Swedish. *S/n:* 1269486 (Sgt); 120677 (Officer) RAFVR. *Rank:* Sergeant; Pilot Officer on 30 December 1941. *Squadron:* 263. *Flight:* A. *In:* 15 September 1941 from 56 OTU. *First Whirlwind Op:* Not operational. *Out:* 8 October 1941 to 137 Squadron. *Squadron:* 137. *Flight:* B. *In:* 8 October 1941 from 263 Squadron. *First Whirlwind Op:* 5 November 1941. *Out:* 12 February 1942 MIA. *Hours:* 48:35 on 40 ops. *Nickname:* Haggie. *Remarks:* One of twenty-six pilots who served with both Whirlwind Squadrons, he was born on 14 March 1922, in Stockholm. Schooled in England he joined the RAF in October 1939. Missing during 'Operation Fuller' in *P7093 SF-A*, possibly shot down by Oblt. Egon Mayer of 7/JG.2, north of Oostende. His promotion to Flying Officer arrived after his death. Aged twenty-one, his name appears on Panel 69 of the Runnymede Memorial.

HANDLEY William Anthony

Nationality: British. *S/n:* 1509430 RAFVR. *Rank:* Sergeant; Flight Sergeant on 7 October 1943. *Squadron:* 263. *Flight:* B. *In:* 16 June 1943 from 257 Squadron. *First Whirlwind Op:* 23 August 1943. *Out:* 7 February 1945 to 59 OTU. *Hours:* 7:47 on 7 ops. *Nickname:* Tommy or ITMA. *Remarks:* His brothers engineering company manufactured the Whirlwinds tail wheel assembly for Westland. He flew eighty-one Typhoon ops during which time he shared in the destruction of a Do.217 on 20 April 1944 with F/L Rutter, F/O Purkis and P/O Green, and damaged a He.111. Inevitably nicknamed '*ITMA*' after the popular Radio Show starring Tommy Handley, he was posted to 59 OTU on Rest, then to Singapore as an Equipment Officer for a month before being demobbed and becoming a teacher. He passed away in January 2012.

HARRIS Douglas
Nationality: British. *S/n:* RAFVR. *Rank:* Sergeant. *Squadron:* 137. *Flight:* B. *In:* 1 April 1943 from 58 OTU. *First Whirlwind Op:* Not operational. *Out:* 22 May 1943 to 197 *Squadron: Remark:* With 137 for seven weeks.

HARVEY Philip DFC
Nationality: Republic of Ireland. *S/n:* 102571 RAFVR. *Rank:* Pilot Officer; Flying Officer on 28 June 1942. *Squadron:* 263. *Flight:* A. *In:* 13 September 1941 from 56 OTU. *First Whirlwind Op:* 8 November 1941. *Out:* 18 April 1943 MIA: *Awards:* DFC on 1 May 1943. *Hours:* 120:15 on 105 ops. *Incidents: P7013* undercarriage collapsed at Charmy Down on 1 October 1941; *P7112* crashed at Fairwood Common on 1 April 1941; *P7100* burst tyre on at Fairwood Common on 15 April 1942. *Nickname:* Tim. *Remarks:* Born in 1919, in Dublin he enlisted in 1940. Attached to the US 8th Air Force on Liaison Duties from 30 August to 30 September 1942. He disappeared off Ouistreham in *P7090*, probably shot down by an armed trawler (*see also* Basil Abrams). Described as a person of rare charm and goodness he had been married for just five weeks and his DFC was awarded posthumously. Aged twenty-three, his name appears on Panel 125 of the Runnymede Memorial. His father, Lord Bishop of Cashel, was an exceptional sportsman; he dismissed W. G. Grace for a duck in a Dublin University v London County XI game, and played Rugby for Ireland.

HAYES John Furnival DFC
Nationality: New Zealander. *S/n:* 77019 RAFVR. *Rank:* Pilot Officer. *Squadron:* 263. *Flight:* A. *In:* 21 January 1941 from 56 OTU. *First Whirlwind Op:* Not operational. *Out:* 25 January 1941 to 247 Squadron. *Remarks:* With 263 for four days, he finished the war as Squadron Leader and retired 9 February 1958.

HEATON William Whittaker
Nationality: British. *S/n:* 156653 RAFVR. *Rank:* Flight Sergeant; Pilot Officer on 26 August 1943. *Squadron:* 263. *Flight:* B. *In:* 25 May 1943 from 55 OTU. *First Whirlwind Op:* 20 July 1943. *Out:* 9 June 1944 KIA. *Hours:* 22:15 on 19 ops: *Incident: P7097* hit by flak on 8 October 1943. *Nickname:* Bill. *Remarks:* Attended 1 SLAIS at Milfield in early 1944, and after converting to Typhoons flew thirty-seven ops before failing to return from the St Lo area in *MN449*. The ORB noted, 'F/O Bill Heaton is missing in circumstances which offer nothing but guess work. We hope to see him again, but…' He is buried in Bayeux War Cemetery, Calvados, France, Plot III.F.4.

HICKS Francis Leslie
Nationality: Australian. *S/n:* 408207 RAAF. *Rank:* Flight Sergeant. *Squadron:* 263. *Flight:* A. *In:* 31 July 1942 from 87 Squadron. *First Whirlwind Op:* Not operational. *Out:* 19 February 1943 KIFA. *Hours:* 57:00. *Nickname:* Butch. *Remarks:* Born on 12 August 1918, in Latrobe, Tasmania, he worked for the Goliath Cement Company before enlisting on 25 April 1941. Attached to A&AEE, Boscombe Down between 15 August and 31 October 1942 during the trials of the Whirlibomber, but on 19 February 1943 on an Army Co-Op Exercise he hit a tree and crashed in *P7062 HE-L* south of Chiseldon. An engine failure probably caused the crash. Aged thirty, he is buried in (St John the Baptist and Helen) Churchyard, Wroughton, Wiltshire, Plot 2, Row EE. His brother Pat was an Air Gunner.

HOARE

Nationality: British. *S/n:* RAFVR. *Rank:* Sergeant. *Squadron:* 263. *Flight:* A. *In:* 6 March 1943 from 195 Squadron. *First Whirlwind Op:* Not operational. *Out:* 29 May 1943 to Warmwell Target Towing Flight. *Remarks.* With 263 for seven weeks.

HOLMAN Eric John

Nationality: British. *S/n:* 125518 RAFVR. *Rank:* Flying Officer. *Squadron:* 263. *Flight:* A. *In:* 4 July 1943 from 53 OTU. *First Whirlwind Op:* 12 August 1943. *Out:* 30 December 1943 Injured. *Hours:* 17:45 on 15 ops. *Remarks:* Born on 7 June 1918, he was a Flying instructor in the US at Cochran Field during 1942 and married on 28 October 1942, in New York. He took F/O Green the MO and Cpl Hamer to Biggin Hill in the Oxford on 19 November 1943 but it swung on landing, and as he tried to take off again, it hit a building and burst into flames. Badly injured, he was posted to ground duties and finished the war as a Flight Lieutenant. He passed away in Norwich in January 1991.

HOLMES Joseph William Ernest DFC

Nationality: British. *S/n:* 938843 (Sgt); 114291 (Officer) RAFVR. *Rank:* Sergeant; Pilot Officer on 24 October 1941; Flying Officer on 1 October 1942; Flight Lieutenant on 18 September 1942. *Squadron:* 263. *Flight:* B. *In:* 1 April 1941 from 501 Squadron. *First Whirlwind Op:* 27 April 1941. *Out:* 18 September 1942 to 137 Squadron. *Squadron:* 137. *Flight:* A Commander. *In:* 19 September 1942 from 263 Squadron. *First Whirlwind Op:* 25 October 1942. *Out:* 16 February 1943 to 263 Squadron. *Squadron:* 263. *Flight:* B Commander. *In:* 17 February 1943 from 137 Squadron. *First Whirlwind Op:* 28 February 1943. *Out:* 20 June 1943 Rested: *Awards:* DFC on 2 June 1943. *Hours:* 155:25 on 135 ops. *Incidents: P7000* hit farm machinery at Filton on 15 June 1941; *P7005 HE-A* struck a balloon cable off Barry on 15 June 1941; *P7110 HE-E* tail wheel collapsed at Charmy Down on 12 January 1942; *P7110 HE-E* damaged on 19 February 1941; *P7000* crashed at Fairwood Common on 1 April 1942; *P7040* instrument failure on 21 March 1943. *Remarks:* Born on 22 April 1916, in Yorkshire, he joined the RAF in 1939. He was one of twenty-six pilots who served with both Whirlwind Squadrons. Posted from 263 to 29 Pilot Gunnery instructors Course, Sutton Bridge, he was awarded an AFC on 8 June 1944 and was later CO of 266 Squadron. Promoted to Wing Commander in January 1952, during the Malaysian Emergency, he ditched a 1 Squadron RAAF Lincoln off Singapore, then led the crew to safety through shark-infested waters, for which he was Mentioned in Despatches. He later served at the Air Ministry; as Air Attaché, Bangkok; Senior Operations Officer at Supreme Headquarters Allied Powers Europe and retired as a Group Captain. He was an English teacher at Victoria College, Jersey, and passed away in 1993.

HOSKINS Ormonde John Horace

Nationality: British. *S/n:* 69485 RAFVR. *Rank:* Pilot Officer. *Squadron:* 263. *Flight:* A. *In:* 13 September 1941 from 56 OTU. *First Whirlwind Op:* Not operational. *Out:* 9 October 1941 KIFA. *Remarks:* Born in September 1915, in Laverstock, Wiltshire, the eldest of six brothers, 'Well liked on the squadron for his good humour and cheerful personality' he was killed after colliding with F/L Coghlan over Bath. He attempted to force land *P6968 HE-H* but stalled whilst avoiding houses and crashed onto a railway weighbridge at Saltford. Aged twenty-six, he is buried in Laverstock (St Andrews) Churchyard.

HOWE Bernard
Nationality: British. *S/n:* 33427 RAF. *Rank:* Flying Officer. *Squadron:* 263. *Flight:* B. *In:* 3 January 1941 from 25 Squadron. *First Whirlwind Op:* 6 March 1941. *Out:* 20 April 1941 KIFA. *Hours:* 19:10 on 18 ops, 37:00 total: *Claims:* He.111 of I/KG27 damaged on 6 April 1941, in *P7002. Nickname:* Bunny. *Remarks:* He graduated as a Kitchener Scholar from the RAF College, Cranwell on 29 July 1939, and fought with 25 Squadron during the Battle of Britain but was killed when *P6992 HE-C* broke up during a beat-up of RAF Wittering, and crashed in the grounds of Burghley House. Aged twenty-two, he is buried in Plot 4, Row C of Wittering (All Saints) Churchyard, Northamptonshire.

HUGHES Joseph Grantley
Nationality: British. *S/n:* 41706 RAF. *Rank:* Sgt; Pilot Officer on 28 December 1939; Flying Officer on 30 September 1940; Flight Lieutenant on 28 November 1941. *Squadron:* 263. *Flight:* A; B Commander. *In:* 2 October 1939 from 3 FTS. *First Whirlwind Op:* 7 December 1940. *Out:* 20 September 1941 to 137 Squadron. *Squadron:* 137: *Flt:* B Commander. *In:* 22 September 1941 from 263 Squadron. *First Whirlwind Op:* 26 October 1941. *Out:* 18 November 1941 to Central Flying School. *Hours:* 108:30 on 93 ops: *Incident: P7096* tail wheel would not lower at Charmy Down on 26 October 1941. *Nickname:* Joe. *Remarks:* Born on 27 December 1919. He flew two ops on Hurricanes then converted to Whirlwinds, and was 'A' Flight Commander from 1 April 1941, before being posted to 137 where he was 'B' Flight Commander. From 137 he went to the Central Flying School. He was one of twenty-six pilots who served with both Whirlwind Squadrons, survived the war and passed away in Aylesbury in February 1991.

HUGHES Richard John
Nationality: British. *S/n:* 1387105 RAFVR. *Rank:* Sergeant; Flight Sergeant on 10 September 1943. *Squadron:* 263. *Flight:* A. *In:* 8 June 1943 from 56 OTU. *First Whirlwind Op:* Not operational. *Out:* 20 September 1943 to 616 Squadron. *Nickname:* Dickie. *Remarks:* On 20 June 1943, on landing after his first solo in *P7013*, he selected 'up' undercarriage instead of flaps. Despite the damage he was exonerated, the locking device on the undercarriage lever had malfunctioned. Posted to 616 Squadron in exchange for F/L Snalam, he finished the war as a Flying Officer and received the Order of Leopold II with Palme and Croix de Guerre on 27 June 1947.

HULL Caesar Barraud
Nationality: Rhodesia. *S/n:* 37285 RAF. *Rank:* Flight Lieutenant. *Squadron:* 263. *Flight:* B Commander. *In:* 9 May 1940 from 43 Squadron. *First Whirlwind Op:* Not operational. *Out:* 30 August 1940 to 43 Squadron. *Remarks:* Born on 23 February 1913 at Leachdale Farm in Shangani, Rhodesia, he was a member of the 1934 Springbok boxing team at the Empire Games, Wembley. Unable to join the SAAF as he did not speak Afrikaans, he was granted a Short Service Commission in the RAF in 1935 and was posted to 43 Squadron on completion of his training on the 5 August 1935 and represented the squadron in aerobatics at the 1937 Hendon Air Display flying a Hawker Fury. He shared in the destruction of a He.111 on 30 January 1940, and the 28 March 1940 and destroyed one on the 13 February during the first raid on Scapa Flow. He then fought in the second Norwegian Campaign, but was seriously wounded on 27 May by return fire from a Ju.87 and Me.110 and crash-landed. Thrown clear,

he was rendered unconscious for a while but on coming round he walked away from the wreckage despite wounds to his head and knee. Taken to Bödö Hospital, he was moved to a hospital ship and evacuated back to the UK in a Sunderland flying boat on the 30 April 1940. Whilst on sick leave he was awarded the DFC and Mentioned in Despatches. Posted to command 43 Squadron he claimed a Me.109 destroyed and two Me.110s probably destroyed but was killed leading them into action on 7 September, his Hurricane – *V6641* – crashed in the grounds of Purley High School. Aged twenty-seven, he is buried in Tangmere (St Andrews) Churchyard Plot E, Row 1, Grave 477.

HUNT Henry Norman

Nationality: British. *S/n:* 82655 RAF. *Rank:* Pilot Officer. *Squadron:* 263. *Flight:* B. *In:* 23 June 1940 from 6 OTU. *First Whirlwind Op:* Not operational. *Out:* 11 July 1940 to 504 Squadron. *Remarks:* Born in 1919, in Harrow, Middlesex, he was with 263 for eighteen days, but he was killed with 504 Squadron on 13 May 1941. Aged twenty, his name appears on Panel 33 of the Runnymede Memorial.

HUNTER Robert Charles

Nationality: British. *S/n:* 150009 RAFVR. *Rank:* Flying Officer. *Squadron:* 263. *Flight:* B. *In:* 16 July 1943 from 55 OTU. *First Whirlwind Op:* Not operational. *Out:* 22 February 1944 MIA. *Nickname:* Bob. *Remarks:* Born in 1920, his family were in the motor trade and he always drove an expensive sports car. Last seen in Typhoon *JR304* eight miles north-west of Guernsey, whilst circling S/L Geoff Warnes and F/O Tuff. He was on his first operational sortie and either stalled and spun in whilst trying to keep them in sight; had fuel feed problems or was shot down by fighters (*see also* Robert Tuff *and* Geoff Warnes). Aged twenty-three, his name appears on Panel 207 of the Runnymede Memorial.

HUNTER Thomas

Nationality: British. *S/n:* 1001262 RAFVR. *Rank:* Sergeant. *Squadron:* 263. *Flight:* B. *In:* 10 June 1941 from 52 OTU: *First Op:* 23 June 1941. *Out:* 29 September 1941 KIA. *Hours:* 17:25 on 15 ops. *Remarks:* Abandoned *P7009* five miles south of the Eddystone Light after a dusk attack on Morlaix aerodrome. His body was later washed ashore at Poldhu Cove, Mullion. Aged twenty-one, he is buried in Monk Helseden (Blackhall) Cemetery, Durham.

JARDINE Peter Alastair

Nationality: South African. *S/n:* 711019 RAFVR. *Rank:* Flight Sergeant. *Squadron:* 263. *Flight:* A. *In:* 28 January 1942 from 51 OTU. *First Whirlwind Op:* Not operational. *Out:* 21 September 1942 KIFA. *Hours:* 44:00. *Remarks:* A Lieutenant in the SAAF *(s/n 103692)* prior to transferring to the RAF, he fractured his back in a heavy landing in *P7039* and was hospitalised between 7 March and 4 August 1942. 'Very well liked in the squadron for his quiet good humoured disposition' he was killed on a Sector recce when *P7003* dived into the ground between Wool and Wareham. Aged twenty, he is buried in Warmwell (Holy Trinity) Churchyard, Dorset.

JOHNSTONE Arthur Norman William DFC

Nationality: British. *S/n:* 42313 RAF. *Rank:* Flight Lieutenant. *Squadron:* 263. *Flight:* A. *In:* 4 September 1942 as a supernumerary. *First Whirlwind Op:* 16 September 1943. *Out:* 3 November

1942. *Hours:* 5:25 on 6 ops. *Remarks:* He served in the Western Desert before joining 263 and received the DFC on 29 April 1941 for destroying an enemy bomber on an airfield with a Verey cartridge fired at it as he flew past. Posted to 263 as a supernumerary, he attempted to take-off in course pitch on 8 October 1942 and crashed into Knighton Wood at Warmwell, writing off *P7014 HE-T* in the process. He left 263 for the Far East, was Mentioned in Despatches on 1 January 1945, finished the war as a Wing Commander and retired on 24 December 1965.

JOWITT Douglas St John

Nationality: British. *S/n:* 968039 (Sgt); 114169 (Officer) RAFVR. *Rank:* Sergeant; Pilot Officer on 15 November 1941; Flying Officer on 1 October 1942. *Squadron:* 263. *Flight:* B. *In:* 25 January 1941 from 56 OTU. *First Whirlwind Op:* 9 March 1941. *Out:* 15 September 1941 to 137 Squadron. *Squadron:* 137. *Flight:* B. *In:* 22 September 1941 from 263 Squadron. *First Whirlwind Op:* 30 October 1941. *Out:* 31 October 1942 MIA. *Hours:* 166:00 on 142 ops. *Incidents: P6973* faulty tail wheel at Exeter on 2 February 1941; *P6999* hit by flak on 12 August 1941; *P7013* wingtip hit ground at Charmy Down on 12 September 1941; *P7035* landed with tail wheel retracted at Charmy Down on 30 September 1941; *P7106 SF-D* crashed at Horsham St Faith on 25 December 1941; *P6982 SF-S* instrument failure on 24 March 1942; *P7109 SF-N* the undercarriage of failed to retract on take-off from Matlaske on 1 July 1942. *Nickname:* Gorgeous George. *Remarks:* Born in India in 1919, where his father was a tea planter. He was one of twenty-six pilots who served with both Whirlwind Squadrons. On 29 May 1942 he abandoned Whirlwind *P7118 SF-O* when an engine cut at 800 feet on approach to Matlaske. The aircraft crashed in water meadows at Binty Farm, Itteringham – he landed outside the Mess, tucked his parachute under his arm and went in for breakfast! He disappeared in *P7115* on 137's first Rhubarb operation. Aged twenty-three, his name appears on Panel 67 of the Runnymede Memorial.

KENNEDY Irving Farmer

Nationality: Canadian. *S/n:* J/15273 RCAF. *Rank:* Sergeant; Flight Sergeant on 1 February 1942; Pilot Officer on 20 March 1942. *Squadron:* 263. *Flight:* B. *In:* 30 September 1941 from 55 OTU. *First Whirlwind Op:* 15 December 1941. *Out:* 14 June 1942 to 421 Squadron. *Hours:* 33:10 on 27 ops. *Nickname:* Hap. *Remarks:* Born on 4 February 1922, in Cumberland, Ontario, he attempted to join the RCAF at the outbreak of the war but being seventeen he was told to come back when he was eighteen – he finally enlisted in Ottawa on 21 October 1940. Not happy flying defensive patrols on Whirlwinds, he volunteered to go to Malta, and joined 421 Squadron flying Spitfire Mk.Vs. Awarded the DFC on 22 June 1943, he was shot down by flak near Dreux on 26 July 1944, in Spitfire IX *MK311 YO-D* as CO of 401 Squadron, but evaded capture. On his return he was Rested and returned to Canada, received the Bar to his DFC on 3 November 1944, and finished the war with ten confirmed kills. Post-war he graduated from medical school and practiced for thirty-seven years in his home town. In 1994 he published an autobiography, *Black Crosses off My Wingtip* and passed away on 6 January 2011.

KING Cecil Percy DFM

Nationality: West Indian. *S/n:* 958932 (Sgt); 128999 (Officer) RAFVR. *Rank:* Sergeant; Flight Sergeant on 16 January 1942; Pilot Officer on 10 September 1942; Flying Officer on 20 December 1942 *Squadron:* 263 *Flight:* A. *In:* 25 January 1941 from 56 OTU. *First Whirlwind*

Op: 2 March 1941. *Out:* 18 April 1943 MIA: *Awards:* DFM on 11 September 1942. *Hours:* 193:15 on 173 ops. *Nickname:* Rex: *Claims:* Me.109E-7 of 1/JG.2 destroyed on 7 November 1941 in *P7112*. *Incidents: P7004* hit by flak on 8 September 1941; *P7112* hit by flak on 15 November 1941; *P7052* hit by flak on 3 October 1942, *P6974 HE-X* faulty flaps on 21 March 1943. *Remarks:* Born on 12 February 1920 in British Guiana, he was studying Law before joining up. He failed to return from a Night Armed recce near Airel in *P7117 HE-H*. Aged twenty-three, his name appears on Panel 125 of the Runnymede Memorial.

KITCHENER Herbert Horatio DFM

Nationality: British. *S/n:* 740755 RAFVR. *Rank:* Pilot Officer. *Squadron:* 263. *Flight:* B. *In:* 11 October 1939 from 605 Squadron. *First Whirlwind Op:* 17 December 1940. *Out:* 11 March 1941 Injured: *Awards:* DFM on 7 August 1940. *Hours:* 28.30 on 31 ops, 68:00 total: *Claims:* Ju.88 damaged on 5 March 1941 in *P6985 HE-J*; Ju.88 damaged on 11 March 1941 in *P6985 HE-J. Nickname:* Kitch. *Remarks:* Born on 30 August 1914, in Crowborough, East Sussex, he was named after Field Marshal Lord Kitchener, but never liked his Christian names and was always known as 'Kitch'. He joined the RAFVR in October 1937, served with 605 Squadron before transferring to 263 and fought in both Norwegian Campaigns where he destroyed three He.111s and a Ju.87 on 2 June 1940 (shared with F/L Alvin Williams) for which he was awarded the DFM (and the Norwegian War Cross with Swords on 6 October 1942). He flew thirty-one ops on Hurricanes before converting to Whirlwinds, but was severely injured when *P6985 HE-J* crashed at Portreath after combat with a Ju.88. Following six months in hospital he went to the ops Room at 60 OTU East Fortune, then the Flying Accident Investigation Branch, Cairo where he served until the end of the war. Demobbed as a Flight Lieutenant in November 1945 he worked in local government until 1979 and passed away in July 2010.

KNOTT Leonard James

Nationality: British. *S/n:* 1386897 RAFVR. *Rank:* Sergeant. *Squadron:* 263. *Flight:* B. *In:* 8 June 1943 from 56 OTU. *First Whirlwind Op:* Not operational. *Out:* 13 July 1943 Injured. *Hours:* 31:00. *Remarks:* Injured when *P7110 HE-C* crashed during an emergency landing at Warmwell he was treated by Sir Archibald McIndoe at East Grinstead and became a member of the Guinea Pig Club. Posted to ground duties, he retired as a Flight Lieutenant in the early 1960s.

LaGETTE Paul Milton

Nationality: American. *S/n:* J/107776 RCAF. *Rank:* Pilot Officer. *Squadron:* 137. *Flight:* A. *In:* 21 December 1941 from 57 OTU. *First Whirlwind Op:* 21 December 1941. *Out:* 31 July 1942 Posted. *Hours:* 22:00 on 19 ops: *Incident: P7092* crashed on take-off at Matlaske on 11 January 1942. *Nickname:* Jeep: *Claims:* Ju.88 destroyed on 27 May 1942 in *P7046* shared with F/S Brennan. *Remarks:* Born on 12 January 1919, in California. The Ju.88 destroyed with F/S Brennan was actually Blenheim *V5568* of 1401 Meteorological Flight, Bircham Newton. He survived the war and passed away in January 1963.

LATHAM Norman

Nationality: British. *S/n:* 122304 RAFVR. *Rank:* Pilot Officer. *Squadron:* 263. *Flight:* A. *In:* 24 June 1942 from 59 OTU. *First Whirlwind Op:* Not operational. *Out:* 4 July 1942 Posted

Overseas. *Remarks:* With 263 for ten days, he remained in the RAF, retiring as a Flight Lieutenant on 30 August 1954.

LAWSON Graham Lewis

Nationality: British. *S/n:* 920311 RAFVR. *Rank:* Sergeant. *Squadron:* 263. *Flight:* A. *In:* 19 February 1941 from 56 OTU. *First Whirlwind Op:* Not operational. *Out:* 4 July 1941 to RAF Yatesbury: *Incident: P6991 HE-R* collided with a motor roller at Portreath on 23 March 1941. *Remarks:* He remained in the post-war RAF, being commissioned as a Flying Officer in the RAFVR on 20 May 1947, and relinquishing his Commission as a Flight Lieutenant on 21 May 1957. He joined the RAFVR Training Branch as a Flying Officer on 26 March 1959 before again relinquishing his Commission on 25 March 1979.

LAWTON John Clifford

Nationality: British. *S/n:* 65584 RAFVR. *Rank:* Pilot Officer. *Squadron:* 263. *Flight:* B. *In:* 13 September 1941 from 56 OTU. *First Whirlwind Op:* Not operational. *Out:* 8 October 1941 to 137 Squadron. *Squadron:* 137. *Flight:* B. *In:* 8 October 1941 from 263 Squadron. *First Whirlwind Op:* 17 November 1941. *Out:* 24 April 1942 to 51 OTU. *Hours:* 45:55 on 41 ops: *Incident: P7090* hit a maintenance hangar at Coltishall on 10 November 1941. *Nickname:* Gladys. *Remarks:* One of twenty-six pilots who served with both Whirlwind Squadrons, he was killed in a flying accident at 51 OTU on 15 October 1942. Aged twenty-six, he is buried in Section E, Row P, Plot 5 of Cirencester Cemetery.

LEE Patrick Henry

Nationality: British. *S/n:* 39796 RAF. *Rank:* Squadron Leader. *Squadron:* 137 *Flight:* A. *In:* 20 March 1943 as supernumerary. *First Whirlwind Op:* 1 April 1943. *Out:* 23 May 1943 to 257 Squadron. *Hours:* 3.20 on 3 ops. *Remarks:* Born on 2 August 1918, he joined the RAF in 1937 and was an instructor at the Central Flying School until 1941. Commended for bravery 1 July 1941, he was posted to 263 as a supernumerary then to 257 Squadron as CO and later to India as S/L Flying 165 Wing where he shot down three Japanese aircraft. Awarded the DFC on 8 September 1944 and an OBE on 23 May 1946 for distinguished service in south-east Asia, he finished the war as a Wing Commander and passed away in May 2002, in Herefordshire.

LEE-WHITE Arthur Henry DFC

Nationality: Peruvian. *S/n:* 121791 RAFVR. *Rank:* Pilot Officer; Flying Officer on 22 November 1942. *Squadron:* 263. *Flight:* B. *In:* 13 October 1942 from 59 OTU. *First Whirlwind Op:* 10 November 1942. *Out:* 29 June 1943 to 1453 Flight AFDU: *Awards:* DFC on 13 June 1943. *Hours:* 45:35 on 35 ops: *Claims:* Fw.190 of NAG.13 damaged on 16 May 1943 in *P7059*. *Incidents: P7040* hit by flak on 27 April 1943; *P7059* hit by flak on 23 May 1942. *Remarks:* Born in Peru. Attached to the US 8th Air Force at Goxhill on liaison duties on 9 February 1943, he crash-landed a P-47 whilst there then on leaving 263 he was posted to 1453 Flight AFDU Wittering flying captured German aircraft. On D-Day he flew a smoke laying Boston, and on his second tour he became the personal pilot of Sir Archibald Sinclair the Secretary of State for Air. He later flew C-47s with Transport Command ferrying troops to India and left the RAF in November 1946, then flew for Faucett Airlines in Peru before retiring to Canada.

LILLEYSTONE John Thomas
Nationality: British. *S/n:* 128644 RAFVR. *Rank:* Flying Officer. *Squadron:* 263. *Flight:* A. *In:* 31 October 1943 from 1 TEU. *First Whirlwind Op:* Not operational. *Out:* 10 November 1944 Posted. *Remarks:* Born in 1922, in Billericay, Essex. On 10 November 1943 he was sat on a bench in Torquay with a girlfriend when they were hit by a lorry and severely injured. He did not return to the squadron until 20 February 1944 but was not operational on Typhoons. He finished the war as a Flight Lieutenant, and by 1 July 1968 was a Wing Commander. He retired on 25 December 1976.

LINTERN Donald William
Nationality: British. *S/n:* 60079 RAFVR. *Rank:* Pilot Officer. *Squadron:* 263. *Flight:* A. *In:* 11 March 1941 from 56 OTU. *First Whirlwind Op:* Not operational. *Out:* 26 April 1941 to 504 Squadron. *Remarks:* Born on 19 June 1914, in Farnham, he was with 263 for just six weeks. Shot down in 185 Squadron Hurricane *Z5265* off Gozo by the Macchi 202 of Ten. Frigerio on 29 September 1941. Aged twenty-seven, his name appears on the Malta Memorial, Floriana, Panel 1 Column 1.

LONG Carl Arthur
Nationality: British. *S/n:* 918717 RAFVR. *Rank:* Sergeant. *Squadron:* 263. *Flight:* A. *In:* 19 February 1941 from 56 OTU. *First Whirlwind Op:* Not operational. *Out:* 12 June 1941 to 10 Group Flight. *Hours:* 12:30. *Remarks:* Born on 19 October 1918. He flew twelve training sorties on Whirlwinds. Posted to Malta, he survived ditching a Spitfire, finished the war as a Flight Lieutenant with Transport Command and relinquished his Commission on 1 July 1953 prior to joining the Airfield Construction Branch. He retired on 27 July 1956 and passed away in January 2001.

LOVELL Stuart James
Nationality: British. *S/n:* 107258 RAFVR. *Rank:* Pilot Officer; Flying Officer on 20 September 1942. *Squadron:* 263. *Flight:* B. *In:* 16 December 1941 from 55 OTU. *First Whirlwind Op:* 16 February 1942. *Out:* 1 March 1942 to 2 Delivery Flight. *In:* 1 May 1942 from 51 OTU. *Out:* 22 April 1943 to 257 Squadron. *Hours:* 90:20 on 83 ops. *Nickname:* Stu. *Remarks:* Born in Ceylon in 1916, he was short sighted and had a pair of corrective goggles made, but when someone pointed out a distant feature, he could be heard saying 'Where? Where?' He requested a Posting to 257 Squadron and was later transferred to 183 Squadron but was shot down by flak on 29 January 1944 over Guipavas aerodrome in Typhoon *MM970*. Aged twenty-seven, he is buried in Brest (Kerfantras) Cemetery, Lambezellec, Finistere. His brother W/C Anthony Desmond Lovell DSO* DFC* DFC (US) also died on active service.

LOVELL William Albert
Nationality: American. *S/n:* J/15275 RCAF. *Rank:* Sergeant; Flight Sergeant on 1 February 1942; Pilot Officer on 20 April 1942. *Squadron:* 263. *Flight:* A. *In:* 9 October 1941 from 55 OTU. *First Whirlwind Op:* 7 January 1942. *Out:* 29 September 1942 to USAAF. *Hours:* 105:05 on 96 ops. *Nickname:* Bill. *Remarks:* From Pennsylvania, he crossed the border into Canada in June 1940 to join the RCAF and arrived in England in July 1941. Discharged

from the RCAF to join the USAAF, *s/n O-885238*, he was posted to the 94th *'Hat in the Ring'* Fighter Squadron, 1st Fighter Group flying P-38s in North Africa and was awarded the Air Medal with three Oak Clusters and a Purple Heart. He failed to return from a combat near Bizerte, Tunisia, on 11 February 1944, in P-38F *41-7581*, and his name appears on the tablet at the North African American Cemetery, Carthage, Tunisia.

LUING John Frederick

Nationality: British. *S/n:* 745317 (Sgt); 121527 (Officer) RAFVR. *Rank:* Sergeant; Flight Sergeant on 1 December 1941; Pilot Officer on 22 May 1942; Flying Officer on 1 November 1942. *Squadron:* 263. *Flight:* A. *In:* 15 September 1941 from 56 OTU. *First Whirlwind Op:* Not operational. *Out:* 8 October 1941 to 137 Squadron. *Squadron:* 137: *Flt:* B. *In:* 8 October 1941 from 263 Squadron. *First Whirlwind Op:* 15 November 1941. *Out:* 5 October 1943 to Personnel Despatch Centre. *Hours:* 113:25 on 100 ops: *Claims:* Ju.88 damaged on 18 August 1942 in *P7055* shared with Sgt O'Neill. *Incidents: P7005 SF-S* undercarriage damaged at Snailwell on 26 August 1942; *P7051* crashed and caught fire at Manston on 17 January 1943 he was unhurt but John McClure noted, 'Boy did he run' just before the bombs which exploded. *Nickname:* Jack or Lou. *Remarks:* Born on 7 February 1917, he learnt to fly with a University Air Squadron in Derby before the war and was an electrical engineer. He served with 604 Squadron during his first tour before being rested to 56 OTU. He was one of twenty-six pilots who served with both Whirlwind Squadrons. Posted for Liaison Duties with US 8th Air Force between 24 October 1942 and 1 January 1943, he flew one Op on Hurricane IVs before being posted to 24 then 221 Squadron in Burma, but was shot down in Beaufighter *LZ364* on 8 March 1944. He died in a Japanese POW camp on 24 October 1944 aged twenty-seven, and is buried in Plot 6, H.10, Rangoon Cemetery, Burma. His brother Peter flew with the Fleet Air Arm.

MACAULAY John Gray

Nationality: British. *S/n:* 1113286 RAFVR. *Rank:* Sergeant. *Squadron:* 263. *Flight:* A. *In:* 1 September 1942 from 175 Squadron. *First Whirlwind Op:* 3 September 1942. *Out:* 14 April 1943 MIA. *Hours:* 14:00 on 13 ops. *Incidents: P6991 HE-R* his starboard engine failed on take-off in. He avoided high tension cables but hit a tree and crash-landed in a field on 9 February 1943. *Remarks:* His childhood friend, Bob Mathewson, noted that he was a bit of a dare-devil and was not surprised he became a fighter pilot. Missing in *P7010*, he was shot down by a Me.109 of 8/JG52 flown by Leutnant Wilhelm Godt. Aged twenty-three, his name appears on Panel 157 of the Runnymede Memorial.

MADDOCKS Jack

Nationality: British. *S/n:* 522229 RAFVR. *Rank:* Sergeant. *Squadron:* 263. *Flight:* B. *In:* 1 July 1941 from 56 OTU. *First Whirlwind Op:* 18 September 1941. *Out:* 8 October 1941 Posted. *Squadron:* 137. *In:* 8 October 1941 from 263 Squadron. *First Whirlwind Op:* 15 November 1941. *Out:* 7 January 1942 Injured. *Hours:* 23:20 on 20 ops. *Incidents: P6982* undercarriage collapsed at Charmy Down on 25 August 1941; *P7061 HE-A* crashed at Coltishall on 7 December 1941; *P7062* he overshot a landing in bad visibility at Coltishall and was badly injured in the subsequent crash on 7 January 1942. *Remarks:* He was one of twenty-six pilots who served with both Whirlwind Squadrons. After recovering from his crash on 7 January 1942 he returned to flying as an instructor but was killed on 14 January 1945 when he crashed at Melsbroek, Belgium in fog on return from a Raid on Berlin in 571 Squadron Mosquito XVI *ML976*. Aged thirty-one, he is buried in Brussels Town Cemetery in grave X.27.43.

MALIA, William
Nationality: British. *S/n:* RAFVR. *Rank:* Warrant Officer. *Squadron:* 137. *Flight:* A. *In:* 10 March 1943 from 59 OTU. *First Whirlwind Op:* Not operational. *Out:* 10 April 1943 to 91 Squadron. *Remarks:* Born in Rotherham, he was with 263 for one month. Whilst with 91 Squadron he was involved in an accident with Spitfire Mk.V *BL714*. Caught by a gust of wind whilst taxiing, she ground looped and the undercarriage collapsed. He passed away in 1976.

MARSLAND Guy
Nationality: British. *S/n:* 41940 RAF. *Rank:* Flight Lieutenant. *Squadron:* 263: *Flt:* B. *In:* 1 October 1941 from RAF Sutton Bridge. *First Whirlwind Op:* 15 October 1941 *Out:* 16 December 1941 to 137 Squadron. *Squadron:* 137 *Flight:* A Commander. *In:* 16 December 1941 from 263 Squadron. *Out:* 17 February 1942 Posted Overseas. *First Whirlwind Op:* 23 December 1941. *Hours:* 31.50 on 30 ops. *Remarks:* Born on the 5 November 1919, in Rotherham, Yorkshire, he fought with 245 and 253 Squadrons during the Battle of Britain, and destroyed a Me.110 on the 29 October 1940, before becoming a Gunnery instructor at Sutton Bridge. One of twenty-six pilots who served with both Whirlwind Squadrons, he was later posted to the Far East. He shot himself in a bizarre accident as he tried to draw his revolver cowboy style. He finished the war as a Squadron Leader, retired from the RAF in 1958 as a Wing Commander and became a successful antiques dealer. He passed away in 1983.

MARTIN George William
Nationality: British. *S/n:* 102619 RAFVR. *Rank:* Pilot Officer. *Squadron:* 263: *Flt:* B. *In:* 13 September 1941 from 56 OTU. *First Whirlwind Op:* Not operational. *Out:* 8 October 1941 to 137 Squadron. *Squadron:* 137. *Flight:* B. *In:* 8 October 1941 from 263 Squadron. *First Whirlwind Op:* 17 November 1941. *Out:* 12 February 1942 MIA. *Hours:* 48:45 on 41 ops. *Nickname:* Gus. *Remarks:* He graduated from Queens College, Cambridge in 1938, and was one of twenty-six pilots who served with both Whirlwind Squadrons. Missing in *P7106 SF-D* during 'Operation Fuller', he was twenty-two and his name appears on Panel 70 of the Runnymede Memorial.

MASON Dennis William
Nationality: British. *S/n:* 550478 (Sgt); 45726 (Officer) RAF. *Rank:* Sergeant; Pilot Officer on 8 May 1941. *Squadron:* 263. *Flight:* B. *In:* 14 November 1939 from 11 Group Pool. *First Whirlwind Op:* 12 January 1941. *Out:* 10 September 1941 KIA. *Hours:* 87:10 on 82 ops. *Remarks:* Born 19 July 1918 he joined the RAF in 1937 and joined 263 shortly after its formation. Seconded to 141 Squadron between 7 December 1939 and 9 May 1940, he converted to Whirlwinds after flying twenty-six Hurricane ops and when he was shot down by flak near Lestré in *P7001*, S/L Donaldson wrote of him 'His cool, courageous and aggressive flying has been an inspiration to us all. He has flown in action with me on many

occasions and I am sure you will be proud to know that the part he has played towards winning the war is a debt which no one can repay. The Country has lost one of her most promising young Fighter Pilots; we have lost a very firm and popular friend.' Aged twenty-three, he is buried in Plot 6, Row G, Grave 12, Cherbourg Old Communal Cemetery.

McCLURE John Edward DFC

Nationality: Canadian. *S/n:* J/15505 RCAF. *Rank:* Sergeant; Flight Sergeant on 2 February 1942: Pilot Officer on 6 July 1942: Flying Officer on 24 January 1943: Flight Lieutenant on 20 June 1943. *Squadron:* 263. *Flight:* B. *In:* 9 October 1941 from 55 OTU. *First Whirlwind Op:* Not operational. *Out:* 22 October 1941 to 137 Squadron. *Squadron:* 137. *Flight:* B. *In:* 22 October 1941 from 263 Squadron. *First Whirlwind Op:* 24 November 1941. *Out:* 20 June 1943 to 263 Squadron. *Squadron:* 263. *Flight:* B Commander. *In:* 20 June 1943 from 137 Squadron. *First Whirlwind Op:* 18 July 1943. *Out:* 13 October 1943 Posted: *Awards:* DFC on 6 July 1943. *Hours:* 182:25 on 156 ops, 533 total: *Claims:* Ju.88 destroyed on 25 July 1942 in *P7104 SF-V* shared with W/O Robert Smith. *Incidents: P7104 SF-V* battle damage on 22 July 1942; *P7047* engine failure on 17 September 1943. *Nickname:* Mac. *Remarks:* Born in London, Ontario in 1921, he was one of twenty-six pilots who served with both Whirlwind Squadrons. His DFC was awarded for offensive operations with 137 Squadron and he later became Aide-de-Camp to the Governor and C-in-C of the Dominion of Canada on 23 November 1944. A distinguished post-war RCAF career included Commanding a Sabre Squadron.

McDERMOTT Irving Francis

Nationality: Canadian. *S/n:* 41719 RAF. *Rank:* Pilot Officer. *Squadron:* 263. *Flight:* B. *In:* 2 October 1939 from 3 FTS. *First Whirlwind Op:* Not operational. *Out:* 8 September 1940 to Central Flying School. *Hours:* 13.00. *Remarks:* Born in Winnipeg, Canada, he arrived in the UK on the *'Ascania'* on 27 December 1938 and was Posted to 263 on its formation. On 7 August 1940 he abandoned *P6966 HE-X* near Stenhousemuir when a tyre burst on take-off and jammed the undercarriage; it was the first Whirlwind loss. Not operational on the aircraft, he flew thirteen hours on training sorties. Posted to CFS then 36 SFTS in Canada as an instructor, he later flew Wellingtons with 104 Squadron in Italy but was killed on 1 November 1943 – his DFC was awarded posthumously on the 23. Aged twenty-seven, he is buried in Plot 1.C.9, Biguglia War Cemetery, Corsica.

McFADGEN Robert Alex

Nationality: American. *S/n:* R/58420 RCAF. *Rank:* Sergeant. *Squadron:* 263. *Flight:* A. *In:* 28 December 1941 from 51 OTU. *First Whirlwind Op:* Not operational. *Out:* 10 May 1942 to RAF Uxbridge. *Nickname:* Bob or Don. *Remarks:* Born on 19 April 1919, he enlisted on 9 August 1940, in Vancouver, and trained at 2 ITS; 13 EFTS and 8 SFTS before being awarded his Wings on 7 April 1941. He was discharged from the RCAF on 12 October 1942 and joined the USAAF.

McPHAIL Donald Burton

Nationality: Canadian. *S/n:* R/67887 RCAF. *Rank:* Sergeant; Warrant Officer on 12 March 1942; Pilot Officer on 1 October 1942. *Squadron:* 137. *Flight:* B. *In:* 1 December 1941 from 59 OTU. *First Whirlwind Op:* 16 February 1942. *Out:* 9 October 1942 to 263 Squadron. *Squadron:*

263. *Flight:* B. *In:* 9 October 1942 from 137 Squadron. *First Whirlwind Op:* 7 November 1942. *Out:* 7 December 1942 MIA. *Hours:* 63:35 on 55 ops. *Remarks:* Born in Ontario to Scottish parents he was one of twenty-six pilots who served with both Whirlwind Squadrons. He was shot down attacking a convoy in the Baie du St Brelade, Jersey in *P9687 HE L* and the ORB noted, 'Of sober habits he was well liked [...] an excellent amateur photographer he was i/c Squadron Photographic Records.' (*See also* Robert Woodward.) Aged twenty-five, his name appears on Panel 101 of the Runnymede Memorial.

MERCER Charles Eldred
Nationality: Canadian. *S/n:* J/15738 RCAF. *Rank:* Sergeant; Warrant Officer on 12 March 1942; Pilot Officer on 25 October 1942. *Squadron:* 137. *Flight:* B. *In:* 1 October 1941 from 56 OTU. *First Whirlwind Op:* 1 February 1942. *Out:* 18 February 1943 KIFA. *Hours:* 89:00 on 83 ops, 266:00 total: *Claims:* Do.217 of 3/KG.2 destroyed on 20 June 1942 in *P6972* shared with F/S Ashton: *Incident: P7048* damaged on 19 January 1943. *Nickname:* Merce. *Remarks:* Killed in *P7119 SF-W* when he hit 2 Lt. Freeman in *P7114* at Manston. Aged twenty-four, he is buried in Margate Cemetery, Plot 16197, Section 50, next to his colleague. (*See also* 2nd Lt Neville Freeman.)

MERCER Paul Thomas Richard
Nationality: British. *S/n:* 127883 RAFVR. *Rank:* Flying Officer. *Squadron:* 263. *Flight:* B. *In:* 25 February 1943 from 56 OTU. *Out:* 24 October 1943 KIA: *First Op:* 14 May 1943. *Hours:* 21:05 on 16 ops. *Remarks:* Hit by flak in *P6986 HE-Q* during the low-level attack on the *M/V Münsterland* in Cherbourg Harbour then shot down into the sea by flak near St Vaast. He was described as being 'very brave and very petrified' and was married a week before being killed. His name appears on Panel 126 of the Runnymede Memorial.

MEREDITH John Eutychus
Nationality: British. *S/n:* 1100657 RAFVR. *Rank:* Sergeant. *Squadron:* 263. *Flight:* A. *In:* 1 July 1941 from 56 OTU. *First Whirlwind Op:* 30 July 1941. *Out:* 7 June 1942 to 175 *Squadron: Whirlwind Hours:* 48:20 on 41 ops. *Incidents: P7039* collided with *P6996* and a Nissen hut at Charmy Down on 15 September 1941; *P7117 HE-E* wingtip hit ground at Fairwood Common on 16 April 1942; *P7035* undercarriage collapsed at Fairwood Common on 30 April 1942. *Nickname:* Paddy. *Remarks:* Born on 20 March 1920. Posted on a Navigation Course at RAF Cranage then to 175 Squadron, where he destroyed a He.111 on 19 August 1942, he finished the war as a Flight Lieutenant and passed away in Stoke in September 1996.

MILLIGAN George Stanley
Nationality: British. *S/n:* 742070 (Sgt); 87030 (Officer) RAFVR. *Rank:* Sergeant; Pilot Officer on 29 October 1940. *Squadron:* 263. *Flight:* B. *In:* 2 October 1939 from 11 Group Pool. *First Whirlwind Op:* 20 December 1940. *Out:* 30 April 1941 KIFA. *Hours:* 47:20 on 45 ops, 144:00 total: *Incident: P6968 HE-H* ran over an unmarked pot hole at Exeter on 16 February 1941. *Remarks:* Born in Great Shelford, Cambridge on 2 September 1918, he was a typewriter mechanic before enlisting in September 1938. Posted to 263 on its formation he took part in both Norwegian Expeditions during which he claimed 2½ victories, and then flew twenty-eight sorties on Hurricanes before converting to the Whirlwind. He was

killed when *P7008* broke up in the air and crashed near Aldermaston during a Co-Op Exercise with 15 OTU Wellingtons. Aged twenty-two, his name appears on column 2 at Cambridge Crematorium.

MILLS Randolph Stuart
Nationality: British. *S/n:* 36067 RAF. *Rank:* Flight Lieutenant. *Squadron:* 263: *Flt:* A Commander. *In:* 2 October 1939 from HQ Fighter Command. *First Whirlwind Op:* Not operational. *Out:* 18 August 1940 to 87 Squadron. *Nickname:* Milly. *Remarks:* Born on 20 October 1909, he graduated from the Imperial Service College as an Aero engine Fitter in December 1929, later applying for flying training and on 21 May 1936 he became a Pilot Officer. Posted to 263 as a Flight Commander on its formation, he was wounded on 21 April 1940 during the first Norwegian campaign when his section of three aircraft flew into a mist covered mountain. He was awarded the DFC on 10 May 1940 for his work in Norway. Posted as CO 87 Squadron, then Assistant Air Attaché to the USA, where he helped develop British training facilities and briefed President Roosevelt on European air operations. He finished the war as a Wing Commander, retired as a Group Captain on 20 October 1956 and passed away in 1999.

MITCHNER John Davidson
Nationality: Canadian. *S/n:* J/16799 RCAF. *Rank:* Sergeant. *Squadron:* 263. *Flight:* A. *In:* 9 October 1941 from 55 OTU. *First Whirlwind Op:* Not operational. *Out:* 29 June 1942 to 55 OTU. *Hours:* 7:20. *Nickname:* Mitch. *Remarks:* Born in Saskatoon, Canada on 3 July 1914, he was a book keeper before enlisting on 26 October 1940. A diagnosis of diabetes prevented him becoming operational on Whirlwinds and he was posted back to 55 OTU at Usworth as an instructor, but later flew two tours on Spitfires, received a DFC and Bar and the Netherlands Cross, and claimed eleven victories before returning to Canada on 31 March 1946. He remained in the post war RCAF, commanding 434 Squadron on Sabres in June 1952, retired as a Wing Commander in November 1960 and passed away on 8 December 1964.

MOFFET Alan Ormerod
Nationality: British. *S/n:* 40736 RAF. *Rank:* Pilot Officer. *Squadron:* 263. *Flight:* A. *In:* 26 June 1940 from 6 OTU. *First Whirlwind Op:* Not operational. *Out:* 22 July 1940 to RAE. *Nickname:* Moff. *Remarks:* Born in Chorlton, Lancashire, he was with 263 for five weeks. Awarded an AFC on 11 June 1942 he died in an accident on 21 July 1945 as a Squadron Leader. Aged twenty-five, he is buried in Skelsmergh Cemetery, near Kendal, Plot A, Grave 36.

MOGG Douglas Edwin George
Nationality: British. *S/n:* 123605 RAFVR. *Rank:* Flying Officer. *Squadron:* 263. *Flight:* B. *In:* 4 July 1943 from 53 OTU. *First Whirlwind Op:* 24 October 1943. *Out:* 26 December 1943 KIFA. *Hours:* 7:40 on 8 ops. *Incidents:* *P7046* flak damage on 26 November 1943. *Nickname:* Pussy. *Remarks:* Born in Poole in 1920. Flew into high ground at Melbury near Shaftsbury in poor visibility in Typhoon *JR239*. Aged twenty-three, he is buried in Plot 25, Section CC, Poole (Parkstone) Cemetery.

MOODY Vincent Kenneth

Nationality: Canadian. *S/n:* J/15362 RCAF. *Rank:* Flying Officer. *Squadron:* 263. *Flight:* A. *In:* 1 July 1943 from Air Fighting Development Unit. *First Whirlwind Op:* Not operational. *Out:* 10 July 1943 to 610 Squadron. *Remarks:* Born in Taunton, Massachusetts in 1920, he became a Canadian citizen in 1940. With 263 for nine days, he later fought on Malta with 249 Squadron and received the DFC on 25 January 1944 with 610 Squadron, but was shot down by flak in Spitfire IX *MD123 NX-M* of 131 Squadron when attacking Le Mans aerodrome on 12 June 1944. In avoiding the village of L'Eveque he crashed and was killed. Aged twenty-four, he is buried in Yvre L'Eveque Communal Cemetery. A street and the village nursery school are named in his honour.

MORTON Frank

Nationality: British *S/n:* 580250 RAF. *Rank:* Sergeant. *Squadron:* 263. *Flight:* A. *In:* 1 July 1940 from OTU. *First Whirlwind Op:* 12 December 1940. *Out:* 9 January 1941. *Hours:* 2:55 on 4 ops. *Remarks:* Born on 19 May 1917, in Birmingham, he was a talented artist, and was 'well liked by everyone.' After taking the Adjutant, F/O Hiscock, to his new posting at Warmwell in Blenheim *L1223* he crashed near Ebford during his return to Exeter. Aged twenty-four, he is buried in Plot 78, Section 2, Boldmere (St Michael) Churchyard, Warwickshire.

MUIRHEAD Harvey Donald

Nationality: Canadian. *S/n:* R/79587 RCAF. *Rank:* Sergeant; Flight Sergeant on 14 April 1942. *Squadron:* 263. *Flight:* A. *In:* 9 October 1941 from 55 OTU. *First Whirlwind Op:* 26 December 1941. *Out:* 28 September 1942 to 286 Squadron. *Hours:* 85:30 on 81 ops: *Incident: P7013* hit *P7120 HE-R* at Portreath on 5 July 1942; *Nickname:* Mick. *Remarks:* Born in Estevan, Saskatchewan, he was killed when *BM346*, his 401 Squadron Spitfire, collided with *W3839* on 17 February 1943. Aged twenty-four, he is buried in Plot 9, Row OO, Catterick Cemetery, North Yorkshire.

MUNRO John Gray

Nationality: British. *S/n:* 36016 RAF. *Rank:* Squadron Leader. *Squadron:* 263 *Flight:* A; Commanding Officer. *In:* 7 August 1940 from Air Ministry. *First Whirlwind Op:* 8 December 1940. *Out:* 18 February 1941 to AGME. *Hours:* 4:10 on 5 ops. *Nickname:* Jack. *Remarks:* The son of a Lawyer, he was born in Aberdeen on the 24 March 1913 and graduated with an Honours in Mechanical Sciences from Cambridge University, having learned to fly with the University Air Squadron. His RAF career began on the 29 September 1934 and on the 5 September 1935 he joined 47 Squadron in Khartoum. On his return to the UK he served with the Aircraft Armament Co-operation Flight; Air Armament School and the R&D Dept of the Air Ministry where he helped with the design of the servo fed 20-mm cannon and wrote the original armament installation specification for the Whirlwind. Posted to 263 to resolve firing problems with the cannons, he became CO on 17 December 1940. Although not shown in the 263 Squadron ORB, he flew the statutory sortie to be eligible for the Battle of Britain clasp. Due to his specialist technical knowledge he was screened from ops and posted to Command the Air Gun Mounting Establishment at Duxford, and was also involved with the Air Fighting Development Unit. Promoted to Wing Commander Fighters he was posted to the Telecommunications Flying Unit at Hurn where he was engaged in further secret work with the Radar Research Establishment. Following an Army Staff Course in August 1942 he was posted to the Air Ministry where he held several Staff roles until the 25 June 1943 when he was posted to Air HQ India and was involved in logistical support in Burma. He finished the war as a Group Captain and in June 1946 became Wing Commander Flying RAF Wyton which housed Lincoln bombers, but retired from the RAF on 21 February 1949 due to ill health and he passed away in on 23 January 1951.

MUSGRAVE Edward Lancelot DFC

Nationality: Australian. *S/n:* 403528 RAAF. *Rank:* Pilot Officer; Flying Officer on 25 March 1942. *Squadron:* 137. *Flight:* A. *In:* 13 January 1942 from 61 OTU. *First Whirlwind Op:* 15 March 1942. *Out:* 17 May 1943 KIA: *Awards:* DFC on 26 February 1943. *Hours:* 105:15 on 92 ops: *Claims:* Fw.190A-4 *'Black 2'* of 8/JG.26 destroyed on 28 January 1943 in *P7058 SF-G*. *Incidents: P7063* crashed at Matlaske on 30 July 1942; *P7114* hit by flak on 10 February 1943; *P7092 SF-Q* hydraulic failure on 14 March 1943; *P7048* hit by flak on 17 April 1943. *Nickname:* Eddie. *Remarks:* Born on 26 February 1918, in Sydney, he was a Furniture Salesman before he enlisted on 1 February 1941 and trained in Canada prior to shipping to the UK. Hospitalised between 11 November and 11 December 1942, he was seconded to 268 Squadron for a week in March 1942. Awarded the DFC for, amongst other things, his attack on the blockade runner *Tojo* he failed to return from a night attack on a convoy in *P7063*. A keen and efficient pilot, and very popular with the squadron, he was named Lancelot after his mother's favourite literary character. Aged twenty-five, he is buried in Pihen-lès-Guînes War Cemetery, Pas de Calais, Plot 1.C.1.

NEAL Clarence

Nationality: Australian. *S/n:* 413236 RAAF. *Rank:* Flight Sergeant. *Squadron:* 137. *Flight:* A. *In:* 26 May 1943 from 55 OTU. *First Whirlwind Op:* Not operational. *Out:* 31 August 1943 to 1 SLAIS, Milfield. *Remarks:* Born on 25 June 1919, in Taree, New South Wales, he was a clerk with Aladdin Industries before enlisting on 16 August 1941. After one Hurricane IV Op he went to 1 SLAIS, then 66 Squadron where on 22 June 1944 he was listed as missing. He returned safely after five days however and was repatriated to Australia. Discharged as a Flying Officer on 5 November 1945, he passed away in December 1967.

O'DOWD Kevin Patrick

Nationality: British. *S/n:* 1033310 RAFVR. *Rank:* Warrant Officer. *Squadron:* 263. *Flight:* A *In:* 19 January 1943 from 535 Squadron. *First Whirlwind Op:* Not operational on Whirlwinds. *Out:* 22 February 1943 to 141 Squadron. *Remarks:* Posted in from 535 Turbinlight Squadron, he was with 263 for five weeks. Missing in 264 Squadron Mosquito II *DD643* over the Bay of Biscay on 14 June 1943, he was twenty-two, and his name appears on Panel 138 of the Runnymede Memorial.

O'NEILL Hugh Leo

Nationality: British. *S/n:* 530323 RAF. *Rank:* Sergeant; Flight Sergeant on 1 November 1942. *Squadron:* 263. *Flight:* A. *In:* 15 September 1941 from 56 OTU. *First Whirlwind Op:* Not operational. *Out:* 8 October 1941 to 137 Squadron. *Squadron:* 137: *Flt:* A. *In:* 8 October

1941 from 263 Squadron. *First Whirlwind Op:* 11 November 1941. *Out:* 22 May 1943 Posted Overseas. *Hours:* 68:35 on 55 ops: *Claims:* Ju.88D-1 *F6+EL* of 3(F)/122 destroyed on 29 July 1942 in *P7005 SF-H* shared with P/O Rebbetoy; Ju.88 damaged on 18 August 1942 in *P7037* shared with P/O Luing. *Incidents: P7094* crashed near Matlaske on 23 December 1941; *P7005* battle damage on 29 July 1942. *Nickname:* Paddy or Clarry. *Remarks:* Born in Dundee in1921, he joined the RAF in March 1936. Posted from 263 to the Far East, he was killed on 12 July 1945, in 110 Squadron Mosquito *RF672/V*. Aged twenty-eight; he is buried in Plot B2.A.2, Tanbyuzayat War Cemetery, Burma.

OGILVIE Donald Bruce

Nationality: British. *S/n:* 83287 RAFVR. *Rank:* Flying Officer; Flight Lieutenant on 17 August 1942. *Squadron:* 263. *Flight:* B. *In:* 10 February 1942 from 56 OTU. *First Whirlwind Op:* Not operational. *Out:* 20 April 1942 to 137 Squadron. *Squadron:* 137. *Flight:* B Commander. *In:* 20 April 1942 from 263 Squadron. *First Whirlwind Op:* 28 April 1942. *Out:* 7 June 1942 to HQFC. *Squadron:* 263. *Flight:* B Commander. *In:* 10 December 1942 from HQFC. *Out:* 17 February 1943 to RAF Milfield. *Hours:* 23:00 on 21 ops, 54:35 total. *Remarks:* Born on 22 September 1920, in Warrington, he enlisted in 1938 and fought with 601 Squadron during the Battle of Britain. Injured in a crash-landing on 24 September 1940 he later flew P-39 Airacobras and was Mentioned in Despatches on 17 March 1941. On 22 May 1941 he shot down the Me.109F-2 of Gefreiter Hans-Günther Kärger of 7/JG3, and was attached to Westland as a test pilot in January 1942 prior to joining 137 as 'B' Flight Commander. He was one of twenty-six pilots who served with both Whirlwind Squadrons, and left 137 to act as Liaison Officer for 1st Fighter Squadron 94th Fighter Group 8th USAAF. He flew several missions on their P-38s before returning to Whirlwinds as 263 'B' Flight Commander, followed by a spell as an instructor at SLAIS, Milfield; then with 6 Squadron in the Middle East; and Air Support Officer to the SAS, SBS and LRDG at HQ Eastern Mediterranean. His final appointment was as Senior Air Officer on Kos but he was captured when the Germans invaded the Island, and spent the rest of the war as a POW at Barth Vogelsang, Germany. Released from Vogelgesand by the Russians in May 1945 he was invalided out of the RAF in July and later received the US Silver Star and Air Medal with two Oak Leaves. He passed away in January 1993.

OLIVIER Harold Antony

Nationality: British. *S/n:* 39388 RAF. *Rank:* Flying Officer; Flight Lieutenant on 3 September 1940. *Squadron:* 263. *Flight:* A; B Commander. *In:* 21 April 1940 from 5 OTU. *First Whirlwind Op:* 11 December 1940. *Out:* 22 December 1940 to North Africa. *Hours:* 1:25 on 3 ops. *Remarks:* Born in Paddington on 6 November 1917, he fought in the Second Norwegian Campaign then flew one operational sortie on Hurricane Is before converting to Whirlwinds. 'An efficient and competent pilot, as well as being a steadying influence on the younger pilots' he became a Squadron Leader on 1 July 1954.

PARSONS Lamont Maroy

Nationality: Canadian. *S/n:* J/11551 RCAF. *Rank:* Flight Lieutenant. *Squadron:* 263. *Flight:* B. *In:* 1 July 1943 from 3 Personnel Reception Centre. *First Whirlwind Op:* Not operational. *Out:* 2 July 1943 to 610 Squadron. *Remarks:* Born in Newfoundland on 12 August 1919, he enlisted in Toronto on 17 May 1940 and served with 118 Squadron in Canada. An

Instructor before being posted to the UK on 22 May 1943, he was with 263 for just one day before moving on. Promoted to Flight Lieutenant on 30 April 1944, he returned to Canada on 31 July 1944 and was discharged on 1 December 1944.

PASCOE Reginald Gunn
Nationality: British. *S/n:* 927360 RAFVR. *Rank:* Sergeant. *Squadron:* 263. *Flight:* B. *In:* 17 May 1941 from 56 OTU. *First Whirlwind Op:* Not operational. *Out:* 11 June 1941 KIFA. *Hours:* 16:00. *Remarks:* Born on 30 November 1920, in Gravesend, he received his 'Wings' at 15 FTS on 23 March 1941. He overshot a landing and crashed in a Hurricane at 56 OTU in April 1941; he then flew sixteen hours on training sorties in the Whirlwind, but was killed when *L6845* crashed on Cefn Coed Farm, Kincoed following an engine failure. Aged twenty, he is buried in Plot 3162 of Swanscombe Cemetery, Kent. His brother, Douglas, was killed with 108 Squadron in Palestine in 1942.

PESKETT Maurice John
Nationality: British. *S/n:* 934165 RAFVR. *Rank:* Sergeant. *Squadron:* 263. *Flight:* A. *In:* 15 September 1941 from 56 OTU. *First Whirlwind Op:* Not operational. *Out:* 8 October 1941 to 137 Squadron. *Hours:* 18:00. *Squadron:* 137. *Flight:* A. *In:* 8 October 1941 from 263 Squadron. *First Whirlwind Op:* Not operational. *Out:* 30 October 1941 Posted. *Incidents: P7063* crashed Charmy Down on 3 October 1941. *Nickname:* Mike. *Remarks:* Born on 21 September 1921, in Ipswich, he was one of twenty-six pilots who served with both Whirlwind Squadrons. On 28 October 1941 he returned to base in a badly damaged *P7058 SF-G* following a collision with *P7053* in which S/L Sample was killed. Posted immediately, he finished the war as a Flight Lieutenant and received an AFC on 1 January 1946.

PRIOR Derrick Ellis
Nationality: British. *S/n:* 166018 RAFVR. *Rank:* Sergeant. *Squadron:* 263. *Flight:* A. *In:* 15 September 1941 from 56 OTU. *First Whirlwind Op:* 15 October 1941. *Out:* 14 December 1941 KIFA. *Hours:* 5:35 on 5 ops, 51:00 total. *Incidents: P6983* undercarriage collapsed at Charmy Down on 16 September 1941; *P7061* tail wheel would not lock down on 5 December 1941. *Remarks:* Received his 'Wings' on 5 April 1941 at 31 SFTS, Canada. 'A very popular member of the squadron due to his sense of humour and excellent spirit,' he died on a Searchlight Co-Op Exercise when *P7044* crashed near Coleford, Gloucestershire. Aged twenty-one, he is buried in Plot 9, Block C, Row A at Yiewsley & West Drayton Burial Ground, Middlesex.

PROCTOR Harold Medd
Nationality: British. *S/n:* 159873 RAFVR. *Rank:* Sergeant; Flight Sergeant on 13 September 1943; Pilot Officer on 17 October 1943. *Squadron:* 263. *Flight:* B; A. *In:* 25 February 1943 from 56 OTU. *First Whirlwind Op:* 11 May 1943. *Out:* 24 August 1944 KIA. *Hours:* 33:05 on 26 ops: *Incident: P6971* heavy landing on 11 May 1943; *P7097* hit by flak on 24 October 1943. *Nickname:* Percy or Proc I. *Remarks:* Born in Stokesley, Yorkshire, he was a 'very able pilot and excellent leader, he was not only liked but admired for his laid-back approach to life and although not noted for high jinks or unruly behaviour, he was always one of the team.' He flew fifty-two ops on Typhoons, received the DFC on 28 July 1944 and became 'A' Flight Commander on 19 August. Five days later in *MP153* he led his section in an attack

on a Ferry on the Seine which they left on fire. During the attack he was hit by flak and went 'straight in' near Quillebeuf. 'His was a very grave loss to the squadron, Proc I was a grand fellow, very popular with all the pilots and was an excellent Flight Commander.' Aged twenty-three, his name appears on Panel 203 of the Runnymede Memorial.

PUGH Thomas Patrick DFC

Nationality: British. *S/n:* 40137 RAF. *Rank:* Flying Officer; Flight Lieutenant on 12 February 1941; Squadron Leader on 22 August 1941. *Squadron:* 263. *Flight:* B; B Commander; Commanding Officer. *In:* 1 July 1940 from RAF Uxbridge. *First Whirlwind Op:* 9 January 1941. *Out:* 12 February 1942 to 82 Group HQ: *Awards:* DFC on 8 October 1941. *Hours:* 74:50 on 60 ops. *Incidents: P6977* engine failure on 9 January 1941; *P6984 HE-H* following double engine failure he was forced to abandon her over Middlemore, South Devon on 19 January 1941; *P7041* hit by flak and on 28 September 1941. *Nickname:* Puff. *Remarks:* Born in Farnborough in 1920, his brothers also served in the RAF. (Robert flew Wellingtons with Coastal Command, but John was killed in May 1940, in a Spitfire). He joined the RAF in July 1937 and fought with 103 Squadron in France. Posted to 1 RAF Depot then 263 on his return to Britain, he became 'B' Flight Commander on 30 August 1940. He was the first to suggest hanging bombs on a Whirlwind, and was posted as Squadron Leader Tactics 82 Group HQ. In 1943 he formed and led 182 Squadron but was shot down over Dunkerque Harbour on 2 August 1943, in Typhoon *EK395*, as an Acting Wing Commander. Aged twenty-three, his name appears on Panel 64 of the Runnymede Memorial.

PURKIS John Barrie

Nationality: British. *S/n:* 1388276 (Sgt); 158700 (Officer) RAFVR. *Rank:* Sergeant; Flight Sergeant on 13 September 1943; Pilot Officer on 24 September 1943. *Squadron:* 263. *Flight:* A. *In:* 25 February 1943 from 56 OTU. *First Whirlwind Op:* 2 August 1943. *Out:* 31 August 1944 Rested. *Hours:* 20.30 on 17 ops. *Remarks:* Born 29 April 1921. He flew sixty-one ops on Typhoons in 1944 during which he crash-landed *MN136* after hitting a tree near Loudeac on 31 March; shared in the destruction of a Do.217 with F/L Rutter, P/O Green and F/S Handley on 20 April; became 'A' Flight Commander on 17 July; received the DFC on 28 July and was shot down by flak in *MN878* near Vimoutiers on 16 August. Heard to say over the R/T that he had been hit, he baled out over enemy territory and was captured by SS troops. Held briefly in Bernay prison, he was overlooked when the Germans left, and was treated like royalty by the French Commandant until British troops arrived when he walked out through the main gate to meet them. A stockbroker after the war, he passed away on 7 April 2011.

RACINE Gerry Geoffrey

Nationality: Canadian. *S/n:* J/5800 RCAF. *Rank:* Flying Officer; Flight Lieutenant on 21 December 1943. *Squadron:* 263: *Flt:* A; B. *In:* 28 October 1943 from 51 OTU. *First Whirlwind Op:* Not operational. *Out:* 31 March 1944 Rested. *Remarks:* Born on 21 May 1920, in St Boniface, Manitoba, Canada, he was an animation artist before the war and enlisted in Montreal on 11 November 1940. He graduated in the same class as Irving Kennedy and John Mitchner but was retained in Canada as an instructor. On 31 March 1944 he was hit by return fire from a Me.410 which he then destroyed, but was forced to abandon Typhoon *MN170* over the French coast. Aided by the Resistance, he returned to Britain on 16 April, received a DFC, but was Rested and returned to Canada where he was discharged on 8 February 1946. He passed away in March 1998.

RAMAMURTHY O.
Nationality: Indian. *S/n:* 1330624 RAFVR. *Rank:* Sergeant. *Squadron:* 263. *Flight:* A. *In:* 16 March 1943 from 58 OTU. *First Whirlwind Op:* Not operational. *Out:* 25 May 1943 to 286 Squadron. *Nickname:* The Maharajah of Strawberry Jam Pot. *Remarks:* Posted to 286 Squadron at Weston-super-Mare, then to 1624 Anti-Aircraft Co-operation Flight on 9 September 1943.

REBBETOY James Reginald
Nationality: Canadian. *S/n:* J/15741 RCAF. *Rank:* Sergeant; Flight Sergeant on 1 March 1942; Pilot Officer on 1 October 1942; Flying Officer on 4 April 1943. *Squadron:* 137. *Flight:* A. *In:* 28 October 1941 from 56 OTU. *First Whirlwind Op:* 1 February 1942. *Out:* 25 April 1943 KIA. *Hours:* 112:45 on 101 ops: *Claims:* Ju.88D-1 *F6+EL* of 3(F)/122 destroyed on 29 July 1942 in *P7058 SF-G* shared with F/S O'Neill; Fw.190 probably destroyed on 19 December 1942 in *P7005 SF-H* shared with F/O Bryan. *Incidents: P7097* crash-landed near Coltishall on 8 February 1942; *P7111 SF-E* engine failure on 3 September 1942. *Remarks:* Born in Cayuga, Ontario, he was French Canadian. On 25 April 1943 he was shot down and killed attacking a flak train near Tielt, Belgium in *P7058 SF-G*. S/L Coghlan wrote to his father, 'Your son joined my Squadron a year and a half ago as a Sergeant, and from the very moment of joining had shown himself to be a very fine pilot, exceptionally keen and most efficient, and six months after his joining I was very happy to recommend him for a commission, so that he could become one of my Officers. Since that time he has done extremely well and was in line for being recommended for the DFC, and but for his unfortunate loss he would have certainly earned this distinction. He was very much beloved by the squadron and he had a personality which we will always remember.' Aged twenty-six, he was buried in the Adegem Canadian War Cemetery, Adegem, Oost-Vlaanderen, Belgium, Plot 1.E.2.

REED Richard Irl
Nationality: American. *S/n:* R/67827 RCAF. *Rank:* Sergeant; Flight Sergeant on 12 February 1942. *Squadron:* 263. *Flight:* A. *In:* 9 October 1941 from 55 OTU. *First Whirlwind Op:* 21 October 1941. *Out:* 29 September 1942 to USAAF. *Hours:* 67:35 on 60 ops. *Incidents: P7017* ran into a ditch at Charmy Down on 21 November 1941; *P7051* heavy landing at Charmy Down on 22 November 1941; *P7117 HE-D* hit a lorry at Angle on 9 August 1942. *Remarks:* Born in Florida. He was discharged from the RCAF to fly P-38s with the USAAF 94th *'Hat in the Ring'* Fighter Squadron, 1st Fighter Group, s/n O-885326,, then later P-47s with the 335 Fighter Squadron but was killed on 20 February 1944 in *42-75051 WD-R* shortly after sharing in the destruction of a Me.110 over Belgium.

RÉMY Mauiritius
Nationality: French. *S/n:* 30.656 FFF. *Rank:* Lieutenant. *Squadron:* 263. *Flight:* A. *In:* 17 February 1941 from 56 OTU. *First Whirlwind Op:* Not operational. *Out:* 20 February 1941 to 238 Squadron. *Remarks:* His real name was Roger Motte, he was born on 15

August 1912, in Neuilly-on-Seine, and he was a teacher. With 263 for just three days, he later crash-landed his 32 Squadron Hurricane in the Irish Republic and was interred for sixteen months before escaping. Post-war he served in the La Armée de l'Air but was killed in an air crash on 26 October 1962.

RIDLEY Kenneth Charles DFC DFM

Nationality: British. *S/n:* 756303 RAFVR. *Rank:* Sergeant; Flight Sergeant 1 October 1942. *Squadron:* 263: *Flt:* A. *In:* 15 September 1941 from 56 OTU. *First Whirlwind Op:* 25 October 1941. *Out:* 29 June 1943 to AFDU: *Awards:* DFC; DFM on 3 July 1943. *Hours:* 135:40 on 132 ops. *Incidents: P6971* hit an obstruction at Charmy Down on 15 October 1941; *P6994* engine failure on the 30 October 1941; *P7013* hit by flak on 3 October 1942: *P6974 HE-X* hit by flak on 15 June 1943. *Remarks:* He was born on 13 May 1921, in Northfleet, Kent. Detached to 1 SLAIS Milfield on 20 March 1943 he received the DFC and DFM for work on Whirlwinds. Rested to AFDU Wittering, he returned to fly Meteor IIIs with the re-formed 263 Squadron in late 1945 before emigrating to South Africa where he passed away in Durban in November 1980.

RILEY William

Nationality: Republic of Ireland. *S/n:* 37422 RAF. *Rank:* Flight Lieutenant. *Squadron:* 263. *Flight:* A. *In:* 3 May 1940 from 610 Squadron. *First Whirlwind Op:* Not operational. *Out:* 11 July 1940 to 302 Squadron. *Remarks:* Born in Manorhamilton, County Leitrim, he joined the RAF in August 1935. His first Squadron was 54, and by December 1938 he was with HQ RAF Far East in Singapore. On his return, he joined 263, was wounded in Norway, and then fought with 302 Squadron during the Battle of Britain, claiming two Ju.88s and a Me.109. He received a DFC on 31 October 1941 and later flew with 272 Squadron in the Middle East. He was killed on the 16 July 1942 as a Wing Commander when his Beaufighter collided with another just after take-off and crashed into the sea. Aged twenty-five, his name appears on column 24 of the Alamein Memorial.

ROBERTS Desmond Arthur

Nationality: New Zealander. *S/n:* 411994 RNZAF. *Rank:* Sergeant; Flight Sergeant on 1 August 1942; Pilot Officer on 20 February 1943. *Squadron:* 137. *Flight:* A. *In:* 1 March 1942 from 57 OTU. *First Whirlwind Op:* 5 April 1942. *Out:* 2 June 1943 to 485 Squadron. *Hours:* 48:05 on 46 ops: *Claims:* Do.217E-4 *F8+BN* of 5/KG.40 destroyed on 19 August 1942, in *P7046* shared with F/O Bryan. *Incidents: P7048* tail wheel collapsed at Matlaske on 8 April 1942; *P7047* instrument failure on 17 April 1943. *Nickname:* Red. *Remarks:* Repatriated to New Zealand on 1 November 1944 as a Flying Officer, he passed away in 1970.

ROBERTSON Basil Lionel

Nationality: British. *S/n:* 748333 RAFVR. *Rank:* Sergeant; Flight Sergeant on 1 November 1941; Warrant Officer on 7 February 1942. *Squadron:* 263. *Flight:* A. *In:* 15 September 1941 from 56 OTU. *First Whirlwind Op:* Not operational. *Out:* 8 October 1941 to 137 Squadron. *Squadron:* 137. *Flight:* A. *In:* 8 October 1941 from 263 Squadron. *First Whirlwind Op:* 26 October 1941. *Out:* 12 February 1942 MIA. *Hours:* 39.05 on 34 ops. *Nickname:* Robbie. *Remarks:* He joined 54 Squadron on 22 August 1940. One of twenty-six pilots who served with both Whirlwind Squadrons, he went Missing during 'Operation Fuller' in *P7107*.

Aged twenty, his name appears on Panel 73 of the Runnymede Memorial.

ROBINSON John Joseph

Nationality: British. *S/n:* 1057469 RAFVR. *Rank:* Sergeant. *Squadron:* 263. *Flight:* B. *In:* 15 September 1941 from 56 OTU. *First Whirlwind Op:* 2 October 1941. *Out:* 6 November 1941 MIA. *Hours:* 3:05 on 3 ops. *Remarks:* 'A quiet and efficient person, his loss was recorded with very great regret,' he was shot down off Cap Barfleur in *P6970* by Oberfeldwebel Magnus Brunkhorst of 9/JG2. Aged twenty-one, his name appears on Panel 51 of the Runnymede Memorial.

ROSS David George

Nationality: British. *S/n:* 84001 RAFVR. *Rank:* Flight Lieutenant. *Squadron:* 263. *Flight:* B/A Commander. *In:* 16 July 1943 from 55 OTU. *First Whirlwind Op:* 4 August 1943. *Out:* 9 February 1944 to 198 *Squadron: Awards:* DFC on 28 March 1944. *Hours:* 37:45 on 33 ops. *Incidents: P6997* hit by flak on 26 November 1943. *Remarks:* Born in 1920, in Ecclefechan. Posted to 263 as a supernumerary and given command of 'A' Flight on 8 August 1943, he crash-landed a flak damaged *P6974 HE-X* at 180 mph on 24 October 1943 following the attack on the *M/V Münsterland.* Awarded the DFC for his work with Whirlwinds, he was posted as CO 198 Squadron. On the evening of 5 June 1944 he abandoned flak damaged Typhoon *MN761* south-east of the Isle of Wight, he was never found. Aged twenty-four, his name appears on Panel 201 of the Runnymede Memorial.

RUDLAND Clifford Percival DFC

Nationality: British. *S/n:* 745446 (Sgt); 65998 (Officer) RAFVR. *Rank:* Sergeant; Pilot Officer on 8 May 1941; Flying Officer on 8 May 1942; Flight Lieutenant on 9 September 1942. *Squadron:* 263. *Flight:* B; A Commander. *In:* 8 August 1940 from 6 OTU. *First Whirlwind Op:* 10 January 1941. *Out:* 1 September 1942 to 19 *Squadron: Awards:* DFC on 7 September 1941. *Hours:* 202:55 on 190 ops: *Claims:* Two Me.109Es of JG.2 destroyed on 6 August 1941 in *P7002. Incidents: P6979 HE-Q* tail wheel collapsed at Exeter on 8 February 1941; *P6979 HE-Q* tail wheel collapsed at Exeter on 29 August 1941; *P7002 HE-L* battle damage on 6 August 1941; *P6998* hit by flak on 26 August 1941. *Remarks:* Born on 12 December 1915, in Islington, London, he joined the RAF in March 1939. He tested the first Whirlwind fitted with bombs and immediately afterwards requested a posting, saying, 'If I had wanted to drop bombs I would have flown a Lancaster.' He joined 19 Squadron and was later detached to Vickers Supermarine at Southampton where he tested Spitfires until October 1943 before joining 131 Squadron. His next posting was as CO of 64 Squadron in August 1944, and in March 1945 he became Wing Commander Flying at Andrews Field, Essex until the end of the war. He received the US DFC on 15 May 1945 and a Bar to his DFC on 17 August 1945, and served as Planning Officer at 11 Group HQ between May and August 1945 before being sent to America on a Command & General Staff School course. Returning to the UK in November 1945, he was released from the RAF as a Wing Commander although he served in the RAFVR from 1946 to 1951 as a Flight Lieutenant. He passed away in March 1996.

RYAN Alton James

Nationality: Canadian. *S/n:* R/149115 RCAF. *Rank:* Sergeant. *Squadron:* 263. *Flight:* B. *In:* 1 September 1943 from 55 OTU. *First Whirlwind Op:* Not operational. *Out:* 24 June 1944 KIA. *Nickname:* Buck. *Remarks:* Born in Calgary, Canada in 1921. He was not operational on Whirlwinds but flew thirty sorties on Typhoons before being shot down by flak in *MN524* on 24 June 1944 during an attack on St Malo harbour. Aged twenty-three, he is buried in the Dinard British Cemetery, Row G, Grave 14. His 'Wings' were awarded posthumously on 28 May 1947.

SAINSBURY James Edwards

Nationality: British. *S/n:* 911888 RAFVR. *Rank:* Sergeant. *Squadron:* 263. *Flight:* A. *In:* 11 March 1941 from 56 OTU. *First Whirlwind Op:* Not operational on Whirlwinds. *Out:* 6 April 1941 1941 to RAF Uxbridge. *Remarks:* Born in Erlestoke, he was with 263 for twenty-six days. He received an AFM on 25 June 1942, but died in an accident on 28 June, in 87 Squadron Tiger Moth *T7474* at East Carlton, Northants and is buried in Erlestoke (Holy Saviour) Churchyard, Wiltshire.

SAMANT Dattatraya Anant

Nationality: Indian. *S/n:* 108597 RAFVR. *Rank:* Pilot Officer; Flying Officer on 1 November 1942. *Squadron:* 137. *Flight:* A. *In:* 21 January 1942 from 61 OTU. *First Whirlwind Op:* 18 March 1942. *Out:* 9 October 1942 to 263 Squadron. *Squadron:* 263. *Flight:* A. *In:* 19 October 1942 from 137 Squadron. *First Whirlwind Op:* 17 October 1942. *Out:* 18 January 1943 to 118 Squadron. *Hours:* 52:30 on 50 ops. *Nickname:* Sammy. *Remarks:* Born in Bombay, he received his Aero Club Licence in April 1937 at the Bombay Flying Club. One of twenty-six pilots who served with both Whirlwind Squadrons, he crashed on landing in *P7056* on 5 October 1942 leading to his posting to 263. He ended the war as a Flight Lieutenant, and was an Area Manager with Indian Airlines in Bombay in the 1960s.

SAMPLE John DFC

Nationality: British. *S/n:* 90278 RAF. *Rank:* Squadron Leader. *Squadron:* 137. *Flight:* Commanding Officer. *In:* 20 September 1941 from RAF Colerne. *First Whirlwind Op:* 24 October 1941. *Out:* 28 October 1941 KIFA. *Hours:* 2:35 on 2 ops. *Remarks:* Born in Longhirst, Northumberland in February 1913, he was a land agent for the Duke of Portland, working from Bothal Castle and in 1934 was the fifth person to join 607 (County of Durham) Auxiliary Squadron. On the 17 October 1939 as 'B' Flight Commander he led the only successful interception of an enemy aircraft by UK based Gladiators when he and two others destroyed the first enemy aircraft since the First World War, a Dornier Do.18, fifty miles off the Northumberland coast. He fought with the squadron in France, baled out of mortally damaged Hurricane *P2615*, became its CO and received the DFC on 4 June 1940. Posted to command 504 Squadron during the Battle of Britain, he destroyed a Do.17Z-2 on 15 September 1940 then became 2nd Controller at Colerne before forming 137 Squadron. He collided with Sgt Peskett on a practice flight but abandoned *P7053* too late and was killed. Such was the esteem in which he was held that wreaths were sent from 137 Squadron, Officers of Colerne and Charmy Down, and the tenants of the Manor House and the villagers of English Coombe where he crashed. Aged twenty-eight, he is buried in St Andrews Churchyard, Bothal, Northumberland.

SANDY John Anthony William
Nationality: British. *S/n:* 1051978 (Sgt); 116508 (Officer) RAFVR. *Rank:* Sergeant; Pilot Officer on 9 February 1942. *Squadron:* 263. *Flight:* B. *In:* 15 September 1941 from 56 OTU. *First Whirlwind Op:* Not operational. *Out:* 8 October 1941 to 137 Squadron. *Squadron:* 137. *Flight:* B. *In:* 8 October 1941 from 263 Squadron. *First Whirlwind Op:* 15 November 1941. *Out:* 12 February 1942 MIA. *Hours:* 37:35 on 31 ops. *Incidents: P7005 HE-A* undercarriage collapsed at Charmy Down on 20 September 1941; *P7107* damaged on 6 December 1941. *Remarks:* He was one of twenty-six pilots who served with both Whirlwind Squadrons, but went Missing during 'Operation Fuller' in *P7050*, his name appears on Panel 71 of the Runnymede Memorial.

SHELLARD John Walter
Nationality: British. *S/n:* 1338885 RAFVR. *Rank:* Sergeant. *Squadron:* 263. *Flight:* B. *In:* 1 December 1943 from 55 OTU *First Whirlwind Op:* Not operational. *Out:* 30 August 1945 Renumbered. *Nickname:* Johnny. *Remarks:* Born in the West Country, he decided to join the RAF after being 'buzzed' by Whirlwinds as a young LDF volunteer. By sheer coincidence he joined the very Squadron that prompted his decision, just as they converted to the Typhoon, so he was not allowed to fly a Whirlwind. He flew 103 ops on Typhoons during the course of which he was hit by flak on 27 April 1944 in *MN250 HE-M* and crash-landed at Harrowbeer. Then on 26 April 1945 he shared in the destruction of a Me.262 jet with F/O Gus Fowler, P/O David Morgan and W/O Barrie. He left the RAF as a Flying Officer and became a teacher.

SHEWELL Stanley Joseph
Nationality: Canadian. *S/n:* J/16103 RCAF. *Rank:* Flying Officer. *Squadron:* 263. *Flight:* B. *In:* 1 July 1943 from AFDU. *First Whirlwind Op:* Not operational. *Out:* 10 July 1943 to 610 Squadron. *Remarks:* Born 13 October 1919, in Ontario, he was with 263 for nine days. Killed on 2 October 1943 with 610 Squadron, aged twenty three, he is buried in Bath (Haycombe) Cemetery, Plot 39, Section H, Row C, Grave 25.

SIMPSON James Ian DFM
Nationality: British. *S/n:* 155239 (Sgt); 656521 (Officer) RAFVR. *Rank:* Sergeant; Flight Sergeant on 1 May 1943; Pilot Officer on 31 July 1943. *Squadron:* 263. *Flight:* A. *In:* 1 July 1942 from 175 Squadron. *First Whirlwind Op:* 21 September 1942. *Out:* 9 October 1943 KIA: *Awards:* DFM on 26 September 1943. *Hours:* 55:00 on 44 ops, 234:00 total: *Incident: P6979 HE-Q* crash-landed at Fairwood Common on 6 March 1943. *Nickname:* Simmy. *Remarks:* Accidentally shot by F/S Thould on 26 May 1943 he was treated in Bovingdon Military Hospital. Engine failure in *P7047* on approach to Tangmere caused him to crash into an anti-landing post a hundred yards from the runway. The ORB noted, 'He was very well liked and is a loss both as a pilot and a friend.' Aged twenty-four, he is buried in Glasgow (Eastwood) Cemetery, Section H (New Part), Grave 45.

SKELLON Robert Burton
Nationality: British. *S/n:* 967895 RAFVR. *Rank:* Sergeant. *Squadron:* 263. *Flight:* A. *In:* 25 January 1941 from 56 OTU. *First Whirlwind Op:* Not operational. *Out:* 19 May 1941 to 2 Delivery Flight. *Hours:* 7:00. *Remarks:* Born on 22 March 1920 in Cardiff. On 15 February

1941 he ran out of fuel on a cross-country exercise and crash-landed *P6976 HE-X* near Cannington, Bridgwater. Posted as not suitable for Whirlwinds, he later flew Air Sea Rescue Lysanders and survived one more crash before left the RAF as a Flight Lieutenant on medical grounds on 24 April 1945. He passed away in 1973.

SLATTER John Peyto Shrubb

Nationality: British. *S/n:* 89815 RAFVR. *Rank:* Flying Officer. *Squadron:* 263: *Flt:* B. *In:* 26 January 1942. *First Whirlwind Op:* Not operational. *Out:* 2 February 1942 to 2 Delivery Flight. *Remarks:* Born on 12 February 1922, he was with 263 for seven days. Transferred to the Admin Branch on 17 November 1944, he retired due to ill health on 6 May 1945 and passed away in November 1996.

SMALL Douglas Francis

Nationality: British. *S/n:* 112034 RAFVR. *Rank:* Sergeant. *Squadron:* 263. *Flight:* B. *In:* 15 September 1941 from 56 OTU. *First Whirlwind Op:* 13 February 1942. *Out:* 11 August 1942 to 2 Delivery Flight. *Hours:* 72:10 on 63 ops. *Incidents: P7035* tail wheel failed to lower at Charmy Down on 19 October 1941. *Nickname:* Sammy. *Remarks:* On 11 August 1942 he was attached to 2 Delivery Flight Colerne and Posted there permanently on 19 September 1942. He died on 9 November 1942 as a passenger in Defiant *N3444* when it crashed on the edge of Harrowbeer aerodrome near the *'Leg O' Mutton'* pub. A memorial stone marks the spot. Aged twenty-two, he is buried in Plot 18, Section J of Tollcross Churchyard, Glasgow.

SMITH Aubrey Cartwright

Nationality: British. *S/n:* 1340628 RAFVR. *Rank:* Sergeant. *Squadron:* 137. *Flight:* A. *In:* 23 July 1942 from 53 OTU. *First Whirlwind Op:* 30 April 1942. *Out:* 19 March 1944 to 3 Tactical Exercise Unit: *Awards:* DFM on 9 September 1943. *Hours:* 23:30 on 24 ops. *Incidents: P7051* tail wheel collapsed at Manston on 5 October 1942: *P6976 SF-X* wing tip hit ground at Manston on 1 May 1943. *Nickname:* Smithy. *Remarks:* Born on 15 February 1922, in Dunblane, Perthshire, he was a decorator before enlisting in 1941, and received the first award to an NCO with 137 Squadron. On 24 February 1943 he married, and his friend Tom Sutherland was his Best Man. He flew thirteen sorties on Hurricane IVs and six on Typhoons, then after 3 TEU he went to 84 GSU then 193 Squadron on the 18 October 1944 but on 1 April 1945 his Typhoon was hit by flak and caught fire. He baled out over enemy held territory. Freed from Stalag Luft 1 in June 1945, he was promoted to Flight Lieutenant on 24 August 1945. He passed away on 24 September 1997.

SMITH Graham Natt

Nationality: Australian. *S/n:* 416719 RAAF. *Rank:* Flight Sergeant. *Squadron:* 263. *Flight:* B. *In:* 2 May 1943 from 55 OTU. *First Whirlwind Op:* 18 July 1943. *Out:* 12 March 1944 KIFA. *Hours:* 19:10 on 16 ops. *Incidents: P7012* hit by flak on 26 November 1943. *Nickname:* Smudger. *Remarks:* Born in Strathalbyn, South Australia on 30 September 1922, he was a Station Hand on a sheep station, and enlisted on 16 August 1941. He converted to Typhoons and flew ten ops as a Pilot Officer. The Squadron shared Warmwell with an American P-38 Group, and both would regularly beat up the aerodrome, he was killed during one of these in *MN129*. He attempted a slow upward roll at low level, but the engine cut whilst inverted and he was unable to correct before crashing south-west of Knighton Wood. 'A person of quiet voice and genial ways and was very well liked by all who knew him.' Aged twenty-one, he is buried in Plot 39, Section H, Row B, Grave 249 of Bath (Haycombe) Cemetery.

SMITH Hubert Kenneth

Nationality: British. *S/n:* 88714 RAFVR. *Rank:* Pilot Officer. *Squadron:* 263. *Flight:* A. *In:* 21 January 1941 from 56 OTU. *First Whirlwind Op:* Not operational. *Out:* 25 January 1941 to 247 Squadron. *Remarks:* With 263 for four days. Killed as an instructor at 52 OTU on 7 April 1942 in Master II *AZ315* with his pupil Sgt Lloyd Brown RCAF, he is buried in Swindon (Christ Church) Burial Ground, Central Section, Grave 877.

SMITH Robert Leslie DFC DFM

Nationality: British. *S/n:* 742902 (Sgt); 129958 (Officer) RAFVR. *Rank:* Sergeant; Pilot Officer on 24 July 1942; Flying Officer on 24 January 1943. *Squadron:* 137. *Flt:* B. *In:* 22 April 1942 from 82 Squadron. *First Whirlwind Op:* 30 April 1942. *Out:* 22 May 1943 Rested: *Awards:* DFC on 12 February 1943. *Hours:* 41:25 on 37 ops: *Claims:* Ju.88 of 3(F)/122 destroyed on 25 July 1942 in *P7012* shared with P/O John McClure; Fw.190 damaged on 15 December 1942 in *P6976*. *Incidents: P6976 SF-X* hit by flak on 15 December 1942. *Nickname:* Pop. *Remarks:* Born in Dartmouth, he received the DFM with 82 Squadron, and then a DFC with 137, the Squadron's first decoration. Rested and posted to 52 OTU as a Flight Lieutenant.

SMITH Wynford Ormonde Leoni

Nationality: British. *S/n:* 37366 RAF. *Rank:* Flight Lieutenant. *Squadron:* 263. *Flt:* A Commander; C Commander. *In:* 20 June 1940 from 1 FTS. *First Whirlwind Op:* 7 December 1940. *Out:* 29 December 1940 KIA. *Hours:* 1:40 on 5 ops. *Nickname:* Smithy. *Remarks:* Born in Worthing in 1915, he joined the RAF on a Short Service Commission in October 1935, trained at 6 FTS, and received his Wings in July 1936. He was Posted to the Aircraft Depot, Karachi on 11 February 1937 then to 5 (Army Co-Op) Squadron at Risalpur before returning to the UK. He crash-landed Hurricane I *P2991* in the grounds of Carstairs Junction Public School on 13 July 1940 before converting to Whirlwinds and leading 'C' Flight which was tasked with bringing the aircraft to operational status. He was killed when *P6975 HE-L* crashed on Fox Tor Mire near Princetown, Devon in bad weather, but was not found until 9 March 1941 (*see also* Donald Vine). Aged twenty-five, he is buried in Exeter Higher Cemetery, Plot 80, Section ZK, next to Donald Vine.

SNALAM Frederick Donald

Nationality: British. *S/n:* 86725 RAF. *Rank:* Flight Lieutenant. *Squadron:* 263. *Flt:* B Commander. *In:* 20 September 1943 from 616 Squadron as supernumerary. *First Whirlwind Op:* 30 October 1943. *Out:* 1 February 1944 Posted Overseas. *Hours:* 7:45 on 8 ops. *Incidents: P7097* hit by flak on 26 November 1943. *Remarks:* Born in Preston in 1920 he was posted to 263 as a supernumerary from 616 Squadron in exchange for F/S 'Dickie' Hughes. He finished the war as a Flight Lieutenant and joined the Royal Auxiliary Air Force on 27 December 1947.

SOULSBY Bernard

Nationality: British. *S/n:* 126629 RAFVR. *Rank:* Pilot Officer; Flying Officer on 17 July 1943. *Squadron:* 137. *Flight:* B. *In:* 1 April 1943 from OTU. *First Whirlwind Op:* 15 May 1943. *Out:* 7 October 1943 KIA. *Hours:* 3:25 on 4 ops. *Remarks:* He flew eleven ops on Hurricane IVs, but was killed on a low level shipping strike in *KZ620*. Aged twenty-eight, his name appears on Panel 129 of the Runnymede Memorial.

STEIN David

Nationality: British. *S/n:* 84299 RAFVR. *Rank:* Pilot Officer; Flying Officer on 27 July 1941. *Squadron:* 263. *Flight:* B. *In:* 1 August 1940 from OTU. *First Whirlwind Op:* 12 January 1941. *Out:* 30 October 1941 MIA. *Hours:* 100:56 on 93 ops: Claims: Ju.88 destroyed on 12 January 1941 in *P6972*; Me.109E of JG2 damaged on 4 September 1941 in *P6990*. *Remarks:* Forced to abandon Hurricane *L1803* on 25 August 1940 due to engine failure. It crashed on mudflats near Kincardine Bridge and he landed in Grangemouth Docks. He flew thirty operational sorties on Hurricane Is before converting to the Whirlwind and scored the types first 'kill' – a Ju.88 on 12 January 1941, although it was not confirmed until after P/O Graham had been given the accolade almost a month later. Missing in *P7015* following an attack on Morlaix aerodrome, he crashed at Kerdiny but although his body was seen in the wreckage, he has no known grave and his name appears on Panel 30 of the Runnymede Memorial. 'His loss to the squadron was inestimably great, as a pilot, humourist or friend'

STONE Cedric Arthur Cuthbert DFC

Nationality: British. *S/n:* 39424 RAF. *Rank:* Flying Officer. *Squadron:* 263. *Flight:* A. *In:* 10 June 1940 from 3 Squadron. *First Whirlwind Op:* Not operational. *Out:* 13 July 1940 to 245 Squadron. *Nickname:* Bunny. *Remarks:* Born on 8 December 1916, in Amritsar, India he joined the RAF in November 1936 and fought with 3 Squadron in France, claiming five victories and receiving a DFC on 31 May 1940. Following his thirty-three day posting to 263 he flew with 245 Squadron during the Battle of Britain then led 17 Squadron in Burma where he claimed two Japanese 'Sally' bombers and a 'Nate' fighter, and received a Bar to his DFC on 10 April 1942. He finished the war as a Wing Commander with 222 Group, Ceylon and left the RAF in 1946. A talented artist, he emigrated to South Africa in a single-engine Auster but returned to the UK in the 1960s and passed away in 1990.

STURGEON Douglas Wallis

Nationality: British. *S/n:* 51115 RAF. *Rank:* Flying Officer. *Squadron:* 263. *Flight:* B. *In:* 16 July 1943 from 55 OTU. *First Whirlwind Op:* 25 August 1943. *Out:* 30 December 1943. *Hours:* 5:40 on 5 ops. *Nickname:* Lofty. *Remarks:* Born on 4 December 1919, he was an armourer with 19 Squadron before the war, and was always seen smoking a pipe. He was put in charge of the Squadrons many mascots. Posted from 263 as a Flying instructor, he later flew Typhoons and Mosquitoes, finished the war as a Flight Lieutenant and post-war flew Tempests and de Havilland Hornets, an aircraft he described as 'everything the Whirlwind could have been.' He abandoned a Tempest over the Mediterranean after engine failure, and spent five days in a dinghy before being rescued. He retired from the RAF in the late 1950s.

SUTHERLAND Thomas Arthur

Nationality: British. *S/n:* 655932 RAFVR. *Rank:* Sergeant. *Squadron:* 137. *Flight:* A. *In:* 1 September 1942 from 56 OTU. *First Whirlwind Op:* 21 October 1942. *Out:* 5 April 1944 Posted. *Hours:* 19:40 on 20 ops. *Incidents: P7005 HE-A* tail damaged at Matlaske on 16 August 1942 after his second flight on type; *P6998* crash-landed at Lympne on 22 December 1942; *P7063* engine failure on 7 February 1943; *P7005 HE-A* engine failure on 12 February 1943. *Nickname:* Tom. *Remarks:* Born in Chingford, Essex, he was Best Man to Aubrey Smith on 24 February 1943, he flew eleven ops on Hurricane IVs, eight on Typhoons, finished the war as a Flying Officer and later emigrated to New Zealand.

TEBBIT Donald Frank Jellicoe

Nationality: British. *S/n:* 951767 (Sgt); 156650 (Officer) RAFVR. *Rank:* Sergeant; Flight Sergeant on 7 October 1941; Warrant Officer on 1 August 1942; Pilot Officer on 11 August 1943. *Squadron:* 263. *Flight:* A. *In:* 19 February 1941 from OTU. *First Whirlwind Op:* 2 May 1941. *Out:* 12 June 1941 10 Group Flight. *In:* 7 October 1942 from Tactical Exercise Unit. *Out:* 17 January 1944 Posted. *Hours:* 70:20 on 63 ops. *Incidents: P7100* hit by flak on 26 November 1943. *Nickname:* Tebby. *Remarks:* Born on 23 July 1914, in Ipswich, he enlisted on 3 August 1939. On 29 May 1941 he crashed on the River Severn mudflats in Gwent after hitting a balloon cable whilst attempting to fly under the Sharpness Bridge. *P7006* was burnt out and although arrested he was later released for lack of evidence and posted to 10 Group Flight, an Anti-Aircraft Co-Op Unit that later became 286 Squadron, as a punishment. He then went to Tactical Exercise Unit before returning to 263 where he became Deputy 'A' Flight Commander on 3 October 1943. In January 1944, the 'A' Flight Diary noted, 'We are losing Granpappy Tebbit, who has been deemed worthy of a Rest. We bid farewell to Tebby regretfully. Besides being the oldest member of the squadron, apart from S/L Warnes, he was definitely one of the most valuable, being an excellent organiser, and he will be sorely missed.' He joined 92 Squadron on 21 July 1944 but on 5 October an engine fire on take-off forced him retract the undercarriage whereupon the 90 gallon drop tank caught fire and he suffered burns to his face. He spent time at East Grinstead Hospital as one of the 'Guinea Pigs.' On 22 February 1945 he was shot down by flak in Spitfire XIV *RM789 FL-W* near Coesfeld and spent the remaining weeks of the war as a POW in Stalag Luft VIIA Moosburg. Repatriated in early May 1945 he was Mentioned in Despatches on 14 June 1945 and joined the Fighter Control Branch on 24 September 1950. He retired from the RAF on 23 April 1965 as a Wing Commander.

THORNTON Cyril Brooking

Nationality: British. *S/n:* 117692 RAFVR. *Rank:* Flying Officer. *Squadron:* 263 *Flight:* A. *In:* 19 January 1943 from 535 Squadron. *First Whirlwind Op:* Not operational. *Out:* 22 February 1943 to 141 Squadron. *Remarks:* Born in 1918, in Croydon, he received a commission on 21 February 1942 after serving with the Worcester Regiment and was posted to 263 when 535 Turbinlight Squadron disbanded. Awarded the MBE on 14 March 1944 for rescuing the crew of a Mosquito from their burning aircraft, he served with FIU's Tempest Flight in June 1944 then 501 Squadron when they merged and shot down nine V-1s. He was killed in a flying accident on 21 August 1944 when Tempest *EJ602 SD-P* crashed at Woodnesboro, Kent in bad weather and was buried in Margate Cemetery Section 50, Grave 16251.

THORNTON-BROWN Patrick Glynn

Nationality: British. *S/n:* 81639 RAF. *Rank:* Pilot Officer. *Squadron:* 263. *Flight:* B. *In:* 7 June 1940 from RAF Drem. *First Whirlwind Op:* 13 January 1941. *Out:* 14 March 1941 Injured. *Hours:* 32:19 on 38 ops: *Claims:* Ju.88 damaged on 1 March 1941 in *P6989 HE-J*. *Remarks:* Born in Weston-super-Mare in 1919, he joined the Royal Engineers in 1938 but transferred to the RAFVR in spring 1939 and was posted to 263 in June 1940. Seriously injured when *P6988 HE-J* crashed at RAF Portreath on 14 March 1941, he was hospitalised for several months and later joined 56 Squadron. He took command of 609 Squadron at Lympne on 21 August 1943 but on 21 December 1943 was shot down by USAAF Thunderbolts in Typhoon *R8845*. He baled out near Doullens, but was shot and killed by troops whilst in his parachute. His DFC was promulgated two days after his death, along with a recommendation for promotion to Wing Commander and he was recognised by the Belgian Government with the award of a posthumous Croix de Guerre avec Palme on 18 June 1946. Aged twenty-four, he is buried in Caumont Churchyard, Pas de Calais.

THOULD John

Nationality: British. *S/n:* 1246400 RAFVR. *Rank:* Sergeant. *Squadron:* 263. *Flight:* A. *In:* 24 February 1943 from 61 OTU. *First Whirlwind Op:* Not operational. *Out:* 13 October 1944 KIA. *Hours:* 26:00 on 32 training sorties. *Remarks:* Born in Upton on Severn, Worcestershire. He wrote off *P7057* on 7 May 1943 in a heavy landing resulting in a posting to an Aircrew Refresher Course in Brighton. Shortly after his return he accidently shot F/S Simpson in the stomach at the firing range and was posted to Target Towing Duties on 27 May 1943. He returned to the squadron on 9 December 1943 and flew sixty-seven ops on Typhoons, during which time he attended 1 SLAIS and destroyed a Me.410 near Brétigny on 18 April 1944. He was shot down in flames by flak near Hoogstraten, Holland on 13 October 1944 in Typhoon *MN476 HE-D 'The Hawk.'* Aged twenty-four, he is buried in Plot 1, Merkplas Communal Cemetery, Antwerp, Belgium.

THYAGARAJAN Sayana Puram Duraiswamy

Nationality: Indian. *S/n:* 1339499 RAFVR. *Rank:* Sergeant. *Squadron:* 263. *Flight:* A. *In:* 20 October 1942 from 56 OTU. *Out:* 25 May 1943 to 286 Squadron. *In:* 1 January 1944 from 286 Squadron. *First Whirlwind Op:* 13 March 1943. *Out:* 25 August 1944 KIA. *Hours:* 13:20 on 10 ops. *Nickname:* Tiger or Billy. *Remarks:* Posted to 286 Squadron on 18 May 1943 he did not leave until 25 May 1943 but returned in January 1944 as a Pilot Officer to fly fifty ops on Typhoons. Hit by flak in *MN477 HE-T* on 25 August 1944, he attempted to force land but the aircraft turned over and blew up. La Lande, the nearest village had only been liberated the previous day, and the Priest insisted that he should be buried in the Churchyard. Aged twenty-six, his is the only war grave in the cemetery, and the only CWGC headstone with inscriptions in English, Hindi and French.

TOBIN James Richard

Nationality: British. *S/n:* 39909 RAF. *Rank:* Flying Officer. *Squadron:* 263. *Flight:* A. *In:* 26 June 1940 from 6 OTU. *First Whirlwind Op:* Not operational. *Out:* 22 July 1940 to Royal Aircraft Establishment. *Nickname:* Toby. *Remarks:* He was with 263 for five weeks before being posted to RAE, Farnborough where he received the AFC on 11 June 1942 for testing captured German aircraft and his study on the physiological effect of high 'G' on air crews. Promoted to Squadron Leader and posted to Blackburn Aircraft as a test pilot on 21 January 1944 he was killed on 16 March 1945 when the Firebrand he was flying broke up in the air. 'As a result of this accident the country lost a test pilot of far above the average quality'; he was posthumously awarded the King's Commendation for Valuable Service in the Air on 14 June 1945. Aged thirty, he is buried in Section A, Grave 14, Carlisle (Dalston Road) Cemetery.

TODD Denis Charles
Nationality: British. *S/n:* 1335350 RAFVR. *Rank:* Sergeant; Flight Sergeant on 10 September 1943. *Squadron:* 263. *Flight:* A. *In:* 16 June 1943 from 59 OTU. *First Whirlwind Op:* 8 September 1943. *Out:* 31 January 1945 Rested. *Hours:* 11:15 on 11 ops. *Incidents: P6983 HE-H* engine failure on 25 November 1943. *Nickname:* Two-Pint. *Remarks:* Born on 14 May 1922, in Eltham, London. After converting to Typhoons, he flew seventy-six ops and led a charmed life in the process, surviving no less than three crash-landings. After the war he flew Dakotas out of Hong Kong, retired from the RAF in 1963 and passed away in Hexham in May 1994.

TOOTH Albert
Nationality: British. *S/n:* 88469 RAFVR. *Rank:* Pilot Officer. *Squadron:* 263. *Flight:* A. *In:* 21 January 1941 from 56 OTU. *First Whirlwind Op:* 26 February 1941. *Out:* 1 June 1941 to ASR RAF Warmwell. *Hours:* 50:50 on 52 ops, 100:00 total: *Claims:* He.111 of I/KG.27 damaged on 6 April 1941 in *P7004. Remarks:* Born on 7 January 1918 in Manchester. He flew Mosquitoes with 82 Squadron in the Far East; was an Air Liaison Officer to the 1st Chindit operation *'Operation Longcloth'* and ended the war as a Flight Lieutenant. Awarded the DFC on 17 August 1945 he remained in the RAF as a Squadron Leader but died on 2 July 1948 when A&AEE Lincoln *RF560* crashed near Wylye, Wiltshire.

TORRANCE Alexander
Nationality: British. *S/n:* 64932 RAFVR. *Rank:* Pilot Officer; Flying Officer on 27 April 1942; Flight Lieutenant on 27 April 1943. *Squadron:* 137. *Flight:* A; B; B CO. *In:* 1 October 1941 from 56 OTU. *First Whirlwind Op:* 16 December 1941. *Out:* 5 October 1943 to PDC. *Hours:* 80:30 on 77 ops. *Incidents: P7096* damaged on 6 April 1943. *Nickname:* Scottie. *Remarks:* En-route to Malta in HMS *Furious* he was amongst a group watching a Hurricane take off, when one of its long range tanks fell off and sprayed them with burning fuel. Posted to 137 following hospitalization he took command of 'B' Flight on 3 December 1942 and later flew five ops in Hurricane IVs. Posted to Burma as a Flight Commander with 27 then 45 Mosquito Squadron, he was acting W/C Flying, Seletar, Singapore for four months. In 1971 he planned Sheila Scott's record polar flight.

TUFF Robert Bruce
Nationality: Australian. *S/n:* 409257 RAAF. *Rank:* Flying Officer. *Squadron:* 263. *Flight:* A. *In:* 22 June 1943 from 59 OTU. *First Whirlwind Op:* 12 August 1943. *Out:* 22 February 1944 MIA. *Hours:* 12:50 on 12 ops. *Remarks:* Born on 11 July 1922, in Seddon, Victoria he was a Tax clerk, and enlisted on 20 July 1941. He attended 1 SLAIS between 13 October and

3 November 1943 and later converted to Typhoons on which he flew five ops but made the ultimate sacrifice in possibly the most selfless act of the war. When S/L Geoff Warnes ditched off Guernsey and was seen to be in difficulties, he abandoned *JR302* to help him – neither man was seen again. For this courageous act he was Mentioned in Dispatches on 8 June 1944, the citation read:

> On the 22 February 1944, F/O Tuff was returning from a shipping reconnaissance when he observed that his CO who had been compelled to alight on the sea twenty miles northwest of Guernsey, was in difficulties and some fifty yards away from his dinghy. F/O Tuff informed the Flight Leader that he intended to abandon his aircraft and go to the assistance of S/L Warnes, who also appeared to be injured. He undoubtedly realised that, in view of the rough sea and poor visibility, it would be extremely unlikely that he would be able to alight on the sea close to S/L Warnes, and that to reach him he would probably have to swim a long distance in a perilous sea. He was a strong swimmer and was evidently prepared if necessary to discard his own dinghy. Even if he reached S/L Warnes the chances of being picked up were extremely small in view of their distance from Guernsey and the roughness of the sea. Nevertheless, F/O Tuff, in cold blood, took the risk in order to try and save the life of his CO. He showed extreme bravery and his self-sacrifice was worthy of the highest praise.

They may have been strafed by German fighters whilst in the water. Aged twenty-one, his name appears on Panel 258 of the Runnymede Memorial. (*See also* Geoff Warnes *and* Robert Hunter.)

UNWIN Leonard Arthur
Nationality: British. *S/n:* J/10393 RCAF. *Rank:* Flying Officer. *Squadron:* 263. *Flight:* A. *In:* 18 September 1943 from 55 OTU. *First Whirlwind Op:* 24 October 1943. *Out:* 24 December 1944 KIA. *Hours:* 2:20 on 3 ops. *Nickname:* Uncle Lem. *Remarks:* Born in January 1917, in Ecclesall, Yorkshire, his family emigrated to Canada in 1918. On 5 December 1943 he took S/L Baker to a Fighter Leaders Course at Ashton Down in the Oxford but force landed near Worth Maltravers on his return. He flew ninety-eight ops on Typhoons and was promoted to Flight Lieutenant, but was killed when *RB335* was hit by flak and blew up. Aged twenty-seven, he is buried in Plot 180 of Woudenberg General Cemetery, Netherlands.

UNWIN Philip Herbert Buxton
Nationality: British. *S/n:* 111127 RAFVR. *Rank:* Flying Officer. *Squadron:* 137. *Flight:* B; A. *In:* 30 June 1943 from 59 OTU. *First Whirlwind Op:* Not operational. *Out:* 30 November 1944 to 164 Squadron. *Remarks:* Wrote off Hurricane IV *KW918* when she ran out of fuel and crashed near Manston on 17 August 1943.

VAN SCHAICK John Edward DFM
Nationality: British. *S/n:* 114086 RAFVR. *Rank:* Pilot Officer; Flying Officer on 21 June 1942; Flight Lieutenant on 13 February 1942. *Squadron:* 137. *Flight:* B; B Commander. *In:* 1 December 1941 from 59 OTU. *First Whirlwind Op:* 17 February 1942. *Out:* 3 December 1942 to 59 OTU. *Hours:* 66:40 on 58 ops. *Incidents:* *P7054* engine failure on 12 July 1942. *Nickname:* Van or Shaky-Do. *Remarks:* Born in 1921 in Prescot, Liverpool. He received the DFM with 609 Squadron, and

was shot down over the Channel on 21 July 1941 in Spitfire *W3372*. He became 137 'B' Flight Commander on 13 February 1942, and on 31 October 1942 took another dip in the Channel when he ditched *P7064* off Le Touquet due to flak damage. He was rescued from a minefield after five hours in his dinghy. Rested to 59 OTU Crosby on Eden to command 'B' Flight he had been married for five weeks when he was killed on 20 February 1943 in Miles Master *T8553* with his pupil Sgt Harold Gleadall, when it crashed near Berrington, Northumberland. Aged twenty-two, he is buried in St Peter's Churchyard, Littleover, Derbyshire.

VAN ZELLER Christopher Peter
Nationality: British. *S/n:* 109495 RAFVR. *Rank:* Pilot Officer. *Squadron:* 263. *Flight:* A. *In:* 1 February 1942 from 56 OTU. *First Whirlwind Op:* 19 February 1942. *Out:* 14 October 1942 RAF Uxbridge. *Hours:* 56.45 on 57 ops. *Remarks:* Born in Wandsworth. On 25 June 1942 whilst taxiing to take off in *P6987 HE-L*, the aircraft in front stalled and as his own engines were overheating he tried to taxi around it but as he did so the tail wheel collapsed. A quiet but reliable pilot, he was invalided out of the RAF on 17 November 1942 after losing a hand in an accident. Post-war he emigrated to Spain.

VINE Donald Martin
Nationality: British. *S/n:* 83718 RAFVR. *Rank:* Pilot Officer. *Squadron:* 263. *Flight:* B. *In:* 1 August 1940 from 6 OTU. *First Whirlwind Op:* 29 December 1940. *Out:* 29 December 1940 KIA. *Hours:* 0:45 on 1 Op; 9:00 total. *Remarks:* Born in Eastbourne, he was awarded his 'Wings' on 19 June 1940 at 5 FTS and flew twenty-eight ops on Hurricanes before converting to Whirlwinds. Killed when *P6978* crashed on Fox Tor Mire near Princetown, Devon in bad weather, but he was not found until 9 March 1941 (*see also* Wynford Smith). Aged twenty-three, he is buried in Plot 81, Section ZK of Exeter Higher Cemetery, next to Wynford Smith.

WADDINGTON Walter David
Nationality: British. *S/n:* 754687 RAFVR. *Rank:* Sergeant. *Squadron:* 263. *Flight:* B. *In:* 13 January 1941 from 56 OTU. *First Whirlwind Op:* 14 March 1941. *Out:* 19 May 1941 to RAF Colerne. *Hours:* 2.00 on 2 ops. *Remarks:* Born on 20 April 1921, in Sculcoates near Hull, he was a Car Salesman before the war. Noted for always wearing his .38 Smith & Wesson revolver; it was rumoured he even wore it to bed! He remained in the post-war RAF as a Flight Lieutenant, and passed away in September 1993, in Beverley, Yorkshire.

WAECHTER John d'Arcy
Nationality: British. *S/n:* 88715 RAFVR. *Rank:* Pilot Officer. *Squadron:* 263. *Flight:* B. *In:* 21 January 1941 from 56 OTU. *First Whirlwind Op:* Not operational. *Out:* 25 January 1941 to 247 Squadron *Remarks:* Born on 16 November 1915, in Bognor, Sussex. With 263 for four days, he later served in the Middle East and finished the war as a Squadron Leader. A noted archaeologist, he passed away in Plymouth in January 1978.

WALDRON Francis Gordon
Nationality: British. *S/n:* 1287168 RAFVR. *Rank:* Sergeant. *Squadron:* 137. *Flight:* B. *In:* 1 January 1942 from 59 OTU. *First Whirlwind Op:* 30 April 1942. *Out:* 31 October 1942

POW. *Hours:* 39:10 on 34 ops. *Nickname:* Jack. *Remarks:* Born in Hull on 25 October 1923 he was an Accountant before enlisting on 3 September 1940. Missing in *P7109 SF-N* near Etaples, he was reported as a POW on 9 November 1942. Held in Stalag Luft I, IV and VI, Heydekrug, Lithuania, he was liberated in February 1945. He passed away in Beverley, Yorkshire in October 2000.

WALKER Gerald Oscar Harrington
Nationality: British. *S/n:* 138247 RAFVR. *Rank:* Sergeant. *Squadron:* 137. *Flight:* A. *In:* 25 October 1942 from 55 OTU. *First Whirlwind Op:* 4 December 1942. *Out:* 2 March 1943 POW. *Hours:* 5:40 on 7 ops. *Incidents: P6993 SF-A* ran over an unmarked pothole at Manston on 20 December 1942. *Nickname:* Gerry. *Remarks:* Born on 23 July 1920, in Mirfield, Yorkshire, he enlisted in November 1940. Missing in *P7005 SF-H* near Neufchâtel, he was captured north of Boulogne and held in Stalag 344 and IXA Lamsdorf, Poland. Freed by the US Army on 30 March 1945 he weighed just five stone. He passed away in April 1957.

WALKER John James
Nationality: British. *S/n:* 1163975 (Sgt); 119013 (Officer) RAFVR. *Rank:* Sergeant; Pilot Officer on 20 March 1942. *Squadron:* 263. *Flight:* B. *In:* 18 May 1941 from 56 OTU. *First Whirlwind Op:* 30 May 1941. *Out:* 23 July 1942 MIA. *Hours:* 83:45 on 82 ops. *Nickname:* Johnny. *Remarks:* Crash-landed the Station Commanders Master at RAF Angle on 15 June 1942 when he forgot to lower the undercarriage. He was shot down in *P7060* off Ile de Batz by Unteroffizer Freidrich Steinmüller of 11/JG2. Aged twenty-two, his name appears on Panel 72 of the Runnymede Memorial.

WARNES Geoffrey Berrington DSO DFC
Nationality: British. *S/n:* 78429 RAFVR. *Rank:* Pilot Officer; Flight Lieutenant on 9 November 1942; Squadron Leader on 9 December 1941. *Squadron:* 263. *Flight:* B; B Commander; Commanding Officer. *In:* 15 September 1941 from 56 OTU. *First Whirlwind Op:* 19 September 1941. *Out:* 15 June 1943 to 10 Group. *In:* 7 December 1943 from 10 Group. *Out:* 22 February 1944 MIA: *Awards:* DFC on 17 February 1943; DSO on 13 June 1943. *Hours:* 150:00 on 130 ops. *Incidents: P7110 HE-E* hit by flak on 7 November 1941; *P7110 HE-E* tail wheel collapsed on 23 June 1942; *P7043 HE-A* stern frame broke at Brough on 4 June 1942. *Nickname:* The Blind Ace. *Remarks:* Born on 22 October 1914, in Leeds, he was taught to fly at the Yorkshire Aeroplane Club by 'Ginger' Lacey, but was rejected by the Air Crew Selection Board for defective eyesight, and Commissioned in the RAFVR in April 1940 as an Equipment Officer. He served in France, then on 1 November 1940 he joined a Flying Refresher Course and became a Flying instructor but when it was noticed that he always wore glasses he was ordered to take an eye test. He had himself fitted with contact lenses however and passed the test by memorizing the chart. Awarded the DSO and DFC for his work on Whirlwinds, the latter at the same time as F/L Blackshaw, he was posted to 10 Group for Sector Gunnery Duties, but returned as CO in December 1943 to fly fourteen operational sorties on Typhoons, destroying a Do.217 and a Me.109F in the process. Forced to ditch *MN249* eight miles north-west of Guernsey he was never seen again, and may have been strafed by German fighters whilst in the water (*see also* Robert

Hunter *and* Robert Tuff). The ORB noted, 'The development of dive bombing and the success obtained by the squadron as an anti-shipping unit owed much to his leadership and tactical brilliance. F/O Tuffs tribute to him leaves no more to be said – he was regarded and admired as a friend of all ranks throughout 10 Group. In the hearts of intimate friends, he leaves a place that cannot possibly be filled.' Aged twenty-nine, his name appears on Panel 201 of the Runnymede Memorial.

WATKINS William Edwin
Nationality: British. *S/n:* 1317496 (Sgt); 162644 (Officer) RAFVR. *Rank:* Sergeant; Pilot Officer on 26 November 1943. *Squadron:* 263. *Flight:* B. *In:* 24 February 1943 from 61 OTU. *First Whirlwind Op:* 19 May 1943. *Out:* 6 January 1945 to 56 OTU. *Hours:* 20:30 on 17 ops, 129:50 total. *Incidents: P7110* hit tree with the wingtip, jamming the ailerons and force landed at Stoney Cross on 21 June 1943; *P7096* hit tree at Warmwell on 27 August 1943. *Remarks:* On 13 February 1944 he was hit by flak and abandoned Typhoon *JR309* near Rambouillet. He evaded capture, and helped by the Resistance, returned via Spain and Gibraltar on 31 May 1944, the squadron's third evader. After a Refresher Course, he returned to the squadron on 15 July 1944 and flew a total of fifty-seven ops. Rested to 56 OTU as an instructor he was then posted to Khartoum with George Wood to test the Tempest II in tropical conditions and finished the war as a Flight Lieutenant. Mentioned in Despatches on 14 June 1945, he became a Headmaster.

WATSON Ivor Ashley St Clair
Nationality: British. *S/n:* 89627 RAFVR. *Rank:* Pilot Officer. *Squadron:* 263. *Flight:* A. *In:* 21 January 1941 from 56 OTU. *First Whirlwind Op:* Not operational. *Out:* 25 January 1941 to 247 Squadron. *Remarks:* With 263 for four days. He was Mentioned in Despatches on 11 June 1942, and received a DFC on 21 November 1944 with 165 Squadron.

WATSON-PARKER Patrick Ian
Nationality: British. *S/n:* 741433 RAFVR. *Rank:* Sergeant. *Squadron:* 263. *Flight:* B. *In:* 11 October 1939 from 605 Squadron. *First Whirlwind Op:* Not operational. *Out:* 13 July 1940 KIFA. *Remarks:* Crashed Gladiator *K6145* in the River Severn on 21 October 1939 attempting to fly under the Sharpness Bridge. He fought in the Second Norwegian Expedition and was temporarily detached to 5 OTU to convert to twins, but whilst there he was attached to 6 MU then 610 Squadron. He crashed in Spitfire I *R6807* at Skid House, Tatfield near Biggin Hill whilst on a patrol, and is buried in Section NN, Grave 24, Cudham (St Peter & Paul) Churchyard, Orpington, Kent.

WILLIAMS David John
Nationality: British. *S/n:* 1314587 RAFVR. *Rank:* Sergeant. *Squadron:* 263. *Flight:* A. *In:* 21 August 1942 from 56 OTU. *First Whirlwind Op:* 17 October 1942. *Out:* 12 February 1943 MIA. *Hours:* 10:15 on 9 ops. *Nickname:* Dai or Wingtip. *Remarks:* Hit by flak in *P7052*, he ditched four miles off Cap de Carteret and was seen organizing his dinghy, but was not found by an ASR search. Aged twenty, his name appears on Panel 170 of the Runnymede Memorial.

WILLIAMS George
Nationality: British. *S/n:* 1502741 RAFVR. *Rank:* Sgt; Flight Sergeant on 10 September 1943. *Squadron:* 263. *Flight:* A. *In:* 16 June 1943 from 59 OTU. *First Whirlwind Op:* 29 August 1943. *Out:* 13 February 1944 KIA. *Hours:* 13:20 on 10 ops. *Incidents: P7040* hit by flak on 24 October 1943. *Nickname:* Willy. *Remarks:* Flew five ops on Typhoons, but was shot down in flames by flak over Chartres aerodrome in *JR215* and is buried in Plot 1, Guillerval Communal Cemetery, Essonne, France.

WITHAM Albert
Nationality: British. *S/n:* 1336599 RAFVR. *Rank:* Sergeant. *Squadron:* 137. *Flight:* A. *In:* 24 February 1943 from 55 OTU. *First Whirlwind Op:* 3 April 1943. *Out:* 25 May 1944 KIA. *Hours:* 6:50 on 6 ops. *Nickname:* Bert. *Remarks:* He flew fifteen ops on Hurricane IVs and forty on Typhoons, but was shot down by flak in *MN469* off Oostende and is buried in Adegem Canadian War Cemetery, Maldegem, Oost-Vlaanderen, Belgium, Plot III.AB.11.

WOOD George Albert
Nationality: British. *S/n:* 1334647 RAFVR. *Rank:* Flight Sergeant. *Squadron:* 263. *Flight:* B. *In:* 24 February 1943 from 61 OTU. *First Whirlwind Op:* 18 July 1943. *Out:* 5 January 1945 to 56 OTU. *Hours:* 15:05 on 12 ops, 103:40 total. *Incidents: P7110 HE-C* stern frame damaged in a heavy landing at Warmwell on 18 May 1943. *Nickname:* Timber. *Remarks:* Born on Wimbledon in 1922. Shot down over Morlaix aerodrome on 23 September 1943 in *P7113 HE-W* he returned to Britain on 1 November with aid of the Resistance, the squadron's first evader. He went on to fly forty-seven ops on Typhoons, an aircraft he considered a brute compared to the Whirlwind which was a lady. In January 1944 he was ordered to report to the AOC 10 Group for an interview pending his Commission. When the AOC was called out of the office George took the opportunity to read his personnel file and saw that he had been recommended for the CGM by Geoff Warnes. The request was rejected however. Posted to 56 OTU as an instructor, then to Khartoum with Bill Watkins, where they tested the Tempest II in tropical conditions, he finished the war as a Flight Lieutenant and due to his wartime experiences was ordained into the Church in 1954. (*See Chapter 14*)

WOODHOUSE Robert
Nationality: British. *S/n:* 551782 RAFVR. *Rank:* Flight Sergeant. *Squadron:* 137. *Flight:* B. *In:* 26 June 1942 from 58 OTU. *First Whirlwind Op:* 13 August 1942. *Out:* 30 June 1943 to RAF Milfield. *Hours:* 8:25 on 8 ops. *Incidents: P7012 SF-V* damaged when he selected up undercarriage instead of up flaps on landing at Rochford on 4 December 1942. *Nickname:* Woody. *Remarks:* Posted as an instructor, he remained in the post-war RAF, joining the Fighter Control Branch on 26 July 1950 and retiring as a Flight Lieutenant on 7 February 1956.

WOODWARD Robert Sinkler DFC
Nationality: British. *S/n:* 74698 RAFVR. *Rank:* Flight Lieutenant; Squadron Leader on 10 February 1942. *Squadron:* 137. *Flight:* B Commander. *In:* 7 November 1941 from 600 Squadron. *First Whirlwind Op:* 17 November 1941. *Out:* 11 February 1942 to 263 Squadron.

Squadron: 263. *Flight:* Commanding Officer. *In:* 12 February 42 from 137 Squadron. *First Whirlwind Op:* 15 February 1942. *Out:* 7 December 1942 MIA. *Hours:* 76:35 on 73 ops. *Incidents: P7105 HE-N* hit by flak on 3 October 1942. *Nickname:* Woody. *Remarks:* Born on 31 March 1919, in India where his father was a Major in the Army, he learned to fly with the Oxford University Air Squadron; joined the RAF on 22 June 1939 and fought with 600 Squadron during the Battle of Britain. He claimed three night victories for which he received the DFC in August 1941 but was injured baling out of his damaged Beaufighter and following several months recuperating he joined 137. Posted to 263 as Commanding Officer, he was one of twenty-six pilots who served with both Whirlwind Squadrons and was shot down by flak from a convoy in Baie du St Brelade, Jersey in *P7105 HE-N,* the ORB noted, 'As CO something of his record may be gleaned from the effective programme of training as well as the intense convoy activity in the spring of 1942 and the development of the Whirlibomber. In ops he showed his keenness both in persuading Group to lay them on and in his own leadership; his exploits were both gallant and successful.' Aged twenty-three, his name appears on Panel 65 of the Runnymede Memorial.

WRAY John Basil DFC
Nationality: British. *S/n:* 37874 RAF. *Rank:* Squadron Leader. *Squadron:* 137. *Flight:* A; CO. *In:* 20 September 1942 as a supernumerary. *First Whirlwind Op:* 17 October 1942. *Out:* 5 December 1943 to HQ 13 Group. *Hours:* 11:15 on 13 ops: *Claims:* Fw.190 damaged on 15 June 1943 in *P7111. Remarks:* Born on 21 August 1917, he joined the RAF in May 1936 and flew Beaufighter night fighters with 25 Squadron during his first tour. Rested to Church Fenton, his second tour commenced when he was posted to 137. Detached on liaison duties to the USAAF on 1 January 1943, he then flew with 181 and 174 Squadrons and was posted back to 137 as a supernumerary until assuming Command on 23 May 1943. He flew fourteen ops on Hurricane IVs and received the DFC on 23 October 1943, followed by a spell with HQ 13 Group, then as Wing Commander Flying 122 Tempest Wing he shot down two Me.262s. Awarded the Order of Orange Nassau with Swords from the Queen of the Netherlands on 23 January 1948 he retired as a Group Captain on 21 August 1967, to become a prominent member of the Conservative Party. He passed away in February 1997, in Poole.

WRIGHT Robert Elmer Douglas
Nationality: Canadian. *S/n:* R/83069 (Sgt); J/15147 (Officer) RCAF. *Rank:* Sergeant; Pilot Officer on 14 January 1942. *Squadron:* 137. *Flight:* B. *In:* 1 December 1941 from 59 OTU. *First Whirlwind Op:* 10 February 1942. *Out:* 4 May 1942 KIFA. *Hours:* 35:40 on 32 ops, 106:00 total: *Incident: P7105* the wingtip hit the ground at Matlaske on 5 January 1942. *Remarks:* Born in Lethbridge, Alberta in 1916, he died when *P7103* broke up near Aylesham. His quiet and unassuming manner made him popular with everyone. Aged twenty-six, he is buried in Grave 271, Scottow Cemetery.

WRIGHT Walter Roylance
Nationality: South African. *S/n:* 1380712 RAFVR. *Rank:* Sergeant; Flight Sergeant on 1 August 1942; Flying Officer on 8 February 1943. *Squadron:* 263. *Flight:* B. *In:* 17 November 1941 from 57 OTU. *First Whirlwind Op:* 15 February 1942. *Out:* 13 April 1943

Posted Overseas. *Hours:* 90:45 on 74 ops. *Incidents:* Damaged *P7040* on 23 March 1943. *Nickname:* Chop-Chop

WYATT-SMITH Peter
Nationality: British. *S/n:* 41768 RAF. *Rank:* Pilot Officer, Flying Officer on 23 September 1940. *Squadron:* 263. *Flight:* B. *In:* 2 October 1939 from 3 FTS. *First Whirlwind Op:* Not operational. *Out:* 15 December 1940 to 261 Squadron. *Hours:* 10:30 on 13 training sorties. *Remarks:* Born on 9 June 1918, in Tsinan-Foo, China where his father was serving in the British Consul. He force landed Gladiator *K6145* on 12 October 1939 and crashed another on 2 January 1940 following a forced landing near Porthcawl. Wounded by shrapnel on 14 May 1940 on *M/V Delius* during the 1 Norwegian campaign, he was replaced by Lt. Lydekker of the Fleet Air Arm. Not operational on Whirlwinds, he flew thirteen training sorties before being posted to 261 Squadron on Malta then to the Middle East with 73 Squadron. He was killed on 5 January 1945 delivering Mustang III *KH555* to 165 Squadron at Aston Down. Aged twenty-six, he is buried in Bath (Haycombe) Cemetery, Plot 39, Section H, Row C, Grave 236.

WYLDE Geoffrey Higson
Nationality: British. *S/n:* 1450890 RAFVR. *Rank:* Warrant Officer. *Squadron:* 263. *Flight:* A. *In:* 26 May 1941 from 66 Squadron. *First Whirlwind Op:* Not operational. *Out:* 29 May 1941 to 58 OTU. *Remarks:* Born on 15 January 1923, in Macclesfield, he was with 263 for three days. He finished the war with 5½ V-1 kills in Tempest Vs with 56 Squadron, retired on 22 September 1948, he passed away on 17 January 1994, in Cheadle.

YATES Jocelyn Ivan
Nationality: Republic of Ireland. *S/n:* 1381800 (Sgt); 137257 (Officer) RAFVR. *Rank:* Sergeant; Flight Sergeant on 1 August 1942; Pilot Officer on 25 November 1942. *Squadron:* 263. *Flight:* A. *In:* 31 December 1940 from 56 OTU. *First Whirlwind Op:* 21 February 1942. *Out:* 5 April 1943 to 286 Squadron. *Hours:* 58:13 on 52 ops. *Remarks:* Posted to 286 Squadron to fly Martinet Target tugs, he transferred to the Admin Branch on 30 May 1944 as a Flying Officer and survived the war.

5
Groundstaff of 263 & 137 Squadrons

ASH Oswald – Engineering Officer
Nationality: British. *S/n:* 116029 RAFVR. *Rank:* Pilot Officer; Flying Officer on 13 November 1942. *Squadron:* 263. *In:* 14 May 1942. *Out:* 30 September 1943 to 29 Squadron. *Remarks:* Retired on 2 November 1954 as a Flight Lieutenant.

BARNETT Leslie William – Intelligence Officer
Nationality: British. *S/n:* 102743 RAFVR. *Rank:* Pilot Officer; Flying Officer on 25 August 1942. *Squadron:* 137. *In:* 1 October 1941. *Out:* 20 December 1943 to 3 Squadron. *Nickname:* Barny. *Remarks:* Resigned his Commission on 22 February 1946.

BLICK John Francis – Adjutant
Nationality: British. *S/n:* 74431 RAF. *Rank:* Pilot Officer; Flying Officer on 26 September 1940. *Squadron:* 263. *In:* 25 March 1940 from 145 Squadron. *Out:* 15 December 1940 to RAF Grangemouth. *Remarks:* He served in the RFC as an Observer in the Great War and was released as a Lieutenant on 16 May 1920. Mentioned in Dispatches on 17 March 1941 and 8 June 1944, he finished the war as a Squadron Leader.

CLAYTON Richard Barnett – Medical Officer
Nationality: British. *S/n:* 102264 RAFVR. *Rank:* Flying Officer. *Squadron:* 137. *In:* 1 October 1941. *Out:* 18 July 1942.

COLE Clifford William Douglas – Medical Officer
Nationality: British. *S/n:* 89036 RAFVR. *Rank:* Flight Lieutenant. *Squadron:* 263. *In:* 26 January 1942. *Out:* 22 May 1942 to RAF Zeals. *Nickname:* Bill. *Remarks:* Born in Plymouth. Always interested in flying matters he was popular with the squadron. Finished the war in Italy as a Wing Commander, was Mentioned in Dispatches on 14 June 1945, and became a respected chest physician but died in a car crash in 1986.

EADIE Eric Comissiong – Medical Officer
Nationality: British. *S/n:* 120050 RAFVR. *Rank:* Flying Officer; Flight Lieutenant on 13 March 1943. *Squadron:* 263. *In:* 22 May 1942. *Out:* 30 June 1943.

FLEET Charles Stanley – Adjutant
Nationality: British. *S/n:* 83945 RAFVR. *Rank:* Pilot Officer; Flying Officer on 20 August 1941. *Squadron:* 263. *In:* 9 April 1941 from RAF Exeter. *Out:* 26 November 1941 to 600 Squadron. *Remarks:* Fell off a bus and broke his leg on 6 November 1941, and resigned his Commission on 8 August 1942.

FLYNN Robert Smollett – Medical Officer
Nationality: British. *S/n:* 128008 RAFVR. *Rank:* Flying Officer; Flight Lieutenant on 24 April 1943. *Squadron:* 137. *In:* 18 July 1942. *Out:* 30 June 1943 Posted Overseas.

FOWLER Denis Herbert – Medical Officer
Nationality: British. *S/n:* 75567 RAF. *Rank:* Flying Officer; Flight Lieutenant on 24 October 1940. *Squadron:* 263. *In:* 1 March 1940. *Out:* 10 February 1941 to RAF Filton. *Remarks:* On 20 December 1940 he was 'brought to notice' for distinguished services in Norway. Finished the war as a Squadron Leader, he resigned his commission on 5 March 1948.

FREEMAN Norman Emery – Adjutant
Nationality: British. *S/n:* 104865 RAFVR. *Rank:* Flying Officer. *Squadron:* 137. *In:* 2 October 1942. *Out:* 17 November 1942. *Remarks:* He retired on 11 February 1944 due to ill health.

GARLAND John Charles – Engineering Officer
Nationality: British. *S/n:* RAFVR. *Rank:* Pilot Officer; Flying Officer on 15 April 1941. *Squadron:* 263. *In:* 25 March 1941 from 92 Squadron. *Out:* 1 October 1941. *Remarks:* He finished the war as a Flight Lieutenant and joined the Auxiliary Air Force on 2 June 1947.

GRANT Bertrum Robert – Engineering Officer
Nationality: British. *S/n:* 149152 (Sgt); 44144 (Officer). *Rank:* Warrant Officer on 11 November 1939; Pilot Officer on 6 July 1940. *Squadron:* 263. *In:* 2 October 1939. *Out:* 25 March 1941 to RAF West Malling. *Remarks:* The ORB noted, 'His going was a great loss.' He retired on 10 February 1946 as a Squadron Leader.

GREEN Peter Roland – Medical Officer
Nationality: British. *S/n:* 139309 RAFVR. *Rank:* Flying Officer. *Squadron:* 263. *In:* 1 July 1943. *Out:* 16 August 1944. *Remarks:* Born 12 June 1914. Injured in the Oxford at Biggin Hill on 19 November 1943, he retired on 16 October 1946, and passed away in July 1988.

HADLEY Geoffrey Hugh – Adjutant
Nationality: British. *S/n:* 87522. *Rank:* Pilot Officer. *Squadron:* 263. *In:* 9 January 1941 from RAF Filton. *Out:* 9 April 1941 to RAF Exeter. *Remarks:* Finished the war as a Flight Lieutenant.

HAY Alfred Arthur BEM – Engineering Officer
Nationality: British. *S/n:* 46415 RAFVR. *Rank:* Pilot Officer; Flying Officer on 19 April 1942. *Squadron:* 263. *In:* 1 October 1941. *Out:* 13 May 1942 to RAF Zeals. *Remarks:* He

was awarded the BEM on 11 July 1940 prior to joining 263, and it was due to his efforts that serviceability remained high, especially during the 3-way oil union problems. He remained in the RAF after the war, was granted a permanent Commission as a Squadron Leader in 1949 and retired on 28 January 1954.

HAYMAN William Frank – Adjutant
Nationality: British. *S/n:* 67748 RAFVR. *Rank:* Flying Officer *Squadron:* 137. *In:* 28 May 1943. *Out:* 1 October 1943 to 511 Airfield and Motor Transport Repair Unit *Remarks:* Finished the war as a Flight Lieutenant

HENDRY Francis Harold Arthur – Intelligence Officer
Nationality: British. *S/n:* 80919 RAF. *Rank:* Pilot Officer. *Squadron:* 263. *In:* 3 July 1940 from Air Ministry. *Out:* 22 July 1940 to RAF Catterick. *Remarks:* Commissioned as a 2nd Lieutenant in the Highland Light Infantry on 29 August 1917, and Commissioned into RAF as a Pilot Officer on 17 June 1940, he retired on 22 December 1940.

HISCOCK Leslie Robert – Adjutant
Nationality: British. *S/n:* 77223 RAF. *Rank:* Flying Officer. *Squadron:* 263. *In:* 17 December 1940 from 55 OTU. *Out:* 9 January 1941 to 152 Squadron. *Remarks:* Born in London, he gained his Aero Club Certificate on 6 February 1939 at Brooklands. He passed away in January 1996.

HOGAN Philip Lewis – Adjutant
Nationality: British. *S/n:* 83751 RAF. *Rank:* Flight Lieutenant. *Squadron:* 137. *In:* 28 September 1941 from RAF High Ercall. *Out:* 1 October 1942. *Remarks:* He retired on 9 July 1954 as a Flight Lieutenant.

MOORE Dennis Lionel Patrick – Engineering Officer
Nationality: British. *S/n:* 50326 RAFVR. *Rank:* Pilot Officer. *Squadron:* 137. *In:* 1 October 1941. *Out:* 31 May 1943. *Nickname:* Dinty. *Remarks:* He remained in the RAF on a Short Service Commission from 13 May 1949.

MORGAN James Lawson – Medical Officer
Nationality: British. *S/n:* 60982 RAFVR. *Rank:* Flight Lieutenant. *Squadron:* 137. *In:* 30 June 1943. *Out:* 1 November 1944 to RAF Goxhill. *Remarks:* Mentioned in Despatches on 2 June 1943, he retired as a Squadron Leader on 20 May 1956 and passed away in March 1992.

ORMEROD Arthur Hereward – Intelligence Officer
Nationality: British. *S/n:* 80693 RAF. *Rank:* Pilot Officer; Flying Officer on 17 June 1941. *Squadron:* 263. *In:* 22 July 1940 from RAF Catterick. *Out:* 2 September 1941 to RAF Colerne. *Remarks:* Born in Halifax, he joined the Legal Branch on 22 February 1943 as a Flight Lieutenant and was involved in the Nuremburg Trials. Secretary to the Master of Rolls in the 1960s, he wrote several books on the English Legal System.

OWENS Eugene Charles – Adjutant
Nationality: British. *S/n:* 77280 RAFVR. *Rank:* Flight Lieutenant. *Squadron:* 263. *In:* 26 November 1941 from RAF Predannack. *Out:* 31 May 1944 to RAF Predannack. *Nickname:* The Bish. *Remarks.* Born in St Pancras, London he served in the RFC. Mentioned in Dispatches on 17 March 1941, the 263 ORB noted, 'the immemorial figurehead of the squadron. Despite his years, which trebled those of most members of the squadron, he was an excellent companion and an inimitable raconteur. It goes without saying that he was adept and able to penetrate and control all the mysteries of the squadron's 'bumph'. As a man of the law and an inveterate weigher up of sporting chances, he was particularly helpful to anyone involved in any sort of sticky or delicate situation. He retired as a Squadron Leader on 27 July 1954, and passed away in 1966.

PARRY Rheon Thomas – Engineering Officer
Nationality: British. *S/n:* 83378 RAFVR. *Rank:* Flying Officer; Flight Lieutenant on 1 July 1943. *Squadron:* 263. *In:* 1 June 1943. *Out:* 22 December 1944 to 145 Wing. *Remarks:* Joined the Technical Branch of the reconstituted RAFVR as a Flying Officer on 1 March 1950.

PRIEST Gordon Edmund William – Adjutant
Nationality: British. *S/n:* 65066 RAFVR. *Rank:* Flying Officer. *Squadron:* 137 *In:* 17 November 1942. *Out:* 30 April 1943 Posted Overseas.

THOMAS John Douglas – Adjutant
Nationality: British. *S/n:* 100716 RAFVR. *Rank:* Flying Officer *Squadron:* 137 *In:* 30 April 1943. *Out:* 28 May 1943. *Remarks:* Commissioned as a Flying Officer in the RAFVR on 2 June 1952.

WALLIS Geoffrey – Engineering Officer
Nationality: American. *S/n:* 47635 RAFVR. *Rank:* Pilot Officer; Flying Officer 1 October 1942. *Squadron:* 137. *In:* 23 January 1942. *Out:* 31 July 1943 to RAF Southend: *Awards:* Mentioned In Dispatches on 2 June 1943. *Nickname:* Why. *Remarks:* Remained in the post-war RAF.

WEIR Walter Pollock – Medical Officer
Nationality: British. *S/n:* 87994 RAFVR. *Rank:* Flying Officer; Flight Lieutenant on 5 November 1941. *Squadron:* 263. *In:* 10 February 1941. *Out:* 26 January 1942 to RAF Goxhill. *Remarks:* Born in Greenock, he received the OBE on 31 December 1982 for Services to Forensic Sciences in Scotland; he passed away in November 1986.

WORDSWORTH Andrew Sigfrid – Intelligence Officer
Nationality: British. *S/n:* 62464 RAFVR. *Rank:* Pilot Officer; Flying Officer on 30 March 1942; Flight Lieutenant on 1 July 1943. *Squadron:* 263. *In:* 2 September 1941. *Out:* 1944. *Remarks:* Son of the Bishop of Winchester, he was born in Salisbury. He retired on 29 November 1955 and passed away 1978.

6

Awards to Whirlwind Pilots

ASHTON Joel Hilton – Distinguished Flying Cross – 23 October 1943

This Officer has completed a very large number of sorties including successful attacks on airfields, shipping and rail communications. He has displayed great skill and determination, setting an example worthy of high praise. These qualities were well illustrated in a recent attack on an installation at Hansweert. P/O Ashton attacked his objective from such a low level that his aircraft was struck in places by the flying debris.

BAKER Ernest Reginald DFC – Bar to Distinguished Flying Cross – 27 September 1943

BLACKSHAW Herbert John – Distinguished Flying Cross – 17 February 1943

S/L Warnes and F/L Blackshaw have participated in a great number of sorties, achieving many successes. On one occasion, they attacked and sank an armed trawler, whilst on another attack they delivered a destructive attack on a distillery. In low-level raids on enemy airfields and other ground targets, they have invariably pressed home their attacks with great determination. S/L Warnes, who wears contact lenses to correct his sight for flying, and F/L Blackshaw, have displayed high qualities of leadership and outstanding keenness.

BRUNET Arthur Gaston – Distinguished Flying Cross – 14 August 1943

This Officer who has completed many sorties both by day and night in an extremely able and determined pilot. In the course of his activities, P/O Brunet has attacked many locomotives and rolling stock with success. In addition, he has attacked many barges and several E-Boats with telling effect. He has set a very commendable example.

BRYAN John Michael – Distinguished Flying Cross – 12 March 1943

This Officer has taken part in a large number of sorties and patrols. On one occasion, he assisted in the destruction of a Dornier Do.217. In attacks on enemy transport in Northern France and Belgium, he has damaged fifteen locomotives. His skill and keenness have been worth of high praise.

BRYAN John Michael – Bar to Distinguished Flying Cross – 1 August 1943

F/L Bryan is a skilful and tenacious pilot. Since being awarded the DFC, he has damaged two minesweepers, three barges and an E-Boat. In addition he has executed thirteen destructive attacks on locomotives; he has also participated in several successful attacks on enemy airfields. He has displayed high qualities of leadership, setting an inspiring example.

COGHLAN Humphrey St John – Distinguished Flying Cross – 8 October 1941

This Officer has displayed excellent qualities as a fighter pilot and has participated in many sorties. In one attack on Lannion aerodrome, he destroyed two Ju.88s on the ground. In another attack on the same aerodrome he successfully accomplished his mission and was compelled to return to this country in darkness. Nevertheless, he flew back with great skill and, although his petrol supply ran out, he executed a skilful landing. F/O Coghlan has displayed great courage and initiative.

COGHLAN Humphrey St John – Mentioned in Despatches – 1 January 1943

COTTON Maxwell Tylney – Distinguished Flying Cross – 13 June 1943

P/O Cotton has taken part in numerous and varied operational missions, some of which have been completed at night. His sorties have included dive bombing of enemy airfields, attacks on railway objectives and against shipping in convoy. On three occasions his aircraft has been seriously damaged by anti-aircraft fire, but he did not fail to fly back to this country and to land safely. He has displayed a complete disregard of intense enemy opposition and has at all times pressed home his attacks with the greatest determination.

COYNE James Patrick – Distinguished Flying Cross – 2 June 1943

This Officer has completed numerous sorties involving low-level attacks on airfields, dock installations and rail communications. His courageous leadership, tenacity and keenness have been inspiring.

DeHOUX Joseph Laurier – Distinguished Flying Cross – 1 August 1943

This Officer has participated in many sorties including attacks on enemy airfields, both by day and night, on military installations and shipping. In the course of his activities, he has inflicted damage on nineteen barges, three minesweepers, and five locos. He has displayed great skill and fighting qualities.

DONALDSON Arthur Hay – Distinguished Flying Cross – 21 August 1941

This Officer has shown himself to be an excellent leader and has carried out seven offensive operations against the enemy over Northern France and Belgium. During these operations, he has destroyed and damaged a number of aircraft on the ground and inflicted damage to buildings and dispersal pens. Once whilst returning to base with his Squadron, he attacked six anti-aircraft barges, one of which was sunk and three damaged. S/L Donaldson has by his leadership, gallantry and initiative in action, set an excellent example and is largely responsible for the successful operations carried out by the squadron.

HARVEY Philip – Distinguished Flying Cross – 1 May 1943 posthumous

This Officer has taken part in twenty-six sorties during which successful attacks have been made on shipping and on railway installations. During an attack on railway installations, an aircraft of the formation in which he was flying was it by anti-aircraft fire. Displaying great determination, he escorted the damaged aircraft on the return flight until its pilot was compelled to bring it down on to the sea. He flew on and landed at an airfield and then set out again as the navigator of an aircraft of the air/sea rescue service in an endeavour to find his comrade. During an operational flight one day in April 1943, he observed the crew of a bomber afloat in their dinghy. As a result of information supplied by him, the crew were subsequently picked up. The same afternoon he took part in a successful attack on a ship off Brest. He has invariably displayed skill and courage of a high order.

HOLMES Joseph William Ernest – Distinguished Flying Cross – 2 June 1943

This Officer has taken part in many operations during which attacks have been made on such targets as airfields, gun positions, and military installations. He is a first class leader, whose skill and courage have set an excellent example.

KING Cecil Percy – Distinguished Flying Medal – 11 September 1942

In the course of many sorties, he has inflicted much damage on enemy targets. He is a skilful and determined pilot whose example has been most praiseworthy. He has destroyed one enemy aircraft.

LEE-WHITE Arthur Henry – Distinguished Flying Cross – 13 June 1943

This Officer has taken part in numerous and varied offensive operations, a number of which have been at night. His sorties have included attacks on shipping and industrial targets. On one occasion, when attacking enemy vessels in convoy, the starboard engine of his aircraft was set on fire. Undaunted, he bombed an armed trawler before successfully flying back to this country where he made a safe landing while the fire still burned in the engine. He has shown complete contempt for enemy opposition and has always pressed home his attacks with great determination.

McCLURE John Edward – Distinguished Flying Cross – 6 July 1943

This Officer has completed much operational flying, including a number of reconnaissances and attacks on shipping. In attacks on enemy lines of communications, he has destroyed four locomotives and damaged several more. In addition, he has destroyed a barge and caused damage to rolling stock. F/O McClure has displayed skill, keenness and determination of a high order.

MUSGRAVE Edward Lancelot – Distinguished Flying Cross – 26 February 1943

This Officer has taken part in a large number of operational missions. In attacks on the enemy's communications in Northern France and Belgium, he has damaged seven locomotives. One night in February 1943 he took off to search for a large merchant vessel, escorted by five armed ships, reported in the Channel. Although the night was very dark, he sighted the vessels sailing close to the shore south of Boulogne. Skilfully approaching the merchant vessel, he flew in to attack but was frustrated by heavy fire from the coastal defences. Despite this, he persisted and, after diving through the searchlights from the shore he attacked his objective, releasing his bombs from a low level. Although his aircraft was damaged by opposing fire from the ships, he flew it safely to base. He displayed great courage, skill and determination in the execution of his task.

PUGH Thomas Patrick – Distinguished Flying Cross – 8 October 1941

During August and September 1941, this Officer participated in many sorties during which a variety of targets were attacked, including shipping and wireless stations as well as enemy aerodromes on which he personally destroyed two Ju.88s on the ground. On one occasion, whilst participating in an escort to a force of bombers which attacked a convoy, he attacked a 500 ton enemy escorting vessel and set the decks and superstructure on fire. One day in September 1941, during an attack on an enemy aerodrome he destroyed a Me.109 on the ground. Throughout these operations, which have necessitated the most accurate navigation and skill, often in the face of heavy enemy fire, S/L Pugh has shown great courage and determination.

RIDLEY Kenneth Charles – Distinguished Flying Medal – 3 July 1943

This airman has taken part in thirty sorties involving attacks on airfields, industrial targets, rail communications and shipping. He has displayed great skill and determination throughout, and on three occasions, when his aircraft has been severely damaged by enemy action, he has flown it back to base.

RIDLEY Kenneth Charles – Distinguished Flying Cross – 1943

For his many gallant and successful offensive operations with 263.

ROSS David George – Distinguished Flying Cross – 28 March 1944

RUDLAND Clifford Percival – Distinguished Flying Cross – 7 September 1941

This Officer, who recently assumed command of his Flight, has performed exceptionally fine work in the course of offensive operations against the enemy, including a determined attack on an enemy aerodrome, a successful attack on a wireless station and important operations carried out in the Cherbourg area. On one occasion he destroyed a Me.109 which was taking off. On another occasion, P/O Rudland displayed great coolness and courage when engaging and destroying one of a vastly superior number of enemy fighters. In August 1941, whilst leading a section on an offensive operation, he attacked an enemy aerodrome at ground level. P/O Rudland has displayed a high standard of leadership and courage.

SIMPSON James Ian – Distinguished Flying Medal – 26 September 1943

In recognition of gallantry and devotion to duty in the execution of air operations.

SMITH Aubrey Cartwright – Distinguished Flying Medal – 9 September 1943

This airman has completed many sorties during which he has attacked a variety of targets, including shipping, airfields and mechanical transport. On one occasion he executed a determined attack on a convoy of some forty lorries causing much destruction. On another occasion he destroyed an E-Boat and a minesweeper. This airman has invariably displayed outstanding keenness and determination.

SMITH Robert Leslie DFM – Distinguished Flying Cross – 12 February 1943

Since being awarded the DFM, P/O Smith has taken part in numerous operational flights, including attacks on shipping and railways. On one occasion he engaged four Fw.190s and seriously damaged one of them. Although his own aircraft also received severe damage during the combat, he flew it safely to base and affected a masterly landing.

WARNES Geoffrey Berrington – Distinguished Flying Cross – 17 February 1943

S/L Warnes and F/L Blackshaw have participated in a great number of sorties, achieving many successes. On one occasion, they attacked and sank an armed trawler, whilst on another attack they delivered a destructive attack on a distillery. In low-level raids on enemy airfields and other ground targets, they have invariably pressed home their attacks with great determination. S/L Warnes, who wears contact lenses to correct his sight for flying, and F/L Blackshaw, have displayed high qualities of leadership and outstanding keenness.

WARNES Geoffrey Berrington – Distinguished Service Order – 13 June 1943

Since the award of the DFC this Officer has been engaged on numerous operational sorties, both day and night, which have included low level attacks on heavily defended railway targets and attacks on enemy shipping. One night in May 1943 S/L Warnes participated in the destruction of a medium sized motor vessel. He has displayed considerable powers of leadership and his skill and enthusiasm have been an example to others.

7
Whirlwind Commanding Officers

263 Squadron

Henry Eeles
6 July – 16 December 1940
John Gray Munro
17 December 1940 – 18 February 1941
Arthur Hay Donaldson AFC DFC
18 February – 21 August 1941
Thomas Patrick Pugh DFC
21 August 1941 – 12 February 1942
Robert Sinkler Woodward DFC
12 February – 7 December 1942
Geoffrey Berrington Warnes DSO DFC
9 December 1942 – 15 June 1943
Ernest Reginald Baker DFC*
15 June – 5 December 1943

137 Squadron

John Sample DFC
20 September – 28 October 1941
Humphrey St John Coghlan DFC
2 November 1941 – 23 May 1943
John Basil Wray DFC
23 May – 5 December 1943

8

Whirlwind Losses

263 SQUADRON

1940	24 July	P/O Eric Wilfred Bell – Killed in a Flying Accident – Blenheim *L1105*
	12 December	F/O Allan Walter Naylor Britton – Killed in a Flying Accident – *P6980*
	29 December	F/L Wynford Ormond Leoni Smith – Killed in a Flying Accident – *P6975 HE-L*
	29 December	P/O Donald Martin Vine – Killed in a Flying Accident – *P6978*
1941	9 January	Sgt Frank Morton – Killed in a Flying Accident – Blenheim *L1223*
	8 February	P/O Kenneth Arthur George Graham – Missing in Action – *P6969 HE-V*
	11 March	P/O Herbert Horatio Kitchener DFM – Badly Injured – *P6985 HE-J*
	14 March	P/O Patrick Glynn Thornton Brown – Badly Injured – *P6988 HE-J*
	1 April	F/L David Alexander Cummins Crooks DFC – Killed in Action – *P6989 HE-C*
	20 April	F/O Bernard Howe – Killed in Flying Accident – *P6992 HE-C*
	30 April	P/O George Stanley Milligan – Killed in Flying Accident – *P7008*
	11 June	Sgt Reginald Gunn Pascoe – Killed in Flying Accident – *L6845*
	12 June	P/O Roy Frederick Ferdinand – Killed in Flying Accident – *P7045*
	4 September	Sgt Geoffrey Leighton Buckwell – Prisoner of War – *P7042*
	10 September	P/O Dennis William Mason – Killed in Action – *P7001*
	29 September	Sgt Thomas Hunter – Killed in Action – *P7009*
	9 October	P/O Ormonde John Horace Hoskins – Killed in Flying Accident – *P6968 HE-H*
	30 October	P/O David Stein – Killed in Action – *P7015*
	6 November	Sgt John Joseph Robinson – Missing in Action – *P6970*
	14 December	Sgt Derek Ellis Prior – Killed in Flying Accident – *P7044*
1942	23 July	P/O Vernon Lester Currie – Missing in Action – *P7035*
	23 July	P/O John James Walker – Missing in Action – *P7060*

	21 September	Sgt Peter Alastair Jardine – Killed in Flying Accident – *P7003*
	7 November	F/O Donald Ross Gill RCAF – Missing in Action – *P7043 HE-A*
	7 December	S/L Robert Sinkler Woodward DFC – Missing in Action – *P7105 HE-N*
	7 December	P/O Donald Burton McPhail RCAF – Missing in Action – *P6987 HE-L*
1943	12 February	Sgt David John Williams – Missing in Action – *P7052*
	19 February	F/S Francis Lesley Hicks RAAF – Killed in Flying Accident – *P7062 HE-L*
	13 March	Sgt John Gray Macaulay – Missing in Action – *P7010*
	17 April	F/O Edger Brearley – Missing in Action – *P6995*
	18 April	F/O Philip Harvey DFC – Missing in Action – *P7090*
	18 April	P/O Basil Courtney Abrams – Missing in Action – *P7099*
	18 April	P/O Cecil Percy King DFM – Missing in Action – *P7117 HE-H*
	15 May	F/L Herbert John Blackshaw DFC – Killed in Action – *P7094 HE-T*
	15 June	P/O Maxwell Tylney Cotton DFC RAAF – Missing in Action – *P7000*
	13 July	Sgt Leonard James Knott – Badly Injured – *P7110 HE-C*
	9 October	P/O James Ian Simpson DFM - Killed in Action – *P7047*
	24 October	F/S Leonard Scott Gray – Prisoner of War – *P6979 HE-G*
	24 October	F/O Paul Thomas Richard Mercer – Killed in Action – *P6986 HE-Q*

137 SQUADRON

1941	28 October	S/L John Sample DFC – Killed in Flying Accident – *P7053*
	30 October	F/O Colin Anthony Gordon Clark – Killed in Action – *P7091*
1942	7 January	Sgt Jack Maddocks – Badly Injured – *P7062*
	12 February	P/O Ralph Otto Gustaf Häggberg – Missing in Action – *P7093 SF-A*
	12 February	P/O George William Martin – Missing in Action – *P7106 SF-D*
	12 February	P/O John Anthony William Sandy – Missing in Action – *P7050*
	12 February	W/O Basil Lionel Robertson – Missing in Action – *P7107*
	9 March	P/O Charles Wilbert DeShane RCAF – Killed in Flying Accident – *P7036 SF-X*
	4 May	P/O Robert Elmer Douglas Wright RCAF – Killed in Flying Accident – *P7103*
	27 May	F/S John Robert Brennan RCAF – Missing in Action – *P7122*
	31 October	P/O Douglas StJohn Jowitt – Missing in Action – *P7115*
	31 October	Sgt Francis Gordon Waldron – Prisoner of War – *P7109 SF-N*

1943	23 January	W/O Alexander Ivan Doig – Prisoner of War – *P7054*
	23 January	P/O Alfred Edward Brown – Missing in Action – *P7095 SF-H*
	18 February	P/O Charles Eldred Mercer – Killed in Flying Accident – *P7119*
	18 February	2nd Lt Neville Austin Freeman SAAF – Killed in Flying Accident – *P7114*
	2 March	Sgt Gerald Oscar Harrington Walker – Prisoner of War – *P7005 SF-H*
	15 April	F/O John Maude Hadow – Killed in Flying Accident – *P7121 SF-C*
	25 April	F/O James Reginald Rebbetoy RCAF – Killed in Action – *P7058 SF-G*
	17 May	F/O Edward Lancelot Musgrave DFC RAAF – Missing in Action – *P7063*

9	Killed in Action
20	Missing in Action
17	Killed in Flying Accident
5	Prisoner of War
4	Badly Injured

9
Whirlwind Victories

1941

12 January	Ju.88 of K.Gr.806 – Destroyed – David Stein *P6972*
8 February	Ar.196 of 5/Ku.Fl.Gr.196 – Destroyed – Kenneth Graham *P6969 HE-V*
1 March	Ju.88 – Damaged – Patrick Thornton-Brown *P6989 HE-J*
5 March	Ju.88 – Damaged – Herbert Kitchener DFM *P6989 HE-J*
11 March	Ju.88 – Damaged – Herbert Kitchener DFM *P6985 HE-J*
1 April	Do.215 – Damaged – Arthur Donaldson *P6998*
6 April	He.111 of I/KG.27 – Damaged – Bernard Howe *P7002 HE-L* [1]
6 April	He.111 of I/KG.27 – Damaged – Albert Tooth *P7004* [2]
7 April	Ju.88 of KG.54 – Damaged – Roy Ferdinand *P6996*
6 August	Me.109 of JG.2 – Destroyed – Robert Brackley *P6983 HE-H*
6 August	Me.109 of JG.2 – Damaged – Arthur Donaldson *P7001*
6 August	Me.109E-7 of JG.2 – Destroyed – Clifford Rudland *P7002 HE-L*
6 August	Me.109E-7 of JG.2 – Destroyed – Clifford Rudland *P7002 HE-L*
4 September	Me.109E of JG.2 *White 15* – Damaged – David Stein *P6990*
7 November	Me.109E-7 of 1/JG.2 – Destroyed – Cecil King *P7112*

1942

15 May	Ju.88 – Damaged – Robert Brennan *P7055 SF-S*
27 May	Ju.88 – Destroyed – Robert Brennan *P7122* & Paul LaGette *P7046*[3]
20 June	Do.217 of 3/KG.2 – Damaged – Joel Ashton *P7012 SF-V* & Charles Mercer *P6972*
6 July	Ju.88 – Damaged – Len Bartlett *P7111 SF-E*
25 July	Ju.88 *8H+KL* of 3(F)/122 – Destroyed – John McClure *P7104 SF-V* & Robert Smith *P7012*
29 July	Ju.88D-1 *F6+EL* of 3(F)/122 – Destroyed – Leo O'Neill *P7005 SF-H* & James Rebbetoy *P7058 SF-G*
18 August	Ju.88 Damaged – Leo O'Neill P7037 SF-J & John Luing *P7055 SF-S*
19 August	Do.217E-4 *F8+BN* of 5/KG40 – Destroyed – Mike Bryan *P7121* & Des Roberts *P7046*
19 August	Ju.88 Damaged – Alfred Brown *P6976 SF-X*
20 August	Ju.88 Damaged – John Barclay *P6982*
14 December	Fw.190 of 10/JG.2 – Damaged – Max Cotton *P7052*
14 December	Fw.190 of 10/JG.2 – Damaged – James Coyne *P7057 SF-S*

15 December Fw.190 – Damaged – Robert Smith *P6976 SF-X*
19 December Fw.190 – Destroyed – John Bryan *P7114* & James Rebbetoy *P7005 SF-H*

1943
28 January Fw.190-4 '*Black 2*' of 8/JG.26 – Destroyed – Eddie Musgrave *P7058 SF-G* [4]
16 May Fw.190 of NAG 13 – Damaged – Arthur Lee-White *P7059*
16 May Fw.190 of NAG 13 – Damaged – James Coyne *P7110 HE-E*
15 June Fw.190 – Damaged – John Wray *P7111 SF-E*
14 August Ju.88 of KG.26 – Destroyed – Reginald Baker *P7113*

13 Destroyed (5 Ju88; 4 Me.109; 2 Fw190; 1 Do217; 1 Ar.196)
18 Damaged (6 Ju.88; 6 Fw190; 2 He111; 2 Me.109; 1 Do215; 1 Do217)
[1, 2] & [4] – No claim made; [3] – was actually Blenheim V5568 of 1401 Met Flight, Horsham St Faith

10
Sorties – Flying Hours – Scrambles – Patrols

	TOTAL		SCRAMBLES		CONVOY PATROLS		YARMOUTH PATROLS	
263 SQUADRON	Sorties	Hours	Sorties	Hours	Sorties	Hours	Sorties	Hours
December 1940	28	20:50	11	6:50	2	1:50		
January 1941	63	55:10	38	35:10				
February 1941	70	58:05	38	32:40				
March 1941	182	183:30	92	84:05	56	72:55		
April 1941	179	267:20	21	25:20	142	100:50		
May 1941	210	239:30			191	227:35		
June 1941	156	194:00	6	6:00	133	173.25		
July 1941	103	130:05	15	12:10	87	121:30		
August 1941	104	119:50	10	9:00	47	55:55		
September 1941	58	65:50	10	9:30	12	14:20		
October 1941	16	18:35	9	9:45	4	5:10		
November 1941	37	37:20						
December 1941	6	5:30						
January 1942	16	10:40						
February 1942	419	458:50	69	54:15	343	392:55		
March 1942	206	256:00	24	18:50	119	149:40		
April 1942	307	382:10			222	270:25		
May 1942	433	535:55						
June 1942	400	489:10	12	6:20				
July 1942	379	325:10	52	51:10	288	328:55		
August 1942	98	89:20	27	17:50	54	57:00		
September 1942	42	37:30	10	7:10				

October 1942	43	46:45			14	17:10		
November 1942	82	92:20			45	60:00		
December 1942	26	27:25						
January 1943	29	35:40						
February 1943	100	115:50						
March 1943	74	101:10						
April 1943	121	174:50						
May 1943	96	117:50						
June 1943	10	12:05						
July 1943	16	18:50						
August 1943	112	148:00			36	48:10		
September 1943	82	99:35						
October 1943	83	91:10						
November 1943	95	104:25						
December 1943								
	4481	**5166:15**						

	TOTAL		SCRAMBLES		CONVOY PATROLS		YARMOUTH PATROLS	
137 SQUADRON	Sorties	Hours	Sorties	Hours	Sorties	Hours	Sorties	Hours
October 1941	6	6:50						
November 1941	78	92:20	4	5:40	28	35:25		
December 1941	145	185:00	22	20:55	4	6:40	105	139:45
January 1942	111	114:05	48	32:10	34	45:20	8	8:20
February 1942	211	236:30	89	89:10	23	30:10	2	81:15
March 1942	105	121:40	24	16:10	35	50:30	15	19:40
April 1942	191	198:50	70	48:05	63	83:20	48	59:50
May 1942	257	284:20	121	121:25	55	67:40	19	21:25
June 1942	195	213:45	66	56:25	43	70:10	6	6:00
July 1942	245	297:50	91	85:30	105	152:15		
August 1942	110	130:25	44	37:25	24	53:20		
September 1942	22	21:35						
October 1942	52	43:05	10	7:50				
November 1942	39	39:05						
December 1942	72	59:55						
January 1943	59	42:35						
February 1943	47	45:35						
March 1943	51	46:50						
April 1943	107	115:05						
May 1943	66	76:00						
June 1943	54	53:40						
	2223	**2429:00**						

11
Whirlwind Bases

263 Squadron

Drem	10 June 1940 – 28 June 1940
Grangemouth	28 June 1940 – 2 September 1940
Drem	2 September 1940 – 28 November 1940
Exeter	28 November 1940 – 24 February 1941
St Eval	24 February 1941 – 18 March 1941
Portreath	18 March 1941 – 10 April 1941
Filton	10 April 1941 – 7 August 1941
Charmy Down	7 August 1941 – 19 December 1941
Warmwell	19 December 1941 – 23 December 1941
Charmy Down	23 December 1941 – 28 January 1942
Colerne	28 January 1942 – 10 February 1942
Fairwood Common	10 February 1942 – 18 April 1942
Angle	18 April 1942 – 15 August 1942
Colerne	15 August 1942 – 13 September 1942
Warmwell	13 September 1942 – 20 February 1943
Harrowbeer	20 February 1943 – 15 March 1943
Warmwell	15 March 1943 – 19 June 1943
Zeals	19 June 1943 – 12 July 1943
Warmwell	12 July 1943 – 7 September 1943
Manston	7 September 1943 – 10 September 1943
Warmwell	10 September 1943

137 Squadron

Charmy Down	20 September 1941 – 8 November 1941
Coltishall	8 November 1941 – 31 November 1941
Matlaske	31 November 1941 – 2 August 1942
Drem	2 August 1942 – 11 August 1942
Matlaske	11 August 1942 – 17 September 1942
Snailwell	17 September 1942 – 12 June 1943
Southend	12 June 1943

12
S/L Warnes' Tactical Memorandum

HINTS AND TIPS FOR BEGINNERS (AND OTHERS) IN SHIPPING ATTACKS WITH WHIRLIBOMBERS

Make sure of your bomb fusing. Remember: –

The 3-second detonator will vary between 2 & 4-seconds in its delay.

The 11-second detonator may give as little as seven seconds delay.

Know the call signs & numbers of aircraft escorting you and doing anti-flak.

Make sure the escort knows the method of your attack.

Be two minutes early for the rendezvous. Far better to do a circuit than keep the Wing waiting.

OUTWARD FORMATION – ANTI-FLAK FIGHTERS

Anti-flak fighters leading, in Flights line abreast, with aircraft line abreast 1,200 yds between the Flights, 50 yds between aircraft & 100 feet above sea-level.

BOMBERS

In sections line abreast 50 feet above sea level & 400 yds behind the anti-flak fighters. #2s in each section flying two spans out and one length behind their #1s. In this formation, the leaders are in the best position to choose the targets. If eight aircraft are used, repeat the formation for four aircraft, Flights astern.

ATTACKING

Fuse bombs & put both selector switches to the 'on' position immediately on setting course.

Swing into the best position on sighting the enemy (i.e. abeam or up sun). It is better to spend 2 minutes doing this than to attack without thought immediately on sighting. In the formation given above, each section of bombers will be able to follow the corresponding anti-flak Flight onto the target.

Time your attack so that you are about on the target as the anti-flak fighters break away. If both you and the Spit boys have your finger out, the last anti-flak cannon shell should beat your bombs to the target by a short head. In this way, less flak will be experienced as often the fighters draw the ships fire.

Concentrate on your bombing run, make this absolutely on the deck. Fly straight at your ship, and plant your bombs on the waterline.

Keep your camera button pressed on your run in so that you can prove to the Intelligence Officer that it was a 4,000 tonner not a 150 ton coaster. Most Intelligence Officers have never heard of a ship of more than 1,000 tons anyway, and you will be able to say, 'I told you so' when the combat film comes back.

Do not jink it serves no purpose, & only spoils your aim.

Do not fire your cannon, it is nice to hear the noise, but you cannot do both jobs at once, and will only make a cock of both. Leave the anti-flak to the Spits.

Both aircraft in a section must attack the same ship. Better one ship at the bottom than two damaged. Both aircraft should pass over the ship practically together. In this way the early demise of the #2, who might otherwise be blown up by his leader's bombs, will be avoided.

After bombing, pull over the masts (recommended) & get down on the deck again. DO NOT career wildly over the sky under the impression you are taking evasive action. This only makes everyone else's job, particularly the escort, more difficult.

Keep station. The Leader will throttle back immediately after leaving the target area to make this easier.

If attacking at night you will naturally attack into the moon. Bank sharply right or left, keeping low, immediately after. If you keep straight on you will make a nice target silhouetted against the moon.

REMEMBER – FLAK LOOKS A LOT WORSE THAN IT IS

RETURNING HOME

Bombers leading, sections line abreast & 100-150 yds apart. The #2s 100 yds behind & 100 feet above their #1s.

Anti-flak will escort, the former escort giving rear cover.

Defuse Selector switches to 'off' before crossing the coast.

Do not shoot a line to the Intelligence Officer about the size of the ship. An M class minesweeper looks like a Destroyer. A Destroyer looks like the Scharnhorst. Be modest, halve your estimate of tonnage, & wait until your camera films have been developed (provided of course you are a 'Good type' and have followed Hint #5).

13
Sgt Geoffrey Leighton Buckwell

Geoffrey Leighton Buckwell emigrated to Australia after the war where he practiced as a GP. This is his account of Thursday 4 September 1941.

It was a bright sunny afternoon without a cloud in the sky and the view from the cockpit was awe inspiring. The Whirlwind was a great aircraft to fly; we really were a privileged few. We joined the Hurricanes and Spits and flew down the west coast of the Cherbourg Peninsula with the Blenheims, turned east then north and approached Cherbourg from the south at 6,000 feet and 180 mph. We flew with the bombers through the flak, by which time I was straggling badly. Suddenly, tracer flashed past me, there was a sound like gravel on a mudguard, the starboard engine burst into flames and the inner part of the wing began to burn furiously and partly melted away. I radioed that I was on fire and bailing out, which I did with difficulty as I had been wounded in one leg. I was furious with myself for having 'had my finger well and truly in,' and being caught by 'the Hun in the sun.' My wound was painless as my leg was numb, but it bled furiously in the dinghy and I had to use my tie as a tourniquet. I was picked up by an armed trawler and taken to the Kriegsmarine Lazaret [Pasteur Institute] in Cherbourg where my shattered leg was operated on and encased in plaster.

The next day, I was visited by one Oberleutnant Siegfried Schnell, the pilot who had shot me down. Apparently I was his fiftieth victim. The nuns at the Kriegsmarine Lazaret repaired my clothes, and I was given them back on 7 September when I was flown in a Ju.52 ambulance with German sick and wounded to Le Bourget, Paris. It was here I saw my first Fw.190; she looked a most formidable machine. Whilst at the Luftwaffen Lazaret at Clichy [Hospital Beaujean] I underwent a further operation on my leg, and was well cared for. I also met several Luftwaffe pilots who were admitted from time to time. We agreed not to discuss military or technical matters, but played chess and discussed life in general and women in particular. They enjoyed a god-like status in the hospital and there was never shortage of pretty girls around. I went by train to the Dulag Luft Hospital about 7 January 1942, then via Frankfurt General Hospital, to Meiningen [IXC] Hospital run by British Army personnel. The facilities there were very basic indeed but, on 26 August 1942, I was sent to a convalescent Hospital at Kloster Haina which was part of a mental institution and eye hospital. Towards the end of August, we thought that the end was in sight, but instead a large number of wounded Canadians arrived from Dieppe, and I became a blood donor for the first time. By the middle of February 1943, I had recovered enough to be discharged from hospital and went to Dulag Luft. From there I went to Stalag Luft III [M. Stammlager VIIIB] at Lamsdorf south of Breslau. This was an Army Camp of some 20-30,000 men with a central compound of 2,000 aircrew, a few paratroopers and a few hundred French

Above left: Sgt Geoffrey Buckwell. (*Dr Geoff Buckwell archives*)

Above right: Oberleutnant Siegfried Schnell. He was shot down on 25 February 1944, in combat with Russian fighters near Narva. His aircraft crashed in marshy ground and he was never found. At the time of his death, he had ninety-three victories. (*Dr Geoff Buckwell archives*)

Canadians from Dieppe. It was around this time that I decided to attempt an escape, and along with two Canadians, John Patterson and Frank Linklater, began to make plans. We could see the Czechoslovak mountains in the distance, but as there was no hope of going through or under the wire, we decided to swap places with soldiers who were detailed for working parties, as we thought it would be easier to escape once away from the camp. It was not difficult to find soldiers willing to swap, and although not an original idea, it worked. We left Lamsdorf in September 1943 for Poland. There were five other 'swapovers' with us, two French Canadians and three RAF men. One, a Kenyan, was detected, and returned to the camp, and sixteen of the party were later killed in an air raid. Travelling in closed railway trucks, we passed through the industrial area of Gleiwitz, and eventually arrived at Arbeits Commando E715, Auschwitz, to work on the I. G Farben synthetic rubber plant being built there. We soon learned about the concentration camp, and reluctantly decided that although we had planned on escaping, if we were to be caught in this sensitive area, it would not prove too healthy. In February or March 1944, 250 of us were transferred to Stammlager 344 Arbeits Commando 711a, at Heidebrech. Here we worked on the Blechhammer North synthetic oil plant, though never did a good day's work. When news came through of the Normandy invasion, we decided to abandon our escape and await the early end to the war.

Between July and December 1944, there were many air raids by B-24 Liberators from Italy, which caused much damage, although a great many bombs were way off target and many failed to explode; these were removed by Jewish disposal squads. We saw several bombers shot down, and managed to build a radio from parts surreptitiously salvaged from one of them. Then, towards the end of January 1945, we were suddenly evacuated from the camp due to the sudden breakthrough of the Russians, and over the next few months moved slowly westwards through Sudetenland and Czechoslovakia to Bayreuth, then Nuremberg and Munich.

Finally on 28 April 1945, we were liberated by General Patton's troops near Moosberg and moved to Stalag VHA where we received medical treatment. On 11 May, I was flown back to Britain and in June was interrogated by MI6 as a possible war crimes witness, but as Auschwitz was in the Russian zone and no exact names, dates or places were recorded, no further action was taken.

For many years after the war, I did not take part in any service-related activity, being thoroughly sick and tired of it, especially the political aspect, and was also greatly disturbed by Auschwitz, and man's inhumanity to man. I have since met survivors from there whilst in medical practice, although I did not think anyone could have survived that particular hell.

Dr Buckwell passed away peacefully in 2006.

14
F/S George Albert Wood

George Wood's remarkable story began at 14,000 feet as he pushed Whirlwind *P7113* over into a dive bombing attack on the German occupied aerodrome at Morlaix, on 24 September 1943. Seconds after his two 250lb bombs left their racks at 4,000 feet, one of them was hit by flak and detonated; the aircraft bore the brunt of the explosion and disintegrated. One of the escorting Spitfire pilots described the sight as 'just like a flower opening up' and as no one saw his parachute, George was posted 'Missing in Action'. S/L Baker, who was on leave at the time of the raid and whose aircraft it was, wrote in George's logbook, 'A grand pilot, whose loss we can ill afford.' In his own diary he noted that:

> I am feeling somewhat depressed, one of my boys was killed on a job this morning, he blew up over the target. He wouldn't have known what hit him – I suppose that is some consolation.

Iain Dunlop was following George in the dive:

> It was my first operational sortie. One second he was there the next he just blew up and I remember thinking to myself, 'Bloody hell, this is a dangerous job.'

The obituaries however, were premature: F/S George Albert Wood was very much alive. Trapped in the tumbling, burning wreckage he fought to open the canopy, it could not be jettisoned but had to be wound back using a lever, and it would not move.

> Finally in desperation I cried out, 'Oh God, help me!' and He did. Suddenly, I was falling free and instinctively pulled the ripcord.

Watching the attack through binoculars was Captain Lucien Marzin, a veteran of the First World War, and by luck he had focused on George's aircraft seconds before it disintegrated. He said later that there were so many bits falling to earth that he thought two aircraft had collided, but as the wreckage fell, he recognised one of the pieces as a parachute. George remembers little after pushing over into the dive, until realising that he was being shot at by a soldier from a nearby light-flak battery as he hung beneath his parachute. 'There were bullets whistling past my lughole and I was just hoping they wouldn't hit the parachute or me.' His landing on the perimeter of the aerodrome was cushioned by trees, and as he was still being shot at he quickly released his harness and left it hanging in the tree then:

F/S George Wood. (*Revd George Wood archives*)

…ran like hell until I came to a barbed wire fence, and followed it until I came to a tree where I was able to shin up the trunk and drop over the other side of the wire. I then continued to run across a field, discarding my gloves and helmet and hid my Mae-West under some sheaves of wheat in another field. I was surprised that no one followed me, but this was due to me running across a minefield.

He was only told of this later, but as they were anti-tank mines it is doubtful his weight would have set one off.

I crossed several more fields and passed through an orchard where I picked an apple which I ate as I walked across the next field until I came to a quiet lane with several pheasants in it. Reasoning that where there were birds there were no people I began walking along it, hiding the remainder of my gear as I did so. Further down the lane I passed a farmer working in a field.

Six locals, including this farmer, were arrested and told they would be shot if they could not produce George. They were later released unharmed. Meanwhile, a panel bearing the legend 'Lochinvar' (S/L Baker's call sign) had been found amongst the smouldering wreckage of *P7113 HE-W* and, thinking they had a VIP in their midst, the Germans had mobilised a full battalion of some 900 men to search for him.

I hid in a hedge and ate a Horlicks tablet whilst I took stock of my situation. Knowing I should avoid such an exposed position I descended a hillside through some woods until I reached Morlaix estuary, and, although the tide was in, it looked an easy swim, which I decided to attempt after dark. It was about 1430, so I began to walk southwards towards Morlaix whilst searching for a hiding place. Eventually I found a fir tree set back from the road and after climbing it surveyed the surrounding countryside. To the east was a slight depression running down the side of the valley towards the estuary. On the other side of this and about thirty yards from my tree were several farm buildings. There was a woman feeding chickens, and at an upper storey window, a man sat painting. Further up the hillside was a chateau, and after watching for a while I could see that there were no Germans there, although their patrols were by now everywhere. They had the disconcerting habit of prodding hedges and bushes with their bayonets and at one point a patrol even stopped beneath my tree for a rest and a cigarette before continuing their search. Luckily not one of them looked up! After they had gone I climbed down and found a better hideout, a taller fir tree covered in ivy, which commanded an excellent view in every direction. Once settled in, I again took stock of my situation. During the day, I heard a church bell ringing on the opposite bank of the estuary, and decided to make for it after my forthcoming midnight swim. At OTU, I had attended a lecture on evasion and those most likely to help an aviator on the run were, oddly, either a priest or a prostitute. My decision to choose the convent must have been subconscious – I joined the priesthood after the war! I found out later that it was the Convent of St Francois Cuburien et la Salette.

Two hours after sunset I climbed down from the tree, hungry and stiff, and set out for the estuary. I picked up a branch to help me find my way in the dark, but on reaching the river, the tide had gone out leaving only thick glutinous mud into which I sank waist deep at every attempt. Having been thwarted I decided to head back along the road towards Morlaix, hoping to find a bridge or stepping stones. This walk was fraught with danger as the German patrols increased

The Convent of St Francois Cuburien et la Salette. (*Revd George Wood archives*)

the nearer I got to the town. Luckily, many of them were very noisy, but had progressed from bayoneting bushes to shooting them! I had the impression that many of the men were drunk, but at least I had adequate warning of their approach. When taking cover from one patrol I jumped over a wall into a six-foot deep ditch with muddy water at the bottom. Luckily, the splash I made was not heard, but I quickly realised that even if there was a bridge I would be unable to cross it with so many guards about and in daylight it would be impossible. I retraced my steps to the farm buildings I had seen earlier, crept into one and tried to get some sleep but this was difficult in my wet uniform.

Next morning after a night of trying to sleep on a cold concrete floor I was awakened by the farmer's wife as she collected grain for her chickens. She did not see me, but as I moved several barrels into a corner to make a better hiding place, I was discovered. The young man who found me, André Cras, fetched Mr Gueguen, the farmer, who led me to a haystack in the farmyard. He made a hollow between the stack and the wall it was leaning against and gestured me to get in. My uniform was still wet so I was given clean dry clothes although they were a little on the small side, a little bread, fruit and wine, the first food I had eaten in twenty-four hours. Mr Gueguen contacted a local sailor who could speak a little English. He would not reveal his name to me [it was Marot] as the Germans were always trying to infiltrate the escape organizations.

Certain that the young pilot was genuine; the sailor contacted a local bus driver, Albert Huet, and asked if he knew anyone who would be prepared to hide George. Unbeknown to the sailor, Huet was a member of the local Resistance cell, and immediately reported to his superior – Captain Marzin, the same man who had watched George parachute to safety. From that moment on, he was in safe hands.

Later in the day, Monsieur Gueguen handed me a note that read, 'Wait two or three days. Courage.' I was moved to the top floor of the stable, where I had seen the owner painting, and where I spent a more comfortable night. Next day I was visited by Doctor Le Duc. He was possibly one of the bravest men I ever met. We spoke briefly before he left promising to return at four in the afternoon. He duly arrived in a small car with Lulu Rault, a well-known Breton artist and we set off for the latter's home which was some twenty miles away in Carantec. I lay across the back seat covered by blankets as the journey entailed driving into the centre of Morlaix, crossing the river onto the West Bank and heading north again. During the journey, I mentioned my original intention of reaching the Convent, only to be told it had been requisitioned by the Germans, and was being used as a fuel dump! We passed several patrols, and at every bend, the doctor stopped the car and Lulu jumped out to see if the next patrol were stopping and searching cars – luckily none were.

As we entered Carantec, I sat up, but no sooner had I done so than we encountered two patrols. In my beret and blue mac however I did not arouse any suspicions and we were not stopped. Lulu's house overlooked the mouth of the estuary, and once there I was introduced to Madame Le Duc, the doctor's wife, and Mademoiselle Yvonne Rothschild, Lulu's sister. The first thing they did was to forge papers for me, and I became Pierre Floch, a deaf and dumb seventeen-year-old student from Montpelier University, Santec. Madame Le Duc took the documents to the local Register Office and asked for information, which she knew would take the clerk to the other side of the office, and in those few moments he was away, she leaned over the counter and stamped the false documents!'

The stamp said Carentec, but this was soon altered to Santec. Despite the precautions taken by his hosts however, a rumour reached the Gestapo and ten days later, they took Madame Le Duc away for questioning, accusing her of hiding an Allied airman. Despite the shock she must have received, she told her captors that as she had a young family she would be stupid to hide Allied airmen.

She even invited them to search her home! She must have been convincing, as she was quickly released. After such a narrow escape, I was moved further down the line to the Villa Kerjoaic on the southern outskirts of Morlaix. This was the home of Captain and Madame Marzin, their twenty-one-year-old daughter Simone, eight-year-old son Lulu, and the children's grandparents, Monsieur and Madame Boucherie. The grandmother though bedridden, kept lookout from her room and would bang on the floor with her walking stick if she saw a German approaching. Dr Le Duc's petrol ration was only enough for his visits to patients, so this time he arrived on a motor scooter. The journey back to Morlaix about twenty miles away was begun at night, strictly against the curfew, but as the machine was not powerful enough to carry two of us up even the slightest incline, we spent most of the night pushing it. Consequently, we arrived in Morlaix just as the soldiers were leaving their billets. Two people riding a scooter was strictly forbidden, but the sight of the well known doctor and a friend pushing one up the steep streets of the town did not arouse curiosity. By this time, I had apparently been officially reported as drowned.

George was to stay with the family for three weeks, and although he was unable to speak French, he and young Lulu did share a common interest – scouting. George had been in Groningen, Holland on the outbreak of war, and his scout troop was lucky to get a place on the last ship to leave for Britain. The summer before the war he had been to a jamboree at a place called Bolt Head – a few years later it was the aerodrome he took off from on his last flight. Young Lulu was in the Wolf Cubs.

George with Madam LeDuc and Mme Yvonne Rothschild. (*Revd George Wood archives*)

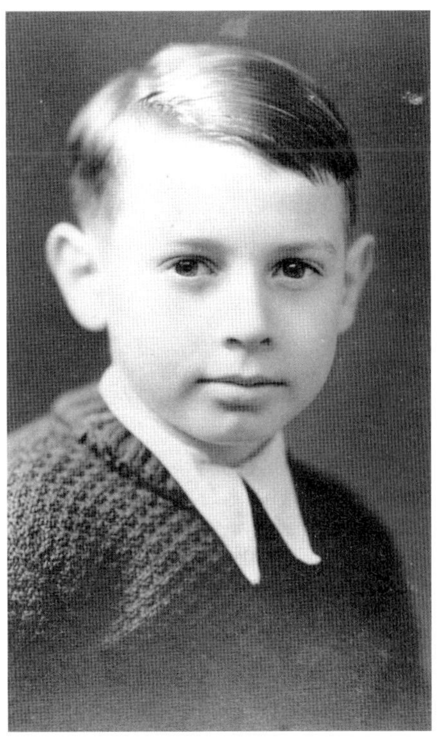

Lulu Marzin. (*Revd George Wood archives*)

> I recognised the badge on his jacket, the head of a wolf cub. It was worn in defiance of the Germans, who had banned the Boy Scout Movement. Members of the scouts shake hands with each other using their left hand and when I did this on meeting Lucien, his eyes lit up with great delight. We amused ourselves with pillow fights and made so much noise that we could be heard outside the house, which must have been a worry for the Marzins, although they did not say anything. Lucien kept it a secret from his school friends that he had pillow fights with the British pilot that the Germans were looking for; he did not say a word. Before doing his homework, he went on guard duty loitering outside his home, and if danger approached he would whistle the popular song 'Frere Jacques'.

Conversations between George and the family were difficult, but were greatly helped by Captain Marzin's sterling efforts to speak English, though George admits that he very often fell about in discourteous laughter at some of the captain's phrases. George's efforts at French were little better, however, and he managed to tell Simone that she was a 'sack of wine' and one of his first sentences was, 'Avez vous la biere pour le facteur?' ('Have you a beer for the postman?'), a phrase that was to come in useful later.

A few days later, they had a nasty shock. A German staff car escorted by two motorcycle outriders pulled up at the house and a senior Luftwaffe officer and his orderly knocked at the door. George was quickly rushed upstairs before Simone calmly opened the door. The officer entered and explained that he was from Morlaix aerodrome and had been sent to thank Captain Marzin for his help in pulling two airmen from their burning crashed aircraft a few weeks previously. As soon a Simone realised they had not come to look for George, she quietly went upstairs to tell him, and they stood by the window watching the car and the two outriders. Downstairs Captain Marzin had taken offence at the officer's tone and told him that if he had 'been sent' then his mission was complete. A long conversation then took place with the officer apologising and explaining that he had only come to express his gratitude. Eventually, honour satisfied, the captain showed him to the door. Unfortunately, that was not the end of the matter. The orderly was unable to start the car, and George and the family watched through the curtains for thirty minutes before the engine finally fired up and the Germans left.

In an attempt to keep George occupied, Madame Marzin would 'borrow' books in English from the library. One day as she was dropping a book into her shopping bag, Dr Le Duc sneaked up behind her, put his hand on her shoulder and in German said loudly 'Feldgendarmerie' ('Field Police'). Despite the obvious shock she must have received, she did not flinch. Dr Le Duc said that her conscience was obviously clear, although quite what she said to the doctor was not recorded!

In the meantime, arrangements were being made for George's escape. Despite the obvious risks involved with having him in her home, Madame Marzin had grown used to him and regarded him as one of the family, so much so, that when he followed Dr Le Duc up the lane for the last time, instead of breathing a sigh of relief, she and Simone stood in the kitchen and wept.

The doctor took George back to Lulu Rault's house, which overlooked the sea near the mouth of the estuary in Carantec and was nearer to the boatyard from which he was to escape. Once again they made the journey by motor scooter, but because the machine needed to be pushed so much, the journey took longer and they were obliged to travel in daylight. They passed several patrols and flak batteries, but as before, no one challenged them. George stayed with Lulu for three days, during which time the artist toured the local coastline checking on possible targets such as flak batteries and radar stations. Despite the dangers, he made sketches of them and marked their position on a map.

George was to return to England by boat, but not just any boat. In Carantec there was a small boat yard run by two brothers – Ernest and Leon Sibiril. During the Occupation, all boats had to be registered as they were built, but to overcome this, as soon as they finished one, the Sibiril brothers replaced it on the stocks with a partly finished example. In this way, they completed eighteen vessels, which ultimately took almost two hundred people across the Channel to safety in Britain. The boat due to take George and three other escapees was named *Le Requin* ('the shark') and was the final boat built by the brothers as they were also wanted by the Gestapo and were to escape on her.

Word was sent to George and Madame Le Duc, who took him to the boatyard. They had to be quiet because they were on the streets after the curfew, so she asked George to remove his clogs. Unfortunately, this slowed their progress even further so she allowed him to put them back on as long as he walked as quietly as possible. At the boatyard things were not going to plan. As they prepared to launch *Requin*, she fell off the slipway, and turned turtle as she hit the water. Immediately, several men jumped into the icy water up to their necks and righted her. Luckily the sound of the waves hid the noise and commotion. George and Madame Le Duc missed this excitement; they were busy dodging the patrols in the town and were consequently very late in reaching the boatyard. So late in fact that Dr Le Duc and the Sibirils thought that they may miss the tide. George remembers:

The Sibiril Brothers. (*Revd George Wood archives*)

> I had mentioned that I would have liked a souvenir of my 'visit', especially from the Feldgendarmerie whose job it had been to catch me. Consequently, Doctor LeDuc went into the centre of town, to their headquarters and ripped their nameplate off the wall. It measured some thirty inches in length, and he presented it to me as I boarded the boat!

They set sail much later than planned. The *Requin* was a twenty-four foot Breton cutter with a single sail and small engine and she made good progress in the calm waters of the estuary. They passed several flak positions unobserved, but when they got out into the Channel the sea became rough and pretty soon the passengers were all sea-sick.

> The brothers were unaffected and ate raw oysters the whole time. Only when we were in mid-Channel would they start the engine, as they believed that the noise would be picked up by German radar. The fact that we were not picked up anyway was something of a surprise, and throughout the journey, I kept a sharp lookout for E-Boats, as I had the sketches made by Lulu Rault in a suitably weighted bag, and was ready to throw them overboard at any hint of trouble. Thankfully, after thirty hours, the first ship we saw was a Royal Navy minesweeper – HMS *Loch Park* - that had been vectored onto us near the Eddystone lighthouse and we were towed into Plymouth.

Whilst George was happy to be home, he received a less than enthusiastic welcome. 'On arrival I was given a cursory medical, the doctor was more interested in whether I had any Gauloises cigarettes on me.' As F/S George Albert Wood had been reported missing in action, and his obituary had been published in the press, it was understandable the Duty Intelligence Officer at Plymouth viewed him with suspicion. 'During our conversation it transpired he came from Southfields and as I came from Wimbledon, as proof of my identity I described – in some detail – the physical attributes of every barmaid in the area. His manner changed immediately and he offered me a glass of Scotch – a rare treat in wartime.'

The next day, George and his fellow passengers were escorted by two Plymouth Police Inspectors by train to Paddington, where they were met by a Black Maria – the authorities were still not taking any chances.

> The Frenchmen were taken to what was known as 'Patriotic School' whilst I was taken to MI5 Headquarters. It was early evening and I was told I would be interviewed by Major Buckmaster the following morning, so I asked if I could go home for the evening as I lived not far away. It was made plain that until I could prove otherwise I was being treated as a spy passing himself off as George Wood and might be planning to blow up the Houses of Parliament, and I was therefore to remain with MI5. However, I borrowed two-bob from the duty corporal, phoned my dad and slipped out to catch a train home to Wimbledon. I bumped into a WAAF I knew at Waterloo Station – she nearly passed out, believing me dead. Even though I was unshaven and still wearing a French beret, clogs, and an old overcoat, none of my fellow passengers gave me even a cursory glance. That evening, the BBC informed the Resistance of the safe arrival of the *Requin* in their nightly broadcast, 'The Pacific Sharks (*Les requines Pacifiques*) have arrived' and for the benefit of the Marzin family, 'Avez vous la biere pour le facteur?
>
> I had intended to return to MI5 early the next morning before Major Buckmaster arrived. Unfortunately, there was a thick fog and the trains were not running so I was late. Needless to say, the Major was not amused. [Maurice Buckmaster was head of F-Section at SOE.] During my debriefing, I passed on the maps and sketches made by Lulu Rault. After that, I phoned Reggie Baker and apologised for pranging his aircraft. His response, 'That's alright old chap. I would only have done it myself later on. Come down, let's have a party.' Typical Reggie.

In 1994 George was presented with the Carantec town medal and a replica of *Le Requin*, whilst he in turn presented the 'Feldgendarmerie' sign to the town as a tribute to the bravery of Dr. Le Duc. It now resides in the museum at Pegasus Bridge near Caen, the first objective captured on D-Day. He also learnt that *Le Requin* had been built in a record eleven days by Ernest and Leon Sibiril's father, and had put to sea – in winter – without any trials, thus putting great faith in the craftsmanship of the builders. But then the Sibiril family have been building boats since 1790. After the war she was returned to France and is now on display at Carantec Museum. The Mae-West which he hid in a wheat field was found by a farm labourer and hidden properly, and after the war was used in teaching the children of Ploujean to swim. Dr. Le Duc's son told George that in early 1944, the Gestapo arrested his mother and father. Madame Le Duc was put under house arrest and an elderly soldier kept guard on her and her three children. At first the children resented him, but Madame Le Duc told them to be nice to him, he was an old man and probably had children of his own, and eventually they became quite friendly – he even brought them chocolate and treats. There was a small hollow statuette of the Virgin Mary

F/S George Wood, F/S Denis Todd, and F/S William Handley with the 'Feldgendarmerie' sign at RAF Beaulieu February 1944. (*Tommy Handley archives*)

in the house, inside of which was a list of the names and addresses of the local Marquis. Although the house had been searched, it was never found, but one day the old soldier picked up the statue to look at and, after he had left, Madame LeDuc, fearful that the list may be discovered, removed and destroyed it. Dr Le Duc was taken by train to Paris for interrogation, but during the journey it was attacked by Typhoons. Although wounded in the leg, an injury which left him with a permanent limp, he helped other wounded before slipping away in the confusion, and disappeared until after the liberation. There is a good chance that George was one of the pilots who attacked that train, as 263 were operating in the area that day.

George returned to Britain on 1 November, and after debriefing returned to the squadron and converted to Typhoons. In January 1944, Geoff Warnes recommended him for a Commission, and he was invited to 10 Group HQ for an interview with the AOC. Part way through, the AOC was called away so George took a look at his personnel file, and was surprised to learn he had been recommended for a Conspicuous Gallantry Medal. In the end, though, he only received a Commission. After flying forty-seven ground attack sorties on the Typhoon, he reached the end of his tour in January 1945.

> Bill Watkins and I were rested and posted to Khartoum, along with four other pilots, to test the Tempest Mk. II under tropical conditions. All of us had first-hand experience of the war in Europe; three had been shot down like myself, and had evaded capture, but for the resident personnel in Khartoum the war had passed them by. Servants, afternoon tea parties and the like

were the norm. Life was good, unaffected by the war, and seemingly they neither knew nor cared what was taking place in Europe. We rebelled somewhat and would fly low over the flat rooftops when the locals were enjoying an afternoon siesta, and on one occasion we circled round the open air cinema at night, drowning out the soundtrack. Next day the newspapers branded us 'Sky Hogs of Khartoum' even whilst admitting that the residents probably owed the RAF their liberty, if not their lives. Shortly after our arrival we were ordered on parade, and after being told that hostilities in Europe had ceased, three cheers were called for, the only recognition given to the end of the war in Europe – the resident personnel realising, no doubt, that their luxurious lifestyle was at an end. As no official celebrations were laid on, we six pilots went to the airmen's mess and joined the Erks, most of who, like ourselves, had served in Europe. We showed them how to make a pyramid of chairs, and plant your backside covered in shoe polish on the ceiling, known as a 'bum print.' The whole pyramid would then usually collapse. Suffice to say that we caused a lot of damage – £36 worth, a lot of money in those days – and each pilot was charged £6 – a week's wages – to cover the bill, plus a reprimand, but what a fantastic way to celebrate the end of the war in Europe, after three half-hearted hip-hoorays.

As a result of his wartime experiences, George was ordained into the Church of England in 1954.

George Wood (*right*) and Bill Watkins (*left*) met at 61 OTU and became life-long friends. Their subsequent careers with 263 Squadron were remarkably similar. Both were shot down over France by flak. George was thrown out of his disintegrating Whirlwind in September 1943 whilst Bill baled out of his burning Typhoon in February 1944. Both evaded capture and returned with the aid of the Resistance, George across the Channel and Bill via Gibraltar, and both were rested in January 1945 and posted to Khartoum to test the Tempest II in tropical conditions. Post-war, George became a priest and Bill a headmaster. (*Bill Watkins archives*)

15
F/S Leonard Scott Gray

The following account was taken from an interview with Scotsman Len Gray.

I left school the year war broke out, began training as a gardener, and joined the Local Defence Volunteers, the LDV (also known as 'Look, Duck and Vanish'). I also thought about joining up. As a child I had been pushed into a pond and didn't like the water, so the Navy was out. I did not fancy carrying a heavy backpack and marching everywhere in hobnail boots, so the Army was out, hence I joined the RAF! After Air Crew Recruitment Centre, London, and Initial Training Wing at Newquay, Cornwall, a short spell in hospital separated me from my original batch of cadets. On recovery I was sent on a grading course at RAF Bumaston, near Derby, flying Magisters. Around Christmas 1941, we travelled to Greenock, where we boarded the *Bergensfjord*, a 16,000 ton liner and our small convoy included two other liners, rumoured to be carrying German and Italian prisoners being transferred from North Africa to Canada. We were escorted by several lend-lease four-stacked American destroyers of First World War vintage.

The weather was cold and miserable for us landlubbers and the discomforts of a North Atlantic winter crossing were compounded by soggy ship's bread and unfamiliar grub, not to mention thoughts of U-boat attacks which to my knowledge did not materialise. Eventually we docked with considerable relief at Halifax, Nova Scotia. After a stay at a transit camp we received news of the best possible posting west of the pond. Our journey to No. 2 BFTS Lancaster, on the edge of the Mojave Desert, took five days by train, through Chicago, Kansas City and El Paso, to name but a few places. After six months of hard work – and play, we once had tea with James Cagney on the set of *Yankee Doodle Dandy* – we got our coveted and hard won brevets and returned to Canada. I must record the great friendliness of ordinary Canadians and Californians during our six months plus in the land of the dollar. I have particularly fond memories of the week's leave that Stevie Stevens and I spent in Santa Barbara, staying at the Hope Ranch with splendid hospitality from Major McLean, a Scots veteran of 1914–18. No. 2 BFTS certainly was by far the best episode in my war.

One Saturday morning we boarded the New Zealand liner, *Awatia*, and set sail. With a long journey ahead we climbed into our hammocks and settled down, but after a few hours, a sea fog was encountered, and around midnight there was loud crash, the ship jolted and the lights went out. Within seconds the emergency blue lights came on and we were ushered to the companionways. There was no panic. After what seemed a long time, we got to the open deck. The ship did not seem to be in serious trouble so I climbed into a lifeboat, still in the dark, and fell asleep. (No line, I was always ready to relax, even as a young man.) I was awakened by a somewhat astonished crew member! An escorting US Destroyer had cut across our bows in the

F/S Len Gray. (*Len Gray archives*)

fog and was sliced in two and lost. With a hole at the bows, the *Awatia* slowly limped back to port and, on arrival, we were confined to barracks for a week to recover and to prevent careless talk about the incident. We were eventually railed south to New York and Pier 90, where we boarded the legendary liner, *Queen Mary*. Even conversion to a troop carrier could not detract from her majesty. She was said to be carrying 7,000 personnel, American troops, crew, and a small number of RAF bods. All the staterooms and cabins had been gutted and bunks installed, and the dining room filled the entire beam, 112 feet, I think. With the huge complement, meals were continuous, a series of breakfasts followed by numerous lunches and so on. The Queen was fast enough to sail unescorted, and especially at night, the whole ship vibrated noticeably, doing well over 30 knots, which was upwards of 40 mph. It was a quick voyage, even though we went far north of the usual shipping lanes for obvious reasons, but it was wonderful to reach the sheltered waters of the Clyde, to see Ailsa Craig, the tiny green fields of Ayrshire, and the islands of the home country, contrasting sharply with the arid Mojave Desert and barren Sierras we had recently left.

I was then posted to 56 OTU, at Tealing, and did fifty very enjoyable hours on Hurricanes before joining 263 Squadron. This was a bit daunting as they were equipped with twin-engine Whirlwinds which we had to convert to without a proper conversion course, but eventually our entire intake managed this without too much panic! There followed a protracted period of familiarisation, formation flying and gunnery practice. The aircraft had bomb racks fitted and was generally known as the 'Whirlibomber'. It was a delight to fly. The squadron usually had about twenty pilots and we all liked the machine. We flew convoy escort, attacked German 'E' and 'R' Boats, coastal and bridge targets. The greatest fun (and very dodgy) was attacking German airfields in Normandy and Brittany. The general idea was for six to eight aircraft with 1,000lb of bombs to sneak across the Channel at very low altitude – to avoid enemy Radar. Then, a steep climb to about 13,000 feet, locate the target and dive. On one such operation, we came back without my friend George Wood. We thought that his aircraft had disintegrated due to the speed of the dive, we reached 450 mph, but later it transpired that it was a direct hit from flak.

It had been a busy few days, and I had flown several sorties, including bombing a railway bridge over the River Vire, near Isigny in Normandy as No. 2 to 'Tebby' Tebbit [22 October]. After we had released our bombs, I heard Tebby's voice over the intercom warn me to 'Weave like hell, Jock!' Then, on Sunday 24 October 1943, we were briefed for an attack on a merchant vessel in Cherbourg harbour. This was the *Münsterland*, a blockade-runner which had returned to France with a cargo of tungsten ore and rubber. It was to be my thirteenth op. We could not comprehend why we were being sent into one of the most heavily defended ports in France at low level, after all, what could we do with our small bombs against such a large vessel in the inner harbour of such a very heavily defended port? Apparently, on the direct orders of Churchill, the Allied High Command were told not to overly damage Cherbourg harbour, and to reserve it for 'Operation Overlord'. All this was unknown to us at the time, but in the event, the enemy completely wrecked the port installations and denied Allied use of the harbour until July 1944.

Our formation of eight Westland Whirlwinds, each with its 1,000lb bomb load, took off at approximately 1500 hours and set off at low level for our target. I found myself last in the loose gaggle. As the outer breakwater of Cherbourg harbour loomed up I thought, 'The CO has made a good landfall, he's heading directly towards the *Münsterland*.' We attacked at low level, but unfortunately Jerry was not napping and soon heavy flak was hose-piping in my direction. Now here is the line shoot, 'I came in so low I had to climb before I could drop my bombs!'

I got rid of the bombs but didn't see if they hit anything as my starboard engine was knocked out by flak, in fact it was set on fire, and I dropped back down low over the inner harbour. I'm not entirely sure what took place next, for things were happening very quickly, but I think that a propeller touched the water. Staggering on, the aircraft then fouled a power cable and that was the final straw! I couldn't climb and was heading at about 100 feet towards the eastern suburbs of the town, but saw a small patch of open ground next to a cemetery. For some reason, it must have been a premonition as I'd never done it before; I had tightened the Sutton harness. There was a cable at the back of the seat attached to the harness, with a clip that held it in place. Just prior to the attack I had pulled it as tight as possible and clipped it so I could hardly move in the cockpit. This action saved me from a fate that befell a large number of pilots who crash-landed and suffered fatal cranial injuries by being dashed head first against the reflector gun-sight. As I approached the ground I thought, 'This is it.' I closed my eyes, there was the most disturbing crashing and rumbling, and after what seemed ages we stopped. Then silence…

Dazed and quite confused, I slowly realised that I was not a goner, I had escaped with just some skin removed from my left elbow and a sore neck which persisted for several weeks, due, of course to whiplash. In fact, I still get a pension for that every week, which as you can imagine is really valuable to a Scotsman! The aircraft was not burning. Somehow, the fire in the starboard engine had been extinguished. I got the canopy open and clambered out on to the port wing, then crept quickly away, hoping to hide until dusk which wasn't too far away as it was October. I saw that the graveyard was quite close and I skirted it slowly making my way to what I hoped was open country to the south. Moving quietly along a hedgerow, I was startled by sporadic rifle fire. God knows what they were shooting at, fortunately not me. I soon came upon some cottages, beyond which was a road, but the land beyond that looked a bit too open to traverse in daylight. Time to make myself as inconspicuous as possible, I thought, as I crept into a patch of nettles beneath a leafy hawthorn hedge intending to wait for darkness before pressing on. Just as the rifle fire seemed to be more distant, and I was thinking I had got away with it, I heard the click of a pistol being cocked. Very slowly, I turned my head and saw this Jerry officer pointing his Luger at me. It is definitely not like it is shown in the films! My only weapon was a knife, supplied to use if one's dinghy inflated at an unsuitable time in the cockpit. Slowly, I stood up and a pack of 'Hitler's Best' surrounded me. I was bundled into a truck and driven back to Cherbourg. Just after I arrived, there was another raid. I was standing outside a large pillbox hoping to see something but was quickly hustled into an air raid shelter. Suddenly there was a great bang and cheers from the Jerry soldiers and that was one of our boys hit or worse. [Possibly the Typhoon of S/L 'Gus' Gowers DFC, the CO of 183 Squadron, which was hit by flak and blew up.] So, instead of going to a dance in the sergeants' mess that was taking place at Warmwell that very evening, my supper that night consisted of rye bread, cold sausage and terrible ersatz coffee – nothing like the fare I had been looking forward to at all.

Next morning I was put aboard a train headed for Paris with two old men as guards. As we crossed over a bridge further east in Normandy, the train slowed down and as I looked out I realised we were crossing the bridge over the River Vire that Tebby and I had attacked the previous Friday. We had clearly damaged it, but it was still in use. Having arrived in Paris, we had to change stations as we were headed further east. As I was marched through the streets, towards the Gare de l'Est Station, one or two of the bolder Parisians who could see who I was, gave me a slight nod or wink of encouragement. I thought of doing a bunk up a side street but then reasoned that not only might I get a bullet, but some innocent civilian might get one as well, so I abandoned that idea quite rapidly. Old these guards might have been, but they could cause havoc, not only to me but also to innocent Parisians. And so to Frankfurt, which was Dulag Luft, and the interrogation. It was not very severe and they didn't try any tricks, not that I was aware of anyway, but they did haul in a German trawler skipper to listen in as they wanted to know how we aimed our bombs – there was only a gun sight in the Whirlwind. Needless to say I told them nothing.

German troops inspecting the crashed *P6979 HE-G*. (*Len Gray archives*)

P6979 HE-G, seen at her Knighton Wood dispersal, RAF Warmwell, during the summer of 1943. (*Len Gray archives*)

On arrival at Stalag Luft IVB. (*Len Gray archives*)

'For you the war is over.' This was said quietly and somewhat woodenly by the German facing me when I arrived at Stalag Luft IVB at Mühlburg-am-Elbe in Upper Saxony. 'Blondie', as we came to call him, wore his Iron Cross and the aura of a man who had been seriously wounded on the Eastern front, and was still suffering. I arrived at Stalag IVB around 29 October, only superficiality injured but with my ego somewhat dented, and spent a generally miserable and monotonous year and a half there. It wasn't terribly funny, the Grey Coats were not as hospitable as they might have been had they been Red Coats at Butlin's, and the service was definitely not so good. Many veterans will have seen films portraying POW camps; however, a brief account of the layout may help readers who are not former 'Kriegies'. The camp was rectangular, divided by a main internal road and with compounds, including an RAF one to either side. Other nationals included French, Belgians, Poles, South Africans, and, unforgettably, Russians – around 45,000 of us. Each compound had a number of identical wooden barracks crowded with three-tier wooden bunks, each with a palliasse supported by boards.

Hotplate stoves provided heating and cooking facilities of a very basic nature. There was also an indoor toilet for night use only. In the middle of the large exercise yard was a big communal toilet which I called our forty-valve receiver. The camp picture was completed by a high perimeter fence topped with barbed wire, strong lights and sentry towers at regular intervals. This then was the Teutonic idea of a third-rate Butlin's – but the grey coats were neither friendly nor helpful. The monotony of each day began to bite deeper after the first few weeks of incarceration. We walked round the compound daily to sustain a degree of fitness. Some played football, cards, or studied languages. (Imagine Mrs Gray's boy a tutor of languages?) However, the camp theatre was very helpful in maintaining morale, particularly in winter, when the flow of Red Cross parcels and mail from home was held up by Allied bombing, etc. My hut was the responsibility of a German appointed Barraken-Fuhrer. Our leader is simply remembered by me as 'Lofty', a big capable paratrooper who had been taken years before. I got Lofty into trouble on only one occasion. This was, I think, during my second winter at IVB. Waking early, due to the cold, I attempted to join the queue for the inside toilet, but could not wait. Forgetful as usual, I dashed outside (the barrack doors were never locked), into the pitch dark and headed for the outside latrine. Halfway there came a shout and I had a pistol rammed into my guts and pushed back inside. A lengthy harangue took place between the German and Lofty. The subject – my perceived lack of discipline in leaving the building – strictly verboten at night. Luckily, I was not sent to the cooler, but carefully avoided our hut leader for a while.

There were bags of incidents, some hilarious, others not so. Our compound lay next to the 'vorlaager'. One day a great commotion arose and we all rushed to investigate. A large number of women were seen inside the 'vorlaager', with just a few strands of wire between them and the Brylcreem Boys. It turned out they were Polish slave workers in transit and many of our lads went daft at the sight of all these women. Soon notes and even items of clothing were flying over to the females. I remember one Yorkshireman, with admiration or something in his eyes, singling out some desirable lady and throwing his singlet to her to keep out the cold. Fortunately, they removed the newcomers before the situation got out of hand. Another time, some trigger-happy Yank flying a Thunderbolt shot up the camp. Several hundred of us hit the deck simultaneously, and miraculously there were no injuries, but the Germans removed the barbed wire from the windows and provided bricks and whitewash to make large POW signs to discourage our over enthusiastic Allies. One day we watched a Flying Fortress slowly spinning down from a great height, a lone parachute was observed. There was a very strong wind blowing and the unfortunate flier was almost dragged into the wire, but luckily stayed outside the compound and was dragged along just outside. Sometime later he was marched towards the guardhouse by two captors, seemingly uninjured.

One of my 'muckers' was a Lancashire lad, Frank Street by name, flight engineer by trade. He was very proud of his plentiful fair hair, but in the interests of hygiene, Jerry removed the hair of all incoming POWs with horse/cattle clippers. As poor Frank's prized locks slipped to the deck, he was a broken man. It took ten months to get him back normal. Luckily, I had a silk scarf which I used to cover my shaven head with the remainder round my neck. This arrangement helped my comfort during the first winter.

Every evening, around eight, a hush descended on the barrack whilst we listened to the BBC news by Ralph Saunders, all the time keeping a close look out for the 'Goons'. This daily 'gen' was a great booster for all of us. The Russian POWs were the most vulnerable and abused group in the camp. Stalin's Russia was not a signatory to the Geneva Convention, consequently they received no protection and no food parcels from the International Red Cross. I have vivid memories of Russians scrambling for potato peelings discarded by us. One of those poor devils had both legs off above his knees. Only sections of tyre bound to the stumps kept him out of dust or mud. There were rumours that if one of their number died in the night, his corpse was held upright on the morning parade so that his rations might be available for his comrades. Incidentally, even in 1943, Stalin was no hero, disrespected by all of his long-suffering conscripts. I must also record that I had no idea of what Bomber Command personnel had really been going through until I arrived in Germany. They told me that the average survival rate was one man per crew, usually seven in number. Some were still carrying bits of shrapnel, etc., around. The main part of our rations consisted of potatoes – summer or winter – potatoes boiled in their jackets. Just after we were liberated, we had the Battle of the Potato Pits. Some French or Dutch guys were after our potatoes so we had to guard them as we didn't know how much longer we would be there. There was a tall English lad – I can't recall his name – who was fighting the would be raiders but we were all so tired and undernourished that they couldn't really fight, they just stood there just going through the motions.

Despite all the adverse factors, morale was generally good. We all knew that the Allied cause was just, and there was increasing evidence that we and our allies were slowly but steadily getting the upper hand, though at appalling cost. We knew that the end was near, but did not immediately notice that the Jerry guards had nipped off and were replaced by Romanians. We were liberated in April 1945 by the Russian Army, Mongols I believe, ferocious looking wee devils on ponies carrying Tommy guns; they shot the Romanian guards out of hand.

I owe the fact that I have my German record card [Kriegsgefangenkarte] to Norman Aldridge, a bearded navigator who raided the records office after the Russian army liberated us in April 1945. They marched us some 20km south from Stalag Luft IVB to Reissen, a sizeable town, where we were put up in a former German barracks. They took all our details, some claim that the Russians did all this not only to be proper, but there were stories that they tried to infiltrate agents back to Britain even at that time. I palled up with a couple of glider pilots who were taken at Arnhem, and on the way back, we broke away from this column and tore up a side street. We got away with it and lived as civvies for a few days, but had to give ourselves up as we had no rations. Eventually after a couple of weeks, the Yanks sent a convoy of lorries, they also gave us good rations and sweets, which we hadn't seen in ages and took us back to Halle, where they crammed us fifty at a time into a Dakota and we were flown to Brussels. There the authorities were up to their usual standard – they gave us 800 Belgian Francs and a ten bob note, then put us straight on a plane to England! We flew in a Stirling, and as I did not know anything about them, I was sitting down below where the bomb aimer sat. That was until an officer came along, called me a 'silly bugger' and told me to move. Apparently, the undercarriage on a Stirling could fold up on occasions and if you were down below on one of these occasions, you were butchers meat! The RAF authorities were very efficient and helpful, they had us disinfected, showered, medically examined, fed and debriefed, then issued with rail warrants, and within twenty-four hours of leaving Germany, Mrs Gray's little boy was back home in Dalkeith for the first time in two years. I also had bags of leave, I was owed about eighty-three days and I was made a Warrant Officer. Along with my friend Hebbie Taylor, also a POW, I took a job helping to gather in the harvest. When I came back I was interviewed and asked a lot of stupid questions, including 'Did I know anybody who had collaborated with the Jerries?', 'Had I collaborated?', which I said of course I hadn't. 'Had I tried to escape?' which I hadn't. It was not until much later when I asked for some papers through the RAF Records Office that I realised the interviewer was from MI9.

I was de-mobbed on 22 December 1945 and have to admit to making one serious error of judgement. We were given a choice of de-mob suits, I chose a brown pin-stripe suit, in retrospect I should have chosen a sports jacket and flannels. I gained entry to Edinburgh University reading for a degree in agriculture, at the same time as my friend, Bill Reid, the Bomber VC, was studying the same subject at Glasgow University. Our paths crossed frequently and Bill was my best man when I married Gladys in 1995, having lost my first wife, Mary, in 1989. I was with the Scottish Crops Research Institute for fourteen years, and the Agricultural Training Board for seventeen years.

The above is one man's story who was, as the more modest survivors of 1914-1918 preferred to call their horrific experiences, 'doing one's bit'. We must never forget not only those who were spared, but particularly treasure the memory of the legions that died so young in helping to save their country.

Len Gray passed away following a short illness in February 2012.

16

Accidents & Losses

July 1940
23 *P6966 HE-Z* tail wheel collapsed, Grangemouth – Henry Eeles

August 1940
7 *P6966 HE-X* abandoned near Stenhousemuir – Irving McDermott
12 *P6970* tail wheel collapsed, West Freugh – Henry Eeles

December 1940
5 *P6970* throttle jammed open – Pat Thornton-Brown
P6972 swung off the runway and hit a pile of timber
P6976 swung off runway and hit *P6971* – Roy Ferdinand
P6971 hit by *P6976*
12 *P6980* crashed into Sand Bay, Burnham – Allan Britton
29 *P6975 HE-L* crashed Fox Mine Tor, Devon – Wynford Smith
P6978 crashed Fox Mine Tor, Devon – Donald Vine

January 1941
9 *P6977* engine failure – Tom Pugh
17 P6983 *HE-H* damaged
19 *P6984 HE-H* abandoned near Middlemore, Devon – Tom Pugh

February 1941
2 *P6973* tail wheel failed to lower, Exeter – Douglas Jowitt
4 *P6971* tail damaged, Exeter – Robert Skellon
8 *P6979 HE-Q* tail wheel collapsed, Exeter – Cliff Rudland
P6969 HE-V shot down off Dodman Point – Kenneth Graham
15 *P6976 HE-X* force landed near Cannington, Somerset – Robert Skellon
16 *P6968 HE-H* tail wheel damaged, Exeter – George Milligan
23 *P6986* damaged, St Eval – David Crooks
P6992 HE-C slipped off jacks during maintenance, St Eval
25 *P6998* tail wheel failed to lock down, St Eval

March 1941
11 *P6985 HE-J* crashed, Predannack – Herbert Kitchener
13 *P6983 HE-H* damaged in air raid, StEval
P6996 damaged in air raid, StEval
14 *P6988 HE-J* crashed, Portreath – Pat Thornton-Brown
23 *P6991 HE-R* hit motor roller, Portreath – Graham Lawson
31 *P7000* swung off runway, Portreath – David Stein

April 1941
1 *P6989 HE-C* shot down near Helston, Cornwall – David Crooks
20 *P6992 HE-C* broke up over Wittering – Bernard Howe
30 *P7008* broke up in the air near Aldermaston – George Milligan

May 1941
4 *P7004* tail wheel burst, Filton – Albert Tooth
P6974 HE-Z slat broke away in the air – Cliff Rudland
9 *P6995* damaged, Filton
13 *P6987 HE-L* damaged, Filton
21 *P6982* stood on nose, Filton – Norman Freeman
29 *P7006* crash-landed near Chepstow – Don Tebbit
P6979 HE-Q undercarriage collapsed, Filton – Humphrey Coghlan

June 1941
11 *L6845* crashed near Llandenny, Usk – Reginald Pascoe
12 *P6982* damaged, Filton
P7045 crashed on approach, Filton – Roy Ferdinand
14 *P7001* flak damage – Arthur Donaldson
15 *P7000* hit tractor, Filton – Joe Holmes
P7005 HE-A struck balloon cable off Barry – Joe Holmes
18 *P7040* tail wheel retracted during maintenance at 18 MU
19 *P7037* and *P7048* damaged

August 1941
6 *P6983 HE-H* force landed, Hurn – Robert Brackley
P7001 flak damage – Arthur Donaldson
P7002 HE-L battle damage – Cliff Rudland
12 *P6999* flak damage – Douglas Jowitt
P7013 flak damage – Antony Albertini
21 *P7046* undercarriage collapsed, Charmy Down – Frank Dimblebee
25 *P6982* undercarriage collapsed, Charmy Down – Jack Maddocks
26 *P6998* flak damage – Cliff Rudland
29 *P6979 HE-Q* tail wheel collapsed, Charmy Down – Cliff Rudland

September 1941

4 *P7042* shot down off Cherbourg – Geoff Buckwell
8 *P7004* flak damage – Cecil King
10 *P7001* shot down by flak near Lestré, France – Dennis Mason
12 *P7013* wingtip hit ground, Charmy Down – Douglas Jowitt
15 *P6996* hit by *P7039*, Charmy Down
P7039 hit *P6996*, Charmy Down – John Meredith
16 *P6983 HE-H* undercarriage collapsed, Charmy Down – Derrick Prior
20 *P7005 HE-A* undercarriage collapsed, Charmy Down – John Sandy
26 *P7039* damaged, Charmy Down
28 *P7011 HE-H* flak damage – Frank Dimblebee
P7041 flak damage – Tom Pugh
P7044 flak damage – Arthur Donaldson
29 *P6998* crash-landed near Predannack – Humphrey Coghlan
P7009 abandoned near Eddystone Lighthouse – Tom Hunter
30 *P7035* tail wheel failed, Charmy Down – Douglas Jowitt

October 1941

1 *P7013* undercarriage collapsed, Charmy Down – Philip Harvey
3 *P7063* crashed on approach, Charmy Down – Maurice Peskett
9 *P6968 HE-H* crashed in Saltford Rail Yard – Ormonde Hoskins
P6999 abandoned over Bath – Humphrey Coghlan
10 *P6994* crashed, Charmy Down – Ken Ridley
15 *P6971* hit obstruction, Charmy Down – Ken Ridley
P6995 engine caught fire, Colerne – Eddie Brearley
16 *P6998* damaged
18 *P7011 HE-H* damaged, Charmy Down
19 *P7035* tail wheel failed to lower, Charmy Down – Douglas Small
20 *P7053* damaged, Charmy Down
24 *P6995* engine caught fire in the air, Colerne – Eddie Brearley
26 *P7096* tail wheel failed to lower, Charmy Down – Joe Hughes
28 *P7053* crashed English Coombe, Somerset – John Sample
P7057 SF-S undercarriage collapsed, Charmy Down – Bob Brennan
P7058 SF-G damaged in collision with *P7053* – Maurice Peskett
P7007 damaged, Charmy Down
P7091 ditched in the Channel – Colin Clark
30 *P6994* overshot with engine failure, Charmy Down – Ken Ridley
P7015 shot down by flak near Ploujean, France – David Stein

November 1941

3 *P7041* tail wheel faulty, Charmy Down – Frank Dimblebee
6 *P6970* shot down off Cap Barfleur – John Robinson
7 *P7110 HE-E* flak damage – Geoff Warnes
10 *P7049* damaged, Coltishall
P7090 hit maintenance hangar, Coltishall – John Lawton

11 *P6977* hit by a Blenheim, Coltishall
P7110 HE-E damaged, Coltishall
15 *P7105* damaged, Coltishall – Mike Bryan
P7112 flak damage– Cecil King
16 *P6987 HE-L* hit Spitfire *AD294*, Charmy – Frank Dimblebee
22 *P7051* tail wheel collapsed, Charmy Down – Richard Reed
23 *P7117 HE-A* damaged, Charmy Down
24 *P6986* damaged, Charmy Down
27 *P7038* damaged, Charmy Down

December 1941
5 *P7061 HE-A* tail damaged, Charmy Down – Derrick Prior
6 *P7107* damaged, Coltishall – John Sandy
7 *P7061 HE-A* crashed, Coltishall – Jack Maddocks
12 *P7122* damaged during ferry flight to 20 MU
13 *P7002 HE-L* tail wheel collapsed, RAF Charmy Down – Les Currie
14 *P7044* crashed near Coleford, Gloucestershire – Derrick Prior
16 *P7122* during ferry flight to 20 MU
23 *P7094* crash-landed l ½ mile west of Matlaske – Hugh O'Neill
25 *P7106 SF-D* crashed Horsham St Faith – Douglas Jowitt

January 1942
3 *P7038* caught fire and burnt out, Charmy Down
5 *P7105* wingtip hit ground, Matlaske – Robert Wright
7 *P7062* hit boundary fence, Coltishall– Jack Maddocks
11 *P7092* crashed on take-off, Matlaske – Paul LaGette
12 *P7110 HE-E* tail wheel collapsed, Charmy Down – Joe Holmes
25 *P7056* tail wheel collapsed, Charmy Down – Basil Abrams

February 1942
8 *P7097* force landed near Coltishall – James Rebbetoy
12 *P7046* damaged, Coltishall – Art Brunet
P7050 shot down over the Channel – John Sandy
P7093 SF-A shot down over the Channel – Ralph Häggberg
P7106 SF-D shot down over the Channel – George Martin
P7107 shot down over the Channel – Basil Robertson
P7112 damaged
13 *P7108* overturned, Fairwood Common – James Coyne
14 *P7096* hit fence, Horsham St Faith – Humphrey Coghlan
16 *P7055 SF-S* damaged, Matlaske
19 *P7110 HE-G* damaged, Fairwood Common – Joe Holmes
21 *P7114* damaged, Fairwood Common
27 *P7046* tail wheel collapsed, Matlaske – Mike Bryan
P7121 SF-C damaged, Matlaske

March 1942

7 *P7039* overturned, Fairwood Common – Peter Jardine
9 *P7036 SF-X* crashed White Horse Common – Charles DeShane
14 *P7004* undercarriage collapsed, Fairwood Common – Les Currie
P7037 SF-J damaged, Coltishall
23 *P7041* engine failure – Bas Abrams
24 *P6982 SF-S* instrument failure – Douglas Jowitt
P7058 SF-G crashed, Coltishall – Mike Bryan
26 *P6991 HE-R* damaged, Fairwood Common

April 1942

1 *P7000* wing tip hit ground, Angle – Joe Holmes
P7112 overturned, Fairwood Common – Philip Harvey
2 *P7041* hit dispersal bay, Fairwood Common – Basil Abrams
8 *P7048* tail wheel collapsed, Matlaske – Des Roberts
9 *P7122* hit high tension cables – Mike Bryan
11 *P7005 SF-H* force landed near East Wretham – Frederick Furber
P7060 damaged, Matlaske
14 *P7046* damaged, Matlaske – Art Brunet
15 *P7100* tyre burst, Fairwood Common – Philip Harvey
16 *P7117 HE-G* damaged, Fairwood Common – John Meredith
30 *P7035* undercarriage collapsed, Fairwood Common – John Meredith

May 1942

4 *P7103* broke up in the air near Aylesham – Robert Wright
13 *P7114* damaged, Matlaske
15 *P7111 SF-E* flak damage – Bob Brennan
24 *P6972* damaged, Matlaske
P7121 SF-C crashed, Matlaske – Mike Bryan
26 *P6983 HE-H* damaged
27 *P7122* shot down near Beverwijk, Netherlands – Bob Brennan
29 *P7118 SF-O* abandoned near Matlaske – Douglas Jowitt
P7000 damaged, Matlaske
P7046 tail wheel collapsed, Matlaske – Mike Bryan
30 *P7005 SF-H* tail wheel collapsed, Matlaske – Art Brunet

June 1942

18 *P7012 SF-V* force landed, Manston – Hilt Ashton
23 *P7110 HE-H* tail wheel did not lower, Warmwell – Geoff Warnes
24 *P7043 HE-A* stern frame broke, Brough – Geoff Warnes
25 *P6987 HE-L* tail wheel collapsed, Angle – Christopher van Zeller
27 *P7049* props touched the ground, Matlaske – Frederick Furber
30 *P7101 SF-A* hit Lysander *N1269*, Matlaske – Len Bartlett

July 1942

1 *P7109 SF-N* undercarriage failed to retract, Matlaske – Douglas Jowitt
5 *P7013* hit *P7120 HE-R*, Portreath – Harvey Muirhead
P7120 HE-R hit by *P7013*, Portreath
9 *P7114* damaged, Matlaske
12 *P7054* engine failure – John van Schaick
P7104 SF-V damaged, Matlaske – Neville Freeman
15 *P6991 HE-R* damaged, Portreath
22 *P7104 SF-V* battle damage – John McClure
23 *P7035* shot down over the Channel – Les Currie
P7060 shot down over the Channel – John Walker
25 *P7116 HE-S* damaged, Portreath
29 *P7005 SF-H* battle damage – Hugh O'Neill
30 *P7063* crashed, Matlaske – Eddie Musgrave

August 1942

8 *P7058 SF-G* tail wheel collapsed, Drem – Len Bartlett
9 *P7117 HE-E* collided with a lorry, Angle – Richard Reed
16 *P7005 SF-H* port tyre burst, Matlaske – Tom Sutherland
18 *P7095 SF-H* damaged, Matlaske – Frederick Furber
26 *P7055 SF-S* undercarriage and nacelle damaged, Snailwell – John Luing
31 *P7007* damaged, Matlaske

September 1942

3 *P7111 SF-E* engine failure – James Rebbetoy
9 *P6979* damaged by flak from a Convoy off Cap de la Hague – Eddie Brearley
21 *P7003* dived into the ground near Wool, Dorset – Peter Jardine

October 1942

3 *P7013* flak damage – Ken Ridley
P7052 flak damage – Cecil King
P7105 HE-N flak damage – Robert Woodward
5 *P7051* tail wheel collapsed, Manston – Aubrey Smith
P7037 SF-J hit boundary fence, Manston – John Barclay
P7058 SF-G hit boundary fence, Manston – Dattatraya Samant
8 *P7014 HE-T* ran into trees, Warmwell – Arthur Johnstone
28 *P7120 HE-R* undercarriage retracted, Warmwell – James Cooksey
31 *P7109 SF-N* shot down near Etaples, France – Francis Waldron
P7064 SF-G ditched off the French coast – John van Schaick
P7102 SF-P flak damage – Frederick Furber
P7115 shot down by flak near Etaples – Douglas Jowitt

November 1942

6 *P6998* engine failure – Art Brunet
7 *P7043 HE-A* flew into high ground, France – Don Gill

December 1942

4 *P7012 SF-V* undercarriage retracted, Southend – Robert Woodhouse
7 *P6987 HE-L* shot down, Baie du St Brelade – Don McPhail
P7105 HE-N shot down, Baie du St Brelade – Robert Woodward
9 *P7012 SF-V* damaged, Manston
15 *P6976 SF-X* flak damage – Robert Smith
20 *P6993 SF-A* tail wheel hit a pothole, Manston – Gerald Walker
22 *P6998* crashed due to flak damage, Lympne – Tom Sutherland
23 *P7119 SF-C* flak damage – Frederick Furber

January 1943

13 *P7061 SF-A* hit *P7102 SF-P*, Manston – Edmund Bolster
P7102 SF-P hit by *P7061 SF-A*, Manston
17 *P7119 SF-S* engine failure – Neville Freeman
18 *P7051* port engine caught fire and crashed, Manston – John Luing
19 *P7048* damaged, Manston – Charles Mercer
23 *P7054* shot down by flak near Poperinghe – Alexander Doig
P7095 SF-H shot down near Doullens – Alfred Brown

February 1943

7 *P7063* tail damaged, Manston – Tom Sutherland
9 *P6991 HE-R* crash-landed near Warmwell – John Macaulay
10 *P7114* flak damage – Eddie Musgrave
12 *P7005 SF-H* engine failure – Tom Sutherland
19 *P7062 HE-L* crashed near Chiseldon, Wiltshire – Frank Hicks
P7114 hit *P7119 SF-W* and blew up, Manston – Neville Austin
P7119 SF-W hit by *P7114* and blew up, Manston – Charles Mercer
28 *P7052* ditched off Cap de Carteret – Dai Williams

March 1943

2 *P7005 SF-H* Shot down near Neufchâtel – Gerry Walker
6 *P6979 HE-G* force landed, Fairwood Common – James Simpson
13 *P7010* shot down over the Lannilis estuary – John Macaulay
14 *P7092 SF-Q* tail wheel retracted, Manston – Eddie Musgrave
21 *P6974 HE-X* flaps failed to retract – Cecil King
P7040 instrument failure – Joe Holmes
22 *P7040* engine failure – Herbert Blackshaw
23 *P7040* damaged, Fairwood Common – Roy Wright
25 *P7089* damaged, Fairwood Common
25 *P6986* flak damage – Robert Smith
26 *P7108* flak damage – Jimmy Coyne
30 *P7104 SF-V* undercarriage collapsed, Manston – John Davidson

April 1943

4 *P7002 SF-W* ditched off Dungeness – Norbury Dugdale
P7111 SF-E flak damage – Humphrey Coghlan
14 *P7010* shot down over Llanilis estuary – John Macaulay
6 *P7096* damaged, Manston – Alex Torrance
P7121 SF-C crashed near Manston – John Hadow
17 *P7047* instrument failure – Des Roberts
P7048 flak damage – Eddie Musgrave
P6995 missing – Eddie Brearley
P7099 missing – Bas Abrams
P7117 HE-H missing – Cecil King
18 *P7090* missing – Philip Harvey
25 *P7058 SF-G* shot down by flak near Thielt – James Rebbetoy
27 *P7040* flak damage – Arthur Lee-White
P7108 flak damage – Max Cotton
28 *P6981 HE-B* flak damage – Max Cotton
30 *P6986* engine failure – John Barclay

May 1943

1 *P6976 SF-X* wing damaged, Manston – Aubrey Smith
7 *P7057* undercarriage collapsed, Warmwell – John Thould
8 *P7111 SF-E* engine failure – Humphrey Coghlan
11 *P6971* tail unit damaged, Warmwell – Harold Proctor
16 *P7094 HE-T* crashed near Exeter – Herbert Blackshaw
17 *P7063* shot down off the French coast – Eddie Musgrave
18 *P7110 HE-C* stern frame broke, Warmwell – George Wood
21 *P7059* crashed, Warmwell – Arthur Lee-White
P7108 flak damage – Max Cotton
22 *P6979 HE-G* damaged, Warmwell
23 *P7089* flak damage – Max Cotton

June 1943

6 *P7055 SF-U* flak damage – Joseph DeHoux
14 *P7092 SF-U* flak damage – Art Brunet
15 *P6974 HE-X* flak damage – Ken Ridley
P7000 shot down by flak off Sark – Max Cotton
17 *P7056* flak damage – John Barclay
18 *P7111 SF-E* flak damage – John Barclay
20 *P7011 SF-U* tail wheel collapsed, Southend – John Barclay
P7013 undercarriage collapsed, Warmwell – Richard Hughes
21 *P6993 SF-A* force landed near Manston – John Barclay
P7110 HE-C force landed, Stoney Cross – Bill Watkins
26 *P7011 SF-U* tail wheel collapsed, Southend – John Barclay

July 1943

4 *P6974 HE-X* damaged, Warmwell
13 *P7110 HE-C* crashed on approach, Warmwell – Len Knott

August 1943

1 *P6981 HE-B* crashed, Warmwell – Peter Cooper
14 *P7046* damaged, Warmwell – Iain Dunlop
15 *P7055* tail damaged, Warmwell – Len Gray
P7111 HE-W exactor failure – Reg Baker
17 *P7096* crashed, Warmwell – Bob Beaumont
27 *P7096* wingtip hit a tree, Warmwell – Bill Watkins
30 *P7056* damaged, Warmwell

September 1943

10 *P7096* port undercarriage torn off, Warmwell – Reg Baker
17 *P7047* engine failure – John McClure
23 *P7113 HE-W* shot down, Morlaix aerodrome – George Wood
25 *P7040* engine failure – Fred Green

October 1943

8 *P7097* flak damage – Bill Heaton
9 *P7047* crashed on approach, Tangmere – James Simpson
14 *P7046* damage, Warmwell – Iain Dunlop
19 *P6971* undercarriage retracted, Warmwell – Norman Blacklock
P7055 flak damage – Iain Dunlop
24 *P6973* undercarriage collapsed; due to flak damage – Peter Cooper
P6974 HE-X crash-landed at 180 mph, Warmwell – David Ross
P6979 HE-G shot down by flak over Cherbourg – Len Gray
P6986 HE-Q shot down by flak off St Vaast – Paul Mercer
P6990 flak damage – Reg Baker
P7040 flak damage – George Williams
P7046 flak damage – Bob Beaumont
P7097 flak damage – Harold Proctor
30 *P7108* flak damage – Iain Dunlop

November 1943

7 *P7098* damaged – Iain Dunlop
25 *P6983 HE-H* engine failure – Denis Todd
26 *P6971* flak damage – Iain Dunlop
P6983 HE-H flak damage – Reg Baker
P6997 flak damage – David Ross
P7012 flak damage – Graham Smith
P7046 flak damage – Douglas Mogg
P7097 flak damage – Frederick Snalam
P7100 flak damage – Don Tebbit

17

Whirlwind Histories

Of the 116 Whirlwinds built, at a cost of £27,000 each (approx £900,000 in 2012), 28 (24%) were lost in action; 7 (6%) were Missing in Action; 5 (4%) crashed in the UK with Battle Damage; 53 (46%) were lost in accidents; 19 (16%) were Struck off Charge; 2 (2%) became Instructional Airframes; and 2 (2%) survived the war. The following list gives a brief resume of each aircrafts movements.

Key = *RAE* – Royal Aircraft Establishment; *A&AEE* – Aircraft & Armament Experimental Establishment; *AFDU* – Air Fighting Development Unit; *AGME* – Air Gun Mounting Establishment; *MU* – Maintenance Unit

L6844 – 31 December 1938 → RAE: 24 January 1939 → Westland: 6 May 1940 → A&AEE: 29 May 1940 → Westland: 23 June 1940 → A&AEE: 9 January 1941 → Westland: 22 May 1941 → A&AEE: 28 May 1941 → AGME: 6 January 1942 → Westland: 24 January 1942 → AFDU: 27 February 1942 → 263 Sqn, Colerne: 13 April 1942 → 4 School of Technical Training at St Athan as *3063M*.

L6845 – 30 May 1940 → 25 Sqn, North Weald: 7 July 1940 → 263 Sqn, Grangemouth: 16 October 1940 → Westland: 30 March 1941 → 263 Sqn, Portreath: 7 April 1941 → Westland: 3 June 1941 → 263 Sqn, Filton: 11 June 1941 crashed, near Usk – Reginald Pascoe killed: Ops Hours 4:10: Total Hours 97:30.

P6966 – 12 June 1940 → 25 Sqn, North Weald: 6 July 1940 → 263 Sqn, Grangemouth *(HE-Z)*: 23 July 1940 tail wheel collapsed, Grangemouth: 7 August 1940 *(HE-X)* abandoned, Stenhousemuir – Irving McDermott.

P6967 – 12 June 1940 → 25 Sqn, North Weald: 7 July 1940 → 263 Sqn, Grangemouth: 23 September 1940 → Rolls-Royce: 31 December 1941 → RAE: 18 March 1942 → Westland: 31 December 1942 → 137 Sqn, Manston: 9 April 1943 → 6 School of Technical Training, Hednesford as *3497M*: 4 November 1944 → Scrapped.

P6968 – 18 July 1940 → 263 Sqn, Grangemouth *(HE-H)*: 16 February 1941 ran over pot hole, Exeter – George Milligan: 23 February 1941 → Westland: 24 May 1941 → 263 Sqn, Filton: 10 July 1941 → Westland: 1 September 1941 → 263 Sqn, Charmy Down: 9 October 1941 collided with *P6999* over Bath and crashed on Saltford Rail Yard – Ormonde Hoskins killed: Ops Hours 13:25.

P6969 – 18 July 1940 → 263 Sqn, Grangemouth *(HE-V)*: 8 February 41 shot down off Dodman Point – Ken Graham killed: Ops Hours 8:25.

P6970 – 26 July 1940 → 263 Sqn, Grangemouth. 12 August 1940 tail wheel broke, West Freugh – Henry Eeles: 5 December 1940 throttle jammed open – Pat Thornton-Brown: 15 February 1941 → Westland: 3 April 1941 → 263 Sqn, Portreath: 3 June 1941 → Westland: 23 June 1941 → 263 Sqn, Filton: 6 November 1941 shot down off Cap Barfleur – John Robinson killed: Ops Hours 39:25.

P6971 – 31 August 1940 → 263 Sqn, Grangemouth: 5 December 1940 hit by *P6977*: 4 February 1941 tail damaged – Robert Skellon: 15 October 1941 hit obstruction, Charmy Down – Ken Ridley: 25 October 1941 → Westland: 12 April 1942 → 18MU, Dumfries: 4 September 1942 → 137 Sqn, Snailwell: 13 September 1942 → 18MU, Dumfries: 27 December 1942 → 263 Sqn, Warmwell: 13 February 1943 → Westland: 17 February 1943 → 263 Sqn, Warmwell: 11 May 1943 heavy landing, Warmwell – Harold Proctor: 12 October 1943 → Westland: 14 October 1943 → 263 Sqn, Warmwell: 19 October 1943 crashed, Warmwell – Norman Blacklock: 26 November 1943 flak damage – Iain Dunlop: 11 January 1944 → 18MU, Dumfries: 14 July 1944 → Scrapped: Ops Hours 63:50.

P6972 – 1 September 1940 → 263 Sqn, Grangemouth: 5 December 1940 swung off the runway and hit a pile of timber:15 February 1941 → Westland: 13 March 1941 → 263 Sqn, St Eval: 30 March 1941 → Westland: 12 July 1941 → 39MU, Colerne: 7 August 1941 → Westland: 20 October 1941 → 51MU, Lichfield: 6 November 1941 → 137 Sqn, Coltishall: 24 May 1942 damaged: 8 July 1942 → Westland: 31 July 1942 → 18MU, Dumfries: 14 July 1944 → Scrapped: 30 September 1944 → SOC: Ops Hours 29:45.

P6973 – 17 September 1940 → 263 Sqn, Drem: 2 February 1941 damaged tail wheel, Exeter – Douglas Jowitt: 5 July 1941 → 51MU, Lichfield: 20 May 1943 → 263 Sqn, Warmwell: 24 October 1943 undercarriage collapsed due to flak damage, Warmwell – Peter Cooper: SOC: Ops Hours 10:45.

P6974 – 7 September 1940 → 263 Sqn, Drem *(HE-Z)*: 26 April 1941 → Westland: 4 May 1941 → 263 Sqn, Filton: 4 May 1941 slat broke off - Cliff Rudland: 3 August 1941 → Westland: 25 February 1942 → 39MU, Colerne: 28 March 1942 → 18MU, Dumfries: 27 February 1943 → 263 Sqn, Harrowbeer *(HE-X)*: 21 March 1943 faulty flaps – Cecil King: 15 June 1943 flak damage – Ken Ridley: 4 July 1943 damaged: 24 October 1943 crash-landed at 180 mph due to flak damage, Warmwell – David Ross: Ops Hours 81:40.

P6975 – 21 October 1940 → 263 Sqn, Drem *(HE-L)*: 29 December 1940 crashed on Fox Tor Mire, Devon – Wynford Smith killed: Ops Hours 3:05.

P6976 – 7 November 1940 → 263 Sqn, Drem *(HE-X)*: 5 December 1940 swung off runway and collided with *P6971* – Roy Ferdinand: 15 February 1941 force landed near Bridgwater – Robert Skellon: 15 February 1941 → Westland: 18 August 1941 → 18MU, Dumfries: 1 February 1942 → 137 Sqn, Matlaske *(SF-X)*: 25 August 1942 → Westland: 8 September

1942 → 137 Sqn, Snailwell: 9 September 1942 → Westland: 12 September 1942 → 137 Sqn, Snailwell: 15 December 1942 flak damage – Robert Smith: 1 May 1943 crashed, Manston – Aubrey Smith: 8 May 1943 → Westland: 2 November 1943 → SOC: Ops Hours 83:50.

P6977 – 7 November 1940 → 263 Sqn, Drem: 9 January 1941 engine failure – Tom Pugh: 20 February 1941 damaged: 23 June 1941 → Westland: 17 July 1941 → 39MU, Colerne: 2 October 1941 → 263 Sqn, Charmy Down: 26 October 1941 → Westland: 1 November 1941 → 137 Sqn, Coltishall: 11 November 1941 hit by a Blenheim, Coltishall: SOC: Ops Hours 18:05.

P6978 – 12 November 1940 → 263 Sqn, Drem: 29 December 1940 crashed on Fox Tor Mire, Devon – Donald Vine killed: Ops Hours 13:30.

P6979 – 7 November 1940 → 263 Sqn, Drem *(HE-Q)*: 8 February 1941 tail wheel collapsed, Exeter – Cliff Rudland: 29 May 1941 undercarriage collapsed, Filton – Humphrey Coghlan: 29 August 1941 tail wheel collapsed, Angle – Cliff Rudland: 11 November 1941 → 48MU, Hawarden: 29 June 1942 → 263 Sqn, Angle: 1 September 1942 → Westland: 6 September 1942 → 263 Sqn, Warmwell: 9 September 1942 damaged by flak from a Convoy off Cap de la Hague – Eddie Brearley: 6 March 1943 force landing, Fairwood Common – James Simpson: 22 May 1943 damaged: 1 June 43 → Westland: 3 June 1943 → 263 Sqn, Warmwell *(HE-G)*: 24 October 1943 shot down by flak, Cherbourg – Len Gray POW: Ops Hours 62:55.

P6980 – 16 November 1940 → A&AEE: 7 December 1940 → 263 Sqn, Exeter: 12 December 1940 crashed into Sand Bay, Burnham on Sea – Allan Britton killed: Ops Hours 2:15.

P6981 – 7 October 1940 → 263 Sqn, Drem *(HE-B)*: 15 March 1941 → Westland: 3 April 1941 → 263 Sqn, Portreath: 5 June 1941 → Westland: 5 July 1941 → 51MU, Lichfield: 16 February 1942 → 137 Sqn, Matlaske *(SF-S)*: 5 April 1942 → Westland: 22 April 1942 → 51MU, Lichfield: 25 April 1942 → 137 Sqn, Matlaske: 4 May 1942 → 51MU, Lichfield: 8 April 1943 → 263 Sqn, Warmwell: 28 April 1943 flak damage – Max Cotton: 1 August 1943 crashed at Warmwell – Peter Cooper: SOC: Ops Hours 26:05: Total Hours 186:35.

P6982 – 26 November 1940 → 263 Sqn, Drem: 17 January 1941 → Westland: 15 February 1941 → 263 Sqn, Exeter: 21 May 1941 stood on nose, Filton – Norman Freeman: 12 June 1941 damaged: 25 August 1941 undercarriage collapsed, Charmy Down – Jack Maddocks: 1 September 1941 → Westland: 8 December 1941 → 51MU, Lichfield: 7 February 1942 → 137 Sqn, Matlaske *(SF-S)*: 24 March 1942 instrument failure – Douglas Jowitt: 7 September 1942 → 18MU, Dumfries: 30 September 1942 → 137 Sqn, Snailwell *(SF-F & P)*: 14 July 1944 → Scrapped: 30 September 1944 → SOC: Ops Hours 82:20.

P6983 – 7 October 1940 → 263 Sqn, Drem *(HE-H)*: 17 January 1941 → Westland: 12 February 1941 → 263 Sqn, Exeter: 13 March 1941 damaged in air raid, StEval: 15 March 1941 → Westland: 4 May 1941 → 263 Sqn, Filton: 6 August 1941 force landed, Hurn – Robert Brackley: 16 September 1941 undercarriage collapsed, Charmy Down – Derrick

Prior: 16 September 1941 → Westland: 27 December 1941 → 51MU, Lichfield: 16 February 1942 → 137 Sqn, Matlaske: 26 May 1942 damaged: 22 June 1942 → Westland: 30 July 1942 → 18MU, Dumfries: 19 August 1943 → 263 Sqn, Warmwell: 22 October 1943 → Westland: 27 October 1943 → 263 Sqn, Warmwell: 25 November 1943 engine failure Denis Todd: 26 November 1943 flak damage – Reg Baker: 11 January 1944 → 18MU, Dumfries: 14 July 1944 → Scrapped: 30 September 1944 → SOC: Ops Hours 58:50.

P6984 – 22 December 1940 → 263 Sqn, Exeter *(HE-H)*: 19 January 1941 abandoned near Middlemore, Devon – Tom Pugh: Ops Hours 19:00.

P6985 – 3 January 1941 → 263 Sqn, Exeter *(HE-J)*: 11 March 1941 crashed, Predannack – Herbert Kitchener injured: SOC: Ops Hours 25:00.

P6986 – 4 January 1941 → 263 Sqn, Exeter: 23 February 1941 damaged – David Crooks: 25 March 1941 → Westland: 28 March 1941 → 263 Sqn, Portreath: 28 April 1941 → Westland: 20 June 1941 → 263 Sqn, Filton: 24 November 1941 damaged: 29 November 1941 → Westland: 15 May 1942 → 18MU, Dumfries: 13 September 1942 → 137 Sqn, Snailwell: 18 October 1942 → Westland: 21 October 1942 → 263 Sqn, Warmwell: 16 February 1943 → 137 Sqn, Manston: 25 March 1943 flak damage – Robert Smith: 30 April 1943 engine failure – John Barclay: 24 June 1943 → 263 Sqn, Zeals *(HE-Q)*: 24 October 1943 shot down by flak off St Vaast – Paul Mercer killed: Ops Hours 81:15.

P6987 – 4 January 1941 → 263 Sqn, Exeter *(HE-L)*: 13 May 1941 damaged: 8 July 1941 → Westland: 1 September 1941 → 263 Sqn, Charmy Down: 16 November 1941 struck Spitfire *AD294,* Charmy Down – Frank Dimblebee: 19 November 1941 → Westland: 1 February 1942 → 263 Sqn, Colerne: 2 April 1942 → 51MU, Lichfield: 5 June 1942 → 263 Sqn, Angle: 25 June 1942 tail wheel collapsed, Angle – Christopher van Zeller: 7 December 1942 shot down by flak, Baie du St Brelade, Jersey – Don McPhail killed: Ops Hours 42:45: Total Hours 211:00.

P6988 – 4 January 1941 → 263 Sqn, Exeter *(HE-J):* 14 March 1941 crashed, Portreath – Pat Thornton-Brown injured: SOC: Ops Hours 29:30.

P6989 – 19 January 1941 → 263 Sqn, Exeter *(HE-J & C)*: 1 April 1941 shot down near Helston, Cornwall – David Crooks killed: Ops Hours 41:40.

P6990 – 19 January 1941 → 263 Sqn, Exeter: 8 November 1941 → Westland: 9 November 1941 → 263 Sqn, Charmy Down: 18 December 1942 → Station Flight, Colerne: 8 April 1943 → 263 Sqn, Fairwood Common: 13 April 1943 → Westland: 1 June 1943 → 263 Sqn, Warmwell: 24 October 1943 flak damage – Reg Baker: 19 November 1943 → Westland: 9 December 1943 → SOC: Ops Hours 160:35.

P6991 – 20 December 1940 → 18MU Dumfries: 6 February 1941 → 263 Sqn, Exeter *(HE-R):* 23 March 1941 hit tractor, Portreath – Graham Lawson: : 28 September 1941 damaged, Charmy Down: 28 September 1941 → Westland: 6 February 1942 → 263 Sqn, Colerne: 26

March and 15 July 1942 damaged: 9 February 1943 crash-landed near Warmwell – John Macaulay: 24 February 1943 → Westland: 10 May 1943 → SOC: Ops Hours 96:10: Total Hours 262:00.

P6992 – 30 December 1940 → 18MU, Dumfries: 1 January 1941 → 263 Sqn, Exeter *(HE-C)*: 23 February 1941 damaged during maintenance, St Eval: 20 April 1941 broke up over RAF Wittering – Bernard Howe killed: Ops Hours 3:40.

P6993 – 30 December 1940 → 18MU, Dumfries: 13 February 1941 → 263 Sqn, Exeter *(HE-S)*: 12 March 1941 damaged in air raid, StEval: 13 March 1941 → Westland: 4 May 1941 → 263 Sqn, Filton: 29 May 1941 → Westland: 5 July 1941 → 51MU, Lichfield: 23 July 1942 → 137 Sqn, Matlaske *(SF-A)*: 20 December 1942 hit pot hole, Manston – Gerry Walker: 21 June 1943 crashed, Manston – John Barclay: Ops Hours 53:40.

P6994 – 24 January 1941 → 51MU, Lichfield: 13 February 1942 → 263 Sqn, Exeter: 29 March 1941 → Westland: 12 September 1941 → 263 Sqn, Charmy Down: 30 October 1941 crashed, Charmy Down – Ken Ridley: 1 November 1941 → Westland: Ops Hours 39:55: 14 February 1942 → 48MU, Hawarden: 29 March 1942 → 47MU, Sealand: 5 June 1942 → America on KHL ship '*Waterland*' in convoy ON101: 18 June 1942, arrived Boston: Tested at Pensacola: Scrapped 1944.

P6995 – 25 February 1941 → 51MU, Lichfield: 18 March 1941 → 263 Sqn, St Eval: 9 May 1941 damaged: 9 May 1941 → Westland: 22 October 1941 → 263 Sqn, Charmy Down: 24 October 1941 undercarriage stressed on landing, Colerne – Eddie Brearley: 8 November 1941 → Westland: 24 April 1942 → 18MU, Dumfries: 6 July 1942 → 263 Sqn, Angle: 23 October 1941 damaged: 25 October 1942 → Westland: 1 March 1943 → 263 Sqn, Warmwell: 17 April 1943 Missing – Eddie Brearley killed: Ops Hours 99:00: Total Hours 293:55.

P6996 – 24 January 1941 → 51MU, Lichfield: 13 February 1941 → 263 Sqn, Exeter: 13 March 1941 damaged in an air raid, StEval: 28 May 1941 → Rolls-Royce: 1 June 1941 → 263 Sqn, Filton: 15 September 1941 hit by *P7039,* Charmy Down: 29 September 1941 → SOC: Ops Hours 61:10.

P6997 – 21 February 1941 → 263 Sqn, Exeter: 9 April 1941 → A&AEE: 28 May 1941 → Westland: 18 June 1941 → AFDU: 7 August 1941 → Westland: 16 August 1942 → A&AEE: 17 September 1942 → Westland: 3 January 1943 → 18MU, Dumfries: 26 January 1943 → 137 Sqn, Snailwell: 1 June 1943 → 263 Sqn, Warmwell: 10 July 1943 → Westland: 9 November 1943 → 263 Sqn, Warmwell: 26 November 1943 flak damage – David Ross: 11 January 1944 → 18MU, Dumfries: 14 July 1944 → Scrapped: 30 September 1944 → SOC: Ops Hours 41:45.

P6998 – 24 January 1941 → 48MU, Hawarden: 25 February 1941 tail wheel collapsed, Exeter: 8 March 1941 → 263 Sqn, Portreath: 7 April 1941 → Westland: 4 May 1941 → 263 Sqn, Filton: 5 May 1941 → Westland: 29 July 1941 → 263 Sqn, Exeter: 26 August 1941 flak damage – Cliff Rudland: 29 August 1941 → Westland: 6 September 1941 → 263 Sqn, Charmy

Down: 29 September 1941 crashed, Predannack – Humphrey Coghlan: 16 October 1941 damaged: 16 October 1941 → Westland: 19 March 1942 → 39MU, Colerne: 28 March 1942 → 18MU, Dumfries: 13 September 1942 → 137 Sqn, Snailwell: 6 November 1942 engine failure – Art Brunet: 22 December 1942 crashed, Lympne – Tom Sutherland: 29 December 1942 → SOC: Ops Hours 28:45.

P6999 – 24 January 1941 → 48MU, Hawarden: 25 February 1941 → 51MU, Lichfield: 27 March 1942 → 263 Sqn, St Eval: 21 May 1941 → Westland: 7 June 1941 → 263 Sqn, Filton: 12 August 1941 flak damage – Douglas Jowitt: 9 October 1941 collided with *P6968* and abandoned near Bath – Humphrey Coghlan: Ops Hours 66:05

P7000 – 24 January 1941 → 48MU, Hawarden: 1 March 1941 → 263 Sqn, St Eval: 12 March 1941 damaged in an air raid, St Eval: 31 March 1941 tipped on nose, Portreath – David Stein: 15 June 1941 hit farm machinery, Filton – Joe Holmes: 20 June 1941 → Westland: 28 October 1941 → 39MU, Colerne: 18 February 1942 → 263 Sqn, Colerne: 1 April 1942 wing tip hit ground, Angle – Joe Holmes: 29 May 1942 damaged: 1 June 1942 → Westland: 5 June 1942 → 263 Sqn, Angle: 15 June 1943 shot down by flak off Sark – Max Cotton killed: Ops Hours 102:20.

P7001 – 24 January 1941 → 48MU, Hawarden: 25 February 1941 → 51MU, Lichfield: 13 April 1941 → 263 Sqn, Filton: 14 June and 6 August 1941 battle damage – Arthur Donaldson: 10 September 1941 shot down by flak, Lestré, France – Dennis Mason killed: Ops Hours 55:10.

P7002 – 13 March 1941 → 263 Sqn, St Eval *(HE-L)*: 6 August 1941 battle damage – Cliff Rudland: 22 October 1941 → Westland: 29 November 1941 → 263 Sqn, Charmy Down: 13 December 1941 tail wheel collapsed, Charmy Down – Les Currie: 21 December 1941 → Westland: 30 June 1942 → 18MU, Dumfries: 2 February 1943 → 137 Sqn, Manston *(SF-W)*: 4 April 1943 ditched off Dungeness – Norbury Dugdale: Ops Hours 72:00: Total Hours 278:00.

P7003 – 3 April 1941 → 39MU, Colerne: 15 April 1941 → 263 Sqn, Portreath: 27 April 1942 → Westland: 9 May 1942 → 263 Sqn, Angle: 21 September 1942 crashed near Wool, Dorset – Peter Jardine killed: Ops Hours 131:55.

P7004 – 2 March 1941 → 48MU, Hawarden: 4 March 1941 → 263 Sqn, St Eval: 4 May 1941 stern frame broke, Filton – Albert Tooth: 8 September 1941 flak damage – Cecil King: 14 March 1942 undercarriage collapsed, Fairwood Common – Les Currie: 27 March 1942 → Westland: 5 October 1942 → SOC: Ops Hours 91:00

P7005 – 24 March 1941 → 263 Sqn, St Eval *(HE-A)*: 15 June 1941 hit balloon cable – Joe Holmes: 20 September 1941 undercarriage collapsed, Charmy Down – John Sandy: 10 December 1941 → 137 Sqn, Matlaske *(SF-H)*: 11 April 42 crash landed, East Wretham – Frederick Furber: 30 May 1942 tail wheel collapsed, Matlaske – Art Brunet: 29 July 1942 battle damage – Hugh O'Neill: 16 August 1942 tyre burst, Matlaske – Tom Sutherland:

12 February 1943 engine failure – Tom Sutherland: 2 March 1943 shot down by flak, Neufchâtel – Gerry Walker POW: Ops Hours 93:50: Total Hours 260:50.

P7006 – 13 March 1941 → 18MU, Dumfries: 4 April 1941 → 51MU, Lichfield: 16 April 1941 → 263 Sqn, Filton: 29 May 1941 crashed and burnt out near Chepstow – Don Tebbit: SOC: Ops Hours 24:40, Total Hours 56:55.

P7007 – 24 March 1941 → 263 Sqn, Portreath: 29 October 1941 damaged - Cecil King: 7 August 1942 → Westland: 17 August 1942 → 263 Sqn, Colerne: 31 August 1942 damaged: 22 May 1943 flak damage – Jimmy Coyne: 25 May 1943 → Westland: 27 May 1943 → 263 Sqn, Warmwell: 21 January 1944 → 18MU, Dumfries: 14 July 1944 → Scrapped: 30 September 1944 → SOC: Ops Hours 163:50

P7008 4 April 1941 → 51MU, Lichfield: 5 April 1941 → 263 Sqn, Portreath: 30 April 1941 broke up and crashed near Aldermaston – George Milligan killed: Ops Hours 10:10.

P7009 6 April 1941 → 18MU, Dumfries: 23 April 1941 → 263 Sqn, Filton: 29 September 1941 abandoned near Eddystone Light – Tom Hunter killed: Ops Hours 48:30

P7010 6 April 1941 → 18MU, Dumfries: 25 January 1943 → 263 Sqn, Warmwell: 13 March 1943 shot down, Lannilis estuary – John Macaulay killed: Ops Hours 15:00: Total Hours 65.05.

P7011 – 10 April 1941 → 18MU, Dumfries: 13 May 1941 → 263 Sqn, Filton *(HE-H)*: 4 September 1941 battle damage – Dennis Mason: 28 September 1941 flak damage – Frank Dimblebee: 18 October 1941 damaged: 9 January 1942 → Westland: 17 January 1942 → 263 Sqn, Charmy Down: 10 June 1942 → 137 Sqn, Matlaske *(SF-U)*: 20 June 1943 tail wheel collapsed, Southend – John Barclay: 24 June 1943 → Westland: 24 November 1943 → 263 Sqn, Warmwell: 29 January 1944 damaged: 8 February 1944 → 18MU, Dumfries: 14 July 1944 → Scrapped: 30 September 1944 → SOC: Ops Hours 93:00.

P7012 – 8 April 1941 → 51MU, Lichfield: 15 November 1941 → 137 Sqn, Coltishall *(SF-V)*: 12 February 1942 stern frame damaged:19 February 1942 → Westland: 7 March 1942 → 137 Sqn, Matlaske: 18 June 1942 force landed, Matlaske – Hilt Ashton: 4 December 1942 landed with undercarriage retracted, Southend – Robert Woodhouse: 9 December 1942 damaged: 23 December 1942 → Westland: 8 February 1943 → 137 Sqn, Manston: 24 June 1943 → 263 Sqn, Warmwell: 26 November 1943 flak damage – Graham Smith: 11 January 1944 → 18MU, Dumfries: 14 July 1944 → Scrapped: 30 September 1944 → SOC: Ops Hours 132:45.

P7013 – 10 April 1941 → 51MU, Lichfield: 4 May 1941 → 263 Sqn, Filton: 12 August 1941 flak damage – Antony Albertini: 12 September 1941 wingtip hit ground, Charmy Down – Douglas Jowitt: 1 October 1941 undercarriage collapsed, Charmy Down – Philip Harvey: 16 October 1941 → Westland: 14 April 1942 → 48MU, Hawarden: 18 April 1942 → 263 Sqn, Angle: 5 July 1942 collided with *P7120*, Portreath – Harvey Muirhead: 20 September 1942,

Westland: 25 September 1942 → 263 Sqn, Warmwell: 3 October 1942 flak damage – Ken Ridley: 20 June 1943 undercarriage retracted whilst taxiing, Zeals – Richard Hughes: 9 October 1943 damaged: 4 November 1943 → SOC: Ops Hours 128:50.

P7014 – 10 April 1941 → 51MU, Lichfield: 15 February 1942 → 263 Sqn, Colerne *(HE-T)*: 8 October 1942 ran into trees on take-off, Warmwell – Arthur Johnstone 24 October 1942 → SOC: Ops Hours 46:10.

P7015 – 23 April 1941 → 51MU, Lichfield: 15 October 1941 → 263 Sqn, Charmy Down: 30 October 1941 shot down by flak near Ploujean, France – David Stein killed: Ops Hours 1:00.

P7035 – 15 April 1941 → 39MU, Colerne: 4 September 1941 → 51MU, Lichfield: 26 September 1941 → 137 Sqn, Charmy Down: 30 September 1941 tail wheel faulty, Charmy Down – Douglas Jowitt: 19 October 1941 tail wheel failed to lower, Charmy Down – Douglas Small: 18 January 1942 damaged, Matlaske: 5 April 1942 → 263 Sqn, Fairwood Common: 30 April 1942 undercarriage collapsed, Fairwood Common – John Meredith: 23 July 1942 shot down over the Channel – Les Currie killed: Ops Hours 94:05.

P7036 – 22 April 1941 → 39MU, Colerne: 20 July 1941 → Staweall Farm Dispersal: 28 September 1941 → 137 Sqn, Charmy Down *(SF-X)*: 9 March 1942 crashed on White Horse Common, North Walsham – Charles DeShane killed: Ops Hours 17:35: Total 66:30.

P7037 – 28 April 1941 → 39MU, Colerne: 19 June 1941 damaged: 20 September 1941 → 263 Sqn, Charmy Down: 26 September 1941 → 137 Sqn, Charmy Down *(SF-J)*: 14 March 1942 damaged, Charmy Down:: 5 October 1942 hit boundary fence, Manston – John Barclay: 8 September 1943 → 18MU, Dumfries: 10 October 1943 → 263 Sqn, Warmwell: 8 February 1944 → 18MU, Dumfries: 14 July 1944 → Scrapped: 30 September 1944 → SOC: Ops Hours 117:35.

P7038 – 27 March 1941 → 48MU, Hawarden: 28 April 1941 → 39MU, Colerne: 4 September 1941 → 51MU, Lichfield: 26 September 1941 → 137 Sqn, Charmy Down: 27 November 1941 damaged: 1 January 1942 → 263 Sqn, Charmy Down: 3 January 1942 burnt out, Charmy Down: 5 March 1942 → SOC.

P7039 – 30 April 1941 → 51MU, Lichfield: 11 June 1941 → 263 Sqn, Filton: 15 September 1941 hit *P6996*, Charmy Down – John Meredith: 26 September 1941 damaged: 7 March 1942 overturned, Fairwood Common – Peter Jardine injured: 14 March 1942 → Westland: 21 June 42 → SOC: Ops Hours 42:55.

P7040 – 29 April 1941 → 18MU, Dumfries: 18 June 1941 tail wheel retracted during maintenance, Dumfries: 8 March 1943 → 263 Sqn, Warmwell: 21 March 1943 instrument failure – Joe Holmes: 22 March 1943 engine failure – Herbert Blackshaw: 23 March 1943 damaged – Roy Wright: 27 April 1943 flak damage – Arthur Lee-White: 29 April 1943 → Westland: 3 August 1943 → 263 Sqn, Warmwell: 25 September 1943 engine failure – Fred

Green: 24 October 1943 flak damage – George Williams: 28 October 1943 → Westland: 22 November 1943 → 263 Sqn, Warmwell: 10 February 1944 → 18MU, Dumfries: 14 July 1944 → Scrapped: 30 September 1944 SOC: → Ops Hours 46:10.

P7041 – 7 May 1941 → 18MU, Dumfries: 27 May 1941 → 263 Sqn, Filton: 28 September 1941 flak damage – Tom Pugh: 3 November 1941 tail wheel failed, Charmy Down – Frank Dimblebee: 23 March 1942 engine failure – Bas Abrams: 2 April 1942 hit dispersal bay, Fairwood Common – Bas Abrams: 17 May 1942 → Westland: 14 September 1942 → SOC: Ops Hours 51:15.

P7042 – 12 May 1941 → 18MU, Dumfries: 12 May 1941 → 27MU: 28 May 1941 → 18MU, Dumfries: 20 June 1941 → 263 Sqn, Filton: 4 September 1941 shot down off Cherbourg – Geoff Buckwell POW: Ops Hours 21:55.

P7043 – 12 May 1941 → 18MU, Dumfries: 21 May 1941 → 263 Sqn, Angle *(HE-A)*: 24 June 1942 stern frame broke, Brough – Geoff Warnes: 15 August 1942 → 263 Sqn, Angle: 7 November 1942 flew into high ground, France – Don Gill killed: Ops Hours 24:15: Total Hours 68:45.

P7044 – 3 May 1941 → 51MU, Lichfield: 5 June 1941 → 263 Sqn, Filton: 28 September 1941 flak damage – Arthur Donaldson: 14 December 1941 crashed near Coleford, Gloucestershire – Derrick Prior killed: Ops Hours 24:45.

P7045 – 16 May 1941 → 51MU Lichfield: 8 June 1941 → 263 Sqn, Filton: 12 June 1941 crashed, Filton – Roy Ferdinand killed: Ops Hours 5:55: Total Hours 356:00.

P7046 – 16 May 1941 → 51MU Lichfield: 15 June 1941 → 263 Sqn, Filton: 21 August 1941 undercarriage collapsed, Charmy Down – Frank Dimblebee: 29 August 1941 → Westland: 9 January 1942 → 51MU, Lichfield: 16 February 1942 → 137 Sqn, Matlaske: 27 February 1942 tail wheel collapsed, Matlaske – Mike Bryan: 27 February 1942 → Westland: 7 March 1942 → 137 Sqn, Matlaske: 29 May 1942 tail wheel collapsed, Matlaske – Mike Bryan: 12 February 1943 and 14 April 1943 flak damage – Art Brunet: 30 May 1942 tail wheel collapsed, Matlaske: 6 June 1943 → Westland: 24 June 1943 → 263 Sqn, Warmwell: 14 August 1943 damaged – Iain Dunlop: 24 October 1943 flak damage – Bob Beaumont: 26 November 1943 flak damage – Douglas Mogg: 8 February 1944 → 18MU, Dumfries: 14 July 1944 → Scrapped: 30 September 1944 SOC: Ops Hours 89:10.

P7047 – 22 May 1941 → 51MU, Lichfield: 15 June 1941 tail damaged: 6 April 1943 hydraulic failure during ferry flight, Benson – First Officer Godwin ATA: 11 April 1943 → 137 Sqn, Manston: 17 April 1943 instrument failure – Des Roberts: 6 May 1943 → Westland: 13 July 1943 → 263 Sqn, Zeals: 17 September 1943 engine failure – John McClure: 9 October 1943 crashed, Tangmere – James Simpson killed: Ops Hours 54:50.

P7048 – 27 May 1941 → 39MU, Colerne: 19 June 1941 damaged: 27 November 1942 → 137 Sqn, Coltishall: 8 April 1942 tail wheel hit drain and collapsed at Matlaske – Des Roberts:

19 January 1943 damaged – Charles Mercer: 17 April 1943 flak damage – Eddie Musgrave: Ops Hours 123:25: Registered by Westland as *G-AGOI* post-war: Scrapped → 1951.

P7049 – 27 May 1941 → 39MU, Colerne: 10 September 1941 → 51MU, Lichfield: 22 September 1941 → 137 Sqn, Charmy Down: 10 November 1941 damaged: 27 June 1942 props touched the ground, Matlaske – Frederick Furber: 11 July 1942 → Westland: 19 October 1942 → SOC: Ops Hours 54:55.

P7050 – 24 May 1941 → 18MU, Dumfries: 28 September 1941 → 137 → Charmy Down: 12 February 1942 shot down over the Channel – John Sandy killed: Ops Hours 56:15: Total Hours 108:30.

P7051 Bellows – 2 June 1941 → 18MU, Dumfries: 6 June 1941 → 263 → Filton: 22 November 1941 tail wheel collapsed, Charmy Down – Richard Reed: 29 May 1942 → Westland: 5 August 1942 → 18MU, Dumfries: 4 September 1942 → 137 → Snailwell: 5 October 1942 tail wheel collapsed, Manston – Aubrey Smith: 18 January 1943 port engine caught fire and crashed at Manston, John Luing: 27 January 1943 → SOC: Ops Hours 86:50.

P7052 Bellows Argentina No. ?? – 27 February 1941 → 18MU, Dumfries: 5 November 1941 → 263 Sqn, Charmy Down: 3 October 1942 flak damage – Cecil King: 28 February 1943 ditched off Cap de Carteret – Dai Williams killed: Ops Hours 103:10: Total Hours 354:50.

P7053 – 12 June 1941 → 18MU, Dumfries: 28 September 1941 → 137 Sqn, Charmy Down: 20 October 1941 damaged: 28 October 1941 collided with *P7058* and crashed at English Coombe, Somerset – John Sample killed: Ops Hours 3:05.

P7054 – 17 June 1941 → 39MU, Colerne: 16 July 1941 → Staweall Farm dispersal: 11 February 1941 → 137 Sqn, Matlaske: 15 May 1942 → Westland: 30 May 1942 → 263 Sqn, Angle: 3 June 1942 → 137 Sqn, Matlaske: 12 July 1942 engine failure – John van Schaick: 12 September 1942 → Westland: 23 September 1942 → 137 Sqn, Snailwell: 23 January 1943 shot down by flak near Poperinghe – Alexander Doig POW: Ops Hours 25:35

P7055 Bellows Argentina No. 1 – 17 June 1941 → 39MU, Colerne: 8 July 1941 → Staweall Farm Dispersal: 1 November 1941 → 137 Sqn, Charmy Down *(SF-S):* 12 February 1942 battle damage – Charles Mercer: 26 August 1942 undercarriage and nacelle damaged, Snailwell – John Luing: 1 September 1942 → Westland: 11 February 1943 → 18MU, Dumfries: 18 February 1943 → 137 Sqn, Manston *(SF-U)*: 6 June 1943 flak damage – Joseph DeHoux: 24 June 1943 → 263 Sqn, Warmwell: 15 August 1943 tail damage – Len Gray: 19 October 1943 flak damage – Iain Dunlop: 11 January 1944 → 18MU, Dumfries: 14 July 1944 → Scrapped: 30 September 1944 → SOC: Ops Hours 107:00

P7056 Pride Of Yeovil – 30 June 1941 39MU → Colerne: 17 July 1941 → Staweall Farm Dispersal: 6 October 1941 → 263 Sqn, Charmy Down: 25 January 1942 tail wheel collapsed Charmy Down – Bas Abrams: 18 December 1942 → Station Flt, Colerne: 14 April 1943

→ 137 Sqn, Manston: 17 June 1943 flak damage – John Barclay: 27 June 1943 → 263 Sqn, Warmwell: 20 August 1943 → Westland: 28 August 1943 → 263 Sqn, Warmwell: 30 August 1943 damaged: 30 August 1943 → Westland: 14 October 1943 → SOC: Ops Hours 108:55.

P7057 Bellows Argentina No. ?? – 8 June 1941 → 39MU, Colerne: 9 July 1941 → Staweall Farm Dispersal: 28 September 1941 → 137 Sqn, Charmy Down *(SF-S)*: 28 October 1941 landed with undercarriage retracted, Charmy Down – Bob Brennan: 22 November 1941 → 137 Sqn, Coltishall: 9 January 1942 → 39MU, Colerne: 4 April 1942 → 18MU, Dumfries: 14 July 1942 → 263 Sqn, Angle: 8 August 1942 → Westland: 18 August 1942 → 263 Sqn, Colerne: 7 May 1943 undercarriage collapsed, Warmwell – John Thould: 16 June 1943 → SOC: Ops Hours 63.05

P7058 – 22 June 1941 → 18MU, Dumfries: 20 September 1941 → 39MU, Colerne: 28 September 1941 → 137 Sqn, Charmy Down *(SF-G)*: 28 October 1941 collided with *P7053* – Maurice Peskett: 24 March 1942 crashed, Coltishall – Mike Bryan: 8 August 1942 tail wheel collapsed, Drem – Len Bartlett: 5 October 1942 hit boundary fence, Manston – Dattatraya Samant: 25 April 1943 shot down by flak near Thielt, Belgium – James Rebbetoy killed: Ops Hours 77:45: Total Hours 320:35.

P7059 – 23 June 1941 → 18MU, Dumfries: 1 March 1942 → 263 Sqn, Fairwood Common: 19 April 1943 → Westland: 20 April 1943 → 263 Sqn, Warmwell: 21 May 1943 crashed due to flak damage, Warmwell – Arthur Lee-White: 4 June 1943 → Westland: 16 June 1943 → SOC: Ops Hours 78:40.

P7060 – 23 June 1941 → 18MU, Dumfries: 27 September 1941 → 137 Sqn, Charmy Down: 1 November 1941 → 263 Sqn, Charmy Down: 11 April 1942 damaged: 23 July 1942 shot down over the Channel – Johnny Walker killed: Ops Hours 81:35.

P7061 – 25 June 1941 → 39MU, Colerne: 9 September 1941 → 263 Sqn, Charmy Down *(HE-A)*: 5 December 1941 tail wheel damaged, Charmy Down – Derrick Prior: 7 December 1941 crashed, Coltishall – Jack Maddocks: 29 May 1942 → Westland: 20 August 1942 → 18MU, Dumfries: 7 November 1942 → 137 Sqn, Manston *(SF-A)*: 13 January 1943 hit *P7102*, Manston – Edmund Bolster: 25 January 1943 → SOC: Ops Hours 81:45.

P7062 – 28 June 1941 → 39MU, Colerne: 16 July 1941 → Staweall Farm Dispersal: 20 September 1941 → 263 Sqn, Charmy Down: 26 September 1941 → 137 Sqn, Charmy Down: 7 January 1942 crashed, Coltishall – Jack Maddocks injured: 21 January 1942 → Westland: 11 July 1942 → 18MU, Dumfries: 18 July 1942 → 263 Sqn, Angle *(HE-L)*: 19 February 1943 crashed near Chiseldon, Wiltshire – Frank Hicks killed: Ops Hours 63:20.

P7063 30 January 1941 → 39MU, Colerne: 8 July 1941 → Staweall Farm Dispersal: 20 September 1941 → 263, Charmy Down: 26 September 1941 → 137 Sqn, Charmy Down: 3 October 1941 crashed, Charmy Down – Maurice Peskett: 3 October 1941 → Westland: 9 January 1942 → 18MU, Dumfries: 16 March 1942 → 137 Sqn, Matlaske: 30 July 1942 crashed, Matlaske – Eddie Musgrave: 7 February 1943 tail damaged, Manston – Tom

Sutherland: 18 May 1943 shot down by flak off the French coast – Eddie Musgrave killed: Ops Hours 100:10.

P7064 3 July 1941 → 51MU, Lichfield: 18 November 1941 → 137 Sqn, Coltishall: 21 June 1942 → Westland: 24 June 1942 → 137 Sqn, Matlaske *(SF-G)*: 31 October 1942 ditched off the French coast – John van Schaick: Ops Hours 94:50: Total Hours 248.00.

P7089 2 July 1941 → 51MU, Lichfield: 10 October 1941 → 263 Sqn, Charmy Down: 25 January 1943 → Westland: 25 March 1943 damaged: 23 May 1943 flak damage – Max Cotton: 28 May 1943 → SOC: Ops Hours 124:30.

P7090 6 July 1941 → 51MU, Lichfield: 22 September 1941 → 137 Sqn, Charmy Down: 10 November 1941 hit hangar, Coltishall – John Lawton: 19 February 1942 tail damaged: 5 April 1942 → 263 Sqn, Fairwood Common: 18 November 1942 → Westland: 31 December 1942 → 39MU, Colerne: 31 December 1942 → Station Flt, Colerne: 26 January 1943 → 263 Sqn, Charmy Down: 18 April 1943 Missing – Philip Harvey killed: Ops Hours 80:40: Total Hours 268:00.

P7091 8 July 1941 → 51MU, Lichfield: 22 September 1941 → 137, Charmy Down: 30 October 1941 ditched in the Channel south of The Lizard – Colin Clark killed: Ops Hours 2:00.

P7092 6 July 1941 → 51MU, Lichfield: 17 October 1941 → 137 Sqn, Charmy Down: 11 January 1942 crashed, Matlaske – Paul LaGette: 31 January 1942 → Westland: 4 March 1942 → 137 Sqn, Matlaske: 25 July 1942 → 18MU, Dumfries: 1 August 1942 → 263 Sqn, Angle: 1 October 1942 → 137 Sqn, Manston *(SF-Q & U)*: 14 March 1943 hydraulic failure – Eddie Musgrave: 14 June 1943 flak damage – Art Brunet: 27 June 1943 → 263 Sqn, Warmwell *(HE-D)*: 8 October 1943 damaged: 8 October 1943 → Westland: 22 January 1944 → SOC: Ops Hours 85:50: Total Hours 399:30.

P7093 – 17 July 1941 → 51MU, Lichfield: 17 January 1942 → 137 Sqn, Matlaske *(SF-A)*: 12 February 1942 shot down over the Channel – Ralph Häggberg killed: Ops Hours 26:00: Total Hours 29:45.

P7094 Bellows Fellowship – 17 July 1941 → 51MU, Lichfield: 20 September 1941 → 137 Sqn, Charmy Down: 23 December 1941 crashed near Matlaske – Hugh O'Neill: 31 December 1941 → Westland: 7 September 1942 → 18MU, Dumfries: 22 September 1942 → 137 Sqn, Snailwell: 8 October 1942 → 263 Sqn, Warmwell *(HE-S)*: 27 April 1943 damaged: 27 April 1943 → Westland: 30 April 1943 → 263 Sqn, Warmwell *(HE-T)*: 16 May 1943 crashed near Exeter – Herbert Blackshaw killed: Ops Hours 51:10: Total Hours 165:45.

P7095 – 21 July 1941 → 51MU, Lichfield: 22 June 1942 → 137 Sqn, Matlaske *(SF-H)*: 18 August 1942 damaged – Frederick Furber: 23 January 1943 shot down near Doullens, France, Alfred Brown killed: Ops Hours 25:30.

P7096 – 24 July 1941 → 18MU, Dumfries: 30 September 1941 → 137 Sqn, Charmy Down: 26 October 1941 tail wheel faulty, Charmy Down – Joe Hughes: 14 February 1942 hit boundary fence, Horsham St Faith – Humphrey Coghlan: 27 February 1942 → Westland: 20 November 1942 → 18MU, Dumfries: 3 January 1943 → 137 Sqn, Matlaske: 6 April 1943 damaged – Alex Torrance: 12 April 1943 → Westland: 3 August 1943 → 263 Sqn, Warmwell: 14 August 1943 → Westland: 17 August 1943 crashed, Warmwell – Bob Beaumont: 27 August 1943 hit tree, Warmwell – Bill Watkins: 10 September 1943 crashed, Warmwell – Reg Baker: 26 September 1943 → SOC: Ops Hours 78:15.

P7097 – 24 July 1941 → 18MU, Dumfries: 6 November 1941 → 137 Sqn, Coltishall: 8 February 1942 force landed near Coltishall – James Rebbetoy: 20 February 1942 → Westland: 21 May 1943 → 18MU, Dumfries: 8 January 1943 → 263 Sqn, Warmwell: 22 January 1943 → Westland: 10 June 1943 → 263 Sqn, Warmwell: 8 October, 24 October and 26 November 1943 flak damage – Bill Heaton, Harold Proctor, Frederick Snalam: 8 January 1944 ran off runway, Hawarden: 11 January 1944 → 18MU, Dumfries: 14 July 1944 → Scrapped: 30 September 1944 → SOC: Ops Hours 46:30, Total Hours 93:00.

P7098 – 30 July 1941 → 18MU, Dumfries: 23 October 1942 → 137 Sqn, Manston *(SF-P)*: 13 April 1943 → Westland: 17 April 1943 → 137 Sqn, Manston: 27 June 1943 → 263 Sqn, Warmwell: 27 July 1943 → Westland: 2 August 1943 → 263 Sqn, Warmwell: 7 November 1943 damaged – Iain Dunlop: 10 January 1944 → Westland: 22 January 1944 → SOC: Ops Hours 55:35 Total Hours 350:35.

P7099 – 30 July 1941 → 18MU, Dumfries: 28 July 1942 → 263 Sqn, Angle: 17 April 1943 shot down over the Channel – Basil Abrams killed: Ops Hours 59:10: Total Hours 215:15.

P7100 – 7 August 1941 → 18MU, Dumfries: 5 December 1941 → 263 Sqn, Colerne: 15 April 1942 tyre burst at Fairwood Common – Philip Harvey: 17 April 1942 → Westland: 4 November 1943 → 263 Sqn, Warmwell: 26 November 1943 flak damage – Don Tebbit: 29 January 1944 → 18MU, Dumfries: 14 July 1944 → Scrapped: 30 September 1944 → SOC: Ops Hours 47:10.

P7101 – 7 August 1941 → 18MU, Dumfries: 18 April 1942 → 137 Sqn, Matlaske *(SF-A)*: 30 June 1942 hit Lysander *N1269*, Matlaske – Len Bartlett: 4 July 1942 → Westland: 15 July 1942 → SOC: Ops Hours 67:35.

P7102 Comrades In Arms – 12 August 1941 → 18MU, Dumfries: 22 June 1942 → 137 Sqn, Matlaske *(SF-P)*: 31 October 1942 flak damage – Frederick Furber: 6 November 1942 → Westland: 13 January 1943 hit by *P7061*, Manston: 25 January 1943 → Westland: 14 September 1943 → 263 Sqn, Warmwell *(HE-N)*: 29 January 1944 → 18MU, Dumfries: 14 July 1944 → Scrapped: 30 September 1944 → SOC: Ops Hours 59:40.

P7103 – 18 August 1941 → 18MU, Dumfries: 27 November 1941 → 137 Sqn, Coltishall: 4 May 1942 broke up and crashed near Aylesham – Bob Wright killed: Ops Hours 63:45: Total Hours 155:00.

P7104 – 30 August 1941 → 18MU, Dumfries: 14 January 1942 → 137 Sqn, Matlaske *(SF-V)*, 12 July 1942 damaged – Neville Freeman: 22 July 1942 battle damage – John McClure: 25

August 1942 → Westland: 30 March 1943 crashed, Manston – John Davidson: 8 April 1943 → Westland: 10 May 1943 → SOC: Ops Hours 84:10: Total Hours 319:00.

P7105 – 30 August 1941 → 18MU, Dumfries: 23 September 1941 → 137 Sqn, Charmy Down: 15 November 1941 damaged – Mike Bryan: 5 January 1942 wingtip hit ground, Matlaske – Bob Wright: 21 January 1942 → Westland: 28 July 1942 → 18MU, Dumfries: 12 August 1942 → 263 Sqn, Colerne *(HE-N)*: 3 October 1942 flak damage – Robert Woodward: 7 December 1942 shot down off St Brelade, Jersey – Robert Woodward killed: Ops Hours 44:50 Total Hours 136:05

P7106 – 30 August 1941 → 51MU, Lichfield: 26 September 1941 → 137 Sqn, Charmy Down *(SF-D)*: 25 December 1941 crashed, Horsham St Faith – Douglas Jowitt: 12 February 1942 shot down over the Channel – George Martin killed: Ops Hours 61:35: Total Hours 96:10.

P7107 – 30 August 1941 → 51MU, Lichfield: 26 September 1941 → 137 Sqn, Charmy Down: 6 December 1941 damaged – John Sandy: 12 February 1942 shot down over the Channel – Basil Robertson killed: Ops Hours 63:10: Total Hours 105:35

P7108 – 10 September 1941 → 51MU, Lichfield: 15 December 1941 → 263 Sqn, Exeter: 13 February 1942 overturned, Fairwood Common – Jimmy Coyne: 20 February 1942 → Westland: 18 February 1943 → 18MU, Dumfries: 27 February 1943 → 263 Sqn, Warmwell: 26 March 1943 flak damage – Jimmy Coyne: 30 March 1943 → Westland: 1 April 1943 → 263 Sqn, Warmwell: 27 April 1943 flak damage – Max Cotton: 2 May 1943 flak damage – Max Cotton: 3 June 1943 → Westland: 20 October 1943 → 263 Sqn, Warmwell: 30 October 1943 flak damage – Iain Dunlop: 8 February 1944 → 18MU, Dumfries: 14 July 1944 → Scrapped: 30 September 1944 → SOC: Ops Hours 68:15.

P7109 – 10 September 1941 → 51MU, Lichfield: 15 November 1941 → 137 Sqn, Coltishall *(SF-N)*: 1 July 1942 undercarriage failed to retract, Matlaske – Douglas Jowitt: 31 October 1942 shot down by flak near Etaples – Francis Waldron POW: Ops Hours 76:45: Total Hours 239:00.

P7110 – 26 September 1941 → 39MU, Colerne: 15 October 1941 → 263 Sqn, Charmy Down *(HE-E, G & H)*: 7 November 1941 flak damage – Geoff Warnes: 11 November 1941 damaged: 12 January 1942 tail wheel collapsed, Charmy Down – Joe Holmes: 19 February 1942 damaged – Joe Holmes: 23 June 1942 tail wheel collapsed, Warmwell – Geoff Warnes: 13 April 1943 → Westland: 18 April 1943 → 263 Sqn, Warmwell *(HE-C)*: 18 May 1943 heavy landing, Warmwell – George Wood: 21 June 1943 force landed, Stoney Cross – Bill Watkins: 13 July 1943 crashed, Warmwell – Len Knott injured: Ops Hours 109:50: Total Hours 349:50.

P7111 Bellows Uruguay No. 2 – 28 January 1942 → 39MU, Colerne: 13 March 1942 → 137 Sqn, Matlaske *(SF-E)*: 11 April 1942 damaged: 15 May 1942 flak damage – Bob Brennan: 3 September 1942 engine failure – James Rebbetoy: 11 February 1943 → Westland: 17

February 1943 → 137 Sqn, Manston: 4 April 1943 flak damage – Humphrey Coghlan: 8 May 1943 engine failure – Humphrey Coghlan: 18 June 1943 flak damage – John Barclay: 4 July 1943 → 263 Sqn, Zeals *(HE-W)*: 15 August 1943 exactor failure – Reg Baker: 11 January 1944 → SOC: Ops Hours 107:15.

P7112 – 26 September 1941 → 39MU, Colerne: 15 October 1941 → 263 Sqn, Charmy Down: 15 November 1941 flak damage – Cecil King: 25 November 1941 → Westland: 21 December 1941 → 263 Sqn, Colerne: 12 February 1942 damaged: 1 April 1942 crashed, Fairwood Common – Philip Harvey: 7 April 1942 → SOC: Ops Hours 43:50.

P7113 Condor I – 26 September 1941 → 39MU, Colerne: 25 May 1942 → 18MU, Dumfries: 9 November 1942 → 263 Sqn, Warmwell *(HE-W)*: 13 April 1943 → Westland: 17 April 1943 → 263 Sqn, Warmwell: 23 September 1943 shot down over Morlaix airfield – George Wood evaded: Ops Hours 65:55: Total Hours 270:00.

P7114 – 29 September 1941 → 39MU, Colerne: 5 November 1941 → 263 Sqn, Charmy Down: 21 February and 13 May 1942 damaged: 18 May 1942 → Westland: 23 May 1942 → 263 Sqn, Angle: 9 July 1942 damaged: 19 July 1942 → Westland: 13 September 1942 → 18MU, Dumfries: 22 September 1942 → 263 Sqn, Charmy Down: 17 November 1942 → 137 Sqn, Manston: 10 February 1943 flak damage – Eddie Musgrave: 19 February 1943 hit by *P7119* and blew up, Manston – Neville Austin Freeman killed: Ops Hours 104:30 Total Hours 303:00

P7115 – 13 October 1941 → 39MU, Colerne: 4 May 1942 → 18MU, Dumfries: 16 September 1942 → 137 Sqn, Snailwell: 31 October 1942 shot down by flak near Etaples, France – Douglas Jowitt killed: Ops Hours 4:35: Total Hours 34:00.

P7116 Bellows Argentina No. 2 – 27 October 1941 → 39MU, Colerne: 3 November 1941 → 263 Sqn, Charmy Down *(HE-F, J & S)*: 1 June 1942 → Westland: 20 June 1942 → 263 Sqn, Angle: 25 July 1942 hit by Beaufort *AW274*, Portreath: 28 December 1942 → Station Flight, Colerne: 26 March 1943 → Westland: 26 March 1943 → SOC: Ops Hours 80:50.

P7117 Bellows Argentina No. 3 – 27 October 1941 → 39MU, Colerne: 3 November 1941 → 263 Sqn, Charmy Down *(HE-A, G, E & H)*: 23 November 1941 damaged: 16 April 1942 wingtip hit ground, Fairwood Common – John Meredith: 9 August 1942 hit lorry, Angle – Richard Reed: 3 April 1943 → Westland: 14 April 1943 → 263 Sqn, Warmwell: 17 April 1943 Missing – Cecil King killed: Ops Hours 86:55: Total Hours 267.35.

P7118 Bellows Argentina No. 4 – 11 November 1941 → 48MU, Hawarden: 20 February 1942 → 137 Sqn, Matlaske *(SF-O)*: 29 May 1942 abandoned near Matlaske – Douglas Jowitt: Ops Hours 51:35: Total Hours 111:00.

P7119 Bellows Argentina No. 5 – 11 November 1941 → 48MU, Hawarden: 8 March 1942 → 137 Sqn, Matlaske *(SF-C, S & W)*: 6 January 1942 → Westland: 26 June 1942 → 137 Sqn, Matlaske: 23 December 1942 flak damage – Frederick Furber: 17 January 1943 engine failure – Neville Freeman: 19 February 1943 hit *P7114* and blew up, Manston – Charles Mercer killed: Ops Hours 82:25: Total Hours 279.36.

P7120 Bellows Argentina No. 6 – 8 December 1941 → 18MU, Hawarden: 26 February 1942 → 263 Sqn, Fairwood Common *(HE-R & D)*: 5 July 1942 hit by *P7013*, Portreath – Harvey Muirhead: 28 October 1942 landed with undercarriage retracted, Warmwell – James Cooksey (1487 Flight): 15 November 1942 SOC: Ops Hours 88:10.

P7121 Bellows Argentina No. 7 – 8 December 1941 → 39MU, Colerne: 6 February 1942 → 137 Sqn, Matlaske *(SF-C)*: 27 February 1942 damaged: 24 May 1942 crashed, Matlaske – Mike Bryan: 16 April 1943 crashed, Manston – John Hadow killed: Ops Hours 90:40: Total Hours 325:35.

P7122 Bellows Uruguay No. 1 – 16 December 1941 damaged during ferry flight → 20MU: 5 January 1942 → 39MU at Colerne: 13 March 1942 → 137 Sqn, Matlaske: 9 April 1942 hit high tension cables – Mike Bryan: 27 May 1942 shot down by flak near Beverwijk, Netherlands – Bob Brennan killed: Ops Hours 15:40: Total Hours 93.10.

Endnotes

Introduction

1. Queen Elizabeth II 17th October 1953 on opening the Air Force Memorial at Runnymede.
2. F/S Leonard Scott Gray, 263 Squadron Whirlwind Pilot.

No. 263 Squadron: 'Ex Ungue Leonum' The Lion is Known By His Claws

1. He later designed the Canberra Bomber, Gnat Trainer and supersonic Lightning Interceptor.
2. Aircrew leaving the squadron during this period were F/L William Riley; F/O James Richard Tobin; P/O Ellis Walter Aires; Sub Lt. Robert Francis Bryant; P/O Philip Melville Cardell; P/O George James Drake; Sgt Stanley Allen Fenemore; P/O Henry Norman Hunt; P/O Alan Ormerod Moffet; P/O Denis Geach Parnall; P/O William Albert Alexander Read; Sgt Jack Stokoe; F/O Cedric Stone and Sgt Basil Ewart Patrick Whall. Drake, Parnall and Whall were veterans of the Norwegian Campaigns.
3. Originally the Whirlwind was to have equipped No. 25 Squadron, and *L6845*, *P6966* and *P6967* were delivered for trials in May 1940.
4. From an interview with Henry Eeles.
5. The plaque was stolen in 2001.
6. Although officially recognised as a Battle of Britain pilot, and fully entitled to wear the Battle of Britain clasp, Henry Eeles refused his as he considered as he did not actually fire a shot in anger and so had not really participated in the fighting.
7. From an interview with Henry Eeles.
8. Recovered in 1979, one engine is now on display at the Rolls-Royce Heritage Trust.
9. From an interview with Henry Eeles.
10. From an interview with Cliff Rudland.
11. From an interview with Herbert Kitchener.
12. Confirmed in an interview with Cliff Rudland.
13. From an interview with Herbert Kitchener.
14. From an interview with Cliff Rudland.
15. From an interview with Cliff Rudland.
16. Quote from S/L Arthur Donaldson.

17. Bf 109 E-7 of E/JG 2 was flown by Unteroffizer Helmut Rainer.
18. From an interview with Cliff Rudland.
19. For propaganda purposes the Air Ministry led the public to believe the Whirlwinds escorted the bombers all the way to Cologne. This was impossible on the 134 gallons of fuel carried in her tanks, but the myth persists to this day.
20. AVM Augustus Henry Orlebar flew the Sopwith Camel in WWI and gained seven victories. He was also commander of the winning Schneider Trophy team of 1931
21. From an interview with Jimmy Coyne.
22. From an interview with Cliff Rudland.
23. From an interview with Cliff Rudland.
24. G/C Richard 'Batchy' Atcherley had flown a Supermarine S6 in the 1929 Schneider Trophy race, and had been W/C Flying at Bardufoss during the Second Norwegian Expedition.
25. From an interview with Jimmy Coyne.
26. From an interview with Cliff Rudland.
27. From an interview with Cliff Rudland.
28. From an interview with Cliff Rudland.
29. From an interview with Cliff Rudland.
30. From an interview with Cliff Rudland.
31. From an interview with George Wood.
32. Due to the teething troubles with the Typhoon and its Sabre engine, stop-gap models were employed.
33. From an interview with George Wood.
34. From an interview with Bill Watkins.
35. From an interview with Len Gray.
36. From an interview with William Handley.
37. From an interview with Len Knott.
38. From an interview with Tony Poole.
39. From an interview with Bill Watkins.
40. From an interview with Doug Sturgeon.
41. From interviews with George Wood; Bill Watkins; Len Gray and Doug Sturgeon.
42. From an interview with Len Gray.
43. From an interview with Len Gray.
44. From an interview with Iain Dunlop.
45. From an interview with Bill Watkins.
46. From an interview with William Handley.
47. From an interview with Len Gray.
48. From an interview with Denis Todd.
49. The Squadron used 102 of the 116 Whirlwinds built.
50. From an interview with John Shellard.

No. 137 Squadron: Do Right, Fear Nought

1. From an interview with John Wray.
2. From an interview with Phil Robson.
3. From an interview with John Wray.
4. From an interview with John Wray.

Index